The Difference_____

The Difference ⎯⎯⎯⎯

HOW THE POWER OF DIVERSITY

CREATES BETTER GROUPS, FIRMS,

SCHOOLS, AND SOCIETIES

Scott E. Page

PRINCETON UNIVERSITY PRESS

PRINCETON AND OXFORD

Copyright © 2007 by Princeton University Press

Published by Princeton University Press, 41 William Street, Princeton, New Jersey 08540
In the United Kingdom: Princeton University Press, 3 Market Place, Woodstock,
Oxfordshire OX20 1SY

Library of Congress Cataloging-in-Publication Data
Page, Scott E.
The difference: how the power of diversity creates better groups, firms, schools, and
societies / Scott E. Page.
p. cm.
Includes bibliographical references and index.
ISBN-13: 978-0-691-12838-2 (cloth : alk. paper)
ISBN-10: 0-691-12838-3 (cloth : alk. paper)
1. Diversity in the workplace. 2. Multiculturalism. I. Title.
HF5549.5.M5P34 2007
658.3008–dc22   2006044678

British Library Cataloging-in-Publication Data is available

This book has been composed in Sabon Typeface
Printed on acid-free paper. ∞
pup.princeton.edu

Printed in the United States of America

10 9 8 7 6 5 4 3 2 1

JENNA, *I dedicate this discrete product of our continuous lives to you.*

*From the earliest traceable cosmical changes down
to the latest results of civilization, we shall find that
the transformation of the homogeneous into the
heterogeneous is that in which progress consists.*

—HERBERT SPENCER, *Progress: Its Law and Cause*

The dim boy claps because the others clap.

—RICHARD HUGO, "The Freaks at Spurgin Road Field"

Contents

PART FOUR
THE PUDDING: DOES DIVERSITY GENERATE BENEFITS?

Acknowledgments

THE CONTINUOUS LIFE

Great genius takes shape by contact with another great genius, but less by assimilation than by friction.
—Heinrich Heini

GIVEN the central claim of this book—that diversity produces benefits—I cannot both take credit for it and claim it to be as good as it could be. And, in fact, this book has been a joint effort. Over the past five years, I've presented bits and pieces of this book to a diverse set of audiences: undergraduates, academics, Wall Street investors, Silicon Valley entrepreneurs, health science researchers, government agency employees (some may even have been spies), human resource professionals, Fortune 500 diversity committee members, political activists, and even alumni at a University of Michigan family camp. Those presentations have led to brief comments, long emails, and even copies of books that I "had to read." What I learned from those interactions has been folded into and improved this book.

Though what you're reading consists entirely of my words, my editor, my wife, some graduate students, and more than a few friends have painstakingly rearranged them. Eric Ball, Jonathon Bendor, Scott de Marchi, Patrick Grim, Ken Kollman, Bill McKelvey, Jennifer Miller, Mike Ryall, Cosma Shalizi, Elizabeth Suhay, and Troy Tassier gave detailed comments on earlier drafts. The path from personal friend to personal hero is paved with red pens. The oh-so-many other people who read parts of earlier versions or heard my ideas and provided comments ranging from adoring to critical include Daron Acemoglu, Susan Ballati, Jake Bowers, Aaron Bramson, Elizabeth Bruch, Dan Catlin, Rui de Figueiredo, Patricia Gurin, Erika Homann, Norman Johnson, John Ledyard, Michael Mauboussin, John Miller, Lester Monts, Katherine Phillips, Jeff Polzer, Cindy Rabe, Jim Surowiecki, Bill Tozier, Nick Valentino, Jennifer Watkins and Michael Wellman. Not included in this list are Mita Gibson and Howard Oishi, who run the Center for the Study of Complex Systems at the University of Michigan. Howard and Mita not only handled all of the administrative tasks associated with the writing of the book, they were valuable sounding boards for many of the ideas contained in it.

I have two academic homes: the University of Michigan and the Santa Fe Institute. One has Blimpy Burgers and one has mountains. At Michigan, I have had the opportunity to think on a regular basis with Rick Riolo, Michael Cohen, Bob Axelrod, Carl Simon, Mark Newman, Mercedes Pascual, and a young man named John Henry Holland—the so-called BACH group. Many of the ideas that follow are probably not my own, but belong more properly to BACH. For that, I promise to dedicate a portion of the proceeds to the stock of M&Ms. Many people at the Santa Fe Institute (SFI), especially Susan Ballati, Bill Miller, Ginger Richardson, and Geoffrey West, have nurtured and encouraged this work. SFI has been instrumental in pushing me out into what they call "the real world." Pat Gurin, Julie Peterson, and Lester Monts have played a similar role at Michigan. I'm shy and unassuming, so being forced out of my shell proved good for me.

I also have four academic birthplaces: Middleville Thornapple Kellogg Schools, the University of Michigan, the University of Wisconsin, and Northwestern University. My Ph.D. advisor, Stan Reiter, once told me that the two most important decisions I'd ever make were who my parents were and when I was born. Choosing a good advisor falls not too far behind on that list. Stan offered his usual wisdom and guidance in the writing of the research papers that were the basis for this book. As is true with the BACH group, where my ideas end and where his begin is a blur. Throughout my career, Stan has been an inspiration both as an intellect and as a human being. Among other contributions to my family, he and his wife, Nina, have provided wise counsel, sculpture, and yoga tapes.

Writing a book like this requires resources. The James S. McDonnell Foundation provided funding for this inquiry into the logic of diversity. Few foundations are as innovative and bold as the McDonnell Foundation. Without its support, the book would be just another collection of loose unfinished ideas floating around in my head and in folders on my computer. The University of Michigan Center for Research on Learning and Teaching also provided a seed grant that led to the larger McDonnell Foundation grand. In addition, a National Science Foundation IGERT grant provided financial support for a community of bright, challenging graduate students, who kept me on my toes throughout the writing of this book. Even with all of these overlapping grants, Howard and Mita made sure that none of this money went to the BACH group's M&Ms or to pay for any lunches for Carl Simon and me at Zanzibar.

Writing a book also requires an editor. Mine, Tim Sullivan, was incredible (indeed!). He cut two hundred pages and personally rewrote most of those that remain. What had been a messy, complex tome, destined to be misunderstood by its twelve readers, Tim transformed into what you see. I had only to remove his many insertions of the word *indeed*.

The orginal manuscript was edited by Madeleine Adams, who corrected more punctuation errors in one month than most seventh grade teachers can claim in a lifetime. The final galley proofs were subject to the expert eye of Andrea Jones-Roy, who spent three hours, twenty-six minutes, and fourteen seconds with me on the phone not only explaining the subtleties of subject verb agreement but also helping me to tighten the prose and highlight the main points. My wife, Jenna, also read and edited the final version—more on her later.

While writing this book, I was coauthoring a book with John Miller of Carnegie Mellon University and SFI. John did most of the late heavy lifting on that project, allowing me the space to finish this one. Both books benefited. I can only imagine how good this one might have been had he written it as well! Writing two books at the same time could spell the end of my days as an author of anything longer than fifty pages. For that reason, I'll thank Christine Schad, my favorite grade school teacher, who still sends me postcards on her birthday (it's also my birthday). Mrs. Schad (then Miss Harrison) taught me to say "good morning" in German and to begin each day with the chant "good better best, never let it rest 'til the good is better, and the better is best." (This mantra was later expanded into book form with the title *Good to Great*.) So when Tim, my editor, said that draft number eleven was "better, and good enough," let's just say I wasn't going to let it rest.

The listing of a single author on the title page causes me to feel equal parts shame and embarrassment. Lu Hong deserves equal billing for the bulk of this research. The parts of this book that are original belong as much to Lu as to me. For the two years I spent writing the core of the book, Lu was in Ann Arbor along with her husband, Tom Nohel, and their son, Jeremy, who at three knew more about rockets than I did at forty. My wife refers to Lu's arrival as a psyche-preserving event for me. It was. I hope this book will become Lu's and my second most remarkable achievement. Number one? We once couldn't find Toronto by car from Syracuse. In our defense, Canada is big and it was dark out, really dark. And we missed Toronto only by seventy miles—less than 2 percent of the length of Canada. By golf standards, we left ourselves a tap in.

Many of the names that appear in the book are drawn from friends (yes, Rebecca and Arun, it's you!) and family. My parents, Ray and Marilyn, and my sister Deb play starring roles. My other siblings, Brenda and Jeff, my many nieces and nephews, Noah, Carter, Maggie, Emily, Natalie, Cole, Katie, Joe, Rose, Brody, and Logan, and my mother-in-law, Karen, as well as most of my brothers- and sisters-in-law, Jeff, Mary, Joe, Rick, and Laura, also appear at various places in the book. It's an odd way to say thanks, but it's all I can do—it may not be to each according to his (or her) needs, but it is from me according to my abilities.

Hey, Orrie and Cooper! (I know—I've read Flat Stanley many times—"hay is for horses.") Guess what? The completion of this book means more time for playing with LEGOs and Playmobil, more time for riding bikes and climbing trees, more time to work on our story about pirates, and more time to mix up a little baking powder and vinegar to make explosions in the backyard. In answer to your question, does my book contain pirates and knights? Of course it does. (There they were.) It even includes a dragon that breathes water instead of fire, which makes him no fun at dragon parties. And best of all, some sentences are written in snake crayon. So that only Owls and Coyotes can understand them. Cool, eh?

This book is dedicated to my wife, Jenna. During the time I've been writing this book, she wrote her own book on the design of robust federations. (It's far more scholarly than this one.) She won a teaching award. And she found time to refine and clarify every single idea and model contained in this book (most have been subjected to her ear, eye, and pen several times). Her kindness, intelligence, and patience (especially her patience) have kept her three boys (Orrie, Cooper, and me) on a relatively even keel throughout this entire multiple-book-writing process. Without her, this book would have far less substance, gravity, and wisdom.

And so would I.

Prologue

Oh do not ask what is it. Let us go and make our visit.
—T. S. ELIOT

IN 1993, I got my first real job, as an assistant professor of economics at the California Institute of Technology in Pasadena, California, home of the Tournament of Roses. I lived one block from campus and one and a half blocks from the Caltech gym. I wore shorts to work every day—even when temperatures fell into the sixties. Apart from being hit in the head by a falling palm frond during a spell of Santa Ana winds, I had a wonderful time. Caltech offered me abundant resources and an environment that encouraged freewheeling exploration.

One winter evening in 1995, to have a little fun I constructed a computer model of diverse problem solvers confronting a difficult problem. Put aside for now what counts for fun at Caltech; "fun" at Caltech rarely makes sense to the outside world. In my model, I represented diversity as differences in the ways problem solvers encoded the problem and searched for solutions. I referred to these ways of solving the problem as tools. In working through the implications of my model, I stumbled on a counterintuitive finding: diverse groups of problem solvers—groups of people with diverse tools—consistently outperformed groups of the best and the brightest. If I formed two groups, one random (and therefore diverse) and one consisting of the best individual performers, the first group almost always did better. In my model, *diversity trumped ability.*

This result proved to be no house of cards. With the help of my good friend and coauthor Lu Hong, I unpacked a logic that underpins that finding. In doing so, Lu and I hit on a fundamental insight: *in problem solving, diversity is powerful stuff.* It doesn't always trump ability, but it does so far more often than we'd expect. The power of diversity is not a new idea. (Evolutionary biologists see the selection of fortuitous diversity as the reason we're here. What could be more powerful than that?) However, as became clear to Lu and me, the idea that our individual differences—the differences in how we think, in the cognitive tools we possess, in our perspectives—was far outside the mainstream in a society that prizes individual talent and achievement. It shouldn't be. Progress depends as much on our collective differences as it does on our individual IQ scores.

The claim that diversity should get equal billing with ability is a strong and controversial one. Anecdotes, metaphors, and decorative quotes won't be sufficient to convince skeptics. Hence, in this book, I make the case using frameworks and models. I show with modest rigor how diverse perspectives, heuristics, interpretations, and mental models improve our collective ability to solve problems and make accurate predictions. An advantage of using logic is that it gives conditions—these results hold when and if the following are true. Another advantage is that it provides the greatest chance of getting hit on the head by a palm frond (just a conceptual one). Models and logic don't come without some costs. They limit what we can claim. We're tied to the mast of our assumptions. They also require careful reading. Don't worry, though; the book doesn't read like that undergraduate economics textbook you resold for ten cents on the dollar. It's fun.

This book can be read from multiple perspectives. Parts of this book have strong connections to two recent books on collective wisdom. The first is Howard Reingold's *Smart Mobs*, which describes how emergent collections of people can carry out tasks and can solve problems.[1] The second book is Jim Surowiecki's

Wisdom of Crowds, which shows how crowds of people can make accurate predictions.[2] The words *crowds* and *mobs* are a bit misleading, as these intuitions apply to groups of ten as well as groups of a thousand. A board of directors is not a mob or a crowd, but it too benefits from diversity.

In this book, I also consider a third benefit of diversity: the increased probability of a savant. If we sample widely, we're more likely to find the one person who can solve the problem or who can make the key breakthrough. We did not get the theory of relatively *sp?* from a crowd. We got it from a diverse, novel thinker in a patent office.

This book also has bearing on claims of the legal, instrumentalist benefits of identity diversity arguments. For a long time, my research papers and presentations included no mention of identity diversity. They considered only the differences inside people's heads, not differences in skin color, gender, or ethnicity. Yet, audiences continued to make a connection between cognitive differences (who we are inside our heads) and identity differences (who we are on the outside). Although promoting greater identity diversity in groups—particularly in groups that possess power—has long been the concern of the political left (usually for reasons of justice and fairness), the people who brought up this connection more often than not came from the corporate sector.

This reaction did not surprise me. Though the business world's concern is, and always has been, with the bottom line (we don't see many business leaders chanting "a people united will never be defeated" or anything of the sort), over the past few decades business leaders have moved in the direction of pro-diversity. Two fundamental changes have led to this directional shift: the business world has become more global (and therefore more aware of ethnic diversity) and the practice of work has become more team focused. The homogenous hierarchy has given way to the diverse team.[3] To paraphrase one business executive, "Look, companies spend billions of dollars each year trying to manage diverse employees. That's not going to change."[4]

Some people dismiss claims that diversity is beneficial as empty rhetoric. And people have good reason to be dubious. These claims do not seem to be based on anything more than hope and metaphor (making them easy to dismiss). This book provides a foundation for those claims. Identity diversity does produce benefits—not every time, not in every context—but there is a there there.[5]

This book also provides a logic for greater interdisciplinary research. What, after all, are the different disciplines but collections of different sets of tools and understandings? That said, at the end of the day this book has to be a contribution to social science. That's the job of the social scientist—to add to the base of knowledge.

This book contributes to social science by unpacking the processes of problem solving and prediction, processes that social scientists often ignore or "black box." Two examples help to clarify what I mean. First, most social science models rarely differentiate among problem solving (curing a disease), prediction (estimating the outcome of the next election), and information aggregation (surveying people to find the grocer with the lowest prices). Even though these tasks differ, many economists would respond (perhaps correctly), "Yeah, yeah, yeah, it's all basically information aggregation. People have different information and the noise cancels." Second, many political science models in effect assume that information arrives on people's doorsteps in the form of *signals*. The story goes as follows: the president proposes a tax policy, a voter wakes up and finds a placard that reads "new policy to lead to a 3% increase in economic growth" on her doorstep the next morning. Moreover, each voter gets a *unique* placard and *on average* those placards are correct. But why are they correct? That is what I unpack.

In what follows I nourish these diverse readings. When possible, I point out the linkages to smart mobs, to wise crowds, to identity diversity, to globalization, and to interdisciplinary science. I do this not just to try to make everyone happy, but because the same logic that shows how cognitive diversity improves the performance of a predictive market can show how including identity diverse— and experientially and vocationally diverse—people improves the performance of a problem-solving team. To quote Dan Ackroyd from his *Saturday Night Live* days, "It's a floor wax *and* a dessert topping."

Before starting, I will put what follows in some context by returning to the original finding that diversity trumps ability. Does this logic imply that we should abandon the meritocracy? That we should remove those "my child is an honor student at Neil Armstrong Junior High" bumper stickers from our minivans and randomly allocate spots in our top colleges? Of course not. Ability matters. But—here's the catch—so does diversity. Comparisons between the two (which matters more: diversity or ability?) require some care. We're comparing an apple to a fruit basket. Ability is a property of an individual—a nice shiny apple. Neither a person nor an apple can be diverse. Diversity is a property of a collection of people—a basket with many kinds of fruit. Diversity and ability complement one another: the better the individual fruits, the better the fruit basket, and the better the other fruit, the better the apple. So while we might equally proudly affix "my other child's different" bumper stickers to our vehicles (anyone with two kids can claim that to be true), ideally, our children would be individually able *and* collectively diverse. If so, what they could accomplish would amaze us.

In sum, rather than being on the defensive about diversity, we should go on the offensive. We should look at difference as something that can improve performance, not as something that we have to be concerned about so that we don't get sued. We should encourage people to think differently. Markets create incentives to be different as well as to be able, but perhaps not to the appropriate levels. We should do more.

Of course, difference does not magically translate into benefits. My claims that diversity produces benefits rest on conditions. These conditions require, among other things, that diversity is relevant—we cannot expect that adding a poet to a medical research team would enable them to find a cure for the common cold. Further, for diverse groups to function in practice, the people in them must get along. If not, the cognitive differences between them may be little more than disconnected silos of ideas and thoughts. Diversity, like everything else (excepting, of course, moderation), has its limits.

Understanding diversity and leveraging its potential requires a deeper understanding than we currently possess. We won't get far with compelling anecdotes and metaphors, which in the diversity realm exist in abundance. We have (as Kermit would say) "so many songs about rainbows and what's on the other side." What we need are formal definitions, assumptions, and claims. We need theorems about rainbows. We need a logic of diversity. This book provides that logic—not all of it, but enough to get us started.

I'll end with this observation: as individuals we can accomplish only so much. We're limited in our abilities. Our heads contain only so many neurons and axons. Collectively, we face no such constraint. We possess incredible capacity to think differently. These differences can provide the seeds of innovation, progress, and understanding.

INTRODUCTION

Unpacking Our Differences

You see, wire telegraph is a kind of a very, very long cat.
You pull his tail in New York and his head is meowing in
Los Angeles. Do you understand this? And radio operates
exactly the same way: you send signals here, they receive them
there. The only difference is that there is no cat.
—ALBERT EINSTEIN

ALPH'S WANTED POSTER

IN the summer of 2001, Alpheus (Alph) Bingham, a vice president of Eli Lilly, created a Web site for seekers—not Quidditch-playing adolescents in pursuit of golden snitches à la J. K. Rowling's Harry Potter series—but large pharmaceutical companies in pursuit of solutions to scientific problems. These problems ran the gamut from tracing metal impurities to assessing the risks of breast cancer to detecting organic chemical vapors. Seekers posted their problems on Alph's site along with an award of up to one hundred thousand dollars that they would pay for successful solutions. Anyone willing to register could be a solver. Solvers included dentists from the Far East and physicists from the Midwest. Only the people running Alph's site knew the identities of both seekers and solvers. In the parlance of the Web, the participants were double blind.

Alph called his site InnoCentive. With it, he created a modern-day version of the Wild West wanted poster. But rather than nailing his posters to trees all over the Dakota Territory, Alph pasted his on the Internet. He built it, and they came: by 2005, more than eighty thousand solvers had registered. They hail from more than 170 countries and span the scientific disciplines. And best of all, they've proven themselves up to the task. A study of InnoCentive revealed that solvers found solutions to nearly one-third of the posted problems.[1] A slight majority of these problems required reduction to practice—the solutions had to be demonstrable in the laboratory. For the remaining 40-some percent, pencil-and-paper solutions sufficed. One-third may seem a low success rate, but keep in mind that the typical seeker is not a seventh grader stuck on a chemistry problem, but a company like Proctor and Gamble, which has nine thousand people as its R&D staff and spends nearly two billion dollars a year on research and development. Suddenly, one-third looks good.

How could these individuals and small teams of scientists find solutions that Proctor and Gamble, with its vast and focused resources, could not? In their study, Karim Lakhani, Lars Bo Jeppeson, Peter Lohse, and Jill Panetta discovered that postings that are solved successfully tend to attract a diverse and differentiated pool of solvers. If a problem attracted a physical chemist, a molecular biologist, and a biophysicist, it was far more likely to be solved than if it attracted only chemists. In other words, InnoCentive works because it exploits diversity.

It's not information diversity that the seekers are after—for that they can Google or Ask Jeeves—it's problem solving diversity they seek. Consider this posting:

INNOCENTIVE 3084200:
Reduction of Chemical Vapor Emissions
POSTED: NOV 04, 2005
DEADLINE: DEC 07, 2005
$5,000 USD
The Seeker is looking for creative ideas for reduction of chemical vapor emissions in a specific industry setting. You do not need to be a chemist to work on this problem. What matters most is your creative and practical mind as a scientist.

InnoCentive takes advantage of new technology to exploit an old idea: the use of diverse, talented people to solve problems. We have to be careful here. Alph is not trying to exploit the wisdom of crowds. He's not averaging anything. He's trying to find a needle in a haystack. He's looking for a person or team who can solve the problem or part of the problem.

InnoCentive therefore, differs from Bletchley Park, the famous British code-breaking organization. At Bletchley Park people worked together—not necessarily in peace and harmony either; some of these people had sharp edges. Like InnoCentive, the Bletchley Park idea was to cast a wide net. Unlike InnoCentive, the idea was to have all the diverse fishes swim together.

To see how this worked, we need some background: during World War II, the British brought together twelve thousand people in Bletchley Park, about fifty miles northwest of London, to crack the Nazi Enigma code. The Nazis had distributed ingenious machines, smaller than manual typewriters, among their forces to create random ciphers that allowed them to communicate secretly with one another. Breaking the code was a priority for the Allies, since it allowed the Nazis to coordinate attacks both on land and at sea, deliver needed supplies, and generally coordinate their far-flung military might. The German navy was especially adept at using the Enigma code and sank, on average, sixty supply ships a month.

Many of the people brought to Bletchley Park—Brits, Americans, Poles, Aussies—had training we might think appropriate for code breaking. These included mathematicians (most notably Alan Turing), engineers, and cryptographers. But other people working in secrecy in the James Bond–like trappings of Room 40 and Hut 8 had been trained as language experts, moral philosophers, classicists, ancient historians, and even crossword puzzle experts. Imagine the drama as it unfolded:

> CRYPTOGRAPHER: Quick, we need a five-letter German word, second letter is an *o*, that means explosive device!
> CROSSWORD PUZZLE EXPERT: Bombe. B-o-m-b-e, bombe.
> LINGUIST: It's pronounced BOM-bah!

Bletchley Park cracked the Enigma code (twice). Churchill called it "the goose that laid the golden egg and never cackled." Like the solvers at InnoCentive, the goose consisted of many diverse parts.

As captivating as these examples may be, they do not show the full range of diversity's benefits. Yes, diversity can contribute to problem solving, but it can also enable collections of people to make accurate predictions. Collections of people, none of whom count as experts, none of whom can predict well alone, have proven able to make accurate predictions, not just once in a blue moon, but consistently, as has been shown in analyses of stock prices, betting lines, and information markets, such as the Iowa Electronic Markets. James Surowiecki calls this "the wisdom of crowds."

The existence of smart mobs like those created by InnoCentive and of wise crowds like those described by Surowiecki is not in dispute. Without collective intelligence, decentralized markets and democracies would have little hope of functioning effectively. Yet we do not fully understand the causes of successful collective performance. We tend to think that it rests in ability, that if we make the individuals smarter, we make the group (or mob) smarter, the crowd wiser, and the team more effective. That logic certainly holds true (with some caveats). But here I show that if we make the individuals more diverse, we get the same effects: better teams, smarter groups, wiser crowds. Unpacking this second, subtler logic takes up the bulk of what follows.

The Diversity Conjecture

One place to start our analysis is with the *Diversity Conjecture*. A conjecture is a guess. And to many, that's what this is.

The Diversity Conjecture: *Diversity leads to better outcomes.*

The diversity conjecture, as stated, suffers from vagueness and imprecision. For us, it's a great jumping-off point. We can refine it and identify conditions so that it is no longer a conjecture, but a conditional statement. Clearly, the conjecture fails to hold universally. That's why we will proceed slowly, defining our terms along the way. Speaking of defining our terms, notice that in the conjecture, not only is the term *diversity* not defined, neither are the tasks for which it supposedly produces better outcomes. So our first steps will be to define diversity and to identify those tasks for which we expect it to be beneficial. For instance, if a loved one requires open-heart surgery, we do not want a collection of butchers, bakers, and candlestick makers carving open the chest cavity. We'd much prefer a trained heart surgeon, and for good reason. But in other circumstances, such as constructing a welfare policy, designing a physics experiment, cracking a secret code, or evaluating post–heart attack treatment, we'd want diversity. Understanding when, and why, diversity proves beneficial is the purpose of this book. We learn that often, diversity merits equal standing with ability and that sometimes, although not every time, it even trumps ability.

I show these benefits of diversity by using simple models and frameworks. I do this because simple models can be powerful drivers and clarifiers of intuition. For a glimpse of their power in clarifying thinking, consider these two seemingly conflicting sayings: "Two heads are better than one," and "Too many cooks spoil the broth." Let's construct a model of cooking. Cooking requires a recipe, which lists the ingredients and how we combine them. Most recipes consist of an irreversible sequence of instructions: *simmer the onions until brown specks form around the edges and then add two teaspoons of cayenne pepper.* In cooking, as in life, we cannot go backward. We can't uncook an onion; we cannot remove the cayenne pepper. These irreversible actions require a single course of action, a single recipe. Following multiple recipes simultaneously spoils the broth (so to speak). Too many cooks, as it turns out, aren't a problem at all. Most great restaurants employ more than one cook, but those cooks work from a single set of recipes. Moreover, even though once we have fired up the grill, we want a single plan, we may, in developing that plan, want lots of cooks. Even Julia Child didn't work alone. She had Simone Beck. Thus, it might be better to draw on the expertise of a variety of cooks—before we uncork the wine and tie on our aprons.

This little digression has shown the value of careful, logical thinking. By constructing a skeletal verbal model, we reveal a condition—the presence of irreversible actions—for the saying about the cooks to be true. We know now when to apply it and when to invoke the other pithy saying—the one about two heads being better than one. As Ayn Rand wrote, "Contradictions do not exist. Whenever you think you are facing a contradiction, check your premises. You will find that one of them is wrong."[2]

The main results on the benefits of diversity may strike some as counterintuitive. Common sense suggests that ability should matter more than difference. That intuition holds only if we picture people working in isolation, like our heart surgeon. The image of the lone worker toiling away at his or her craft makes a nice subject for a Norman Rockwell *Saturday Evening Post* cover illustration but increasingly misrepresents the modern economy. Pa Ingalls cleared the field all by himself one hundred thirty years ago. His decendents now interact in groups and with networks of other people. The same is true for most of us. We make partial contributions to larger and more complex tasks. We change a few lines of code in a computer program or a few lines of dialogue in a movie. We pass ideas, proposals, and solutions back and forth with people who possess diverse cognitive skills. We work in Bletchley Parks. And more and more often, we see InnoCentive-style opportunities.

AN OUTLINE OF THE BOOK

The remainder of this book contains two long parts followed by three short parts. In the first part, I define frameworks for modeling diversity, what I call *the diverse toolbox*. In the second part, I analyze if, when, and how diversity produces better outcomes. In the third part, I discuss the problems created by diverse values. In part four, I summarize and interpret the empirical evidence of diversity's benefits. And in the final part,

I (briefly and sweepingly) discuss the implications for teams, organizations, markets, and democracies. In the epilogue, I wax philosophic about ketchup.

Part I: Unpacking the Toolbox

In part I, I unpack the first component of the *Diversity Conjecture*, diversity itself. Without that unpacking, we would be left to wander about in a land of catch phrases and vague metaphors. We cannot say whether diversity is good or bad unless we first know what diversity is. By *diversity*, I mean cognitive differences.[3] The unpacking consists of four formal frameworks.

DIVERSITY: UNPACKED

Diverse Perspectives: ways of representing situations and problems

Diverse Interpretations: ways of categorizing or partitioning perspectives

Diverse Heuristics: ways of generating solutions to problems

Diverse Predictive Models: ways of inferring cause and effect

The first framework captures the idea that people have diverse *perspectives*. Informally speaking, perspectives represent solutions to a problem. When we say that people have diverse perspectives, we mean that they see or envision the set of possibilities differently.

Perspectives embed knowledge: what we know is a function of how we represent things.[4] To provide just one example, Isabelle, an Ann Arbor resident, might represent a location relative to her home—"To get to Zingerman's, go down State Street and take a left in front of the big Catholic Church." Her brother, Nicky, might represent those same locations using a mental map of city streets—"Zingerman's sits on the corner of Kingsley and Detroit." Given their perspectives, Nicky would prove far more capable of telling a visitor how to get from Zingerman's to the Brown Jug, another Ann Arbor landmark. Isabelle might resort to directions that pass by her house. (Or, like the old New Englander, tell you, "You can't get there from here.")

Perspectives provide one framework for how people see the world differently. A second framework, *interpretations*, highlights the different categories people use to classify events, outcomes, and situations. For example, one financial analyst might categorize companies by their equity value, while another might categorize them by industry. One voter might categorize senators by their ideology. Another might categorize them by their home state. The first refers to Olympia Snowe as a Republican. The second refers to her as a Mainer. Formally speaking, interpretations create many-to-one mappings from the set of alternatives that form categories. Informally speaking, interpretations lump things together.

A third framework captures the different tools people use to solve problems. I call these *heuristics*. These can range in sophistication from simple rules of thumb—if it's bleeding put a bandage on it; no blood, no foul—to sophisticated analytic techniques such as Fourier analysis or wavelet transforms.[5] Heuristics must be applied with respect to a particular representation of a problem, a perspective, so I'll often speak of perspective/heuristic pairs. Because people often apply heuristics in combination, a person who knows two heuristics often knows three—the third being the combination of the first two. Often these combined heuristics prove far more powerful than the individual heuristics that form them.

The fourth framework for capturing cognitive diversity, *predictive models*, describes causal relationships between objects or events. Predictive models serve as a shorthand to make sense of the world. When someone says Nebraskans are nice people or Ford trucks are durable, they map categories—Nebraskans and Ford trucks—onto the categories nice people and durable machines. Predictive models can differ: Ben Franklin believed that "cheese and salty meat should be sparingly eat." Doctor Atkins believed differently. Both sold lots of books.

If we combine perspectives, interpretations, heuristics, and predictive models, we create *cognitive toolboxes*.[6] These toolboxes provide a new way to think about intelligence and ability. We often think of people as having a level of intelligence as measured by an IQ test—where they fall on a scale that starts at zero and goes up (way up, in some cases). IQ provides us with a convenient measuring stick. The move from measuring sticks to toolboxes obliges more than a switch of metaphors. Toolboxes change how we conceive of intelligences and how we compare them. Ranking people, as we shall see, can be a dubious exercise in the world of toolboxes.

Part II: The Benefits of Diverse Tools

In part II, I'll demonstrate *how* diversity produces collective benefits. This idea is not new. Plato said it a couple of thousand years ago. The scholar T. C. Chamberlain stated it in the scientific context more than one hundred years ago.[7] When we say that diversity leads to better outcomes, what do we mean? Do we mean better solutions to hydraulic engineering problems? Do we mean better weather forecasts? Do we mean better government welfare policies? Yes, yes, and yes.

We consider two main types of tasks: *problem solving* and *prediction*. These tasks encompass much of what collections of people do: we generate alternatives and we evaluate possibilities. Who performs these tasks? Small work teams, large organizations, and entire societies do. Teams of civil engineers solve water-flow problems (problem solving). Financial analysts predict the stock price of Kodak (prediction). University hiring committees choose a new employee (problem solving—what kind of scholar do we need?—and prediction—can this person do good research?).

If we hope to reap diversity's benefits, we need this logical connection. We need to understand the conditions under which diversity produces benefits. We cannot convene diverse groups and expect an instant utopia bursting with ice cream, ponies, and cedar plank–grilled salmon soaking in a black truffle oil and white wine reduction, but it will help.[8]

In analyzing problem solving, I focus on the roles played by diverse perspectives and heuristics. Diverse perspectives increase the number of solutions that a collection of people can find by creating different connections among the possible solutions. What one person sees as a small step—attaching our mittens to a string of yarn running through our coat sleeves—may seem a giant leap for another. Diverse heuristics have similar effects. Given a solution, more heuristics allow problem solvers to explore more potential improvements.

The analysis of problem solving culminates in two main results. First, I state a claim that *diversity trumps homogeneity*: collections of people with diverse perspectives and heuristics outperform collections of people who rely on homogeneous perspectives and heuristics. Second, I state a conditional claim that *diversity trumps ability*: random collections of intelligent problem solvers can outperform collections of the best individual problem solvers. This result relies on four conditions: (1) The problem must be difficult; (2) the perspectives and heuristics that the problem solvers possess must be diverse; (3) the set of problem solvers from which we choose our collections from must be large; and (4) the collections of problem solvers must not be too small.

I then consider predictive tasks. People might want to predict any number of outcomes: the price of a stock, the winner of an election, the box office receipts of a movie, the winner of a sporting event, or the sales of a new product. In making predictions, people rely on predictive models. Aggregating predictive models differs from aggregating information (where some people know the answer and others do not). Models of incomplete information are commonplace in economics and political science, but those models rely on signals. The predictive model framework provides a plausible source of these signals and, in doing so, establishes a central role for cognitive diversity in the smooth functioning of democracies and markets.

In the chapter on prediction, I show two main results: that diversity and accuracy contribute equally to collective predictive performance, and that a crowd's collective prediction must always be at least as good as the average prediction of a member of the crowd. I call these the *Diversity Prediction Theorem* and the *Crowds Beat Averages Law*. The first result implies that we should not think of predictive ability as of paramount importance and predictive diversity as something that contributes only around the margins. Ability and diversity enter the equation equally. This result is not a political statement but a mathematical one, like the Pythagorean Theorem. In this chapter, I also compare crowds against experts as well as information markets against polls. I show how information markets create incentives for both accuracy and diversity, which may explain why they work better than polls.

Part III: Diverse Values: A Conflict of Interests (Or Is It?)

Up to this point, the results should bring joy and happiness. We might all think diversity is a wonderful thing. That's because we've ignored *diverse preferences*, differences in what we value. Preference diversity differs from toolbox diversity: Toolbox differences do not create conflict. Preference diversity can and does. For this reason, management books stress agreeing on a common goal—a common *fundamental* preference. If people disagree about what they're trying to accomplish, they function poorly as a collective.

Common fundamental preferences need not imply agreement. People can also have diverse *instrumental* preferences. They can differ on how they think it best to cross a particular finish line. In other words, people can disagree over means as well as ends. Instrumental preferences are preferences about means, so they implicitly contain predictive models. We like (or don't like) a policy of a higher minimum wage because we think it helps (hurts) workers. This distinction between fundamental and instrumental allows two people to agree over the destination—a romantic dinner at Charlie Trotter's restaurant in Chicago—but to disagree over how to get there—cab or train.[9]

My treatment of the potential problems created by preference diversity is at best a flyover of the relevant results—"Look, there's the Grand Canyon." The first result, Arrow's Theorem, gives conditions under which individual preferences do not aggregate into a collective preference. The second result, proved by Charles Plott, states that with majority rule voting, any proposed alternative can be defeated by some other alternative. The third result, proved by Richard McKelvey and Norman Schofield, states that if people vote sincerely, then a sequence of majority rule choices could lead anywhere. We could even have action figure governors! The final result, proved simultaneously by Mark Satterthwaite, an economist, and Allan Gibbard, a philosopher, states that people have incentives to misrepresent their preferences.

These four results paint a bleak picture only if we believe preference differences to be fundamental. In many organizations and communities, members all pull for the same goal. What preference diversity does exist is instrumental. If so, I'll argue that the negative results aren't so bad after all.

I complete this third part of the book with a brief analysis of how toolbox and preference diversity interact. In doing so, I turn some of the intuitions from the previous chapters on their heads. Diverse perspectives, which we touted as a panacea, have a dark side—they lead to the discovery of lots of possible alternatives. If people have diverse fundamental preferences, they less likely agree when they have more possible choices. On the flip side, diverse fundamental preferences, which cause so many problems when making choices, prove beneficial for problem solving. What we desire influences how we look at problems, the perspectives we choose. Thus, collections of people with diverse preferences often prove better at problem solving than collections of people who agree. Difference of opinion not only makes a horse race, it also makes for effective, albeit sometimes contentious, teams.[10]

Part IV: Does Diversity Produce Benefits? The Pudding

The first three parts of the book present a logic of diversity. They explain how diversity produces benefits. Yet, many people care about "facts." These people want to know whether the logic has empirical support, if evidence fits the theory. In the fourth part of the book, I take on that question. I do so with some trepidation. If we do not know how something works, demands for empirical support are premature. If we don't understand how or why diversity creates benefits, we may not realize those benefits. Consider the width of the space between knowing that atoms contain enormous power and building a nuclear reactor to harness that power. It is huge. An analogous (though smaller) gap may exist for diversity. The benefits may be there, but we may not know how to unlock them. If we don't, we shouldn't expect empirical evidence. We may as well wonder why people living in the dark ages didn't use electric lights.

This book makes three core claims: (1) *Diverse perspectives and tools enable collections of people to find more and better solutions and contribute to overall productivity*; (2) *Diverse predictive models enable crowds of people to predict values accurately,* and (3) *Diverse fundamental preferences frustrate the process of making choices.*

Reducing the whole book into three claims paints a picture in rather broad strokes. Some may accuse me of making Bob Ross appear to be a pointillist, but so be it. Here's the evidence: whether we look at countries, cities, or teams, the bulk of evidence supports all three claims.[11] This evidence is strong in places and weak in others. No matter; it does not hold this book on its shoulders. It merely reassures us that the insights apply in the real world.

A second empirical question, one that some readers may believe to be a giant elephant sitting in the middle of the page, relates to identity diversity, that is, to differences in race, ethnicity, gender, social status, and the like. We can phrase the question as follows: Do identity diverse groups prove better at solving problems and making predictions? The short answer: yes, they do. But, identity diversity produces better outcomes indirectly. Any claim that identity diversity creates collective benefits requires two links. The first link connects identity diversity to cognitive diversity. The second link connects these diverse talents to relevant problems. Any number of corporate advertisements, university brochures, and organization Web sites contain what we might call the diversity mantra: *diverse identities bring diverse perspectives.*[12] Oddly, this mantra leaves implicit the conjecture that diverse perspectives create benefits. Presumably, the people who write those brochures believe that it does.

And yet, we can take the connection between identity and cognition too far. Identity diverse people can think alike. And people belonging the same race, age, gender, religion, and social class can also think differently. George Bush and Howard Dean, the early leader for the Democratic Party's 2004 presidential nomination, both grew up in wealthy families, went to elite prep schools, and then attended Yale, with Bush graduating three years before Dean. Yet they think about the world and its problems differently. And let's be honest, Bletchley Park was hardly a rainbow gathering. Yet these groups were cognitively diverse (though perhaps not as diverse as they could have been had they included people of diverse identities).

As for the second link, we shouldn't expect diverse teams to be better at eating donuts or mopping floors. Identity difference can contribute to better outcomes only if the task is appropriate—if we're designing a building—but it cannot have much to add if the task doesn't require problem solving or prediction (if we're digging the hole to put the building in)!

If we look at the evidence on whether identity diverse collections of people perform better than more homogeneous collections, we see mixed results at every level. At the country level, we find that in advanced economies, ethnic diversity proves beneficial. In poorer countries, it causes problems. In cities, we see similar effects. Diversity has the same pluses and minuses. Cognitive diversity increases innovation. Preference diversity leads to squabbles.

If we look at groups, the results become even messier and more confusing. Recent, careful, awarding-winning studies show little effect. Even claims that diverse groups are needed to market to diverse customers do not hold up to close scrutiny.[13] One reason for the mangle of outcomes is that group dynamics can create no end of problems. People prefer to hang with people like themselves and tend to stereotype others.[14] In addition, when studying groups, we can test identity effects more finely, which confuses more than it clarifies. We can compare teams with 80 percent men and teams with 75 percent women. We can find groups that consist almost entirely of men between the ages of fifty and seventy. (Hint: they're running a country near you.)

Overall, the group-level findings are similar to what has been found at the city and country level. If well managed, identity diversity can create benefits, provided it correlates with cognitive differences and provided the task is one in which diversity matters.

Summing all this up, yes, race, gender, and ethnicity matter, but so do our *experiences*: the friendships, road trips, chance meetings, and pancake breakfasts that combine to form a life. *Education* and *training* also influence our collections of cognitive tools. Diversity has many causes. That's good.

Part V: Going on the Offensive

Part V takes the logic out into the real world. I show how to go on the offensive, how to leverage diversity to produce better outcomes. Length considerations preclude this part of the book from reaching greater depths. What I cover, though preliminary, provides a useful start. (Given the power of diversity, I'm also guessing that others out there will see even more applications.)

My advice tends to be more general than specific—how organizations might best leverage diversity, how the models might be applied to hiring decisions as well as college admissions. Some of the advice is intuitive—bring in outsiders—but other bits of advice are less so: encourage preference diversity, avoid lumping, and distinguish aggregation from compromise. My final piece of advice is to maintain humility and embrace the mysteries of diversity. We cannot expect to understand the mysterious origins of new ideas and breakthroughs.

THE LOGIC IN CONTEXT

Before continuing, let's stop and situate the contributions in three larger contexts. First, the logic points to potential benefits from globalization beyond great food, awesome music, and amazing art. Yes, cultural awareness prevents boneheaded actions.[15]

But the logic suggests that the benefits of a globalized workforce extend far beyond better understandings of local markets. People with different life experiences and training, people from different cultural backgrounds, likely see the world differently. And those differences—differences in perspectives—can be valuable when solving problems or making predictions.

Second, the logic can and should be read as supportive of interdisciplinary research. People with different disciplinary training naturally bring diverse understandings and tools to problems. That diversity of tools can lead to breakthroughs that would not occur, or would occur more slowly without interdisciplinary research. Many university administrators preach interdisciplinary research. This book provides a logic for continuing to break down the barriers that separate the disciplines.

Finally, the logic applies to recent defenses of affirmative action policies. Affirmative action policies take many forms. The reasons for affirmative action have shifted over time, at least in the eyes of the courts. Initially, affirmative action policies were motivated by the desire to redress past and current discrimination. Later, following rioting in the 1960s, some saw affirmative action policies as a way to hold society together. Police departments were allowed to have racial goals so that their officers reflected the communities they served. Schools have also attempted to have teachers match their communities' demographics, but the courts have not always supported those policies.

The logic in this book can be used to support an *instrumental* argument for affirmative action. If diversity produces benefits, then schools, firms, and organizations should be able to give a leg up to underrepresented people. The instrumental defense has become central in recent court decisions.[16] The extent to which this logic supports race-based affirmative action depends on empirical facts: *either identity diversity correlates with cognitive diversity or it does not.*

Not all advocates of affirmative action view the instrumental argument positively. Some fear that it covers historical injustices and current discrimination under a large multicolored rug.[17] This book helps us to think through when it would and would not hold. It helps us sort the logical from the illogical. For example, in his dissenting opinion on the cases involving the University of Michigan's law school admissions policies, Supreme Court Associate Justice Antonin Scalia wrote that Michigan was suffering from logical dissonance. On the one hand, Michigan wanted a "super-duper" law school (that's legalese meaning "really good"). On the other, it wanted to be diverse. Justice Scalia presented these two facts as contradictory.

They are not. Diversity and super-duperness can go hand in hand: a great law school may require a diversity of perspectives, interpretations, heuristics, and predictive models. A great law school benefits from including people with diverse preferences (law students like to argue, even more so than lawyers). So if we believe that differences in race, gender, ethnicity, physical ability, religion, sexual orientation, and so on correlate with cognitive diversity, then being super-duper *may* require some identity diversity. And, moreover, super-duperness may *always* require identity diversity, long after discrimination ends.

That same logic does not necessarily translate to every sector of the corporate world. Universities have different goals than companies. Despite their reputation as EMOs (endowment maintenance organizations), universities seek to do research, educate, and serve. In a university classroom, students and faculty learn from one another. Far less cross-fertilization of ideas takes place in a firm that employs traveling salespeople.

AND AWAY WE GO

With the requisite captivating example, background, overview, and contextualization in place, we can now turn to the fun part—the frameworks and models. Once built, they allow us to demonstrate that when confronted with a difficult task, be it solving a problem, predicting the future, or making a choice, we benefit by including diverse people. In such situations, we might think about gathering together the best and brightest minds, but that's a flawed approach. We also need to pay attention to the diversity of those minds, all the more so if the old saying that "great minds think alike" holds true.

As a note of warning, what follows contains a little bit of mathematics. Anything difficult has been relegated to the notes. What the editors allowed to remain should be accessible to almost everyone. If you can handle equations like "force equals mass times acceleration" ($F = MA$) and the Pythagorean Theorem ($A^2 + B^2 = C^2$), you'll be fine.[18]

For those more mathematically inclined readers (hint: my professional colleagues), accept in advance this apology for the necessary overgeneralizations. Many of the claims in the book can be stated with greater clarity and precision. Those who want the details in more detail can peruse the academic papers that Lu Hong, Jenna Bednar, and I have written in the stark, cold language of the academy.[19] These papers (all available on my Web site) contain the mathematical chest thumping—the epsilons and sigma algebras—that one expects from a card-carrying mathematical social scientist.

Churchill called Bletchley Park "the goose that laid the golden egg," and so it was. Someday, InnoCentive-inspired organizations may well become gaggles that produce golden eggs by the truck-load. We can hope. But we must keep in mind that as plastic as our brains may be, they're individually limited. Collectively, they're less limited, but only if they're constructed differently. One light bulb, even the one over Edison's head, is not as bright or as interesting as a string of multicolored lights. Those Apple Corporation ads give sound advice: Think different. In difference lies the potential to contribute.

Part One_____

UNPACKING THE TOOLBOX

Of course, it needs the whole society, to give the symmetry we seek. The parti-colored wheel must revolve very fast to appear white.

—RALPH WALDO EMERSON, "Experience"

A BOOK on diversity can find no better place to begin than by visiting Emerson, one of the greatest thinkers on diversity. Not only did Emerson celebrate and encourage differences, he dared mock those who did not think different—"A foolish consistency is the hobgoblin of little minds." In looking at a crowd of people in an auditorium, Emerson saw not a crowd but a collection of individuals. He saw each person as limited and diverse in what and how each perceived. He saw our experiences and moods as constraining our abilities to see the world in its fullness. Ideally, he hoped we would stretch those experiences and expand our horizons to arrive at individual understandings.

> Life is a train of moods like a string of beads, and as we pass through them, they prove to be many-colored lenses which paint the world their own hue, and each shows only what lies in its focus. From the mountain you see the mountain. We animate what we can, and we see only what we animate. Nature and books belong to the eyes that see them. It depends on the mood of the man, whether he shall see the sunset or the fine poem. There are always sunsets, and there is always genius; but only a few hours so serene that we can relish nature or criticism.

As the excerpt from the essay "Experience" makes clear, Emerson believes that how we experience the world influences how we perceive it. That is certainly true. But what are the implications of those differences? To answer that question, we need first to make better sense of what those differences are. In what follows, we too see mountains; we call them rugged landscapes. These represent difficult problems. And to quote Emerson yet again, "The difference between landscape and landscape is small, but there is a great difference in the beholders." Those beholders who see landscapes sublimely we call geniuses. We can quibble about what it means to be a genius, and even about the extent of Emerson's contributions, but we cannot deny his ability to see clearly what for so many others was muddled and confused. And so, it's appropriate that we begin at his front porch. And as we take leave, we remind ourselves to follow his sage advice, to slow down the wheel.

We slow down the wheel for a specific purpose: to understand the potential benefits of diversity. Our goal is to understand when and how diversity is beneficial. We want to move beyond metaphor and reach a deep understanding. Eventually, we do that. I'll state formal results that show that when solving a problem, diversity can trump ability and that when making a prediction, diversity matters just as much as ability. In order to make those formal claims, I need to lay a foundation.

As an analogy, consider the mathematical theorem that the area of a rectangle equals the base times the height. That result makes sense only if we know that we mean by *base* and by *height*. We have to define those terms. The same holds here. To show that diversity is beneficial, we need to define terms and concepts, so we do. I define *perspectives* (ways of representing the world), *heuristics* (techniques and tools for making improvements), *interpretations* (ways of creating categories), and *predictive models* (inferences about correlation and cause and effect).

These formal ways of capturing diversity we then lump together and call them a person's toolbox. That's how we think of people's capabilities—as their collections of tools. We then use this toolbox framework to explore if, why, how, and when toolbox diversity produces benefits. We have to wait to do that, though. First, we must learn about the tools themselves.

CHAPTER 1

Diverse Perspectives

HOW WE SEE THINGS

Those French, they have a different word for everything.
—STEVE MARTIN

WE all differ in how we see and interpret things. Whether considering a politician's proposal for changes in welfare policy, a new front-loading washing machine, or an antique ceramic bowl, each of us uses a different representation. Each of us sees the thing, whatever it is, in our own way. We commonly refer to the ways we encode things as *perspectives*. But if asked what a perspective is, most of us would have only a crude idea. In this chapter I provide a formal definition, but before I get to that I'll present an example of a famous perspective: the periodic table.

In the periodic table each element has a unique number. These numbers help us to organize the elements. They give structure. Compare this perspective to the perspective that uses common names such as oxygen, carbon, and copper. By convention we know what those names mean—copper is a soft brownish metal that conducts electricity—but the names don't create any meaningful structure. They are just names. We could just as well give copper the name *Kamisha*.

Mendeleyev's periodic table gave us a meaningful structure. Coming up with that perspective took hard work. To discover the structure of the elements, Mendeleyev created cards of the sixty-three known elements. Each card contained information about an element including its chemical and physical properties. Mendeleyev then spent hours studying and arranging these cards, transforming the problem into a representational puzzle. Eventually, Mendeleyev pinned the cards to the wall in seven columns, ordering the cards from lightest to heaviest. (Imagine playing solitaire on the wall using thumbtacks.) When he did this, he saw a structure that was completely understood only three decades later with the introduction of atomic numbers. Before Mendeleyev, atomic weight had been considered irrelevant. A scientist could order the elements by atomic weight from lightest to heaviest, but he could also arrange them alphabetically or by the number of letters in their name. Why bother?

As some of the elements had not been found, Mendeleyev's table had gaps. New elements were soon found that filled those gaps. Mendeleyev took information, turned it into the pieces of a puzzle, and showed us that pieces were missing.[1] Mendeleyev's representational puzzle, unlike the problem of finding the chemical composition of salt, lacks a physical analog. He was not searching for an existing structure; he was creating a structure out of thin air. That structure revealed order in the stuff of which we're made. His story is not unique. We can find stories like Mendeleyev's throughout the history of science—think of Copernicus and the heliocentric universe, or of Einstein and the construction of relatively theory. In both cases, someone saw the world differently—Einstein linked space and time—and what had been obscure, confusing, or unseen became clear.

Scholars from a variety of disciplines have studied how people and groups make breakthroughs. The common answer: *diverse perspectives.* As the philosopher of science Steven Toulmin wrote, "The heart of all major discoveries in the physical sciences is the discovery of novel methods of representation."[2] New perspectives, what Toulmin calls "novel methods of representation," are often metaphorical. The canonical model for earthquakes, for instance, involves blocks connected by springs, which can then be analyzed rigorously using mathematics.[3] Though we know perspectives lead to breakthroughs, their sources remain shrouded in mystery. The only necessary ingredient appears to be hard work and a willingness to look at things that others ignore. That's also a recurrent theme. Being diverse in a relevant way often proves hard. Being diverse and irrelevant is easy.

We can now define perspectives formally. They are representations that encode objects, events, or situations so that each gets its own unique name. No two chairs, no two people are represented in the same way. Mathematicians call these "one-to-one" mappings or bijections. That's a strong but necessary assumption. The names that perspectives assign to objects capture underlying structure. If they do not, then the perspectives are not of much use.

In this chapter, we drive home one main insight: *the right perspective can make a problem easy.* We see how most scientific breakthroughs and business innovations involve a person seeing a problem or situation differently. The germ theory of disease transformed what seemed like an intractable confusing mess of data into a coherent collection of facts. Thanks to Adam Smith, we all know the story of the pin factory and how efficient it is. But do many of us know that the first pin factory manufactured brushes with firm steel bristles? The firm began producing pins only when someone realized that the bristles could be cut off and made into pins. Diverse perspectives—seeing the world differently, seeing the brush as a forest of pins—provided the seeds of innovation.[4] Let's begin.

PUTTING OUR DIFFERENT SHOULDERS

TO THE WHEEL

I first provided some hints of how diverse worldviews can be useful in solving a problem such as cracking the Enigma code. We now consider a problem related to cracking a code of a different form. This example will be a bit of a teaser for the second part of the book, when we consider the application of diversity to problem solving, prediction, and choice.

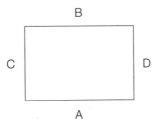

Figure 1.1 The Geometrician's Perspective

Figure 1.2 The Economist's Perspective

We start with a puzzling fact: in every object examined by a team of scientists, they find that the amount of A equals the amount of B and the amount of C equals the amount of D. For the moment, don't worry about what A, B, C, and D are. What might we do with such a fact? How might we make sense of it? Let's put on several different types of academic hats and see what we might do with it.

We might first think like geometricians and imagine that the letters represent the sides of a rectangle (see figure 1.1). If we label the top and the bottom of the rectangle A and B, and label the two sides C and D, we can then exploit the property that the opposite sides of a rectangle must be equal. We have explained our fact. Of course, we don't have any idea what to do with this rectangle, but still, we have an idea that whatever we find might well be rectangular.

Or we might suppose that we are economists (see figure 1.2). If so, we might reason that A is the amount of some good supplied and B is the amount demanded. Or we might reason that A is the

Figure 1.3 The Chemist's Perspective

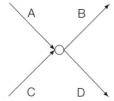

Figure 1.4 The Physicist's Perspective

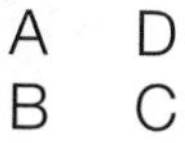

A   D
B   C

Figure 1.5 The Fashion Designer's Perspective

price of the good and *B* is the marginal cost. Or we might think that *A* is the price of an input and *B* is its marginal product. In each of these examples, some force equilibrates the amounts.

Or we might imagine ourselves chemists (see figure 1.3). We might reason that some chemical reaction results in molecules containing equal amounts of *A* and *B*, and of *C* and *D*.

Or we might imagine ourselves physicists (see figure 1.4). We might then reason that *A*, *B*, *C*, and *D* are properties that must be conserved such as energy or matter that can be neither lost nor gained.

Finally, we might imagine ourselves fashion designers with nifty, small glasses (see figure 1.5). If so, we might think of *A* as the number of people wearing argyle sweaters and *B* as the number of people wearing blue jeans. We might think of *C* as the number of people wearing cutoffs and *D* as the number wearing dingy

T-shirts. If everyone wearing an argyle sweater wears jeans and everyone wearing a dingy T-shirt wears cutoffs, then $A = B$ and $C = D$.

Each of these possible perspectives embeds an intelligence based on training and experience. And each of these ways of looking at the problem would prove useful in some cases and not so useful in others.

To see diverse perspectives at work, let's look at the real story: the discovery of the structure of DNA. Francis Crick and James Watson's piecing together of the double helix structure involved many hours of hard work and lots of dead ends. Overcoming these dead ends (what we will later call "local optima": perspectives that look pretty good until you search further) required that they develop new perspectives on their problem. One fact at their disposal, a fact ignored by many others working on the problem, was Chargaff's rules, which stated that a cell's nucleus contained equal amounts of adenine (A) and thymine (T) and equal amounts of guanine (G) and cytosine (C). The natural way to look at these rules was chemical and to think that they happened to be produced in equal amounts by some chemical reaction in the cell. But Crick one day channeled his inner fashion designer and thought to pair the adenine and thymine and the guanine and cytosine. These pairings formed the rungs in the helical ladder that is DNA. In retrospect, the idea to create these pairings seems obvious. At the time, it was a breakthrough.

The most amazing aspect of Crick's pairings idea was not that it led to the solution, but that it solved a second puzzle: the pairings revealed how DNA can be the building block of life. To see how this worked, we use our fashion designer's perspective but replace our blue jeans (B) with trousers (T) and make all of our dingy T-shirts green (G) so that we are using the appropriate letters ($A=T$ and $C=G$).

Imagine a long line of people, some wearing argyle sweaters and trousers and some wearing green dingy T-shirts and cutoff shorts. We can identify each person with a two-letter code. AT is someone wearing an argyle sweater and trousers, and GC is someone wearing a green shirt and cutoffs. To describe the outfits of the entire line of people, we make a long list: *AT, AT, GC, GC, GC, AT,* and so on. In making this list, we've wasted a lot of ink. We don't need two letters to identify each person. If we know what pants a person wears, we know what shirt he wears (and vice versa). Thus, we need only identify one piece of clothing on each person, and we can use logic to fill in the rest. The single piece of clothing list *A, G, T, C, T, T, A, C* provides enough information to reproduce the full list *AT, GC, AT, GC, AT, AT, AT, GC* because the sweaters are always matched with the trousers and the T-shirts with the cutoffs.

This insight explains how our cells reproduce. (Hard to believe, but true.) When the helix splits, each half contains sufficient information to reproduce the missing other half. Every *A* can be matched with a *T*, every *C* can be matched with a *G*, and so on. The single strands of DNA can be thought of as half dressed, but fortunately our cell chemistry completes their outfits by matching appropriate bottoms with tops and tops with bottoms.

With the aid of modern microscopes, any one of us could now uncover the structure of DNA. But Crick and Watson didn't have modern microscopes. All they had were fuzzy pictures taken by Rosalind Franklin. (Franklin didn't share in the Nobel Prize, not because she was a woman, but because she happened to be dead at the time they awarded it.) Crick and Watson's construction was a monumental scientific achievement that required diverse thinking. Crick and Watson may be two white boys, but viewed cognitively, they're a diverse pair. If a person can be diverse, Crick was. Crick's training spanned physics, chemistry, and biology. He did not have Ph.D.s in these areas. In fact, he had no Ph.D. at all. James Watson did have a Ph.D., in zoology. He had been a wunderkind ornithologist, but became obsessed with DNA after studying viruses. Could Crick have unraveled the puzzle without Watson or Watson without Crick? Most doubt it. Historians of science assign credit to their hard work and their diverse skills. They leveraged their differences and together achieved far more than either could have alone. In Robert Wright's brief popular account, he writes, "here is a case where one plus one equals twelve."[5]

To understand this new mathematics, to see how one plus one can be twelve, we need more formalism. We need to begin the harder (and more satisfying) work of building frameworks and models.

THE PERSPECTIVE FRAMEWORK

We now get down to business and consider the perspective framework in detail. In this framework, we'll assume a large set of objects, situations, events, or solutions that must be given a representation. That set could be big. It could contain a billion billion billion things, but it is finite nonetheless.[6] Think stars, atoms, and all creatures great and small. The challenge is that they must be organized. To do this, each person possesses an *internal language* that describes these objects, situations, events, or solutions. An internal language can be written in words, in numbers or symbols, or in abstract shapes and forms. An internal language differs from a spoken or written external language. Internal languages can assign different words to the same object.

What do we mean when we say that these internal languages differ across people? To modify an example from Daniel Dennett, one person could internally represent a right triangle by the length of its two edges. Another person could internally represent the same triangle with a nonright angle and its adjacent edge. These two people can communicate the existence of the triangle by drawing it, but they don't have to translate between their internal languages; they need only translate their internal languages into reality.[7]

So we have some thing, some object or event, and we have an individual's internal language with which they represent that thing. Think of the UPC codes on products as an internal language for scanners. Each item in the supermarket gets a unique code. We call the mapping that takes reality and encodes it in the internal language a *perspective*. Perspectives assign unique names to objects. Mathematicians call them "one-to-one mappings." Each object, situation, problem, or event maps to a unique "word" in the person's internal language.

*A **perspective** is a map from reality to an internal language such that each distinct object, situation, problem, or event gets mapped to a unique word.*[8]

Although perspectives represent solutions in terms of an internal language, from here on I refer to perspectives as both the mapping to the internal language and as the representation itself. This makes the prose much easier to follow, but it comes at a small cost. When we say that two people have different perspectives we could mean one of two things. We could mean that they map reality differently into the same internal language—long strings of zeros and ones—or we could mean that they map reality into different internal languages. But in both cases, the perspectives differ and that's our main focus.

The first perspectives most of us learn are bases—not in baseball but in mathematics. When we say that the speed limit is seventy miles an hour, we use base ten. We mean seven times ten miles per hour. In my older son's kindergarten class, they use the concept of base ten to teach addition. To add seven plus five, a child grabs five straws and then seven more straws. He or she then counts out ten straws, which get traded in for a "bundle." Bundles consist of ten straws tied together. This bundle is then added to the two remaining straws to give an answer of "one ten bundle and two ones" or 12. The teacher might alternatively ask the students to create bundles of size eight. Assigned that task, the child could create one eight bundle with four straws left over. So, in base eight, the answer equals 14. The number of straws could be written in any number of bases. In base four, the answer would be 30, and in base two, the language of computer scientists, the answer would be 1100.

Though we think in base ten, we need not. It is just one of many perspectives we can use to represent numbers. Its use is not universal. The Mayans, who had greater toe awareness, used base twenty. Even more amazing, cultural anthropologists report that one former British colony still uses base sixteen for some weights and measures. Once they reach sixteen ounces, they use the term *pint*.

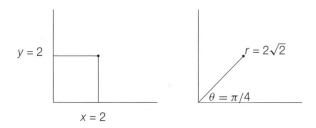

Figure 1.6 Cartesian and Polar Perspectives

The second time that we confront diverse perspectives in mathematics is usually in trigonometry, a subject loved by all. In trigonometry, we learn that a point in space can be represented using Cartesian coordinates, the familiar (x, y), or using something called polar coordinates. Polar coordinates describe a point by an *angle* θ and a distance from the origin called the *radius r*. Figure 1.6 shows a point represented in Cartesian coordinates as the point $(x, y) = (2, 2)$ and in polar coordinates as the point $(r, \theta) = (2\sqrt{2}, \frac{\pi}{4})$.

The Cartesian and polar coordinates systems are both perspectives of points in Euclidean space. Neither perspective is better than the other (despite claims made by those "Polar coordinates are cooler" T-shirts). Cartesian coordinates simplify the description of rectangles by labeling a length and a width. Describing a rectangle using polar coordinates requires a calculator, a clean sheet of paper, and an eraser. But polar coordinates show their worth when we have to describe circles and arcs. A circle is all of the points of some fixed radius. To describe a circle using Cartesian coordinates, we have to rely on complicated functions of x and y. Thus, easy problems in polar coordinates can be difficult in Cartesian, and vice versa.[9] I'll often return to this insight—*the choice of perspective contributes to a problem's difficulty.* It's a touchstone for the more general results.

A second insight is that perspectives often impose structure. For example, if our internal language assigns numbers, we create a complete ordering. One is the smallest number. Two lies between one and three, and so on. Complete and even partial orderings give language power. They simplify identification.[10] If an internal language fails to create structure, if it consists of idiosyncratic names such as *Isabella, Roland, Susan,* and *Hugo,* then, unlike Mendeleyev's periodic table, the language cannot clarify relationships. Even if we were to alphabetize the names, we learn nothing about the relatedness of Roland and Susan. They could be husband and wife. They could be father and daughter. This raises a key point: *Internal languages that fail to create structure do not aid problem solving or understanding. To be of functional value, perspectives must embed meaningful relatedness.* Just assigning names isn't enough.

BEN AND JERRY

To see more concretely how a perspective creates structure, we consider an example that takes some liberties with a story about how Ben and Jerry's Homemade developed a new flavor.[11] In addition to foreshadowing future claims about the benefits of diverse perspectives, this example provides further evidence of the benefits of owning an ice cream company. Suppose that when Ben and Jerry were searching for a good recipe for New York Super Fudge Chunk Ice Cream, they created a two-dimensional array of pints. The two dimensions that they considered were the number of chunks and the size of the chunks. These dimensions impose a structure on the pints that is understandable and manipulable.

Their perspective allows them to compare and maneuver in meaningful ways. They might want more chunks, or larger ones. Given their perspective, they can do that. They have a structure they can exploit. Had they given the pints arbitrary names such as *Captain Crunchy* and *New York State of Mind* and randomly arranged them on the table, then searching among the pints would be nothing more than a random search. But having a structured perspective allows for structured search. Figure 1.7 is a representation of Ben and Jerry's perspective, which is structured. It helps us make sense of how ice cream differs in a meaningful way.

4,1	4,2	4,3	4,4
3,1	3,2	3,3	3,4
2,1	2,2	**2,3**	2,4
1,1	1,2	1,3	1,4

Figure 1.7 Ben and Jerry's Perspective: Number of Chunks (in dozens) and Size of Chunks (cm diameter)

250	252	255	256	258	262

Figure 1.8 Nelly Armstrong's Perspective (in calories)

3,2	**2,3**	**4,1**	3,3	2,4	4,3

Figure 1.9 Nelly's Perspective in Number and Size of Chunks (in calories)

The internal language consists of numbers representing the number of chocolate chunks and the size of those chunks. Their perspective maps the pints into numbers. This perspective, though useful, is just one of many. It just happens to be the one that Ben and Jerry chose. To see a different perspective, suppose that Ben and Jerry hired a consultant named Nelly Armstrong, and that she arranged the pints according to the number of calories per serving (see figure 1.8).

These two perspectives create distinct spatial relationships between the pints of ice cream. We can translate Nelly's perspective into Ben and Jerry's by replacing the calories in each pint with the number and size of chunks (see figure 1.9).

In Nelly's perspective, the pint with two dozen three centimeter diameter chunks lies adjacent to the pint with four dozen chunks of diameter one centimeter (they are typed in **bold** in her perspective). In Ben and Jerry's perspective, these two pints are far apart

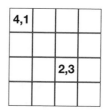

Figure 1.10 Ben and Jerry's Perspective (Number of Chunks, Size of Chunks)

(see figure 1.10). Suppose that Ben and Jerry proposed the pint with two dozen chunks of diameter three, and the consultant then suggested the pint with four dozen chunks of diameter one, and let's suppose that hers tasted better. Ben and Jerry would have perceived this as a cognitive leap, as a brilliant insight by their highly paid consultant. But it is only a giant leap because of the structure imposed by their perspective. It is a small step for Nelly. (If you would like to test these theories in practice, get out your ice cream maker and get cranking.)

Nelly's perspective leads to an improvement, but let's not confuse it with genius. Genius is Einstein linking space and time to create his theory of relativity. Nelly takes into account the fact that people count calories—a good idea but not a great one. We might even speculate on the origin of this perspective. Calories may have been salient for Nelly. Some experience, such as having a father who attended Weight Watchers, could have caused her to focus on calories and not chip size. Nellie also may have gained this perspective from her years of experience in the food industry, which taught her that calories affect taste. Regardless, it gave her a different way of seeing than Ben and Jerry's—and that's what did the trick.

Not all diverse perspectives are helpful. Just because someone brings a different perspective doesn't mean that it will lead to a better solution. To see this, consider a second consultant, Hannah, who organizes the pints of ice cream by the average length of time it takes to chew a spoonful of the ice cream. In order to rationalize being paid some stupendous fee, Hannah might give this attribute some impressive name like *masticity*. For the problem of making ice cream, this perspective would not create meaningful structure. It would be a diverse but not very useful perspective. That doesn't mean it's always a bad perspective. A food industry consultant who saw this example remarked that masticity does matter for breakfast cereals. Cereals should be neither mush nor bark and twigs.

Our Ben and Jerry's example shows a benefit of diverse perspectives in problem solving. Perspectives can also be useful in strategic situations. The difficulty of formulating a strategy depends on how the strategies are represented. To see this, we consider three games.

THREE GAMES

These games that we consider require skill, like chess and Go, although they are not as challenging. Unlike children's board games such as Candy Land or Chutes and Ladders or adult games such as poker, bridge, and backgammon, they involve no luck. The first game is called Sum to Fifteen. Herbert Simon, a computer scientist and political scientist who was awarded the Nobel Prize in economics, created it.

SUM TO FIFTEEN

> **Setup:** Nine cards numbered 1 through 9 are laid out on a table face up.
> **Order of Play:** One player is randomly chosen to go first and then players alternate taking cards.
> **Object:** To collect three cards that sum to 15.

Sum to Fifteen creates two contradicting incentives. A player wants to build combinations that could sum to 15 while simultaneously preventing the other player from doing the same. Walking through a single play of the game reveals some of its complexity.

Suppose that the first player chooses the 5 and the second player chooses the 3. The first player would then not want to choose the 7 because $(5 + 3 + 7 = 15)$ and the 3 has already been selected.

TABLE 1.1:
First player's cards and needs

Cards	Sum	Needed Card
2,4	6	**9**
2,5	7	8
4,5	9	**6**

Suppose then the first player chooses the 2. Her cards now sum to 7, so the second player must choose the 8 to prevent the first player from winning. The second player's cards now sum to only 11, meaning that the first player must choose the 4. After this card has been chosen, the situation looks as follows:

Player 1: Holds 2, 4, 5
Player 2: Holds 3, 8
Remaining Cards: 1, 6, 7, 9

The table above shows all pairs of cards that the first player holds, their sum, and what third card must be added to it in order to sum to 15. For example, cards 2 and 4 sum to six, so card number 9 brings the total to fifteen. The numbers in bold in the last column have yet to be chosen.

Looking carefully at this table reveals that the first player wins. If the second player chooses 6, the first player chooses 9. If the second player chooses 9, the first player chooses 6. In addition, the second player has no card that he can choose that allows him to win. Game over.

The second game is more complicated. In this game, each of nine picnic baskets contains a unique combination of food items. These items are Nachos (N), Eggs (E), Sausage (S), Water (W), Hot dogs (H), Vinegar (V), Lemons (L), and Raisins (R). Across them, the nine baskets contain three of each food item. The goal of this game is to collect baskets that contain all three copies of some food item. If either player gets all three lemons, or nachos, or eggs, and so on, that player wins.

TABLE 1.2:
The Unpacking Game

Basket	Contents
1	H, W
2	S, E, R
3	N, V
4	N, E, L
5	H, V, L, R
6	S, W, L
7	S, V
8	N, W, R
9	H, E

THE UNPACKING GAME

> **Setup:** Nine baskets containing the items as shown in table 1.2 are placed on the table.
>
> **Order of Play:** One player is randomly chosen to go first and then players alternate choosing baskets.
>
> **Object:** To collect all three copies of one of the food items.

In the interests of brevity, we won't walk through a play of this game. You can try it by yourself. It's complicated and requires lots of mental accounting. As in Sum to Fifteen, players in the Unpacking Game must balance offense against defense.

The third game is familiar to all of us. In America we call it Tic Tac Toe, but in England, where it originated centuries ago, they call it Noughts and Crosses. Tic Tac Toe is an easy game. The fun of playing it wears off quickly.

TIC TAC TOE

> **Setup:** Play begins with an empty three-by-three array of boxes. (see figure 1.11)
>
> **Order of Play:** The player randomly chosen to go first places an X in an empty box. The other player places an O in an empty box. Players alternate placing Xs and Os.
>
> **Object:** To get three Xs or Os in a row.

Figure 1.11 Tic Tac Toe

8	3	4
1	5	9
6	7	2

Figure 1.12 A Magic Square

I won't walk you through the play of Tic Tac Toe. It's a simple game. Now, the other games, they were challenging. Or were they?

Suppose someone said that the other games are no harder than Tic Tac Toe. You'd think they were mathematicians, crazy, or both. But, in fact, not only are they no harder than Tic Tac Toe, they *are* Tic Tac Toe—in different perspectives. To see the equivalence of Tic Tac Toe and Sum to Fifteen, we have to learn about magic squares. Some readers may remember these from seventh-grade math. In a magic square, every row and every column sums to fifteen, as do both diagonals (see figure 1.12). Take the top row: $8 + 4 + 3 = 15$. Take the second column: $3 + 5 + 7 = 15$. Take the upward sloping diagonal: $6 + 5 + 4 = 15$. Every row, column, and diagonal sums to fifteen.

Let's play Tic Tac Toe on the magic square. When a player places an X or an O, they must erase the number in the box—which makes the game Sum to Fifteen. Reconsider the play of our game of Sum to Fifteen that we walked through earlier. The first player chose the 5 (put an X in the center box), and the second player then chose the 3 (put an O there). The first player then chose the 2 and the second player the 8. Now when the first player chooses the 4, he has two ways to win, as shown in figure 1.13.

O	O	X
1	X	9
6	7	X

Figure 1.13 Tic Tac Toe on a Magic Square

N,W,R	N,V	N,E,L
H,W	H,V,L,R	H,E
S,W,L	S,V	S,E,R

Figure 1.14 Unpacking Tic Tac Toe

In Sum to Fifteen, the second player's choice of three didn't seem so bad. Seen in the Tic Tac Toe perspective, it looks dumb. Proving that Sum to Fifteen is the same game as Tic Tac Toe requires a little work. The number of sets of three numbers that sum to 15 that include the number 8 equals three. These sets are {8, 2, 5}, {8, 1, 6}, and {8, 3, 4}. All of these are possible in Tic Tac Toe on the magic square. The number 5 belongs to four sets of three numbers that sum to 15 and all four of those also exist on the magic square. Similar arguments can be made for the other seven numbers, establishing the result.

Let's next look at the Unpacking Game. We can see the nine baskets as the nine boxes in Tic Tac Toe. The contents of a box are the paths that contain that box. Instead of having N denoting Nachos, let it denote the Northern path—the three boxes in the top row—and instead of eggs, let E denote the Eastern path. We can similarly define Southern S, Western W, Horizontal H, Vertical V, ladder (upward sloping) L, and ramp (downward sloping) R paths. The eight food items in the Unpacking Game can be seen as equivalent to the eight ways to win at Tic Tac Toe as shown in figure 1.14.

If we place the basket numbers on the Tic Tac Toe board, we again get the magic square (see figure 1.15).

8	3	4
1	5	9
6	7	2

Figure 1.15 Baskets on the Board

This example shows how diverse perspectives cut both ways; for every brilliant perspective that changes a difficult situation into an easy one, there may be a multitude of perspectives that muck up our understanding of even strategic contexts. Different perspectives can simplify, but they can also muddle.

This example also demonstrates the value of being open-minded and listening to new ways of thinking. A person concentrating on playing Sum to Fifteen might ignore some other person prattling on about magic squares and Tic Tac Toe. This other person knows a better way to play the game, but the better way requires adopting a new perspective, which isn't easy.

BUILDING NEW PERSPECTIVES

Novel perspectives on problems do not come from the ether. We often construct them from other perspectives. In this section, we see how that can be done and see evidence of the superadditivity of diversity: how one plus one equals twelve. To be precise, five perspectives create ten pairs of perspectives. Adding a sixth perspective creates, for free, five new pairs of perspectives. These paired perspectives can enable us to solve hard problems. The problems we consider here come from an intelligence test. Spatial and analytic intelligence tests partly attempt to measure the ability to generate perspectives. Thus, many standard questions on IQ tests ask "fill in the missing number" questions. Solving these problems requires encoding the given numbers in such a way that they make sense. This requires finding a perspective that makes the sequence into a pattern. Consider the following three problems taken from actual IQ tests.

IQ Test Questions: *In each sequence, replace the X with the unique number that makes the sequence logically consistent.*

$$\text{Sequence 1:} \quad 1 \quad 4 \quad 9 \quad 16 \quad X \quad 36$$
$$\text{Sequence 2:} \quad 1 \quad 2 \quad 3 \quad 5 \quad X \quad 13$$
$$\text{Sequence 3:} \quad 1 \quad 2 \quad 6 \quad X \quad 1{,}806$$

The first example is the easiest. It is a sequence of squares. The square of 1 equals 1, the square of 2 equals 4, and so on. The missing number is 25. The second sequence appears to be the prime numbers, but that is not correct. One is not considered a prime. Even if it were, the sequence of primes, 1, 2, 3, 5, 7, 11, and 13 requires space for two numbers between 5 and 13. Answering 7 to that question is what is often called a "good wrong answer."

The perspective that makes sense of this sequence is to recognize each number as the difference of the two that follow it. The first number equals the third number minus the second $(1 = 3 - 2)$, the second number equals the fourth minus the third $(2 = 5 - 3)$, and so on. It follows that the fifth should be such that it minus the fourth number, 5, equals the third number, 3. Therefore, the missing number is 8. The number 8 makes sense of the entire sequence because $13 - 8 = 5$, a sequence known as the Fibonacci sequence. It has many nice properties and is taught in many math classes.

People who happened to have seen this sequence in high school math probably get this question right on an IQ test and therefore appear smarter than they are. People who have never seen this sequence before and have had to develop this perspective on the fly can find this problem rather hard. It is not easy to generate this perspective under the stress of an exam.

Our third example is one of the more difficult mathematical sequence problems found on an IQ test. It differentiates those people with extraordinarily high mathematical and logical skill levels from those people who are just good. In this example, the last number, 1,806 seems out of place. It is too large. How could a logical sequence jump from 6 to 1,806? We can find the answer by combining the perspectives developed to solve the first two sequences. In doing so, we'll see the superadditivity of cognitive tools, building on existing tools to make ever more tools. Recall that solving the first sequence requires seeing the numbers as squares. The perspective that makes sense of the second sequence takes differences between successive numbers. Neither of these perspective works on this third sequence. But if they are combined, they reveal the pattern.

First, apply the perspective used in the second sequence: Look at the differences between numbers. The difference between the first two numbers equals 1 $(2 - 1 = 1)$. The difference between the second two numbers is 4 $(6 - 2 = 4)$. This suggests a pattern. That pattern is the perspective used to solve the first sequence: squares. Each number differs from the number after it by an amount equal to its square $1 = 2 - 1^2$, and $2 = 6 - 2^2$. This idea seems cute, but it doesn't seem as though it will get us to 1,806. And yet it does. Using this rule, the next number would be 42, $6 = 42 - 6^2$, and the number after 42 would be (guess what) 1,806: $42 = 1,806 - 42^2$ $(42^2 = 1,764)$. Combining our two perspectives, we can make sense of the third sequence.

Intelligence tests that rely on sequencing problems assume some correlation between intelligence and the ability to create novel perspectives. This may not be a bad assumption. We think of someone as intelligent if they do well in school with little effort and if they have the ability to solve a range of problems. Succeeding at those tasks requires the ability to retain, generate, and combine perspectives. Having a high IQ is not the same thing as being able to use and develop perspectives, but the two are related. We return to this point later.

The ability to solve any one sequencing problem depends on some mixture of ability, experience, and serendipity. All three of these effects can be seen by reconsidering the last, and hardest, sequencing problem. In his cult classic, *The Hitchhiker's Guide to the Galaxy*, the late Douglas Adams wrote that the number 42 was the answer to the Ultimate Question of Life, the Universe, and Everything.[12] Science fiction buffs would be far more likely to guess the number 42 than would people who had never read Douglas Adams. Science fiction buffs who like math might even have seen the pattern once they inserted 42 in the sequence because $42 - 6 = 36$, a perfect square.

In these examples, once the pattern is revealed, the problem seems relatively easy. Herein lies the paradox of novel and useful perspectives. Because they make sense of a problem or situation, because they organize knowledge, they seem obvious after the fact. Of course force equals mass times acceleration. Of course the earth revolves around the sun. Of course we evolved from single-cell organisms. Of course we're composed of little vibrating strings with lots of hidden dimensions—okay, maybe not all perspectives are obvious.

Mount Fuji and Ice Cream Summits

To formalize some of these ideas, consider Alexander Pope's famous epigraph about Isaac Newton: "Nature and Nature's laws lay hid in night / God said, let Newton be! and all was light."

Now extend it to the more general claim that how people see problems determines how hard those problems are. Newton saw physical phenomena clearly. He saw white light as composed of all of the colors. He saw orbiting bodies as attracting. The mysterious made clear. The difficult made easy. We can make the following claim:

The Difficult Eye of the Beholder: *How hard a problem is to solve depends on the perspective used to encode it.*

What does this mean? Formally speaking, it means that we can encode problems so that they are easy. We can encode them so that they are hard. To demonstrate this more precisely, I will introduce the concept of a rugged landscape. Imagine that we want a perspective on houses to help us understand their prices. We consider fourteen houses for sale in West Branch, Iowa (the boyhood home of Herbert Hoover) on www.realtor.com in the fall

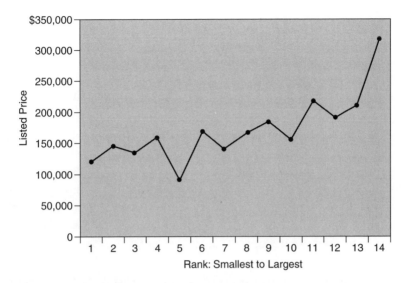

Figure 1.16 West Branch Houses in the Square Foot Perspective

of 2005. The prices of these houses range from a low of $88,500 to a high of $319,000. We can use their square footage to create a perspective on these homes. We can arrange the houses from smallest to largest and plot the prices of the fourteen homes as a function of their ranks. House number 1 is the smallest house, house number two is the next smallest, and so on. We can think of this graph as a landscape: the higher the elevation, the higher the price of the home. This landscape has several *local peaks*. A local peak is a point on the landscape from which any direction you move lowers your elevation. It is, literally, the peak of a hill. The *global peak* is the point of highest value. It's the peak of the biggest hill. On Earth, Mount Washington is a local peak, a windy one at that, but Everest is the global peak.

If square footage were a great perspective for the price of houses, this landscape would have a single local peak, which would be the global peak. But as we see in figure 1.16, our landscape is pretty rugged.[13] Instead of leading gracefully to a single peak (that looks like Mount Fuji), this perspective creates lots of ups and downs. Moving along it would be like hiking in the Adirondacks. The many local peaks imply that square footage doesn't organize the information well. If we wanted to find the least expensive house (assuming that we couldn't just get the information from the Web site) and used the square footage perspective, we'd probably start with the smallest house. If we checked the second smallest, we would find that it is more expensive. We might then think that the smallest house is the least expensive, but it's not; the fifth smallest house is. This perspective isn't helpful.

The best perspectives create landscapes with a single peak—they organize the information in such a way that a single, obvious solution becomes clear. It's easy to imagine a hiker following the various flash marks on a trail (the data points) and getting to the top. But using the square footage perspective on the West Branch houses creates lots of little peaks where our hiker could get stuck (there are five to be exact). Or if we think back to our first consultant's caloric perspective on the ice cream, a person could walk along the pints with a spoon—not a bad day's work—to reach a peak. To use the more flowery language of the late British poet laureate Ted Hughes, that peak would be an "ice cream summit," when neither the pint to the left nor that to the right tasted better.

If we restrict ourselves to one-dimensional perspectives on the fourteen houses (ordering them by their distance from the road, for instance), we can construct 8,192 distinct single-peaked perspectives. How do we know that there are 8,192 such perspectives? We arrive at this number using a perspective on the number of possible perspectives. Here's the trick: assign each house a number from 1 to 14 so that the house numbers increase with price. House number 14 has the highest price and house number 1 the lowest. Note that this is a different numbering than our square footage ranking. A one-dimensional perspective can be thought of as a list of these fourteen numbers. If the perspective creates a single-peaked landscape, the house numbers in the list must increase up to 14 and decrease after it. The perspective 1, 4, 5, 6, 9, 11, 14, 13, 12, 10, 8, 7, 3, 2 is single-peaked, but the perspective 1, 2, 3, 4, 13, 5, 6, 7, 8, 9, 14, 12, 11, 10, is not. It has a second peak at 13. Each distinct single-peaked landscape has a unique subset of houses to the left of the house number 14. So, to compute the number of perspectives that create single-peaked landscapes, we need only compute the number of unique subsets of the numbers from 1 to 13. This equals two raised to the thirteenth power.[14] We can extend this logic to the more general case with any number of objects.[15]

Thus, for any problem, Mount Fuji exists. In fact, many Mount Fujis exist. We can state this as a formal claim. We call it the *Savant Existence Theorem.*[16]

The Savant Existence Theorem: *For any problem, there exist many perspectives that create Mount Fuji landscapes.*

The outline of the proof of this theorem mimics our example. We arrange the solutions from best to worst and then assign them numbers that increase up to the best solution and decrease thereafter. This creates a Mount Fuji landscape. This approach may seem too good to be true, and it is. To use the approach, we need to know the value of every possible solution. If we had all that information, we'd have no need for a perspective. We'd just choose the solution with the highest value.

This does not mean that the theorem isn't important. It is important. It gives hope. For any problem, some Newton-like savant could show up and make everything clear as a bell, creating Mount Fuji out of the Badlands of South Dakota. Nevertheless, for some problems, we don't have good perspectives and we may never have good perspectives. We're waiting for Godot.

The Savant Existence Theorem has a flip side: the number of perspectives is enormous. So, it may not be likely that we find one that creates Mount Fuji. For example, if we return to the West Branch real estate market and place no constraints on the ordering of the houses (we can choose any one of the fourteen to place first, any one of the remaining thirteen to go second, and so on), then the total number of orderings equals 14 times 13 times 12 times 10 times 9 times 8 and so on. If we multiply all these numbers together, we get 87,178,291,200. So, for each perspective that creates a Mount Fuji landscape there exist *ten million* perspectives that do not. Ouch!

In general, the number of one-dimensional perspectives of N objects equals N factorial—N times $(N - 1)$ times $(N - 2)$ and so on, or what mathematicians write as $N!$. This number dwarfs the 2^{N-1} perspectives that create Mount Fuji landscapes. These calculations do get a bit technical, but they have a purpose. They demonstrate that having a unique perspective may not be that hard—we could arrange the houses by their distance from the road or by their house numbers. Both would be unique. They also show that for any problem, many perspectives make the problem simple. They create a Mount Fuji landscape that we can faithfully follow to the top. Unfortunately, relative to the total number of perspectives, these simplifying perspectives are few and far between. Precious few perspectives make problems simple. The vast majority of perspectives create no meaningful structure. People who discover these Mount Fuji perspectives, like Newton, get remembered in poems. The more perspectives we collectively possess, the better our chances of finding a Mount Fuji.

IDENTICAL PERSPECTIVES, COMMUNICATION, AND GROUPTHINK

An implication of what we have covered so far is that when people see a problem the same way, they're likely all to get stuck at the same solutions—if we look at a problem with the same perspective, we're all likely to get stuck at the same local peaks. As we saw in the Ben and Jerry's example, someone who represents the problem differently (and not as well) probably has different local optima—a different peak. This person can help the group get unstuck. We might ask, Why, other than lack of imagination, would people rely on the same perspective? People may share a perspective because it's useful. If someone has a better perspective on a problem, copying it would seem to make sense. As counterintuitive as this advice sounds, copying better perspectives may not be such a good idea. Collectively, we may be better off if some of us continue to use less effective but diverse perspectives.

Another reason for common perspectives is that they allow for quick and error-free communication. An experiment by Colin Camerer and Roberto Weber shows how the incentive to communicate leads people to see the world in the same way, to use the same perspective.[17] In their experiment, two players are shown an identical picture of a nondescript business meeting on a computer screen. On one player's screen, a person in the picture is identified; let's say it's a man in a green Izod shirt. The player then sends a message to the other player, who in turn must click on the identified person. Each time the second player clicks on the correct person in the photograph, both players get a small cash reward. In the experiment, the players were given a fixed length of time to accumulate as many correct identifications, and as much money, as possible.

As you might expect, players developed situational patois, crude languages that helped to identify people quickly and accurately. The man in the green Izod shirt became "gator." The tall woman with the beauty mark above her lip became "Cindy" (after the supermodel Cindy Crawford), and so on. Each pair developed its own unique language.

Camerer and Weber then created havoc by switching the pairings of players. Initially, these new pairs did poorly, much worse, in fact, than the original pairings did. When a player sent the message "gator," his new partner just got confused. Sending the message "green gator" wasn't much help either. The message "the blond guy in his fifties in the green Izod shirt, you idiot!" did work, but that took time (and cost money) to send. Even though the perspectives had been developed only a few minutes earlier, they had resilience.

Similar scenarios play out in business, the academy, and the world of politics. Recall the Steve Martin quotation that begins this chapter. The same might be said of marketers, engineers, accountants, physicists, sociologists, and biologists. We all speak in jargon. We may not be aware of it, but we do. We construct communication shortcuts, often with the help of acronyms. Acronyms are so abundant that people who attend a seminar or meeting outside their own organization or field of specialization often have no idea what people are saying. Acronym overlap makes understanding even more difficult. The acronym ABM represents everything from activity-based management to agent-based models, anti-ballistic missiles, and the Association of Breastfeeding Mothers. This leads many of us to espouse AFC. (That's acronym-free communication.)

Although common perspectives arise because of imitation and the need to communicate, they also arise for less productive reasons. People are social, and insecure, animals. Members of a group sometimes lock into a common perspective because they feel more comfortable thinking about the world the same way that other people do. These common perspectives can be a type of groupthink.[18] The logic of groupthink rests on our desire to conform. If a majority of people thinks of a problem one way, they often compel others to do so. That way could be a good perspective and, if so, the group will do well. Groupthink need not be bad. But it could mean that everyone has adopted an unproductive perspective, and this can lead the group to make bad decisions. Most relevant for our investigation, groupthink—whether good or bad—reduces perspective diversity and stifles the collective ability of the group to find good solutions.[19]

The Last Bite of Ice Cream

In this chapter, we've seen how perspectives organize knowledge. The right perspective can make a difficult problem simple. Hence, we associate clarifying perspectives with genius. They make clear what had been opaque. Perspectives also create superadditive effects. They can be combined to form ever more perspectives.

Thus, if we hope to continue to innovate and reach new understandings, we must encourage the creation of new and diverse perspectives. We should invite physicists into chemistry departments, psychologists into economic departments, and political scientists into business schools. We should include engineers in marketing meetings and marketers in engineering meetings.

And when forming committees and teams, we should choose people who come from different backgrounds and have diverse identities. If not, we're shutting out perspectives. We're slamming the door on potential savants.

Of course, many diverse perspectives won't be useful; they'll make rugged landscapes, not Mount Fujis. We have no guarantee that adding someone different will turn our game of Sum to Fifteen into Tic Tac Toe. A new perspective could just as well transform it into the Unpacking Game. Thomas Edison once optimistically said in the face of the failure of a perspective "we now know a thousand ways not to make the light bulb." Edison rightly saw these failed perspective as a cost worth bearing. So should we, provided we sometimes stumble on a sublime way of seeing a problem.

In this chapter, we've focused on the pragmatic benefits of new perspectives—the scientific understandings, the engineering breakthroughs, the new ways of organizing knowledge. Although those merit our attention and appreciation, they should not cast such a large shadow that we forget the aesthetic joy that diverse perspectives bring. When we look at the periodic table and see the structure of the elements or even when we see how Sum to Fifteen is equivalent to Tic Tac Toe, we experience something sublime.

CHAPTER 2

Heuristics

DO THE OPPOSITE

It is not unreasonable that we grapple with problems. But there are tens of thousands of years in the future. Our responsibility is to do what we can, learn what we can, improve the solutions, and pass them on.
—Richard P. Feynman, *What Do You Care What Other People Think?*

In a classic episode of the television show *Seinfeld*, Jerry's bumbling friend George Costanza comes to the realization that every decision he has made in his life has been the wrong one. When he should have gone left, he went right. When he should have chosen up, he chose down. When he should have quit, he stayed. When he should have stayed, he quit. This realization results in an epiphany: he should *do the opposite*. He should do the reverse of whatever he thinks is best. If the rules in his head tell him to be kind, he should be rude. If they tell him to arrive early, he should show up late. If they tell him to dress casually, he should dress formally. By the end of the show, George has resurrected his once moribund life. He has a girlfriend. And he has a job: with the New York Yankees.

George's "do the opposite" rule is a heuristic. Heuristics are thinking tools used to find solutions to problems. The "do the opposite" heuristic is one of many proposed by Barry Nalebuff and Ian Ayres as useful in finding innovative solutions. Their example: if there exist 900 numbers where you pay to call, why not have 009 numbers where they pay to call you?[1]

Heuristics apply within perspectives. Given a perspective, a heuristic tells a person where to search for new solutions or what actions to take. Heuristics can vary in their sophistication, and they can be immediate, inchoate reactions to situations. Heuristics can be rules of thumb, such as "do the opposite" or "think like your opponent." These simple rule-of-thumb heuristics can be powerful. They can, as Gert Gigerenzer claims, "make us smart" provided that they are logically consistent.[2]

Heuristics need not be simple. They can be elaborate computational search algorithms, such as simulated annealing (which I describe in a few pages), or sophisticated mathematical techniques, such as Newton's method. Academic disciplines and business firms often create heuristics tailored to the problems they confront.[3] These heuristics can be based on pattern matching. The architect Christopher Alexander promotes a set of patterns to follow when designing buildings.[4] Alexander's patterns exploit characteristics of rooms or spaces that in his experience improve their functionality. They form the building blocks (pun intended) of effective spaces. One pattern calls for *different chairs*. People prefer rooms with more than one type of chair. Another pattern requires *light from two sides*. People are most comfortable in rooms in which natural light can enter from two sides. If light can enter from only one side, the resulting dark corners make us uncomfortable, and if light enters from three or more sides we feel too exposed to the world. Even though the word *pattern* evokes a meaning similar to our term *perspectives*, Alexander's patterns are heuristics. They are things we do to a room or a building to improve it.

The sources of heuristics vary. We acquire more sophisticated heuristics through training. Simpler heuristics may come from training, too, but they may more often be developed from experience. And as our experiences are filtered by our identities, our heuristics are also identity dependent. We may not know how we come up with heuristics, what their sources are. They just appear. And we can keep only so many heuristics at our fingertips. This creates a tension between acquiring heuristics that are powerful within a specific domain and heuristics that are less powerful but apply to multiple domains.[5]

APPLYING HEURISTICS

We apply heuristics to problem solving tasks. They are how we search for solutions. For some problems, our heuristics may almost always find optimal solutions, while for others they may be ineffective. Failing to find optimal solutions is no big deal; optimization may be overrated. Some evidence suggests that people who satisfice, who do not obsess about finding the best solution, may be happier than people who try to optimize.[6] Being satisfied with what we get may be a sign of mental health and a good thing, but as a society we may want the bar to be higher. When trying to solve a policy problem, find a business solution, or cure a disease, we seek an optimal solution, or something close to it.

To see how heuristics depend on perspectives, consider the "do the opposite" heuristic. Suppose that the problem under consideration has thirty-two possible solutions. These thirty-two solutions could be represented using the numbers 1 to 32 or they could be represented using strings of five 0s and 1s (that gives us thirty two variations of 1s and 0s): 00000, 11111, and thirty in between. The "do the opposite" heuristic cannot be applied to the first perspective—the numbers from 1 to 32. The opposite of fifteen equals minus fifteen. Minus fifteen lies outside the set of numbers from one to thirty two, and cannot be a solution. But the "do the opposite" heuristic can be applied to solutions in the binary string encoding. The solution 00000 has an opposite: 11111. The solution 10101 also has an opposite: 01010. As this example shows, heuristics can often travel across perspectives. George Costanza probably didn't have binary encodings in mind when developing his heuristic, but it works in that domain as well.

When applying a heuristic, once a new solution is found, it must be evaluated. Thus, in addition to needing a perspective, heuristics also require some evaluative criterion to figure out if they work. This typically takes the form of a value function that assigns a number—a value—to each solution. For a politician the value function might equal the number of votes the politician receives, for a firm it might equal profits, and for a statistician it might equal the number of outcomes predicted correctly. Value functions need not be one-dimensional. A politician could care about getting votes and about remaining true to his principles, and a firm might care about market share and reputation as well as profits. If these various dimensions can be assigned weights, then the multidimensional value function can be collapsed to a single dimension, but sometimes they cannot.

In the simplest cases, value functions can be expressed mathematically, for example, $f(x, y) = x + 2y - xy$. If so, the mathematical representation of the value function can be exploited, a point we'll take up later. If we want to know the value when $x = 2$ and $y = 3$, we just plug those numbers into the formula and we get the answer: 2. However, we often lack an explicit functional form for the value function. Finding the value of a solution requires testing. For example, one evening, my sons and I were making sleds out of LEGOs. We were seeing who could make the sled that would travel the furthest down a track. We didn't have a function that told us how far a sled would travel based on its design. We didn't need one. We could just put the sleds on the track and see how far they traveled. In many situations, we lack a mathematical function or a way to test solutions, and we have to resort to a prediction of the value. Here, though, we assume that the value of any solution is known. It simplifies the analysis. We will define heuristics as operating on *solutions* because we eventually want to apply them to problem solving. Solutions are not just answers to math questions. They're also status quo points. What you are wearing is a solution to the problem of getting dressed.

We can formally define a heuristic as follows:

A **heuristic** *is a rule applied to an existing solution represented in a perspective that generates a new (and hopefully better) solution or a new set of possible solutions.*

This definition of heuristics is limited. It assumes that the heuristic creates a full solution. Many heuristics generate only partial solutions. This definition encompasses only problem solving heuristics. Heuristics can also organize information. The *Rule of 72* is a heuristic that organizes information about interest rates to help people develop good investment strategies.

The Rule of 72: *The approximate number of years required for money invested at x% to double equals* $\frac{72}{x}$.

This rule implies that money invested at 9 percent doubles in eight years, while money invested at 6 percent doubles in twelve years. This rule fails to produce new solutions to problems. Cool and useful as it is, the Rule of 72 lies outside the class of heuristics that we consider here. We mention it, though, because we use it later in showing why small improvements from diversity year after year can produce big long-run benefits.

Our definition of heuristics contains no assumption that the new solutions are better. They need not be. If a new solution has a higher value than the old solution, it should be accepted. If the new solution has a lower value, deciding whether or not to accept it requires some deep thinking. On the one hand, accepting the new solution sacrifices value. On the other hand, the new solution differs, and by being different offers an opportunity to apply the heuristic once again, to search other parts of the space of solutions. Subsequent applications of the heuristic could produce even better solutions. Change for the sake of change need not be bad. We can frame this tension in the language of rugged landscapes. If a perspective generates a rugged landscape, then reaching a high peak may require taking some paths that go downhill. Repeatedly going downhill, however, make little sense. Eventually, a heuristic has to find a peak.

THE TRAVELING SALESPERSON PROBLEM

To see a heuristic in action—beyond George getting a job and finding a girlfriend—we consider a famous problem that recently underwent a name change. Formerly known as the traveling salesman problem, we now call it the traveling salesperson problem. (What's next? Personufacturing, of course.) In this problem, a salesperson has to find a route to visit twenty-five cities and then return to her home. She must complete this trip by traveling as few miles as possible. Traveling salesperson problems such as this one have an enormous number of possible solutions. She could visit any of the twenty-five cities first and then any of the remaining twenty-four second. This selection process would continue until she has a single city left unvisited. If we multiply these numbers together, we obtain a huge number, much larger than a billion times a billion. Except in rare cases, among these billions upon billions of routes, exactly two minimize travel distance. Why two? Because any route can be driven in the opposite direction without changing the distance.

Suppose that this particular salesperson, let's call her Orit, begins and ends her trip in Albuquerque, New Mexico, which we can denote by *A*. The other cities Orit must visit conveniently have names that begin with the letters *B* (Boston) through *Z* (Zanesville, Ohio).

A Possible Route

Albuquerque, NM, to Louisville, KY, to Missoula, MN, to Cairo, IL, to …Eureka, CA, to San Diego, CA, and back to Albuquerque.

A route can be written as a list that begins and ends with the letter *A* with the other twenty-five letters in between them. This provides a *perspective* on the possible routes.

The Route in a Perspective

ALMCVHFNGHUO WZKXQ YWIPBTJRESA

The traveling salesperson problem belongs to a class of canonically difficult problems that computer scientists classify as "NP hard." NP stands for non-polynomial. In an NP hard problem, the number of computations required to solve the problem increases quickly as the number of cities, *N*, increases. It grows faster than

N^2, and faster than N^3. It grows faster than N raised to any power, so finding the optimal routes would take far too much time once N, the number of cities, gets large. Though locating the optimal route takes lots of computational time, Orit might still find a good route or possibly an excellent route by using a search heuristic— just trying different routes. Heuristics don't necessarily lead us to optimal solutions, but they can locate good ones. In the words of Herbert Simon they enable us to satisfice, to find a pretty good solution.

A widely used heuristic for the traveling salesperson problem switches adjacent cities in the route. Starting from the route above, this heuristic might switch Knoxville, Tennessee (K) with Xenia, Ohio (X).

APPLYING A SWITCHING HEURISTIC TO THE ROUTE

ALMCVHFNGHUOWZKXQYWIPBTJRESA

becomes

ALMCVHFNGHUOWZXKQYWIPBTJRESA

If the new route is shorter, it becomes the status quo. This heuristic is said to be *greedy*. It accepts any improvement, and you can apply it to different pairs again and again, accepting those that are shorter. The number of switches that can reduce the length of the route has a limit. Therefore, this heuristic must at some point cease to find improvements. The route eventually located by this heuristic need not be optimal, but most of the time it won't be too bad. Again, it enables us to satisfice.

Switching cities is not the only heuristic that we can apply to the traveling salesperson problem. We might also select a random city and move it to a random place in the sequence. We might accept this random switch only if the new route improves on the old one. Random heuristics like this are not efficient, but they prevent a search from getting stuck at a bad solution. Yet another heuristic might switch cities separated by a single city. This may seem like a strange way to improve on a route but it has an underlying logic. On a map of the United States,

Before

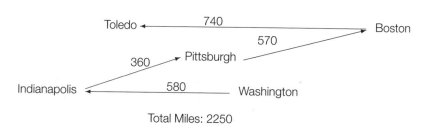

Total Miles: 2250

After

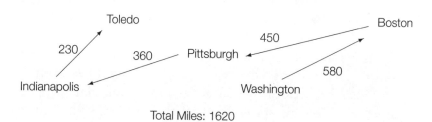

Total Miles: 1620

Figure 2.1 Switching Cities Separated by a City

Pittsburgh (P) lies between Indianapolis (I) and Boston (B). In the routes listed earlier, P sits between I and B. Switching Boston and Pittsburgh or Pittsburgh and Indianapolis would not make much sense. However, if the T stands for Toledo, Ohio, and the W stands for Washington, DC, switching Boston and Indianapolis would cut more than six hundred miles off that subsection of Orit's route (see figure 2.1).

With a little effort, we could extend this example to show the potential for superadditivity from heuristics. A route that is a local peak for the switch-two-adjacent-cities heuristic might be improved on by the switch-two-cities-separated-by-a-city heuristic. This heuristic may in turn get stuck on another route, which the switch-adjacent-cities heuristic then improves on even further. In this way improvements can build on improvements to create superadditive effects.

DIVERSE HEURISTICS

We can choose from many possible types of heuristics. Now that we know what heuristics are, the question is what they have to do with diversity. In what follows, we describe four common classes of heuristics: topological heuristics, gradient heuristics, error-allowing heuristics, and population heuristics. These classes overlap a bit, but they serve our purpose of showing some of the possible diversity of heuristics.

Most of us use all four types regularly. Suppose Carter must cook dinner. He opens the fridge, stares at a chicken breast, and thinks about making curried chicken. Unless his family loved his previous curried chicken (in which case he just makes it exactly as before), he applies some heuristics to his previous best version of chicken curry with the hope of making it even better. Suppose that he decides to add a dash more red chili pepper. If Carter organizes his spices by type, then adding chili pepper would be a topological heuristic since chili lies near curry in the spice drawer. Alternatively, Carter might have heard from his family that the chicken curry was too salty, so he might reduce the amount of salt he adds. This would be applying a gradient heuristic. He's moving in the direction that should most increase satisfaction. Alternatively, Carter might shut his eyes and choose a random spice—perhaps rosemary, perhaps cumin. Maybe this works, maybe it doesn't. In doing so, he's following an error-allowing heuristic (note: his family might not like this approach). Finally, Carter might add the garlic cumin paste he made earlier in the week that worked well with tofu. If so, he's using a population heuristic. He's borrowing part of another solution to help locate a good solution.

Given that there are so many types of heuristics, a natural question to ask is which heuristic works best. It has been shown that comparing heuristics across all problems is a fool's game. No heuristic performs better than any other across all possible problems. This result is known as the No Free Lunch Theorem.[7] We can read this theorem in two ways. It means that for any given problem there will be good heuristics and bad heuristics. It also means that for any heuristic there will be problems on which it performs well and problems on which it fails miserably. Anyone who markets a heuristic as universally good may be full of more than just good intentions. Take for example a heuristic popularized by the life guru Steven Covey: *deal with bigger parts of a problem first*. Imagine you have a bunch of large rocks and a pile of small pebbles that you have to fit in a bucket. If you put the pebbles in first, you cannot later fit in all of the large rocks. But if you put the large rocks in first, you can squeeze the pebbles in around them. This same advice, deal with big problems first, can be applied widely with great effect. Better to put out the grease fire in the kitchen before unloading the dishwasher and not the other way around.

As powerful as this heuristic may be in some contexts, the claim that this heuristic works everywhere bumps up against the logic of the No Free Lunch Theorem. Over the set of all problems, this heuristic is no better than any other. In fact, we could even do the opposite. We could deal with the little things first. Perhaps by taking care of the little things first, the big things will take care of themselves (or become smaller). This do-the-opposite-of-Covey heuristic works well when digging holes in rocky ground. Removing the small pebbles first makes it a lot easier to pull out the large rocks. We don't have to choosing between Covey and Costanza; we should follow both. Each has its place. Successful people have more than seven heuristics.

Topological Heuristics

The simplest heuristics are *topological*. They rely on the perspective's structure and search neighboring solutions. The route-switching heuristics we discussed in the traveling salesperson problem fall into this class, as does the do-the-opposite heuristic. The neighborhood structure created by perspectives often suggests several topological heuristics; you just look for close neighbors. When Ben and Jerry arrayed the pints of ice

	X	
X	S	X
	X	

Figure 2.2 The Von Neumann Neighbors of S

cream in a grid, they could hardly help but look at pints to the north, south, east, and west. Computer scientists call these the Von Neumann neighbors, in honor of John Von Neumann (see figure 2.2).

Topological heuristics exploit the knowledge embedded in the perspective. They search solutions that are near the status quo. Unless the perspective creates a Mount Fuji landscape, topological heuristics get stuck on local optima-peaks in the set of solutions when represented in the perspective. In the Ben and Jerry's example, pints surrounded by pints with lower values are local optima relative to their heuristic.

Even though heuristics differ markedly from perspectives, topological heuristics capture, in a loose way, the idea that people see the world differently. Topological heuristics search directionally. If two people look for solutions in different directions, then they might be thought of as seeing a problem differently, even though they may represent the problem in the same way—they have the same perspective.

Gradient Heuristics

Previously, we discussed how some problems have mathematical functions but other problems, like my building of LEGO sleds with my sons, do not. The topological heuristics we just described do not need a mathematical function. We can apply them provided we can compute the value of solution by putting the LEGO sled on the track. In those cases where we have a mathematical function that gives the value, we can exploit the information contained in that representation using a second class of heuristics, called *gradient heuristics*. These heuristics use calculus to compute the slope of the value function. They then move in the direction of maximal slope.

Sometimes, we can apply gradient heuristics to problems that lack mathematically expressed value functions. A person need not be familiar with calculus to be able to act "as if" she knows calculus, and act "as if" she's calculating a gradient. For example, I sometimes play basketball at the YMCA in Ann Arbor. Before the first game, we divide into teams. We value competitive games. We want the teams as evenly matched as possible. The closer the abilities of the teams, the higher our value. Often (too often) we select teams that are unevenly balanced, and one team wins easily. We must then search for fairer teams. A heuristic we often use to balance teams switches the best player from the better team with the worst player from the other team. When we do this, we follow the gradient. We never say "let's use the gradient heuristic." Guys in gyms don't talk like that.

When a solution has many attributes, the value function has slopes in the direction of each attribute. For example, if the value of a burrito depends on its size and temperature, we can compute how much the value changes as we increase the size and how much the value increases as we up the temperature. At any point in the space of possible solutions there will be one direction that leads to the largest increase in value. The *gradient* tells this direction of steepest ascent at a point.[8] The gradient tells which way is most up. Imagine that you're standing at a random point on the Appalachian Trail. The gradient would point to the steepest slope adjacent to your position. It could be to your left, your right, or directly ahead of you. To coin a phrase, people who do not know the gradient don't know which way is up. Gradient heuristics move in the direction of the gradient, the direction of steepest ascent. By doing so, they climb hills quickly. However, they also often get stuck on local optima. On Mount Fuji problems, gradient heuristics work well: they climb right up the slope. On rugged landscapes, however, they get stuck because they look only locally. Gradient heuristics find peaks, but those peaks may not be of high elevation. Overall, gradient heuristics need not perform better than topological heuristics. The No Free Lunch Theorem still holds.

Gradient search limits diversity in search. The gradient suggests a unique direction of greatest improvement, a single best way to go provided that everyone has the same value function. But, if people differ, even slightly, in what they want in a solution, then their directions of greatest improvement, their gradients, may differ. Here we have an instance of positive feedback. Diverse values lead to diverse heuristics. We will see that this happens frequently. Difference often begets difference.

Error-Allowing Heuristics

The first two classes of heuristics perform poorly when our perspective gives us a problem with lots of local optima, a rugged landscape. By assumption, any hard problem—curing diseases, designing policies—has a rugged landscape. Otherwise, we'd just climb up Mount Fuji, pop open a cold one, and revel in our progress. When our perspective creates a rugged landscape, we need to use a sophisticated heuristic. On rugged landscapes, heuristics that insist on going uphill get stuck. And when a landscape has a large number of local peaks, then upward-striving heuristics get stuck often. One way to prevent getting stuck on local peaks is to crawl down them every once in while. However, while crawling down a small local peak and starting anew would be a good idea, crawling down a large peak would not be.

These two insights suggest that a sophisticated heuristic would take some steps downhill (it would make what appear to be errors), but it would not take too many steps downhill. Such heuristics we call *error-allowing heuristics*. The most widely used error-allowing heuristic is simulated annealing. This heuristic also goes by the name the Metropolis algorithm, not because it will help you find a good restaurant in New York, but because it was invented by Nick Metropolis.

The logic of how errors produce benefits is subtle and worth learning. We so rarely encounter new and unexpected intuitions that we're going to take the time to walk through the logic of the simulated annealing algorithm. Before we start, we note that the algorithm mimics a natural phenomenon—the annealing of glass and metals—and applies it to solving hard problems. To make steel, iron ore is heated and then slowly cooled, or annealed, in such a way that the molecules align to form steel. The heat mixes everything up, and the cooling allows molecules to align. The use of this technique to solve hard problems is an example of the transferability of heuristics.

For the most part, simulated annealing works like hill climbing. It searches for new solutions near the current solution. If it finds one that's better, it moves to that solution. Sometimes, when it finds a solution that is worse, it moves to that solution. The decision whether to accept a solution that's worse depends on a *temperature schedule*. This schedule is just a list of falling temperatures. Think of it as the average daily temperature in Michigan from August through January. It starts warm (in the eighties) and slowly drops down to freezing. When the temperature is high, the algorithm allows mistakes. It accepts new solutions that are worse, provided that they are not a lot worse (we formalize this in the next paragraph). This initial acceptance of all but the largest errors allows the search to wander the space of solutions. But because it rejects large decreases in value, the search algorithm tends toward regions with better solutions.

As the temperature cools, simulated annealing becomes less and less forgiving of worse solutions. Think of it as becoming stricter in the fall and really strict in the cold of winter. By December (when the temperature is really cold), the algorithm rarely accepts solutions that are worse. Eventually (by January), the temperature falls so far that only new solutions with higher values are accepted. At this point, simulated annealing becomes hill climbing (a topological heuristic) and settles on a local peak.

The formal description of the acceptance rule for a new solution looks complicated, but we can follow its logic with ease. Computer scientists and physicists rely on a probabilistic function that contains Euler's constant, $e = 2.71828$, raised to a fraction.[9] Fortunately, we can see the same logic by writing the probability of accepting a new solution as a linear function of *Decrease*, the amount the function value decreases, and *Temp*, the temperature.

To keep things as simple as possible, we assume that all function values lie between zero and one hundred. This assumption constrains our variable *Decrease* to be between zero and one hundred as well. We then write the probability of accepting a solution as a percentage.

Probability of Accepting a Worse Solution $= (Temp - Decrease)\%$

If *Temp* equals 90 (in midsummer) then most new solutions (except those that are bad) will be accepted. This means that search won't get stuck on some little hill in the landscape. As *Temp* falls, the algorithm becomes less likely to accept worse solutions. Suppose that *Temp* equals 50. If a new solution leads to a decrease in value of 40 (*Decrease* equals 40), the algorithm accepts this new solution only 10% of the time. This makes sense. The new solution is so much worse. If *Decrease* equals 1, then the algorithm would accept that solution 49% of the time. Thus, the algorithm accepts small errors but doesn't accept big ones. Eventually, when *T* equals zero, it accepts only new solutions that are better.[10]

As powerful an algorithm as simulated annealing may be, it's not a cure-all. We have to keep the No Free Lunch Theorem in mind. No algorithm is any better than any other on all problems. Simulated annealing, though, is not a single algorithm. It's a family of algorithms. By changing the cooling schedule, we change the algorithm, partially getting around the problem of lunch being costly.

Simulated annealing may be an interesting computational search algorithm, but it seems far removed from something that people would do in their heads. To claim that people approximate taking derivatives on the basketball court may be defensible, but to suggest that people apply cooling schedules might seem a sign of a disconnect from reality. And yet, groups of people use annealing-like heuristics all the time; we just don't call them annealing. We called them brainstorming sessions.[11]

To see how brainstorming mimics simulated annealing, consider a group of people confronted with a perplexing problem—how to design an orchestral hall for a major city. In August, they may first toss out lots of solutions. We can think of the group as having a high temperature. They accept lots of errors. By October, they may settle on a solution and consider only changes that seem approximately as good as the current one. If so, we can think of them as having a cool fall temperature in their annealing algorithm. Near the end of the problem-solving process (which we can assume to be January) they may accept only improving changes. If so, they've further lowered temperature in the annealing algorithm. Although the group never computes a temperature or raises the number e to any fractional powers, they do become more and more discriminating. They anneal.

Individuals also use heuristics that mimic annealing processes. When trying to decide where to go on vacation, initially we let ourselves wander the space possibilities. We then become a little less willing to consider new and less exciting alternatives. Eventually, we don't consider anything unless it improves on our current best solution. Though we anneal, we may not cool at the right speed, however. We may cool too fast and lock into a solution, or we may spend too much time running through the possible alternatives.

The success of error-allowing heuristics in finding good solutions to difficult problems implies a benefit of diverse heuristics and perspectives. If someone with a different heuristic (or perspective) locates a new solution that is worse, that new solution can be beneficial in the long run because it may prevent getting stuck on a bad local optimum. We are not saying that bad solutions are good, but that sometimes, a new solution of lower value can point the way to a better solution. Of course, if we follow a path of solutions that are not as good as a current solution, we could always retrace our steps. But as anyone, or at least anyone who has lost his car keys, knows backtracking isn't as easy as it sounds. So, we have to be careful to leave some bread crumbs along the way.

Population Heuristics

Population heuristics search multiple solutions simultaneously. Evolution can be thought of as a population heuristic. There exists a population of solutions—the members of the species—and some members of the population reproduce more than others. If reproduction rates are correlated with performance, such as speed or robustness, then the population should improve on that performance characteristic over time. John Holland, a colleague of mine at Michigan, developed a population heuristic called a *genetic algorithm* that mimics evolutionary population-based search. Genetic algorithms have proven to be a good general-purpose search heuristic, just as evolution has.[12]

Before we dig more deeply into genetic algorithms, we first consider a simpler population-based search heuristic called *ants*. In this heuristic, a population of ants is randomly tossed out onto the landscape. Each ant lands on a solution, evaluates it, and then applies a topological or gradient heuristic in search of a locally better solution. Over time, each ant finds better and better solutions until it gets stuck. So far, ants are just multiple copies of either a topological or gradient heuristic.

As these ants crawl around they learn what regions of the landscape have higher values. The population heuristic exploits this information. It does this by using airlifts. Those ants at relatively low value solutions get airlifted to locations near those ants at high value solutions. Eventually, once all the ants are in the same place, we stop searching (and allow the ants to picnic on the mountain top). An example helps. Imagine that these ants were trying to find the highest point in the continental United States. The ants would be dropped randomly and start climbing. Soon, helicopters would begin transporting ants roaming Ohio, Indiana, and Iowa, and transport them to California, Colorado, and Wyoming. Eventually, even those ants in the Alleghenies and the Smokies would also get airlifted out West. When the heuristic stops, we have no guarantee that all of the ants will sit atop Mount Whitney, but we can be pretty sure that they'll be at high altitude.

A genetic algorithm builds from the ant heuristic, but rather than airlifting one solution (an ant) so that it becomes the same as another solution, a genetic algorithm *mates* solutions. Mating solutions sounds a bit racy, but it's not. It merely combines parts

Table 2.1:

The best jambalaya recipes

Chef	Paprika	Cayenne	Salt	Pepper	Oregano	Chili	Cumin	Basil	Tabasco	Garlic
Katie	0	0	0	1	1	1	1	1	0	0
Noah	1	1	1	1	0	0	0	1	0	0
Emily	0	0	0	1	0	1	0	1	1	1
Joey	0	0	0	1	0	1	0	1	0	0

Table 2.2:

Creating a new recipe by mating existing recipes

Chef	Paprika	Cayenne	Salt	Pepper	Oregano	Chili	Cumin	Basil	Tabasco	Garlic
Katie	0	0	0	1	1	1	1	1	0	0
Noah	1	1	1	1	0	0	0	1	0	0
Natalie	1	1	1	1	0	1	1	1	0	0

of one solution with parts of another solution. Suppose we're trying to decide which of ten spices to put in jambalaya. Ignoring amounts, the number of possible spice combinations exceeds a thousand. If spices interact in complicated ways, then finding the best spice combinations won't be easy.

We use an obvious perspective on this problem. We encode each combination of spices as a string of zeros and ones with one location in the string for each spice. If we do not use paprika, we assign a zero to paprika. If we use cayenne pepper, we assign a one to cayenne pepper. In this way, we can write a combination of spices as a string of ten zeros and ones.

Suppose that we have a cooking contest with four chefs, each of whom uses a different spice combination, as shown in table 2.1.

We now show how to mate Katie and Noah's recipes. To do this, we first think of these strings of spices as jambalaya DNA. When Noah's recipe mates with Katie's, the offspring recipe takes some of his jambalaya DNA and some of Katie's. In table 2.2, we show an offspring recipe, called Natalie. This recipe combines the first half of Noah's jambalaya DNA with the second half of

Katie's jambalaya DNA. To make this easy to see, we write Noah's jambalaya DNA in **bold**.

We would expect offspring solutions to be good solutions because they can combine good parts of good solutions. If both Katie and Noah have good jambalaya DNA, then each string must contain good combinations of spices. By combining part of Katie's recipe with part of Noah's recipe, we create the possibility of a recipe that joins the good parts of Katie's recipe with the good parts of Noah's. These "good parts" are what John Holland calls "building blocks." Ideally, mating solutions combines these building blocks and locates even better solutions. Suppose, for example, that a company designing chairs has one awkward, sturdy prototype and one flimsy, comfortable prototype. By mating the two prototypes, the company might come up with a sturdy, comfortable design. Or it might come up with an uncomfortable, flimsy design. Such are the risks of reproduction.

To minimize the risks of bad offspring (solutions with low values), genetic algorithms also have a *selection* operator. This operator weeds out low-value offspring. It does not allow them to mate. This creates a bias toward better solutions. In addition, genetic algorithms also allow *mutations*, random changes in the spice combinations. This, along with mating, maintains diversity in the population. Selection keeps the good and drives out the bad.

Genetic algorithms exploit diversity and individual performance. Mating can work only if the solutions are both good and different. If the solutions are not good, mating just leads to jumping around the space of possible solutions. If the solutions do not differ, then mating doesn't create anything new.

THINKING AND SEEING DIFFERENTLY

We conclude by comparing and contrasting diverse heuristics with diverse perspectives. Someone brings a diverse perspective to a problem if she sees the problem differently. By seeing it differently, she creates a different landscape. Peaks for everyone else may not be peaks for her, so she can help find better solutions.

Someone brings a diverse heuristic if he knows a different rule or algorithm for finding solutions. So, perspectives are ways of seeing solutions, and heuristics are ways of constructing solutions, ways of moving around the space of possibilities.

Heuristics may be as simple as "do the opposite." They may be as complex as wavelet transforms. Like Alexander's design heuristic of "light from two sides," a heuristic may be based on experience and theory, or it may be a random thought—"Why not try this?"—whose source has no good explanation. Regardless of where it came from, a heuristic offers hope. It offers the possibility of finding something better. Without a diversity of heuristics, we cannot expect to solve hard problems effectively. If two people use the same heuristic and begin from the same place, they produce similar solutions. If they use different heuristics, they are likely to find different solutions of unequal value.

We can often link perspectives and heuristics. The set of heuristics that can be applied to a given perspective can be large. In fact, the more productively a perspective organizes reality, the more heuristics people create to work with that perspective. Perspectives and heuristics encapsulate some of what is meant by a scientific paradigm. A paradigm can be thought of a collection of widely shared perspectives and heuristics aimed at a common set of problems. Within academic fields, the construction of new heuristics is a constant enterprise. Mathematics, physics, statistics, economics, and accounting—all have a set of core perspectives, and each of those core perspectives has associated with it an enormous set of heuristics that professionals apply regularly.

This buildup of perspectives and heuristics also occurs outside the academy in firms and organizations. Consulting companies, for instance, have a core set of perspectives and heuristics that they teach to their employees. Bain and Company relies on a heuristic it (unfortunately) calls the "80/20 perspective." This heuristic builds from a belief that 80% of the benefits can be found in 20% of the matter at hand. This can be written in heuristic form: *focus on the most important fifth*. Bain's employees then go out and apply this heuristic (and many others) to real problems confronted by real businesses and organizations. In fact, Bain's consultants possess large sets of tools. The perspectives and heuristics that a firm or organization develops encapsulate the firm's competence. Better firms and organizations have more heuristics at their disposal, more arrows in their quivers.

The perspective and heuristic frameworks can be used to refine the popular (and hackneyed) idea of "thinking outside the box." Because perspectives are complete representations of reality, nothing in fact lies outside the box, so we cannot think outside of it. Instead, we should think of new perspectives as *rearranging* the contents of the box. Mendeleyev didn't think outside the box; all of the measures and attributes he considered were already known. But he did rearrange the contents of the box in a marvelous way.

New heuristics, on the other hand, create unexpected movements within the box created by a perspective. This occurs when a heuristic changes a dimension that others have ignored. For a long time, Coca Cola had a market advantage partly attributable to its iconic glass bottle. When Pepsi Cola introduced two-liter plastic bottles, Pepsi remained inside the box—everyone knew that bottles came in different sizes.[13] But it applied a heuristic that changed a dimension—bottle size—that no one had considered. And Coke lost part of its advantage. Green ketchup also represents a movement to an unexpected corner of the box. The innovation came from applying a heuristic—change the color to appeal to children—that had proven effective in the candy market (introducing blue M&Ms and blue Smarties spiked sales of those products). Someone recognized that children were a big part of the ketchup market and came to the deep realization that ketchup, like another children's food, had a color. And this person, following the advice of Nalebuff and Ayres, asked, "Why not change the color?"[14] These two anecdotes suggest a connection between innovation and diversity. Innovations can arise from rearranging the box (new perspectives) or from exploring parts of the box that have been ignored (new heuristics). But innovation also arises from creating finer partitions, from dividing whole numbers into halves, quarters, and eighths, and from looking at dimensions that everyone has ignored. To explain this type of diversity, we need a third framework, one we will call *interpretations*.

CHAPTER 3

Interpretations

OUR OWN PRIVATE FLATLAND

To describe a view from the window, or even a flower in a jug inside the room (a wallflower, dark red, darker at the center, wilting at the edges, lit by the morning sun, spraying out of its jug, reflected in a mirror), one might go on forever and still fail to put into language all that the flower is in its own particular qualities. And if the particularity, concretion, "thingness" even of what we call "concrete objects" is so inaccessible to the probe of our common language, how much less accessible is that of a moment in the mind, or a mood, or a vision, or an attitude.
—WINIFRED NOWOTTNY, *The Language Poets Use*

The poets 'round here don't write nothin' at all.
—BRUCE SPRINGSTEEN, "Jungleland"

MEET A-Square. He lives on a two-dimensional world. Reality has three dimensions, of course, but A-Square sees only two, so he has something of a different interpretation of what he sees than the rest of us do. A-Square is a character in Edwin Abbot's classic *Flatland*. The high point of the book is A-Square's encounters with a sphere. The sphere tries to explain the third dimension to our poor benighted square. We might think of the sphere as not unlike modern string theorists who claim hidden dimensions to our own physical universe—dimensions we cannot see but which exist nonetheless.

Here follows the dramatic scene in which the sphere (known as the stranger) attempts to convince A-Square of the third dimension. Remember that to A-Square, the stranger looks like a circle (a two-dimensional slice of the sphere).

> I (A-SQUARE): "My Lord, your assertion is easily put to the test. You say I have a Third Dimension, which you call 'height'. Now, Dimension implies direction and measurement. Do but measure my 'height,' or merely indicate to me the direction in which my 'height' extends, and I will become your convert. Otherwise, your Lordship's own understanding must hold me excused."
>
> STRANGER: (To himself.) I can do neither. How shall I convince him? Surely a plain statement of facts followed by ocular demonstration ought to suffice.—"Now, Sir, listen to me.
>
> "You are living on a Plane. What you style Flatland is the vast level surface of what I may call a fluid, or in, the top of which you and your countrymen move about, without rising above or falling below it. I am not a plane Figure, but a Solid. You call me a Circle; but in reality I am not a Circle, but an infinite number of Circles, of size varying from a Point to a Circle of thirteen inches in diameter, one placed on the top of the other. When I cut through your plane as I am now doing, I make in your plane a section which you, very rightly, call a Circle. For even a Sphere—which is my proper name in my own country—if he manifest himself at all to an inhabitant of Flatland—must needs manifest himself as a Circle."

We can say that A-Square lacks a full perspective. But he does possess an *interpretation*. An interpretation ignores dimensions. It lumps things together. A-Square lumps together the sphere and a circle.

To avoid confusion, I'll take a moment to clarify the distinction between perspectives and interpretations. The perspectives framework, to make things easier, assumes that people have a different word for every thing. They have a "one-to-one mapping" of reality in their heads. Although that framework provided us with a useful foundation for our discussion of perspectives, it turns out that people make coarse distinctions among the things they see. We don't have separate names for each possible outcome or solution. Instead, we create categories. We lump things together, just as A-Square does. He lumps by ignoring a spatial dimension. We might lump by ignoring color or size.

This lumping is the rule, not the exception; it's just what everyone does. We need only so much detail so we ignore some differences. If people lump, why then did we bother with the perspective framework? We did so for three reasons. First, interpretations are based on perspectives, so we cannot define the one without the other. Second, perspectives are far easier to work with analytically. If two people use diverse interpretations, then they put some objects or solutions in different categories: what Michael calls a sedan, Erica calls a hatchback. This may seem like no big deal but it creates huge problems when we try to analyze problem solving. If the value of an object equals the average value of the objects in its category, then the object's value becomes subjective. It depends on who interprets it. We wanted to avoid that complication when considering problem solving.

Third, the use of perspectives distinguishes two causes of diverse interpretations. Two people can use the same perspective but create different categories within that common perspective. One person may identify birds by their colors. Another may identify them by their songs. For any perspective that creates multiple dimensions, any subset of those dimensions could be an interpretation. In this way, one person may fail to distinguish between two things that another person sees as importantly different. Sam may classify living room tables into two categories—end tables and coffee tables—but Sofia may maintain forty categories of living room tables in her head. In addition, two people may use different perspectives. If so, the interpretations based on those perspectives are bound to differ as well. This distinction between perspective-level and interpretation-level diversity reappears when we discuss projection interpretations.

The interpretation framework was developed jointly with Lu Hong but borrows ideas from computer learning theory.[1] Interpretations allow for partial representations of situations, events, objects, and problems. They are categorizations of reality. In a categorization, each object or event need not get its own word. Instead, distinct events and objects can be interpreted or remembered as identical, as belonging to the same category. The interpretation framework thus has greater empirical plausibility than the perspective framework does. A substantial literature in psychology buttressed with experimental evidence demonstrates that people make sense of the world in this way. We construct categories, and these categories differ.[2]

Despite the widespread usage of the term *category* in the field of psychology, I call these cloudier mappings of reality *interpretations*. I introduce this new terminology because I assume that these interpretations are more than mere partitions. A partition can be any decomposition. An interpretation creates or exploits an underlying structure. For example, there are more than fifty million ways to partition the twenty-six letters of the alphabet into two sets. Most of these create no structure. But the partition into vowels and consonants does create structure. It would be an example of an interpretation. Thus, interpretations can be thought of as structured categorizations. I also use the word *interpretation* because it makes sense. The common usage accords with our formal notion. When people use the word *interpretation*, they imply a structured rendering of events: "that's your interpretation of what happened."

Among our most common interpretations are those based on race and ethnic identity. We classify people as Caucasian, African American, Asian, Latino, and European. We also create categories to contain most of the dimensions of someone's life, from his career (a lawyer), to the house he owns (a McMansion), to the type of car he drives (an American sedan), to his diet (not heart healthy), to his appearance (a slightly overweight George Clooney). We do this to communicate with one another, by highlighting some points and discounting others. We do it to make causal inferences.

Our interpretations often depend on our place or role. The managers of a firm see different parts of the firm's daily activities than the workers do. Producers see a product differently than consumers do. A director interprets a play differently than an audience member does. Differences in preferences can also cause differences in interpretations, an idea we'll take up later. A vegan categorizes restaurants differently than an omnivore does, and environmentalists and capitalists see new nuclear power plants through different lenses. Environmental capitalists see them differently still.

Ralph and Ernst: Bag Boys

To show how the fineness of our interpretations can differ, we consider Ralph and Ernst, Bag Boys. Ralph and Ernst each possess a large stack of paper bags, the kind used to carry groceries. You may call them sacks (the paper bags, not Ralph and Ernst). These bags sit in front of a collection of objects—pieces of a puzzle, maybe, or they could be photographs, birds, books of Russian folktales, or a random collection of all of those things. Ralph and Ernst are charged with the following task: to sort the objects into bags so that the objects in the same bag are similar and the objects in different bags are not.

Let's start with pieces of fruit. Ernst dutifully sorts them into four bags: one for bananas, one for pears, one for oranges, and one for apples. Meanwhile, Ralph puts each piece of fruit in its own bag. He sees each apple and each pear as different from the others, and he ends up using more bags that Ernst does. Next, each is given a paper number line with the numbers one to three hundred. Ernst cuts the number line in two places: at thirty-two and at two hundred and twelve. He puts the three pieces in separate bags with the words: ice, water, and steam on them. Ralph slices the number line into three hundred pieces, one for each integer, and puts each piece in a separate bag.

Ernst is a lumper: he lumps together things into classes that have similar features. The name Ernst is a reference to Ernst Mayr. Mayr helped settle what was known as the nominalism debate of whether species truly existed or people created them. Mayr found that across many cultures, people made exactly the same distinctions between species. In other words, putting robins in one bag and titmice in another was not a product of training or culture but a natural classification. Ralph, on the other hand, is a splitter: he considers each piece of fruit and each number to be different. Ralph refers to Ralph Waldo Emerson. To lump, in Emerson's view, was to diminish.

Neither Ernst nor Ralph should be thought of as correct or incorrect. That said, we see in a moment why Ralph may need to do at least a little more lumping while Ernst may need to do a little less. Otherwise, they may have trouble getting on in the world. We see hints of that in these two examples. Ernst's sorting of the fruit was probably more useful, while Ralph sorted too finely. But Ernst's trisecting of the number line was probably useful only in one context: determining the physical state of water, whereas Ralph's partitioning into individual numbers would be useful almost anywhere.

Though not true in our examples with Ralph and Ernst, the categories that we use to make identifications are often constructed. They do not exist apart from our making them. Consider, for instance, colors. The division into sixteen, thirty-two, and sixty-four colors in our boxes of crayons was arbitrary. Colors are arranged on a spectrum. How we divide up that spectrum is up to us. Thus, aquamarine is not a distinct color in the way that a robin is a distinct bird. The colors are socially constructed lumps. They are snips from a continuum.

In fact, our color lumping is severe. The human perceptual systems can distinguish more than ten thousand distinct colors. That's a lot of crayons. Most of us can get by with far fewer, and our language reflects this. The English language has around three hundred words for colors, and we can create more colors by combining those words. We describe something as reddish brown or greenish blue or even tealish magenta (okay, maybe not tealish magenta).

We can then think of the color red as a convention, a random wavelength pulled out of the interval in the color continuum.

In an alternative rose-colored reality, we might coordinate on a lighter shade of red. We might also replace green with aquamarine, and call our current green "grass green" in our box of sixty-four crayons. Of course, some colors, such as white or black, are not decided on by convention. On these colors we might expect universal agreement across cultures. After all, white is white—or so you might think until you try to match that Martha Stewart "Adirondack Chair White" paint you used on your walls with Benjamin Moore's "Cultured Pearl White."

Though what we call red, blue, yellow, and green may be arbitrary, the basic color categories are similar across cultures. Most cultures rely on the same eleven basic color categories: white, black, red, green, blue, yellow, brown, purple, pink, orange, and gray.[3] Orange in one country is pretty close to orange in another. One reason for this may be that we see the same sky and the same sun. We see similar green leaves and brown animals. We need not come to the same distinctions about continuums other than colors, however. What counts as a big or small piece of pie differs across cultures, across people within a culture, and even within families. What some Americans call a large soda some Europeans would call a bucket.

INTERPRETATIONS

I now describe the formal framework. Interpretations are maps into categories.

An **interpretation** *is a map from objects, situations, problems, and events to words. In an interpretation, one word can represent many objects.*

As was true with A-Square, interpretations often take just a few slices—just a few dimensions—from high-dimensional representations. As we will see, often interpretations take some dimensions of a perspective. Suppose that we are categorizing a collection of LEGO building blocks. Suppose further that each block has a size and a shape and that no two blocks are identical. The encoding of

TABLE 3.1:
The color–size perspective

(Color, Size)	Dogs
(White, Small)	Toy poodle
(Black, Medium)	Labrador
(Black, Large)	Newfoundland
(Brown, Small)	Sharpei
(Brown, Large)	Mastiff

TABLE 3.2:
Color interpretation

Color	Dogs
White	Toy poodle
Black	Labrador
	Newfoundland
Brown	Mastiff
	Sharpei

blocks by their size and color creates a perspective (in the formal sense). Each block is uniquely identified. Interpretations put blocks in groups. One interpretation would be to categorize the blocks by color. Another interpretation would categorize them by size.

We now have a heuristic for creating interpretations: we take a perspective and ignore dimensions. We do this when we refer to the Sonoma Rabbit marinated in a tarragon olive oil broiled over cedar planks and served in a port reduction as "the rabbit dish." A more formal example helps to clarify this point. Suppose that five dogs are playing in a park: a black Labrador retriever, a large black Newfoundland, a brown mastiff, a brown Sharpei, and a white toy poodle. We can construct a perspective that maps each dog into a color and a size (see table 3.1).

This perspective assigns a unique pair of words to each dog, and it can be used to generate two interpretations that are dimensional projections. One of those interpretations is based on color. The other is based on size (see tables 3.2 and 3.3).

TABLE 3.3:
Size interpretation

Size	Dogs
Large	Newfoundland
	Mastiff
Medium	Labrador
Small	Toy poodle
	Sharpei

These interpretations group the dogs differently. Which categorization is most relevant depends on our purpose. If we want to know if the dog will fit under an airline seat we should use the second interpretation. If we're worried about the dog getting too hot if left in the yard, we should use the first. When an interpretation considers only a subset of the possible dimensions, we call it a *projection interpretation*.

A **projection interpretation** *ignores some dimensions of a perspective.*

Not all interpretations are projection interpretations. Some interpretations create clumps in the set of possibilities. For example, if we divide houses into those that satisfy the principles of Feng Shui, we would not get slices in attribute space. We'd get clumps because satisfying those principles requires combinations of attributes coexisting in harmony.

A **clumping interpretation** *creates categories of similar objects, situations, problems, or events that are not simply projections of attributes.*

When we rely on categories such as "insect" or "ant" or "mammal," we're making these clumps. In these cases, what we're doing is ignoring branches upon subbranches of taxonomic distinctions, but we can think of this as carving up the space of possible things into clumps.[4]

The Necessity of Soccer Moms, Bobos, and Yuppies

We can loosely think of interpretations as categories. Interpretations put animals (it's a cat), kitchen items (put that with the other spatulas), movies (it's a romantic comedy), articles of clothing (they're called skorts), and even personalities (he's an INTJ) into categories. We construct these categories to help us make sense of the world. Getting around in the world requires transferring understandings of the particular to the general and from the too general to the more specific. We might at first classify all dogs as frightening, and then refine that inference to one that classifies only large dogs as frightening. That inference may over time become big dogs that don't chase tennis balls are frightening, and little dogs, with the exception of Jack Russell Terriers, are nice.

When pundits analyze an election, when they discuss the voting patterns of Soccer Moms, NASCAR Dads, Union Members, Bobos, and Reagan Democrats, they're doing this to explain why the election turned out as it did. Similar lumpings of people into groups helps explain who buys which products, watches particular television programs, or lives in a particular community. These categories were not handed down from on high. They were not written on stone tablets unearthed from caves. People constructed them.

Consider the dimensions on which people can differ, as well as the distinctions that might be made among people on each of those dimensions (table 3.4). The last column gives an estimate of the number of distinct categories on each dimension.

These categories cannot uniquely identify every individual, yet they create far too many distinct types of people to be useful. The number of different types of people we can distinguish with these categories equals the product of the number of categories: $2*4*10*5*2*4*6*5*5*3*4*2*3$. This number exceeds thirty million. Given that a mere three hundred million people live in the United States, this would create one category for every ten people. If we used all thirty million types, we would have too few people in any one subcategory to draw any inferences that have statistical validity.

TABLE 3.4:
Personal dimensions

Dimension	Categories	Number of Sets
Gender	Male, Female	2
Marital Status	Single, Married, Divorced, Cohabiting	4
Age	By Decade	10
Children	None, One, Two, Three, More than 3	5
Employment	Employed, Unemployed	2
Ethnicity	European, African, Asian, Latino	4
Religion	Christian, Jewish, Buddhist, Muslim, Other, None	6
Income	Quintiles	5
Wealth	Quintiles	5
Education	High School, College, Advanced Degree	3
Region	East, South, Midwest, West	4
Home owner	Yes, No	2
Residence	Urban, Rural, Suburban	3

The number of possible interpretations that we can create from these categories is mind-boggling. Suppose that we want an interpretation that considers a subset of the dimensions listed in table 3.4. We have more than a thousand ways to choose four dimensions and more than two thousand ways to choose five dimensions. Once these four or five dimensions are chosen, we then have thousands of ways to create categories that include these dimensions.

Typically, pundits, marketers, and social scientists rely on big categories so that lots of people fit in them. Hence, we get Soccer Moms: suburban married females between the ages of thirty and forty who have children and working spouses. The Soccer Mom category ignores lots of dimensions—religion, region, education, ethnicity, and even hair color.

Categories such as Soccer Moms have informational value only if the behavior or actions of people of that type differs from that of the rest of society. Otherwise, making the distinction fails to improve predictions. Effective marketing and political campaigning requires identifying relevant categories, what we

TABLE 3.5:
Poll results (Percent)

Voter Type	Voting Republican	Voting Democratic	Still Undecided
All Voters	38	42	20
Soccer Moms	24	22	54
Rich Senior Citizens	54	42	4

would call effective interpretation. If a product sells to affluent white teenagers, then the company targets its advertising toward that type of consumer. In politics, if a candidate lacks appeal to a certain type of voter, or if that type remains undecided, then the candidate tailors speeches, policy proposals, and advertising toward that type. We would not expect political commentators to talk about the Big Foot vote—the voting behavior of people with large feet—because people with big feet don't vote differently than other people.

Suppose, for example, that a poll reveals the estimates shown in table 3.5.

More than half (54 percent) of the Soccer Moms remain undecided. Politicians from both parties should (and would) focus attention on Soccer Moms by targeting advertising or even specific policy programs to that type of voter. Based on these data, politicians would choose to ignore wealthy older people, who have already made up their minds.

Too Much of a Good Thing

Given the awesome number of possible interpretations, it would seem to follow that interpretations, like perspectives, would be easy to create. They are, in fact, even easier to create. For each of the many perspectives that could be created there exists a large number of possible interpretations. An interpretation can ignore a dimension or a branch of a perspective or it can make less fine distinctions. For example, an interpretation used to predict someone's likelihood of buying blueberry Eggo Waffles may ignore education altogether or it could separate out those people with at least a high school education.

Researchers can now program computers to search over the space of possible types and look for aggregate types whose behavior differs from population averages. This technique is called data mining or forensic statistics. Data mining reveals correlation, not causality, which could be spurious. With so many possible dimensions it becomes incredibly likely that some constructed type correlates with the outcome. Episcopalian dog owners who drive more than forty miles to work and recently moved to the suburbs may have an extraordinarily high rate of bladder cancer, but so what? The correlation is probably spurious. Nothing about dog ownership, being Episcopalian, or recently moving to the suburbs would seem to cause bladder cancer. The challenge is to sort through all of the correlations and decide which have a causal basis.

EXPERTS AND THE CHICAGO "EL"

The quality of an interpretation often hinges on its fineness. Experts tend to have finer interpretations than novices. Novices count by fives or tens. Experts count in sixteenths. Like all first approximations, this characterization is not entirely accurate. Experts also learn to ignore dimensions that the rest of us take into account.

This splitting and neglecting embedded in expert interpretations makes discussions with experts fascinating and perplexing at the same time. An expert leading a guided tour of an art museum might mention particulars of a painting (the type of canvas and paint, the style of the brush strokes) as well as details about the painter (his or her personal life, the historical context in which the painting resides, and so on). At the Art Institute of Chicago, the tour stops at Picasso's *Grey Guitarist* and the guide usually mentions a faint sketch of a woman still visible on the canvas

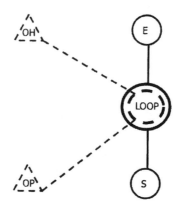

Figure 3.1 Original CTA Routes

even though Picasso painted over it. Yet these same guides often leave out details that we novices find focal. What was that dog doing in the picture? Why do some paintings have gold frames? Experts' ignoring of some dimensions and splitting of others can be seen as related phenomena. Ignoring dimensions allows experts to focus on others and attain deeper understandings and find better solutions. But we still want to know those gross details that experts have seemingly moved past.

To see the value of finer, expert interpretations, let's consider an example involving the Chicago elevated trains, known familiarly as the El. Every day, the El carries tens of thousands of passengers. The Chicago Transit Authority (CTA), a publicly run organization, does its best to keep costs at a minimum and the quality of its service at a maximum. In the early 1990s, the El had three main routes connecting downtown to residential areas and transportation centers. We focus on two of these here (see figure 3.1). One route (denoted by solid lines) began in Evanston, circled around the "Loop" in downtown Chicago, and then proceeded to the south side of Chicago. The other route (denoted by dashed lines) originated at O'Hare Airport, went around the Loop, and headed out to Oak Park.

To determine the number of trains required, the relevant statistic is the maximum number of riders on each route. If the CTA needed

TABLE 3.6:
CTA ridership on two rail lines

Route	Maximum Ridership	Number of Trains
Evanston–South Side	80,000	160
O'Hare–Oak Park	70,000	140

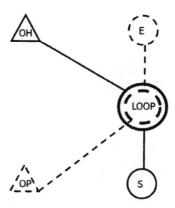

Figure 3.2 New CTA Routes

to carry 80,000 people, and 500 people fit on each train, then the CTA would require at least 160 trains. Maximum ridership for the two lines was approximately as shown in table 3.6.

In 1993, the CTA announced a rearrangement of the tracks that would save money. Instead of thinking of two lines that both traverse the Loop, the CTA reenvisioned the tracks as four lines that all end at the Loop. This was a finer interpretation of the routes. Now, the maximum ridership statistics look as shown in table 3.7.

Looking at the data this way, an obvious solution emerges: hook up the Evanston line with the Oak Park line and the O'Hare line with the South Side line (see figure 3.2). And that's what the CTA did. The costs of doing so were minimal. A small section of track had to be altered and new signs had to be posted explaining the route change. The new routes and the number of trains then looked as shown in table 3.8.

TABLE 3.7:
New CTA routes

Route	Maximum Ridership
Evanston–Loop	80,000
Loop–South Side	35,000
O'Hare–Loop	30,000
Loop–Oak Park	70,000

TABLE 3.8:
Effect of new CTA routes

Route	Maximum Ridership	Number of Trains
Evanston–Oak Park	80,000	160
O'Hare–South Side	35,000	70

Under this new arrangement, the total number of trains required fell from 300 to 230, resulting in an enormous cost savings. Why hadn't this solution been found earlier? Why didn't someone propose this at one of the many public meetings about the CTA? Cutting a train track in half and reattaching it to another line required breaking something apart that most people considered as a whole. It's akin to thinking about the lower portion of our pants legs as separate entities from top parts—a concept also introduced in the 1990s. They're called conversion pants, long pants with detachable legs that transform into shorts.

LUMP TO LIVE

As this chapter makes clear, we often do not assign each situation, event, or outcome its own name. We do not use perspectives. Instead, we lump reality into categories. Unlike the French, we may not have a different word for *everything*! Even so, the perspective model remains of tremendous value. Perspectives form the basis for interpretations. We create interpretations by ignoring some dimensions in a perspective or by dividing the perspective into clumps. Also, as already mentioned, we do construct perspectives for many real-world problems such as the traveling salesperson problem.

Having two frameworks also helps us to differentiate two causes of diversity. Earlier, we saw that perspectives exist in abundance, though only a small percentage captures relevant structure. Each of these perspectives, good or bad, creates many possible interpretations. These diverse interpretations lead us to draw different inferences, to make predictions that differ. So we can see the world the same fundamental way, but divide it up differently. This creates lots of diversity. That diversity affects how we predict outcomes and infer causality, the subject of the next chapter.

CHAPTER 4

Predictive Models

JUDGING BOOKS BY THEIR COVERS

Red cars go fast. —ORRIE PAGE (at age three)

Restaurants in Japan often advertise their fare by featuring plastic versions of their menu items in their windows. When American tourists visit Japan, they often shy away from these restaurants. These tourists predict—incorrectly, it turns out—that these restaurants cannot be good. After all, even Waffle House is too sophisticated to have plastic sausages and waffles in the window. These tourists are using interpretations to gauge a future event: they're making predictions. Whereas an interpretation categorizes the set of possibilities, a predictive model describes what we think will happen in some context in light of our interpretations. We categorize a cloud as a "rain cloud" and correctly predict rain. We categorize lightning as "heat lightning" and correctly predict that we'll remain dry. But, like those tourists in Tokyo, our predictive models can also lead us astray. Nearly every restaurant in Japan features plastic food; in fact, it's so popular that there's even a street in Tokyo called Kappabashi-dori jammed full of stores where you can buy plastic food and other essentials of the Japanese culinary experience.

We use predictive models when we vote, when we buy houses, when we select partners for life or business, and when we invest money for retirement. In each of these instances, we make predictions about the future based on our interpretations of the world. We do not know how events will transpire, whether the market will go up or down, whether learning Russian is a good career move, or whether a particular candidate will make a competent president. We make our predictions and take our chances.

To make a prediction or to infer a causal relationship, we first interpret the situation. To extend an earlier example, when we look into the sky and try to predict the likelihood of rain, we interpret the current weather: the temperature, wind speed, cloud formation, time of day, and the color of the sky. We take a slice of reality that, based on our experience, is relevant to the weather. We then predict a likelihood of rain based on our knowledge and experience. Interpretations influence predictions but they do not determine them. Two people with the same interpretation can make diverse predictions because their experiences or intuitions point them toward different inferences.

Over time we improve and refine our predictive models. We may have economic incentives to do so, or we may just desire deeper understandings. Whether capitalist or Buddhist, we want to know how things work. This constant honing and refinement of models need not lead to convergence of interpretations across different people. We're only likely to converge if presented with abundant data. We learn the causal relationships between fire and heat and ice and cold because fire is always hot and ice is always cold. The less noisy the environment, the more easily we can draw causal inferences. If ice were cold only 51 percent of the time, we might disagree about whether or not it is cold, just as we debate global warming.

Though lots of noise hinders our ability to predict, adding a little noise has an unexpected effect. It reinforces our beliefs in our models. This has practical consequences. If we want to teach a behavior, a bit of randomness can be helpful. For example, to teach a dog to sit, you should not always give her a treat as reward. Most of the time you should, but every once in a while you should withhold it. In doing so, you make the dog think, "I'm sitting, why am I not getting a treat? What is going on here? Didn't he say sit?" This helps her brain make even stronger connections between my command/plea to sit and her response. This may seem like wholly academic research, but it's not. The variable reward schedule is taught in most dog training classes.

Whether we learn them in noisy or clean environments, each of us carries around a set of predictive models in our heads. In what follows, we assume these predictions to be as accurate as possible given the interpretation and available information. Yet this may not always be the case. The theory of evolution has been supported by a century of empirical work. Nevertheless, many people do not believe it. Some government programs, such as Head Start, which most evidence suggests are successful, still have detractors.[1]

Evolution and Head Start remain controversial because of their dimensionality and complexity. When the connections from policies and actions to outcomes become complicated, even experts do not understand them entirely. Therefore, we simplify. We use interpretations. Even experts do. If these interpretations differ, they lead to predictions that differ. Different predictions prove beneficial. Before we show why, we need to understand its sources in more detail.

PREDICTIVE MODELS

Models take many forms. A survey of the vast modeling literature reveals systems dynamics models, regression models, game theory models, factor analysis models, and agent-based models. Models simplify the world. In fact, you're soaking in a model right now. But rather than soften your hands, models interpret reality and then produce outputs. These outputs often take the form of predictions. Here we restrict our attention to these *predictive models*.

A **predictive model** *is an interpretation together with a prediction for each set or category created by the interpretation.*

Just to help keep all of these frameworks and concepts clear, let's think of how predictive models differ from heuristics. A predictive model tells us what we think will happen: "It looks like rain." A heuristic tells us what to do: "It's raining, let's run for cover"—or what not to do: "We get just as wet by running, so let's walk." Predictive models are thoughts. Heuristics are actions.

Predictive models based on crude interpretations can be powerful. In *Blink*, Malcolm Gladwell describes how experts learn to look at just a few features and make expert predictions. Gladwell is describing predictive models based on simple interpretations.[2] Gladwell loads his book with examples, including the story of an expert who instantly recognized a multimillion-dollar sculpture as fake even though scientific analysis had found otherwise, and one of an expert who can accurately predict whether a married couple will stay together by looking at a few dimensions of their relationships. Gladwell's book popularizes ideas that get a more formal treatment in the work of Gerd Gigerenzer and Peter Todd.[3] Using our framework of predictive models, we can make sense of how these brief appraisals can be accurate and also why there may exist environments where even the best "blinker" won't be accurate.

As Gladwell's examples suggest, we should not think of predictive models as applying just to important events such as stock market price changes or the causes of diseases. We apply predictive models almost every time we think. And our predictive models rely on interpretations. A popular predictive model for when a television show has reached its peak relies on categorizing episodes by features of the script. "Jumping the shark" (a reference to Fonzie jumping over a shark on water skis that signified the long decline of *Happy Days*) occurs for many reasons. It could be an event—a wedding, birth, or death—or it could be when the show brings on a special guest star (Nancy Reagan showing up on *Diff'rent Strokes*).[4] In predicting whether a show has jumped the shark, people may rely on diverse models. Some people believe that *American Idol* jumped the shark with William Hung (a singer with no pitch). Others believe that it occurred when Paul Anka appeared as a guest star.

To provide some formalism for predictive models, I construct an example called Screening Success. It's only a little less fun than jumping the shark, but it's much easier to understand. I lean

TABLE 4.1:
The sex and violence interpretation

	Violence			
Sex	*None*	*Low*	*Mod.*	*High*
None				
Low				
Mod.				
High				

heavily on this example, considering it again in the next part of the book when aggregating predictive models.

SCREENING SUCCESS

To see how crude predictive models work, let's consider a context in which quick appraisals are the norm: evaluating movie scripts. In Los Angeles, a shockingly high percentage of the waiters, surfers, valets, mall employees, and even lawyers, doctors, and professors write screenplays. Many of these screenplays get only cursory reads by low-level studio employees (who themselves write screenplays on the side). A few screenplays get passed up the chain, but most get dragged across the computer screen and dumped into the trashcan.

In our example, we consider two employees of a movie production company, Ray and Marilyn, who have the task of reading screenplays. We can assume that they have been assigned the task of accepting only those scripts that will produce profits. Every submitted screenplay can be objectively assigned levels of sex (S) and violence (V). These levels can be classified into one of four categories: none, low, moderate, or high. (See table 4.1.) A complete perspective on the set of all movies would contain more dimensions than these two. So this encoding is an interpretation.

To make this example as simple as possible, we assume a deterministic mapping from these characteristics to whether a

TABLE 4.2:
The screenplay attribute to movie
quality mapping

	Violence			
Sex	None	Low	Mod.	High
None	B	B	G	B
Low	B	B	B	G
Mod.	G	B	G	G
High	B	G	G	G

None	None	None	None
Low	Low	Low	Low
Mod.	Mod.	Mod.	Mod.
High	High	High	High

Figure 4.1 Projection onto Sexual Content

screenplay is good (G) (i.e., can be the basis for a profitable film)
or is bad (B) (i.e., should be dragged into the can). Leave aside the
idea that evaluating film scripts on the criteria of sex and violence
would have deprived us of some great movies. Models require
simplifying reality. Table 4.2 shows the mapping into profits.

Given this construction, if someone knew this map and kept
track of the levels of sex and violence, she could perfectly predict
whether or not the screenplay is good or bad. We're assuming
that Ray and Marilyn don't do this. Each of them lacks the
ability (or time, or inclination) to look at both attributes. In
keeping with gender stereotypes, we assume that Ray keeps track
of the level of sex (figure 4.1) and Marilyn keeps an eye on the
violence (figure 4.2). (We would classify both of these as projection
interpretations.)

To turn these interpretations into predictive models, we need
only attach a prediction to each set in the interpretation. For example, assume that Ray reads a screenplay with no sex. Provided
Ray has lots of experience reading screenplays (a point we take up

None	Low	Mod.	High
None	Low	Mod.	High
None	Low	Mod.	High
None	Low	Mod.	High

Figure 4.2 Projection onto Violence

TABLE 4.3:
Ray's predictive model

Sex Level	Realizations	Prediction
None	3Bs and 1G	B
Low	3Bs and 1G	B
Mod.	3Gs and 1B	G
High	3Gs and 1B	G

shortly), he knows that three times out of four (or 75 percent of the time) the movie will turn out unprofitable. He similarly learns that screenplays with low levels of sex also turn out to be bad 75 percent of the time, but that movies with moderate and high levels of sex turn out to be good 75 percent of the time.

He's not always right, but he's not paid always to be right. He's making a quick appraisal. He's blinking. We can summarize Ray's predictions in table 4.3. This table describes his predictive model. In the first column, we show the level of sex in the films. In the second column, we show what realizations Ray would see. Of those films with no sexual content, three will be Bs and one will be G. The good one will be a film with no sexual content and moderate violence.

Similarly, we can characterize Marilyn's predictive model in table 4.4.

A moment's observation shows that Marilyn will also be correct 75 percent of the time. Note though that she and Ray do not make the same predictions. When evaluating a screenplay with no sex and lots of violence, Ray would predict a flop whereas Marilyn would predict a success. In this instance, Ray would

Table 4.4:
Marilyn's predictive model

Violence	None	Low	Mod.	High
Realizations	3Bs and 1G	3Bs and 1G	3Gs and 1B	3Gs and 1B
Predictions	B	B	G	G

Table 4.5:
Deborah's interpretation

	Violence			
Sex	None	Low	Mod.	High
None	extreme	balanced	balanced	extreme
Low	balanced	dull	dull	balanced
Mod.	balanced	dull	dull	balanced
High	extreme	balanced	balanced	extreme

predict correctly and Marilyn wouldn't. If we average across all cases, it's equally likely that she'd be correct and he wouldn't.

In addition to Ray and Marilyn, we now add a third screenplay evaluator, Deborah. She uses a clumping interpretation, creating sets that allow for variation in both attributes within the same category. Whereas a projection interpretation divides the square into rows or columns, a clumping interpretation divides it into boxes of various shapes.

To construct the correct frame for this interpretation, think of Deborah as someone fueled by large quantities of Diet Coke who wears funky glasses and has serious attitude. Deborah's interpretation clumps screenplays into three sets: dull, extreme, or balanced. Deborah classifies screenplays with low and moderate levels of both sex and violence as dull, screenplays with low or moderate levels of either sex or violence and either a high level or none of the other as balanced, and screenplays with neither a low nor a moderate level of either sex or violence as extreme (see table 4.5).

Assuming that she has lots of experience and makes the more likely prediction for each set in her interpretation, Deborah's

TABLE 4.6:
Deborah's predictive model

| | Violence | | | |
Sex	None	Low	Mod.	High
None	B	G	G	B
Low	G	B	B	G
Mod.	G	B	B	G
High	B	G	G	B

model predicts that balanced screenplays will be good and that all others will be bad. Her predictive model looks as shown in table 4.6.

Relative to Ray and Marilyn's models, Deborah's seems strange. And yet by examining all the cases (which takes a little effort), we can see that she also predicts correctly 75 percent of the time. She's just as accurate as they are. Given their equal proficiency at predicting, Ray, Marilyn, and Deborah would all feel comfortable holding onto their own predictive models. Even under pressure to make good predictions, people need not converge on a common predictive model. *Selective pressure, or what could be called survival of the fittest, need not imply convergence to a single predictive model.* Diversity can persist in a competitive environment. Several predictive models can be close to equally accurate. Each of twenty pundits can analyze an election differently yet compellingly. Was it Ohio evangelicals that swung the 2004 election for Bush or was it the new exurbanites? A case can be made either way. As we will see in part II, when we aggregate these predictive models, this diversity proves beneficial.

THEORY-BASED MODELS

Our discussion so far has assumed that our screenplay readers make the correct predictions that they have learned from experience. But even in the absence of experience, we may still

TABLE 4.7:
Ray's theory-based
predictive model

Sex Level	Prediction
None	B
Low	G
Mod.	G
High	B

have to make predictions based on theories. On their first days of work, for instance, Marilyn and Ray would have had to rely on these experience-free theories. These theories could be no better than random or they could be accurate if underpinned by sound logic. Ray might have theorized that screenplays with low and moderate levels of sex would do well and come up with the predictive model shown in table 4.7.

This model predicts correctly a mere 50 percent of the time. Ray could do equally well flipping a coin and he'd no longer have to suffer through all that terrible dialogue.

This simple example makes an important point: an interpretation that represents the objects or events meaningfully is by itself not enough. An interpretation may capture dimensions or attributes that reveal underlying causality or correlation, but unless that interpretation is combined with an accurate predictive model, possibly one informed by experience, it may not prove useful.

Thus, we can distinguish between the maximal accuracy of a predictive model given an interpretation and the accuracy of a given model. The maximally accurate predictions from an interpretation are those that would be made if the person knew the true probability distribution over outcomes (something we get closer to with experience). As we saw, the accuracy of a particular theory need not achieve this maximum. In addition, maximal accuracy given an interpretation may not be high in some contexts. If so, then it would be impossible to make quick assessments that were highly accurate.

In other words, sometimes we can blink and sometimes we cannot. Suppose we begin with a common perspective that we use to construct projection interpretations and predictive models. We then have at our disposal one predictive model for each dimension. It may be that none of those predictive models works well. If so, blinking—making a quick evaluation based on a single attribute—won't be effective. Good blinking requires the existence of a dimension that makes the task easy. As Gladwell describes in *Blink*, evidence of nastiness is a good predictor of the likelihood a marriage will end in divorce. If our interpretation considers only that single dimension—does a couple make nasty, diminishing comments about each other—it'll allow us to predict pretty well.

But no such dimension may exist for a given predictive task. To take an obvious case, suppose that we want to predict whether a stock price of a company will increase or decrease. If we looked at any one attribute of that company—price–earnings ratio, sales growth, change in stock price over the past year, or the like— we could not predict much better than randomly whether the price would go up or down. The reason no single dimension is of much predictive value rests on a logic of markets. If a simple way to predict rising stock prices existed, someone would find it and raise the price of the undervalued stocks. For this simple reason, people who successfully invest in the stock market use sophisticated predictive models, and we can't "blink" stock prices.

The bulk of the evidence shows that most people, even experts, are less accurate than regression models based on data. The book *Moneyball* popularized this stylized fact by showing how Billy Beane ran regressions and then ran circles around other baseball executives.[5] The *Moneyball* example is not an outlier. More than two hundred studies conducted over the past seventy years demonstrate that simple linear regression models outperform experts in forecasting the future.[6] We should not view these findings as puzzling. Experts are people, too, and they suffer from biases just like the rest of us.

In a decade-long study, Philip Tetlock found that experts could not very accurately predict outcomes of complex economic and political processes. He further found that those experts who relied on fixed ideological interpretations, so-called hedgehogs, performed worse than those who were willing to be flexible. Overall, most experts proved to be more confident than they should have been.[7] Almost everyone suffers from overconfidence. It comes with being human. Most of us feel we're above average in most things. And echoing earlier results, he finds experts worse than regressing.

We shouldn't be too sanguine about Tetlock's findings. We must remember that even experts' heads can hold only so much information. In making predictions, experts rely on a few dimensions at most. They omit variables that matter, and they sometimes include variables that do not. Hence, when the inference task becomes difficult, even the experts must throw up their hands and their predictions may not be much better than tosses at a dartboard.

The fact that experts are not as accurate as regression models begs the question of why we use experts at all. Why don't we just use regression models? We do. Experts do. Successful investors, forecasters, and odds makers do not just get a feel for what is likely to happen using mystical powers, they gather data. They run regressions. These regressions are still based on variables chosen by people—what we call interpretations. The human element is not absent. These interpretations leave out some variables and include others. Given the diversity of possible interpretations, we have lots of diverse experts. And, as we will see, that's beneficial.

CONCLUDING THOUGHTS

At this point, a brief summary helps us keep track of the various concepts that we've covered in the past two chapters. If we want to predict something, we have to have some way of representing those entities whose outcomes we are predicting. Perspectives would give us a full and complete representation, but in most cases people don't use perspectives. We use interpretations—categorizations—based on perspectives. Given these interpretations, we then make predictions based on our experiences or on a theory. We call these predictions, together with the interpretations, a predictive model. Thus, predictive models map the sets (or categories) in our interpretations onto outcomes. Any interpretation has a maximally accurate model, but we have no reason to believe that people use this model. After all, we're human.

Being human, we differ in the interpretations we choose. And as we saw in Screening Success, we therefore differ in our predictive models. Ray thinks the screenplay is good. Marilyn thinks it is not. Sometimes crude predictive models work well. Sometimes they don't. If we confront a complicated predictive task, predictive models based on crude interpretations will be inaccurate most of the time. As we see in the next part of the book, even when individual predictions may not be accurate, collections of diverse inaccurate predictions can be.

CHAPTER **5**

Measuring Sticks and Toolboxes

CALIPERS FOR THE BRAIN

*One only needs two tools in life: WD-40 to make things go,
and duct tape to make them stop.*
—G. WEILACHER

THE four frameworks—perspectives, heuristics, interpretations, and predictive models—turn people, including us, into plumbers. This metaphor has no bearing on how we wear our pants. What it means is that the frameworks are tools that each of us brings to the table or the chalkboard Each of us walks around carrying a toolbox filled with a variety tools. Our toolboxes become a framework for thinking about individual cognitive differences because each of us has a toolbox filled with different cognitive skills. We're not all plumbers, although some of us are; others of us are carpenters, mechanics, aerospace engineers, or musicians. A tool might be a perspective, such as the ability to think in another language. It might be a heuristic or even a set of heuristics, such as knowledge of calculus. It might be an interpretation. It might be a predictive model, or even a class of such models. We then apply these tools to the best of our abilities, regardless of how we wear our pants.

The toolbox framework serves three purposes. First, it helps us think about intelligence in a new way. Normally, we think in terms of IQ scores. With toolboxes, we think in terms of specific tools or collections of tools. Second, the toolbox framework helps us rethink how to rank intelligence. If we think of people in terms of tools, we cannot necessarily say that one person is smarter than another. Third, the toolbox framework allows us to compute collective capabilities. If we think of people as having tools, we can then deduce how a collection of people will perform. We can't perform the same algebra over IQ scores.

Our toolboxes differentiate us: any two people are likely to have different toolboxes. One person may know how to apply Bayes's rule from probability theory. Another person may know how to distinguish species of birds. One person may know how to represent numbers in base two. Another person may know heuristics for combining herbs and spices. Our toolboxes define us, constrain us, and guide us. They determine how we do in school, how we play with others, the careers we choose, how much money we make, whether we are capable of having much fun, and how smart people think we are. A person's toolbox is not fixed for all time. As we go through life, we learn new tools and occasionally forget old ones. At any moment, an individual's collection of tools depends on innate abilities, identity, training, and experiences.

Having tools and being able to apply them correctly are two different things. We keep things simple here and assume people can apply the tools they possess. A more complete framework would also take into account a person's facility with her tools. Facility need not take a single form. One person may be quick to apply her tools. Another may be slow at figuring out which tool to use, but may be better at recombining tools. Many people who have produced interesting insights and breakthroughs have been slow, deliberate thinkers. Then again, some people who think slowly don't think deeply either. The person who said "still waters run deep" never saw a mud puddle.

What can go into a person's toolbox is partly innate. Each of us is born with some constraints and latent abilities for acquiring various tools. Some people can learn languages easily. Some find mathematics intuitive. Some quickly pick up the intricacies of chess. Our genes do not determine or even place hard constraints on our acquired cognitive skills, but they make some skills easier to acquire than others. Whether we choose to nurture those skills for which we have innate abilities is another question altogether.

A toolbox's contents are also a product of identity, experience, and training. We learn what our teachers and parents tell us to learn (at least some of the time) and what opportunities they afford us. How we are trained and what experiences we have are not random. They can be determined by choice. We learn what our friends and we think is exciting to learn. We take up this topic in more detail later in the book. For the moment, we concentrate on the implications of toolboxes for how we think about intelligence.

Though a simplification of how real brains work, the toolbox framework complicates how we think of intelligence. The standard approach to thinking about intelligence relies on measuring sticks, and each of us falls somewhere along the stick. IQ tests use a single stick, while others use more. One expert, Howard Gardner, uses seven sticks and has been contemplating an eighth. Eight measuring sticks may seem like a lot, but we use at least that many to determine the price of a house: square footage, year built, external building material, number of rooms, number of bathrooms, number of bedrooms, lot size, type of flooring, and so on. So why not many more for people?

Our approach assumes that a person's intelligence depends on her toolbox and her ability to retrieve, generate, and apply those tools to problems and situations. All else being equal, the more tools a person possesses, the better she can solve problems, construct theories, and complete other cognitive tasks. Using the toolbox framework complicates how we think about comparing and, more important, combining intelligence, too. If we mean that one person has more tools than another, we can make such comparisons. But we might also require that one person solve any problem that the other person can (plus a few more) and that the first person make more accurate predictions in all cases; if so, we need the first person to possess every tool possessed by the second—not just a different set, but the complete set of the second person, and then some. The superadditivity of tools means that we also need to know all of the combinations of tools that a person might apply. With only a saw or only a hammer, we cannot build anything interesting. With both, we can build homes, tree forts, and fences. As the management guru Peter Drucker wrote, "Effective work is actually done in and by teams of people of diverse knowledge and skills."[1]

In this chapter, we put the toolbox framework through its paces, contrasting it with measuring stick approaches such as IQ scores and multidimensional intelligence scores. Even the multidimensional measures understate the amount of diversity by projecting cognitive differences onto multidimensional spaces. In the toolbox framework, people differ in their capacities and these capacities translate into crude rankings at best. We see why we might be able to rank mathematicians but why we cannot say whether Tolstoy was smarter than Newton. We can rank within domains, but not across them. And we can rank within only some domains—ranking physicists is easier than ranking authors. We cannot say whether Joyce was better than Austen.

A Choice of Metaphors: Measuring Sticks or Toolboxes

Americans love to rank things: cities, schools, cars, airlines, breeds of dogs, and movie stars. We also like to think that we can rank people by their intelligence. But many of us believe that our cognitive abilities cannot be summarized in a single number or vector of numbers. Our analysis of toolboxes argues against complete rankings, but simply to say that everyone differs may be too extreme, too. At a minimum, we may be able to classify people in categories and to make comparisons across those categories. The great novelist or nuclear physicist is, in a real sense, smarter than the rest of us—but one may not be "smarter" than the other.

Different cognitive skills, like the varied attractions of a city, prove beneficial in different contexts. Cognitive skills, like physical skills, apply in some domains and not in others. Anyone who has trouble remembering that physical skills are context dependent need only pick up a Michael Jordan baseball card. Though Jordan was a great baseball player by ordinary standards, he was not up to major league level, even though he was certainly a better all around athlete than almost all major league players. Just as the physical qualities that make for a good figure skater are different from those that make for a good sumo wrestler, the cognitive skills required to be brilliant at one task often overlap little with the skills required for another.

To measure what's under the hood, so to speak, psychologists use general intelligence tests. These tests map the human mind onto a single dimension. That single dimension invites a conceptualization as ability. We think we are smarter than everyone who gets a lower score than we do and dumber than everyone who gets a higher score. We cannot help but do this. But in light of the complexity and diversity of our brains, this ranking of individual people or groups of people on a single measure seems a stretch. Any mapping from something as complex as intelligence into a single number condenses a lot of information. By way of comparison, think of giving cities a quality score. Can we reduce Paris or New York or even Tulsa to a single number? Of course not.

And still, IQ tests measure something meaningful. They capture someone's ability to exhibit a range of cognitive skills in a relatively short time span. People with high IQs should, on average, have more tools, especially tools that allow a person to answer questions quickly and accurately. Thus, the people who score highly may not be diverse.[2]

The toolbox framework fundamentally differs from measuring stick frameworks in how it captures intelligence. IQs and toolboxes are both interpretations. Each interprets a person as a set. In the case of IQs, the sets have numbers. In the case of toolboxes, the sets are combinations of tools. A person's IQ can take at most one of two hundred or so values. By contrast, the number of sets of unique toolboxes can be enormous, as we will see in a few pages.[3] Thus, the toolbox framework embraces our differences more than do measuring stick approaches.

IQ tests determine a person's score by the number of questions she correctly answers. Think back to the city analogy. To assign a single number to Chicago or Boston, we could ask the city questions. Do you have museums? Do you have parks? Is your air clean? Do you have a symphony? To get a high score, a city would have to give the correct answers. The city that scores highest depends on the questions asked. So we cannot say that Chicago is better than Boston or that Boston is better than Chicago. Depending on the questions we ask, either might do better. However, given almost any set of questions, Paris scores better (on average) than Tulsa or Grand Rapids. But, on some questions (are the locals friendly?) Tulsa and Grand Rapids give better answers than Paris. So we cannot say that Paris is better on every dimension.

To push this analogy with cities just a little bit further, suppose that Sarah, who lives in Chicago with her sister Kelly, is thinking of moving to Boston. Sarah knows nothing about Boston except that the magazine *Condé Nast* rates Chicago at 84 and Boston at 85 out of a possible 100. Should Sarah conclude that Boston is a better place to live? Of course not. She should instead conclude that each city has its advantages relative to the other and that on balance they're about the same. If we pull this analogy back to IQ differences, we're drawn to the conclusion that large differences in IQ may signify meaningful differences in intelligence but small differences in IQ do not. And focusing on differences obscures relevant cognitive differences. Two people with identical IQs can make vastly different contributions to society.

Nevertheless, once we have these single numbers, we start making comparisons. Those comparisons create stress and tension. Here's a scenario that gets played out in homes across America every year. David, all six feet two inches of him, receives his SAT scores and compares them to those of his older sister, Jackie, who stands five feet six. His scores are lower. His parents try to calm him by saying, "We're all different. No one is smarter than anyone else." He's thinking, "Yeah, right, I believe that." He can see the scores. His parents may as well have told him that he and his sister are the same height. Yet if we accept the toolbox metaphor, we recognize that David's parents make sense. He's taking these scores too seriously.[4] We can line people up along the wall and make little pencil marks to determine relative heights, but we cannot do the same for intelligence.

Information Loss and Multidimensional Measures

If one number won't do, perhaps we can get closer to capturing intelligence by increasing the number of dimensions. As we will see, this idea moves in the direction of the toolbox approach but doesn't get us all the way there. Nevertheless, it's worth exploring.

As already mentioned, the best-known multidimensional measures are Howard Gardner's seven dimensions of intelligence: linguistic, logical, musical, spatial, kinesthetic, interpersonal, and intrapersonal.[5] Gardner's choices of dimensions hardly can be classified as ad hoc. Each dimension satisfies seven criteria: evidence that the intelligence is located in a specific part of the brain, the existence of prodigies, stages of mastery, and so on.

Robert Sternberg offers a second multidimensional measure of intelligence, one with three dimensions: analytic intelligence, creative intelligence, and practical intelligence.[6] Analytic intelligence can loosely be translated as IQ; it emphasizes the ability to solve test problems. Creative intelligence captures someone's ability to apply past experiences to new problems and to combine ideas, which resonates with our idea of toolboxes. Creative intelligence partially tests the ability to combine tools. Practical intelligence captures a person's ability to apply scholarly knowledge to real-world situations. A person of high practical intelligence can apply her tools when confronted with how much wood to buy to build a deck, but may perform poorly on a math problem. A person with low practical intelligence may be able to solve calculus problems for the area under a graph and then buy five times as much paint as needed when redecorating a room. These two people may marry. If so, all will be fine.

Rankings and Settling Things on the Field

While single dimensional measures of intelligence create rankings, multidimensional measures need not. We can say that

TABLE 5.1:
Sternberg intelligence scores

Person	Analytic	Creative	Practical
Kathleen	60	95	80
Patrick	90	55	85
Paul	55	70	70

someone with an SAT score of 700 verbal and 700 math did better than someone who scored 600 on both sections, but we cannot say whether she did better than someone who scored 800 on the math section but only 600 on the verbal section. Without placing weights on the two sections of the exam, we cannot even say that she did better than someone who scored 710 on the math section and 600 on the verbal section. We could weight the sections to create a combined score—and a one-dimensional ranking—but when we do, we make an implicit value judgment about the parts' relative merit. Even more problematically, if we allow ourselves to vary the weights, we can change the rankings among a group of people.

Suppose that we want to rank Kathleen, Patrick, and Paul based on their test scores. An ordering of Kathleen, Patrick, and Paul is a list with a greater-than relation between their names. The expression

$$\text{Kathleen} > \text{Patrick} > \text{Paul}$$

represents Kathleen coming before Patrick and Patrick coming before Paul. Orderings are transitive so Kathleen must also come before Paul. In this case, the relation > could signify age. Kathleen might be older than Patrick, and Patrick older than Paul. Transitivity implies that Kathleen must also then be older than Paul. Such orderings by age are possible because age is one-dimensional.[7] Let's assume that Kathleen, Patrick, and Paul all take Sternberg's intelligence test and receive the scores shown in table 5.1.

Based on these scores, we cannot rank Kathleen and Patrick. She scores higher on creative intelligence. Patrick scores higher

TABLE 5.2:
Total Sternberg intelligence

Person	Sum of Test Scores
Kathleen	235
Patrick	230
Paul	195

on analytic and practical intelligences. Similarly, Patrick and Paul cannot be ranked. Patrick scores higher on analytic and practical intelligences. And Paul scores higher on creative intelligence. Kathleen and Paul, however, can be ranked (sorry Paul!). Kathleen scores higher on all three measures. These partial rankings invite confusion. Kathleen is more intelligent than Paul, while Patrick isn't. And yet Kathleen is not more intelligent than Patrick. These paradoxes arise because we are squeezing several dimensions down to one. In doing so, we're losing information and obscuring differences.

One way to get a complete ranking is to sum the intelligence scores on the three tests. Their total scores would be as shown in table 5.2.

Now we can rank them. However, this one-dimensional ranking denies the independence of the three types of intelligence. And it weights all three types of intelligence equally. This assumption is arbitrary. In some contexts, analytic intelligence may be more important than creative intelligence and practical intelligence. If we give analytic intelligence double the weight of creative intelligence to create a Double Math Sternberg Intelligence score, we then make Patrick the most intelligent.[8]

This ability to shift weights and alter rankings creates serious problems. Most ranking systems cope with multiple attributes by assigning weights to each attribute and summing them up. For example, *U.S. News and World Report* magazine assigns weights to attributes when ranking colleges and universities. Schools have attributes: test scores of students, graduation rates, faculty–student ratios, and so on. The magazine assigns each attribute a weight that determines the relative importance of the attribute. The score for a school equals the weighted sum of its attributes' values. These one-dimensional scores can then be arranged from highest to lowest. But what if you, as an applicant, would choose to weight various attributes differently than *U.S. News* does? Maybe you want a good school that's within one hundred miles of your house. You'd come up with a different ranking. But of course schools would lose their bragging rights. No school wants to take out an ad saying that it's "closest to Conrad's house for the fifth year in a row."

Granted, if one school outperformed another on every attribute, then regardless of the weights assigned to attributes it would be ranked higher, just as Kathleen would always be ranked above Paul regardless of the weights placed on the three types of intelligence. However, as the number of dimensions becomes large, the odds that one person or school scores higher than another on every dimension become small.

The arbitrariness of the weights makes us uneasy about these rankings. Witness the dissatisfaction with the Bowl Championship Series rankings in college football. These rankings are based on a score that combines polls, computer rankings, win–loss records, strength of schedule, and quality wins. In this particular case, lower scores are better. The two teams with the lowest scores earn the right to play for college football's national championship, a process many consider unfair. Fans want the best team to be determined on the field of play. They want a game to decide the best team.[9]

All this talk of football serves an important purpose. We can show that settling matters "on the field," so to speak, in head-to-head competition, may not work either. A best team may not exist. This same logic applies to people. If we had some way of having people compete to see who was the most intelligent, head-to-head (so to speak), we might have no clear winner for the same reason. With all due apologies to Marilyn Vos Savant, we probably could not find the smartest person in the world even if we produced a game show called *The World's Smartest Person* and determined a champion.

We can use something called the Colonel Blotto Game to call into question the notion that competition reveals the best team.

TABLE 5.3:
Colonel Blotto strategies

Player	Door 1	Door 2	Door 3
USC	40	20	40
Michigan	35	40	25
Florida	20	35	45
Oklahoma	33	33	34

In Colonel Blotto, each of two players has one hundred playing pieces. Each must array these pieces in front of three doors.[10] Whichever player has the most pieces in front of a door wins that door. The objective in Colonel Blotto is to win the most doors. Colonel Blotto has no single best course of action. Any placement of the pieces can be defeated. If one player places fifty pieces in front of the first and second doors and none in front of the third, a second player can place sixty pieces in front of the first and forty in front of the third and win two doors in the process.

To model football using Colonel Blotto, we can let door one represent one team on offense and the other on defense, door two the opposite combination, and door three special teams. To model lawyers, the doors could represent knowledge of the law, charisma, and recall of facts. The Colonel Blotto game doesn't capture competitive situations perfectly—no model does—but it's a decent approximation. Imagine four participants in a Colonel Blotto tournament. I'll call them USC, Michigan, Florida, and Oklahoma. They have the strategies shown in table 5.3.

USC, Michigan, and Florida all defeat Oklahoma because each of the first three schools has more than thirty-four pieces in front of two of the doors. If USC plays Michigan, USC wins by winning Doors 1 and 3. If Michigan plays Florida, Michigan wins the first two doors, and therefore wins. If Florida plays USC, Florida wins. Notice that USC beats Michigan, Michigan beats Florida, and Florida beats USC—a *cycle*. (Cycles reappear later when we cover diverse preference aggregation.) Given this cycle, none of these three teams should be thought of as better than any of the others. All are better than Oklahoma, however.

Suppose that we hold a tournament to determine a national champion from among these four teams. Of the three teams that form the cycle—USC, Michigan, and Florida—one plays Oklahoma in the first round. That team, let's suppose that it is Michigan, defeats Oklahoma. In the other game, Florida defeats USC (in a thriller). Michigan and Florida then play in the Tostitos–Subaru Fiesta Bowl.com, and Michigan wins. Thousands of fans parade in the streets. The next day, students and alumni run to stores to buy hats, T-shirts, and mugs commemorating the event. As they sing it in Ann Arbor, "Hail to the victors valiant, hail to the conquering heroes."

Hold on. If we look closely at the tournament, we see that Michigan won because they played Oklahoma in the first round. If we look at the matchups, we see that whichever teams draws Oklahoma in the first round wins the national championship.[11] So rather than sell shirts that say, "2008 National Champions," Moe's Sport Shop might more honestly sell shirts that say, "The team that got to play Oklahoma first." As titles go, it's not appealing, but at least it's accurate.

Is the Colonel Blotto model reasonable here? Absolutely. Cycles like the USC–Michigan–Florida cycle are widespread. A look at head-to-head competition in almost any conference in any year reveals these cycles, yet we delude ourselves by posting arbitrary rankings and by crowning champions. So long as we know that the title of champion means "winner of the tournament," we're on solid ground. But we should not confuse champion with best.[12]

Let's wrap this all up. With multiple dimensions, no clear winner may exist. Even attempts to settle it on the field won't work. What gets settled on the field depends on the tournament pairings. We cannot expect to find a best team, a best lawyer, or a smartest person. Those soft mumblings that ring hollow when people try to reassure children with lower aggregate SAT scores than their siblings, about everyone being different blah blah blah, should be spoken loudly and clearly. We *are* all different. We have different tools.

The Toolbox Framework

The toolbox framework is pretty simple. First, we think about the set of all possible tools, which consists of all possible knowledge, skills, abilities, heuristics, interpretations, and perspectives that a person might acquire. But an individual can't possibly acquire all of these, so a person's toolbox is the subset of tools that a person has acquired.

We often can apply tools across domains. We use basic arithmetic when balancing our checkbooks, counting change, and buying milk. A drug or surgical procedure developed in one domain often can be applied in others. Botox, a mild form of botulism, was developed to help solve a less-than-dire medical problem—wrinkles. Botox reduces facial wrinkles by numbing muscles—temporarily, so you do have to keep visiting your doctor (or host a Botox party). The ability to numb muscles is just a tool. So once Botox was developed, doctors could apply it to other problems: medical problems that involve overstimulated muscles, such as stuttering, some forms of ulcers, and even cerebral palsy. But then not all tools work on all problems. You can't fix a car with a blender. At least not very well.

That's it. That's the toolbox framework. Unpacking its implications leads to some surprises and insights.

Three Ways to Think about Tools

We now consider two people, Bobbi and Carl, and, using the toolbox framework, try to figure out who's smarter. We pick the smarter person at the end of the chapter. Bobbi and Carl possess distinct, large toolboxes, though Bobbi's contains a few more tools than Carl's. She has twenty and he has fifteen, so she must be smarter. But in the toolbox framework, to be smarter than Carl Bobbi would have to possess each of Carl's tools. If that's not true, Carl may make greater contributions. He may be more successful because he may have more appropriate tools.

We take three approaches to figure out if Bobbi is indeed smarter than Carl. In the first, the tools are unrelated to one another (like cards in a regular playing deck). In the other models, linkages exist—learning one tool may require first learning some others. For instance, mathematicians have an easier time learning physics than do historians. Learning algebra requires a mastery of addition, subtraction, multiplication, and division. We can envision this either as the rungs on a ladder or as branches on a tree.

Model 1: The Deck of Cards

In this first model, Bobbi and Carl choose tools randomly from identical boxes containing fifty-two tools. These boxes represent the set of possible tools someone could acquire. Their choices represent what tools their experiences, opportunities, preferences, and abilities led them to acquire. To help make this more realistic, these fifty-two tools can be associated with the fifty-two cards in a standard deck of playing cards. We want to determine the probability that Bobbi holds every tool (every card) that Carl does. Determining this probability requires three separate calculations:

1. The number of distinct toolboxes Bobbi can choose
2. The number of distinct toolboxes Carl can choose
3. The probability that Bobbi's toolbox contains Carl's

To make these calculations, thinking in terms of cards proves useful. Bobbi chooses twenty cards from the deck, choosing any one of the fifty-two cards first. Using similar logic, she can choose any of fifty-one cards second, and so on. In this way, the number of possible toolboxes she could construct equals fifty-two times fifty-one, times fifty, and so on, all the way down to thirty-three, so that twenty cards are included. However, this calculation takes into account the order in which she chooses the cards. If she chooses the ace of hearts and then the jack of spades, this differs from choosing the jack of spades and then the ace of hearts.

To arrive at the correct figure, we must divide by the number of ways the same twenty cards can be reordered. We could put any of the twenty cards first, any of the remaining nineteen second, and so on. This gives twenty times nineteen times eighteen times . . . times two times one ways to order the cards. Dividing the first number by the second gives the total number of distinct toolboxes Bobbi could acquire:

$$\frac{52 \cdot 51 \cdot 50 \cdot 49 \cdot 48 \cdot \ldots \cdot 33}{20 \cdot 19 \cdot 18 \cdot \ldots \cdot 1}$$

or 125,994,627,894,135, or just shy of one hundred and twenty-six trillion unique collections of toolboxes of size twenty. That's not only more toolboxes than you'll find at Sears and Wal-Mart combined; it exceeds the total number of people who have ever lived on Earth, which can be counted in the billions. Compare this number to the number of possible IQ scores (which is a couple of hundred) and it becomes clear how much more diversity the toolbox framework can capture.

Let's admit that when people, like David's parents a few pages back, say that "everyone is different, everyone has her own unique set of skills," many of us would like to barf. Yet the mathematics reveals that those insipid remarks rest on solid foundations. We can all differ. We have so many toolboxes to choose from that Walt Whitman and Carl Sagan would stand in awe of their diversity and number.

To complete this example, we must make a similar calculation for Carl. We find that he has 4,481,381,406,320, or roughly four-and-a-half trillion toolboxes from which to choose. These first two calculations provide most of the information needed to make the third calculation: the likelihood that Bobbi possesses every tool that Carl does. To calculate this, we assign an arbitrary fifteen tools to Carl and compute the percentage of Bobbi's 126 trillion toolboxes that contain it. Removing Carl's fifteen cards out of the deck leaves thirty-seven cards remaining. Bobbi can choose five more of these. Using the same logic we used to count the number of possible toolboxes for Bobbi and Carl, we can compute the number of possible ways that Bobbi could choose five additional cards:

$$\frac{37 \cdot 36 \cdot 35 \cdot 34 \cdot 33}{5 \cdot 4 \cdot 3 \cdot 2 \cdot 1}$$

This equals a mere 435,897. We've got lots of numbers floating around. Let's walk back through what we've calculated slowly so we don't lose the forest for the trees. Of the 126 trillion toolboxes that Bobbi could choose, fewer than a half million of them contain all of Carl's tools. Dividing the 126 trillion figure by the 435 thousand gives the probability that Bobbi's toolbox contains Carl's. This equals one in 289,046,788. Thus, the odds that Bobbi knows every tool that Carl knows is approximately one in three hundred million. To put this in some context, about three hundred million people live in the United States. So the odds that Bobbi knows every tool that Carl does are about the same as winning a lottery in which each person in the United States has one ticket.

In making these calculations, we assumed only fifty-two possible tools and only a few tools per person. Depending on what we define as a tool, the set of possible cognitive tools could be far larger than fifty-two. It may be in thousands, and the number of tools—even sophisticated ones—that an individual might master probably exceeds twenty by a substantial margin. We used small numbers here so that we could use the deck of card analogy and to make explicit calculations manageable. In reality, the numbers of possible the toolboxes may be beyond comprehension.[13]

COMBINATIONS OF TOOLS

As we have discussed, cognitive tools have value in combination. Tools can be superadditive. Given that the number of tool combinations exceeds the number of tools by a large margin, this superadditivity has implications for how we compare people. A person with twenty tools possesses one hundred ninety pairs of tools and more than a thousand sets of three tools. Not all tool combinations reveal deep insights. Some don't even make sense. It's not clear what doing the opposite of the Rule of 72 would

TABLE 5.4:
Likelihood that Bobbi's toolbox contains Carl's combination of tools

Size of Combination	Carl's Number of Combinations	Bobbi's Number of Combinations	Percentage Bobbi Possesses
One	15	13	87
Two	105	78	74
Three	455	286	63
Four	1,365	715	52
Five	3,003	1,287	43

be (the rule of 27?). And some combinations do not produce new tools. French calculus is still calculus, even though it's called *calcul*. Even so, many tool combinations—evolutionary game theory, physical chemistry, and Bayesian statistics—have proven sublime.

The importance of combinations throws a wrench in attempts to compare ratios of tools. If Bobbi knows thirteen of Carl's fifteen tools, then she possesses $\frac{13}{15}$, or 87 percent, of Carl's tools. So we might think that Bobbi knows almost every tool that Carl knows. But this leaves out the combinations of tools that Carl possesses. Carl's set of fifteen tools creates one hundred five pairs of tools. The thirteen of Carl's tools that Bobbi possesses create only seventy-eight pairs of these same tools. Table 5.4 shows the number of combinations of up to five tools that Bobbi and Carl possess as well as the percentage of Carl's tool combinations that Bobbi possesses, assuming she has thirteen of his fifteen tools.

The numbers in this table make clear that Bobbi knows only a modest percentage of Carl's combinations of tools. Carl's fifteen tools generate more than three thousand unique combinations of five tools. Bobbi's set of thirteen of these tools generates fewer than half of these combinations of size five.

Model 2: Ladders

The calculations of the probability that Bobbi knows all of Carl's tools or combinations of tools rely on an implicit

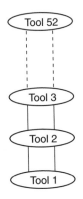

Figure 5.1 A Ladder of Tools

assumption on the relationship between tools. In fact, they depend on the lack of any relationship. Keen observers will notice that we've cheated a bit when making these calculations. We have assumed that any person can acquire any tool. This implies that someone could learn quantum physics without first learning addition. Or that someone could learn to program a computer without first learning the fundamentals of logic. This crude and unrealistic assumption might drive our results. We can emend our model so that tools belong to a topology or network, such as a ladder or a tree, which places an ordering on the tools. Let's see what we get.

To see how much the sequencing of tool acquisition matters, we can arrange the fifty-two tools on a single ladder and number them from one to fifty-two (see figure 5.1). Now, a person must acquire consecutive tools. For a person to acquire tool number seven, she must first learn the tools numbered from one to six. In this ladder model, the number of possible combinations of twenty tools shrinks from more than 126 trillion to just one. Bobbi's twenty tools must be the tools numbered from one through twenty. Similarly, Carl's fifteen tools must be those numbered from one to fifteen.

Now, Bobbi possesses every tool that Carl does, and to say that Bobbi is smarter than Carl would be correct in this case. She has every tool that he has, so she also has every combination of tools that he has. Any problem that he can solve, she could also solve. And given that she has five additional tools, she can also solve problems that he cannot.

MULTIPLE LADDERS

In placing all of the tools in a single ladder, we've erred in the opposite direction. We've placed too much structure on the set of tools. Although people cannot learn whatever tools they choose, as assumed in the deck of cards model, they certainly do not have to learn all tools in a specific order. A person can learn some chemistry without learning physics or learn algebra without knowing how to diagram a sentence. At the same time, learning algebra does require knowing how to add and subtract. So while it is true that more than one ladder exists, it is also true that within many areas of study, we can arrange tools hierarchically.

To capture the existence of some tools being related hierarchically and some not, we can use multiple ladders. Let's first assume that the fifty-two tools can be arranged in two ladders of equal size. On each ladder, the tools can be numbered from one to twenty-six. To master tool number five on either ladder, a person would first have to learn tools numbered one through four on that same ladder.

Calculating the probability that Bobbi's toolbox contains Carl's toolbox becomes a little harder, but we can still do it. We must first partition Carl's fifteen tools across the two ladders. We can do this in sixteen different ways. He can have any number of tools on the first ladder from zero to fifteen. The rest go on the other ladder. This makes for sixteen possible combinations. Similarly, Bobbi has twenty-one ways to allocate her twenty tools across the two ladders. Using the same logic as before, we can assume some random toolbox of fifteen tools for Carl. If Bobbi's toolbox contains Carl's toolbox, then she has five leftover tools to allocate across the two ladders. Of the twenty-one ways that Bobbi can allocate her tools, for each of Carl's allocations exactly six of these contain all of Carl's tools. Thus, the probability that

TABLE 5.5:
Likelihood that Bobbi's
toolbox contains Carl's
as a function of the
number of ladders

Number of Ladders	Likelihood (percent)
One	100
Two	29
Three	9
Four	1
Five	$\frac{1}{200}$

Bobbi's toolbox contains Carl's equals six over twenty-one, or about 28 percent.

The table above shows the probability that Bobbi's toolbox contains Carl's as a function of the number of ladders. As the number of ladders increases from two to three or four, the probability that Bobbi's toolbox contains Carl's decreases significantly (see table 5.5).

With only five ladders, the odds that Bobbi possesses all of Carl's tools falls below 0.01 percent. This number is small to be sure, though not astronomically small as was the case when we assumed no structural relationship between the tools.

Model 3: Trees

The ladder model of tools is mathematically convenient but it does not capture the branching relationships that exist among many tools. If a person learns how to bake crusts, he can then learn how to make pies or quiches. Crusts are a root from which quiches and pies branch. Learning quiche fillings provides no help for making pies and learning to make pie fillings provides few insights into the making of a quiche. Hence, we have branches in a tree and not a ladder. Or, to give a more technical example, if a person learns how to take derivatives, he can then learn how

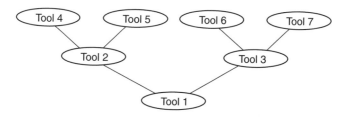

Figure 5.2 A Tree of Tools

to perform integration or how to solve differential equations. Yet to solve differential equations, he need not know how to perform integration and to perform integration he need not know how to solve differential equations.

To capture this branching relationship between tools, we can replace our ladders with trees. We could make this even more complicated, but to keep things tractable, we will assume that these trees have binary branchings: each node has two edges sprouting from it (see figure 5.2).

We will also assume that in accumulating tools, each person follows a single path down each tree. In reality, someone could take multiple paths down the tree, but assuming a single path makes the mathematics far easier. Given these two assumptions, we can again calculate the probability that Bobbi knows every tool that Carl knows. These calculations require only a slight modification of the calculations from the ladder model. First, think of the trees as ladders. In order for Bobbi to know every tool that Carl knows, she has to acquire at least as many tools on each tree as Carl does. The probability of her allocating correctly across the ladders is the same as in the ladder model. Now, in addition, she has to choose the same branches at each node. If Carl picks the left branch initially, then Bobbi must as well. The probability that she does equals $\frac{1}{2}$, but *she has to do this for all branch choices.*

On a single tree, Carl would have to make fourteen branch choices. The probability that Bobbi knows every tool that Carl knows in the tree model equals the probability that she makes the same choice as Carl at each branch. This equals $\frac{1}{2^{14}}$, or approximately one in sixteen thousand. Again, a small number. And this calculation assumes a single tree. With two trees, she would still have to choose each branch correctly. In addition, she would have to assign a sufficient number of tools to each of the two trees. Using our ladder model, the probability that she does that was shown to be 29 percent. With two trees, then, the probability of her knowing all the tools that Carl knows is even lower.

The inference we can draw from these calculations, whether they involve tools arranged on trees, on ladders, or without any structure at all, is that unless the number of possible tools is small and one person knows many more tools than the other, the probability that one person knows all the tools that another knows is small. Given any two people, each probably possesses some tools not known by the other. Yet if one person possesses more tools then the other, we cannot help but think of that first person as more intelligent. She should score higher on standardized tests but would not necessarily perform better at a given task. Nor is she guaranteed to be more successful. The other person could make great scientific discoveries or patent a valuable technology. Whom to hire? Who knows? In difference lies possibility.

INTERPRETING THE NUMBER OF LADDERS AND TREES

We might still ask whether the number of tools that a person possesses can serve as a reasonable proxy for intelligence. If so, people can again be ranked along one dimension, but that dimension corresponds to toolbox size. For the purposes of this discussion, we'll use the term *capacity* to describe how many tools a person has mastered. People differ in their capacities. This could be for innate reasons, because of a person's experiences, or by choice. With only one ladder, capacity would create a complete ranking, but as the number of ladders, or trees for that matter, increases, capacity no longer creates a ranking. One person can have far more capacity than another but possess few of the other person's tools.

This insight, that the number of ladders and trees determines whether capacity generates a ranking, goes a long way toward

TABLE 5.6:
The number of ladders/trees in
the academy

Domain	Number of Ladders/Trees
Mathematics	Few
Physics	Few
Engineering	Few
Social Science	Several
Medicine	Several
Business	Several
Literature	Many
Philosophy	Many

explaining which groups of people believe in objective measures of intelligence. Within an academic field such as mathematics the number of ladders or trees may be relatively small. Algebra requires addition and multiplication, calculus requires algebra, and differential equations require calculus. A mathematician with more capacity may know most of the tools of another mathematician in his or her field who has less capacity. At the other extreme, in a field such as fashion design, many of the tools may be perspectives and interpretations—ways of seeing the world. The number of ladders or trees may be enormous. Hence, someone with larger capacity won't know all the perspectives of someone of lower capacity, unless the capacity gap is a chasm. In academic fields such as literature, in which knowledge of a particular author's techniques or imagery might count as a tool, the number of ladders is again large. We need not understand the use of imagery in Trollope to understand the imagery in Pound. For this reason, a belief in intelligence rankings is not likely to arise in a scholar of literature, art, or philosophy. Rarely will anyone's collection of tools even come close to containing anyone else's. Even though capacity may be seen as differing across people, it will seem no more a measure of intelligence than height or weight. Tables 5.6 and 5.7 crudely categorize the number of ladders/trees across several academic and professional domains.

TABLE 5.7:
The number of ladders/trees across
professions

Domain	Number of Ladders/Trees
Sprinters	Few
Basketball Players	Several
Tax Lawyers	Several
Financial Advisors	Several
Heart Surgeons	Several
Artists	Many
Jazz Musicians	Many
Novelists	Many

These tables help to explain differences of opinion about whether rankings of intelligence are possible. In a university setting, literature professors, art historians, and philosophers tend to dismiss intelligence measures as too reductive. Physicists and mathematicians find them meaningful. Both inferences may be correct within their contexts. Similarly, we accept rankings of sprinters or boxers, professions that have relatively few ladders or trees, but we find rankings of novelists bizarre. Who is to say that Updike is better or worse than Mailer? How do we compare H. A. Rey to either Jean or Laurent de Brunoff with any coherence? We're comparing monkeys to elephants.

SUMMARY

The toolbox framework offers an alternative interpretation to IQ scores for capturing intelligence. Some tools are widely held: lots of people know how to add and subtract, multiply and divide. Fewer people know how to invert a matrix, and only experts know other, more complicated tools, such as how to compute a Lyaponuv exponent to determine the stability of a dynamic system. A person's capabilities are determined by the tools she possesses, and not just by her score on a test. Of course,

IQ tests and other measuring stick measures of intelligence still have value. The criteria that Gardner and others require for an intelligence measure have strong scientific foundations. And IQ tests and SAT tests do prove good predictors of how people do on tests, just as timing people in a hundred-yard dash is a good predictor of how fast these people will be able to run across the street to catch a bus. But intelligence tests are not necessarily good predictors of success generally.

For example, GRE test scores correlate with whether graduate students reach the dissertation stage—which, we might add, often requires passing tests. This explains why so many schools require the test. Why admit students who may fail after just a few years? GRE scores, however, are poor predictors of dissertation quality.[14] GRE scores cannot measure tools whose application requires more thought and time, the kinds of tools necessary to generate research. Writing a dissertation requires creating new knowledge. Being creative requires different tools than test taking.

In general, test scores provide crude measures of success. Small differences do not matter much, even if big ones do. By thinking in terms of toolboxes, we call into question the possibility of ranking people, except in limited domains. Toolboxes enable us to see the differences in people. In addition, when we think in terms of toolboxes, we embrace the possibility of personal growth. We cannot become much more intelligent, or so the test makers tell us. But we can add tools. We can become more and more capable over time. Though these reasons alone would be reason to think in terms of toolboxes rather than measuring sticks, they are not why we constructed the toolbox framework. We built the framework so that we can analyze collective problem solving and prediction by diverse people. That's what we do next.

Part Two

DIVERSITY'S BENEFITS: BUILDING FROM TOOLS

CHAPTER 6

Diversity and Problem Solving

DARWIN'S BRASS TACKS

Talent hits a target that no one else can hit; genius hits a target no one else can see.
— attributed to ARTHUR SCHOPENHAUER

NOW that we've covered what cognitive diversity is— we've defined perspectives, heuristics, and so on—we get to the meat of the book: the demonstration that diversity produces benefits. We see why diversity may be as important as ability in some contexts, and how it can be even more important in others. In short, we show that diversity creates benefits. The proofs rely on the toolbox framework. We'll see how perspectives, heuristics, interpretations, and predictive models aggregate. Throughout, I avoid making blanket statements that diversity is always good or always bad. Blankets cover things, and I do not want to cover the particulars. Whether and how diversity improves performance on a task depends on the type of diversity considered and the type of task. We should not expect any one type of diversity to be beneficial in all contexts any more than we should expect friction to hinder performance in all contexts. When we want to stop the car, we like friction.

In these next three chapters, we see why diversity is such a powerful force. We see how our differences contribute as much to our collective performance as our individual abilities. We will take an abstract, logical approach. By being abstract, we can apply our logic across a variety of contexts—to everything from identity group politics to stock market predictions to interdisciplinary science. Some of what follows may take a little time to absorb, but it's all there for a reason and it all has a big payoff. If you've wondered if, how, and why diversity creates benefits, you're about to find out.

PROBLEM SOLVING

We begin with problem solving. We restrict attention to difficult problems. We don't need diverse perspectives and heuristics to help us with easy ones. Two plus two is easy. Protein folding is difficult. We face no shortage of difficult problems— finding renewable sources of energy, designing health policies, and managing ecosystems receive the most attention, but difficult problems also include designing buildings, writing examinations, and producing movies. Difficult problems are nothing new. Animal domestication and developing the steam engine do not fall into anyone's "easy" category. But many people believe that the dimensionality of current problems and the linkages between them result in greater problem difficulty than existed in the past.[1]

Our analysis highlights the contextual nature of an individual's contribution. How much a person improves a solution depends on how her tools combine with and differ from the tools of the other problem solvers. Yes, her contribution also depends on her ability to find good solutions on her own, but we should not equate intelligence with individual contributions. That's a mistake. Actually, it's two mistakes. First, doing so ignores the difficulty of the problem. We don't want to reward people who happened to have picked or been assigned relatively easy problems, and to underestimate the abilities of people who worked on problems that lie beyond our current collective abilities. Few know the names of the many scientists who unsuccessfully attempted to develop a workable form of fusion in the late 1970s and early 1980s. They've slipped into scientific oblivion because fusion proved too difficult. Had fusion been an easier problem given the perspectives and tools of the day, several people who had modest scientific careers might now be hailed as geniuses. The same is true of all those alchemists who tried to turn lead into gold, and of those people who have tried to build perpetual motion machines. Good try, but hard (in fact, impossible) problems. Second, we assume that the person who makes the discovery has higher intelligence, when that person may just be different. Recall that breakthroughs often come from diverse perspectives. Having a diverse perspective is not the same as being smart. Someone with very few tools—but the right ones for the task—may make a breakthrough.

Our investigation of how individual diversity aggregates culminates in the *Diversity Trumps Ability Theorem*. This theorem provides conditions under which collections of diverse individuals outperform collections of more individually capable individuals. As mentioned in the prologue, this result was not something expected or desired. It just popped out of some experiments with agent-based models that I ran as an assistant professor at Caltech.

A Little Old Logic from Pasadena

I now fill in more of the details of those agent-based models. This detailed analysis helps us see why the theorem holds and what conditions are needed. First, we need some methodological background. An agent-based model consists of artificial agents—computer-based objects that interact in time and space according to rules described in computer code.[2] These agents can represent almost anything: viruses, nations, birds, fish, teenagers, firms, or politicians. The behavioral repertoires of ants and teenagers differ—teenagers are a bit more sophisticated, although not by as much as you might think—but you can model either. In a well-constructed agent-based model, the interactions among the agents and between the agents and the environment tell us something about the real world: how prices emerge in a market or even how riots start. The agent-based models that make the pages of science magazines generate beautiful, structured patterns, like flocking birds, but more often than not these models generate unintelligible muddles.

My model included agents who tried to solve hard problems. We can think of them as making advances on fusion or as trying to figure out how to make every popcorn kernel pop. The objective for the agents in my model was to improve on the existing solutions to a set of predefined problems. The larger the improvement an agent found, the more money the agent received.[3] In the first models, I endowed agents with random perspectives and heuristics. These random assignments created cognitively diverse agents. I did not differentiate the agents by identities. I didn't paint them different colors. Such was my intelligent design.

I had planned to allow the agents to learn from one another and to experiment with new perspectives and heuristics. I hoped to explore the trade-off between exploitation (copying and learning from others) and exploration (searching for new representations and search algorithms). That tension exists in many contexts. Evolution confronts it. Organizations confront it. Individuals confront it. The tension is this. Sure, exploration can be risky (think Magellan), but the benefits can be huge (think Cortez). However, if we explore too much, we never take advantage of what we learn. Exploitation produces guaranteed benefits, but if everyone exploits, they have no new ideas to exploit.

When writing an agent-based model or when proving a mathematical theorem, catching errors is crucial. Computer programs contain hundreds, if not thousands of lines of code. One misplaced semicolon or bracket can alter the model's performance. After writing the initial code, I ran some experiments to check for errors. If I gave an agent greater cognitive ability than the other agents (I did this in the form of more perspectives and heuristics), did that first agent tend to make more money? Yes. If I gave all of the agents more perspectives and heuristics, did the average performance on the problems increase? Yes. If I created more agents, did average performance increase? Again, yes. Finally, I created two economies, one consisting only of agents who performed best individually and another with random, but smart, agents. Did the agents in the first economy, those more able as individuals, on average find better solutions to the problems than did the agents in the second economy?

No.

A Cup of Joe

This last finding, the one I mentioned in the prologue, ran counter to my intuition. I assumed a coding error. I checked and found none, so I rewrote the same model in a different computer language. Same result: the society composed of the better individual agents performed worse. I decided to strip my model down to its core. I created an economy with a single problem. I decided that problem should be something of great importance—making the perfect cup of coffee for my wife. Not being a coffee drinker, I had been greatly vexed by this problem. The coffee problem had only two dimensions to it. Agents tried to find the ideal amount of cream (dimension one) and sugar (dimension two).

This construction allowed me to represent the set of possible solutions on a square. Each point on this square has a horizontal displacement (the infamous x from seventh-grade algebra) and a vertical displacement (x's partner in crime, y). The x value represents the amount of cream in the coffee and the y value as the amount of sugar. In this way, each point within the square represents a unique combination of cream and sugar (see figure 6.1).

Each point in this coffee space also can be assigned a quality—how much my wife liked the coffee. In figure 6.1 quality is shown as the third dimension. I assumed that qualities varied between zero and one hundred: the more she liked the cup of coffee, the higher the value. The problem my agents faced was to find the highest point. Recall from our earlier discussion of perspectives that we can think of the value of each point in the square as an elevation. High-quality cups have high elevations, and low-value cups have low elevations. This representation creates a rugged landscape.

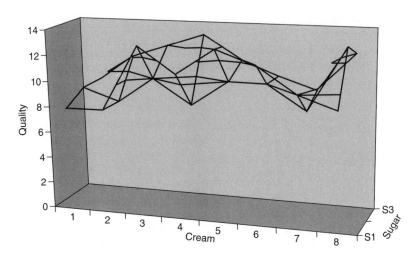

Figure 6.1 The Coffee Space

My agents used search algorithms to roam around this two-dimensional landscape.[4] Placed at any point, an agent would look in two directions. I assigned these directions randomly. If an agent saw a point with a higher value, it would move to that point. An agent followed this search rule until it could not see any cups of higher value. The points at which they got stuck would not necessarily be the best cup, owing to the ruggedness of the landscape. In fact, they rarely were.

To calculate the performance for a group, I allowed one agent in the group to search for a good cup of coffee. That agent continued until it reached a point where it could find no improvement. I then let the next agent start at that point (that cup of coffee) and try to find an even better one. If the second agent found an improvement, the first agent would then try to find further improvements. I continued this process until no agent in the group could find a better cup of coffee.

The model's simplicity made the results more transparent. I could represent an agent graphically by the two directions it searched. When I plotted the two search directions of the best-performing agent, I saw that both directions pointed toward the upper right-hand corner of the square. I then plotted the search directions for each of the best ten agents. I saw a similar pattern in their search directions. They all searched toward the upper right-hand corner of the square. They were all heading to the same place to find coffee. When I plotted the search direction vectors for the random agents, I saw a different pattern. They pointed every which way, like the spokes of a bicycle wheel.

What had been a counterintuitive result now had a logical explanation: The best problem solvers tend to be similar; therefore, a collection of the best problem solvers performs little better than any one of them individually. A collection of random, but intelligent, problem solvers tends to be diverse. This diversity allows them to be collectively better. Or to put it more provocatively: *diversity trumps ability.*

Green Eggs and Ham

I wondered, had I reached into the haystack of possible models and pricked myself on a needle? How general was this finding? To see, I constructed several models of problem solving agents. I varied the space of possible solutions from squares, to lines, to trees, to spheres. And I varied the sophistication of the agents. Most of the time, I found the same result: diversity trumped ability. There did seem to be some necessary conditions, though. I had to create enough agents, I had to assume groups of moderate size, I had to make the problem difficult, and I had to make all of the problem solvers pretty smart. These conditions all made intuitive sense. A collection of third graders probably has little to add to the study of global warming.

These computational experiments were suggestive but not definitive proof that diversity trumped ability. I took to calling this a "green eggs and ham" result in homage to Dr. Seuss's book in which Sam tries to convince his friend to try green eggs and ham in a variety of locales. The friend, as it turns out, will not eat them on a bus or in a box or on a train or with a fox. The same was true of this result. It was true in a box or on a tree or on a graph. It was true anywhere.

But I had a problem, one related to my profession. Although computational experiments persuade most physicists, mathematicians, and biologists, they are not the coin of the realm for economists, and I was paid to be an economist. Economists believe that the computer experiments are correct, but they prefer formal theorems and proofs. Formal logic helps us understand exactly when and why a result holds. To go about constructing a proof, I contacted Lu Hong and pleaded for help. Lu and I hammered out a mathematical proof that provides sufficient conditions for the green eggs and ham result. In 2004, we published these results in the *Proceedings of the National Academy of Sciences.*[5]

The Crowded Chess Table

Could this be true in the real world? Could diverse teams outperform teams of high-ability people? There is one famous example involving the game of chess. On June 21, 1999, Garry Kasparov began a game of chess against approximately 50,000 other players. At the time, Kasparov was the reigning world champion. Some of these people in the group that he was playing were rank amateurs. MSN.com sponsored the game to show the power of the Internet in performing collective problem solving. Kasparov moved first. Each subsequent move took place forty-eight hours later. To determine their move, the people playing Kasparov posted notes to a bulletin board and voted on what to do.

These people had some help. Each time the crowd had to make a move, a team of young chess masters, none older than twenty, proposed an initial set of possible moves. Though great young chess players, they were not of the caliber of Kasparov. At the end of the forty-eight hours, a vote was held. The move that received the most votes was then played. Kasparov then had forty-eight hours to make his next move. After sixty-two moves, Kasparov won. In chess, sixty-two moves suggests a close game. The collection of people performed far better than would be expected of any of its members individually.

Individual Diversity and Collective Problem Solving

It's worth our time and effort to see how a diverse group can outperform a group of more able individuals in solving a problem. To show this result, we need to use perspectives and heuristics. We'll begin with a model of a problem solver with perspectives and heuristics that can be applied to the problem at hand.[6] We consider perspectives first, then heuristics, and then compare the two types of diversity. To keep things as simple as possible, when we study diverse perspectives, we assume that everyone uses the same heuristic, and when we study diverse heuristics, we assume that everyone uses the same perspective.

In undertaking this analysis, we see differences and similarities between diverse perspectives and diverse heuristics. We even see how these two types of diversity can be equivalent. This equivalence can be overemphasized. In a person, perspectives and heuristics operate differently. Diverse perspectives are more likely to lead to breakthroughs and to create communication problems. Diverse heuristics are more likely to lead to smaller, more iterative improvements.

Diverse Perspectives and Problem Solving

Remember, a perspective is a "one-to-one" mapping of reality into some internal language. Two people have diverse perspectives if they map reality into different internal languages, or if they map the reality differently into the same internal language. To capture diverse perspectives and common heuristics, we consider an example in which multiple perspectives map the solutions onto a line. Suppose that we have a lot containing a thousand cars, and the problem is to find the car that gets the best gas mileage. Each car has a fact sheet that contains all relevant information *except* its miles per gallon. Determining gas mileage is costly; it requires taking a car out for a long drive.

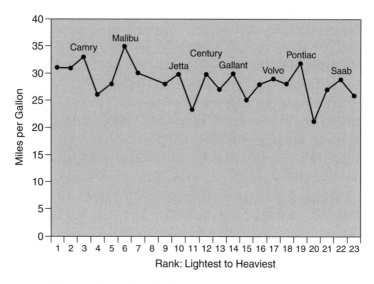

Figure 6.2 MPG in Curb Weight Perspective

Many possible perspectives could be used to arrange these cars. Someone might arrange them by weight, thinking that the heavier the car, the worse the mileage. Someone else might arrange them by height, thinking that aerodynamics matter. A third person might arrange them by their wheelbase, thinking that it is good proxy for the overall size of the car. Each of these perspectives embeds knowledge of the causes of better gas mileage, but none perfectly predicts gas mileage. Therefore, the resulting one-dimensional landscape will be rugged, but not too rugged. Other perspectives that fail to embed understanding—say, arranging the cars by their color or by the diameter of their headlights—would result in very rugged landscapes.

To ground our logic, let's apply these perspectives to actual data on twenty-three 2005 model year midsize sedans (for which we know the official gas mileage).[7] The first graph (figure 6.2) shows the landscape created by curb weight. This perspective has eight local optima: Toyota Camry, Chevy Malibu, Volkswagen Jetta, Buick Century, Mitsubishi Gallant, Volvo S60, Pontiac G6, and Saab 9-5. Our next perspective (figure 6.3) considers the width of the wheelbase. This perspective has seven local

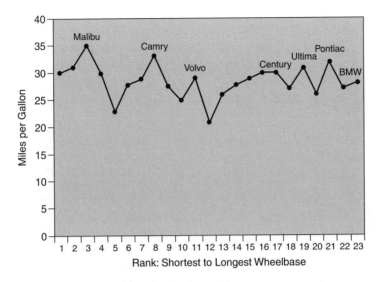

Figure 6.3 MPG in Wheelbase Perspective

optima: Chevy Malibu, Toyota Camry, Volvo S60, Buick Century, Nissan Ultima, Pontiac G6, and BMW 525. Our final perspective (figure 6.4), based on height, creates nine local optima: Dodge Stratus, Hyundai Sonata, Volvo S60 Mazda 6, Pontiac G6, Volkswagen Jetta, Suzuki Verona, Chevy Malibu, and Toyota Camry.

We assume that our testers start at some random point in their landscape (a random car) and test it to determine its miles per gallon. Each then tests a neighboring car. If that car gets better mileage, the problem solver continues in the same direction, testing the next car until finding a local peak. If the second car tested gets worse mileage than the first car tested, the problem solver tests in the opposite direction (if necessary) and searches until reaching a local optimum. Using this heuristic, each problem solver gets stuck on peaks in her landscape. Recall that test-driving these cars to determine their miles per gallon takes time and effort. That's why our problem solvers search locally given their perspectives.

Imagine these three people working as a group. Each landscape has a few local peaks, but a locally optimal solution for one person may not be a local optimum for the others. If they work together,

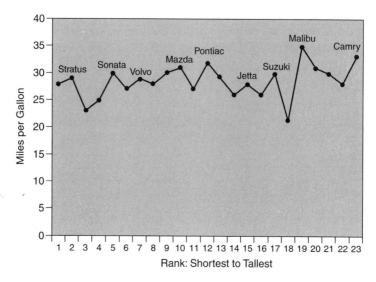

Figure 6.4 MPG in Height Perspective

when one person gets stuck at a local optimum, another person may be able to find a subsequent improvement. That second person's improved solution may then be further improved on by someone else.

For a car to be a local peak for the group, it must be a local peak for *every* member of the group. Putting the names of the local peaks in a table reveals that four cars: the Chevy Malibu (35 mpg), the Toyota Camry (33 mpg), the Pontiac G6 (32 mpg), and the Volvo S60 (29 mpg) are local peaks on all three landscapes. If the problem solvers know this information, they'd pick the best peak, but they don't. They get stuck on one of the peaks. The Malibu, Camry, and Pontiac are ranked first, second, and third in gas mileage, and the Volvo is ranked tied for tenth (see table 6.1).

Note several features of this example. First, any one of these perspectives might locate the Malibu, the car with the best mileage, but the ruggedness of their landscapes prevents them from always locating it. Second, the diverse perspectives create many possible proposed solutions. Of the twenty-three car models, thirteen are local optima for at least one of the three problem solvers. We

TABLE 6.1:
The group's locally optimal car models

Perspective	Model Rankings							
Weight	Malibu	Camry	Pontiac	Volvo	Century	Jetta	Gallant	Saab 9-5
Wheelbase	Malibu	Camry	Pontiac	Volvo	Century	Ultima	BMW 525	
Height	Malibu	Camry	Pontiac	Volvo	Jetta	Suzuki	Stratus	Sonata	Madza6

might then expect the diverse group to generate lots of solutions but not expect all of those solutions to be good. Some might be pretty lousy. That's fine as long as the group can identify the best solution among those proposed. And in this case, they can.

Stringing Us Along

We've taken for granted that these diverse perspectives exist. We might ask why: Why wouldn't people all conform to a common perspective? One obvious reason for diverse perspectives is that each may apply to different parts of a problem. Physicists who study string theory rely on multiple perspectives because each perspective has a set of subproblems for which it is useful. Some people may be surprised to learn that for a long time, physicists didn't know that they were using multiple perspectives. We won't dig deeply into string theory, as it's a knotty subject. We need only these few facts: by the early 1990s, physicists had developed five distinct string theory models—creatively named the Type I, Type IIA, Type IIB, Heterotic-O, and Heterotic-E models. Each of these theories describes our universe as containing six extra dimensions—beyond space and time. These extra dimensions are all folded up so we don't notice them. Yes, string theorists believe that hidden inside that waffle you had for breakfast were six dimensions. Incredible if true, but irrelevant to our larger point. In the mid-1990s, Edward Witten proved that these theories were all the same theory, that they were distinct mathematical representations of the same thing—not competing, but complementary. In our language, they were five distinct perspectives of the same strings. Witten's remarkable discovery led string theorists to embrace all five models. Five perspectives on a set of problems create five landscapes. To quote Brian Greene's *Fabric of the Cosmos*,

> Theorists have found that for certain questions one of the five may give a transparent description of the physical implications, while the descriptions given by the other four are too mathematically complex to be useful. And therein lies the power of Witten's discovery. Prior to his breakthrough, string theory researchers who encountered intractably difficult equations would be stuck. But Witten's work showed that each such question admits four mathematical translations—four mathematical reformulations— and sometimes one of the reformulated questions proves far simpler to answer. Thus, *the dictionary for translating between the five theories can sometimes provide a means for translating impossibly difficult questions into comparatively simple ones.*[8]

Thus, string theory provides yet another example of how diverse perspectives improve problem solving: Different perspectives create different landscapes, and different landscapes have different peaks. Different peaks prevent people from getting stuck at the same point.

Diverse Heuristics and Problem Solving

We now consider how diverse heuristics can aid problem solving by applying some to a trading problem involving men and shoes. We assume that each of five men, Richard, Chauncey, Ben, Rasheed, and Tayshaun, wears size twelve shoes. Each grabs two random shoes from a collection of five pairs: loafers, tennis shoes, sandals, boots, and wingtips. These men don't care which shoes they have, so long as they have matched pairs. We can identify the shoes by the type and the foot so that loafer-L denotes the left loafer, wingtip-R denotes the right wingtip, and so on. The initial random allocation of shoes looks as shown in table 6.2.

TABLE 6.2:
The shoe problem

Person	Shoe 1	Shoe 2
Richard	loafer-L	boot-L
Chauncey	sandal-R	wingtip-R
Ben	tennis-L	sandal-L
Rasheed	loafer-R	boot-R
Tayshaun	wingtip-L	tennis-R

Our first heuristic allows trades between two players only if both players want to make the trade. This heuristic creates a trade between Richard and Rasheed. Richard has the left loafer and the left boot. Rasheed has the right loafer and the right boot. They don't care whether they trade loafers or boots. They just want pairs. Either trade gives each of them a pair. A trade between Richard and Rasheed is the only trade that this first heuristic can find. Any other trade benefits only one of the two people trading.

Our second heuristic allows for trades among exactly three people. As with the first heuristic, a trade takes place only if everyone involved in the trade is strictly happier. Using this heuristic, Chauncey can give the right sandal to Ben, Ben can give the left tennis shoe to Tayshaun, and Tayshaun can give the left wingtip to Chauncey. After this trade, all three have matched pairs. This heuristic would not have found the trade between Richard and Rasheed because that trade involved only two people. Thus, on their own, neither of these two heuristics locates a global optimum, yet together they do.

This example reiterates a point that we discussed earlier: local optima are defined relative to a perspective and the set of heuristics applied to that perspective. If a person has lots of heuristics, she probably is a good problem solver. Think back to the traveling salesperson problem. Some solutions were local optima for one heuristic but not for others. That example hinted at a general insight: *the more tools in our kits, the fewer places we get stuck.*

Interpreting Problem Solvers by Their Peaks

We've now hit upon an important idea: characterizing problem solvers by their local optima, the peaks in their landscapes. A problem solver typically has many local optima—and we know he always has one: namely, the best solution. Everyone agrees that Everest is a peak. A problem solver might not find Everest, but if put there he recognizes it as a peak. I next state three observations that connect characteristics of problem solvers to their local optima. The first describes a correlation between better problem solvers and the values of their local optima.

Better Individual Problem Solvers Have Better Local Optima: *Those problem solvers who perform better individually tend to get stuck at local optima that have relatively good values.*

This observation speaks to the advantage of having relatively high value local peaks. Again, think back to our traveling salesperson problem. If one problem solver has two local optima: one of length 1,400 miles (which is the global optimum) and one of length 1,500 miles, this person will probably do better than someone else with two local optima, one of which has length 1,800 miles (keep in mind that longer is worse). Note that we're assuming that the problem solvers are equally likely to find each of their local optima, an assumption we relax in a moment.

The second observation is that better problem solvers tend to have fewer local optima. They could use perspectives that create less rugged landscapes, which by definition have fewer local optima. Or they could possess more heuristics allowing them to move off from peaks in their landscapes. Either way, they get stuck at fewer points.

Better Problem Solvers Have Fewer Local Optima: *Those problem solvers with better individual performance tend to have fewer local optima.*

The intuition that explains this claim is also straightforward. Local optima are the points at which a problem solver gets stuck.

One of these local optima must be the best solution. The others have values that are not as good. Getting stuck at those other solutions results in worse outcomes. In general, the more local optima, the more likely the search gets stuck on one of them, and the worse the problem solver performs.

We can combine these first two observations. High-performing individual problem solvers should have relatively few local optima, and those local optima should have high values. In contrast, we should expect the poorest performing individual problem solvers to have lots of local optima and many—but not all—of those local optima to have low values.

As convincing as this sounds, the characterization of a problem solver by the number of local optima she has and the value of those local optima gets us only partway to where we need to go. The probability that a problem solver lands on each of those local optima also matters. A problem solver could have only two local optima—the global optimum and a local optimum of relatively low value—but if she almost always locates the low-value local optimum, her average performance will be poor. If she almost always locates the global optimum, her average performance will be great. To capture this insight formally, I introduce the concept of a *basin of attraction*. Loosely speaking, the size of a local optimum's basin of attraction equals the probability that the problem solver gets stuck at that peak.

The word *basin* comes from physics, but we can think of basins in our kitchens or bathrooms and get the idea. Imagine tossing a superball into a room filled with sinks of various sizes and shapes. The ball would ricochet from sink to sink until coming to rest at the bottom of one of the sink's basins. All else being equal, we might expect that the larger and deeper the sink's basin, the more likely the ball lands in that sink. We can apply this same intuition to hill climbing, but we have to invert the imagery. Physicists minimize. Our problem solvers maximize. So, for our problem solvers, the analogs of the depth and size of the basin are the height and width of a peak (see figure 6.5).

Even though we think of people and groups as trying to optimize, let's follow the convention and apply the basin terminology.

Figure 6.5 Basins and Peaks

Let's consider an example to get our bearings. Suppose that two South American banana growers, Karen and Paul, are attempting to breed bananas with a longer shelf life. We will assume that the best possible banana has a shelf life of thirty days after being picked. Karen uses old-fashioned genetic breeding techniques. These techniques are her heuristics, and we assume that they result in three local optima: the best solution, a second solution with a shelf life of twenty-four days, and a third solution with a shelf life of twelve days. Paul has abandoned old-fashioned breeding and relies on genetic modification. His heuristic also has three local optima. They produce bananas with shelf lives of thirty, twenty-five, and twenty days, respectively. If both problem solvers are equally likely to find each of their local optima, then Paul performs better than Karen as the calculations below show.

SHELF LIVES OF KAREN AND PAUL'S BANANAS

$$\text{Karen's Solution's Expected Value: } 22 = \frac{1}{3}(30 + 24 + 12)$$

$$\text{Paul's Solution's Expected Value: } 25 = \frac{1}{3}(30 + 25 + 20)$$

To see the importance of basin size, suppose that Karen has a larger basin of attraction for the best solution—that she finds the best solution two-thirds of the time and that she finds the other solutions only one-sixth of the time each. Her bananas then have a longer expected shelf life. Suppose also that Paul remains equally likely to find each of his three solutions, so that his expected value remains the same. Given these assumptions, Karen performs better on average as the following calculations show.

NEW SHELF LIVES OF KAREN AND PAUL'S BANANAS

Karen's Solution's Expected Value: $26 = \frac{2}{3}(30) + \frac{1}{6}(24 + 12)$

Paul's Solution's Expected Value: $25 = \frac{1}{3}(30 + 25 + 20)$

We can now make a third observation:

Basin Size Matters: *Better problem solvers tend to have larger basins of attraction for their better local optima.*

Based on what we've done so far, we can characterize a problem solver as a set of local optima together with a probability of getting stuck at each of those local optima. In our example, we can identify Karen as having three local optima given by the set $\{30, 24, 12\}$ with probabilities $(\frac{2}{3}, \frac{1}{6}, \frac{1}{6})$, and we can characterize Paul as also having three local optima. But his have values $\{30, 25, 20\}$, and have probabilities $(\frac{1}{3}, \frac{1}{3}, \frac{1}{3})$. Note, of course, that these local optima both contain the global optimum. Everyone has to get stuck at the best solution.

This characterization of problem solvers as sets of local optima and the probability that they locate them proves useful, but it's not a perspective on the set of problem solvers. We next show that two problem solvers can have distinct perspectives and heuristics, yet produce identical sets of local optima and probabilities of attaining them. Thus, the mapping of a problem solver to a set of local optima with probabilities should be thought of as an *interpretation* in the formal sense of that word. It puts problem solvers into categories. This distinction may seem like hairsplitting, but it's not. It allows us to make an important distinction between internal and external problem solving diversity.

Internal and External Problem Solving Diversity

Before turning to that distinction, let's step back for a moment and take stock of what we've learned. A person's

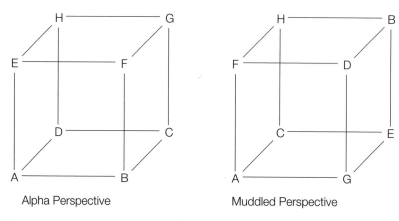

Figure 6.6 Two Perspectives on a Cube

perspective and heuristic define the neighbors of an existing solution—the solutions that a problem solver thinks to search (namely, the solutions, given her perspective, that her heuristics identify). Perspectives and heuristics are *internal* to a problem solver. An outside observer need not know them. What an observer can see, what is *external* to the problem solver, is how the problem solver maneuvers through the solutions. Even knowing this would require some effort on the part of an observer, but we ignore that for the moment.

Our next example requires slow and careful study. It's not difficult, but following it requires patience. Put yourself in the frame of mind you'd be in if looking at a map of a city's public transportation system: it looks like a mess, but there's an underlying logic. In the example, two problem solvers differ both in their perspectives and in their heuristics, and yet they are the same externally—they maneuver in the space of solutions in the exact same way. Let's start with the perspectives. Each of two perspectives shown in figure 6.6 organizes the eight possible solutions, lettered from *A* to *H*, on a cube in a different way. The *alpha perspective* organizes the solutions alphabetically moving counterclockwise around each level. The *muddled perspective* randomly arranges the letters on the cube.

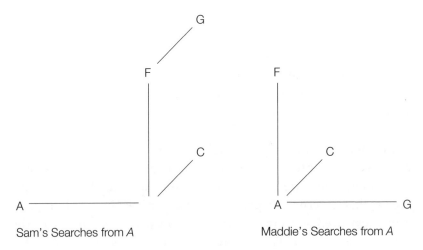

Sam's Searches from *A*   Maddie's Searches from *A*

Figure 6.7 Internal Diversity and External Equivalence

We consider two problem solvers, Sam and Maddie. Sam uses the alpha perspective, and Maddie uses the muddled perspective. Sam and Maddie use different heuristics. Each has three. To define their heuristics, we rely on the edges of the cube. Maddie's three heuristics involve movements along these edges. Starting at solution *A* on the muddled perspective, Maddie checks the three solutions connected along edges of the cube. By inspection these are *G*, *C*, and *F*; *G* lies to the right of *A*, *C* lies behind it, and *F* lies above it.

Sam, in contrast to Maddie, uses sophisticated heuristics. Her first heuristic moves along both the left–right dimension and the front–back dimension. Starting from *A*, Sam checks *C*. Her second heuristic moves along both the left–right dimension and the top–bottom dimension. Again starting from *A*, Sam checks *F*. Finally, her third heuristic moves along all three dimensions. This heuristic moves to the far corner of the cube. It's the cubist version of "do the opposite." Using this heuristic, she jumps from *A* all the way to *G*.

A picture (figure 6.7) helps to make sense of Sam and Maddie's searches over their perspectives.

As this picture makes clear, Sam and Maddie check the same solutions from *A*. With a little effort, it can be shown that this equivalence holds regardless of where they start. Using her heuristic, if Maddie starts at solution *D*, then she checks *F*, *B*, and *G*. The same is true of Sam. Starting at *D*, she goes over and across to *B*, over and up to *G*, and jumps to the opposite corner, which is *F*.

Working through this example required some effort. People who like math probably found it cool, but should anyone else (any nongeeks) care?[9] Yes. They (you) should. This example shows that internal diversity (diverse perspectives and diverse heuristics) need not create external diversity (movements in the space of solutions). People can be different and yet search for solutions the same way. People with diverse perspectives *and* diverse heuristics can solve a problem similarly.[10] Put differently, diverse perspectives and diverse heuristics can cancel each other out. This cancellation may not be likely, but we have no guarantee that two people who use different representations and apply different problem-solving techniques search for solutions differently. The implication: *diverse people may not solve problems differently.*

DIVERSITY TRUMPS ABILITY

With this background in place, I now turn to the claim that diversity can trump ability. I first show how diversity trumps homogeneity. Imagine two collections of people, one diverse and one homogenous. If the "ability" (I formalize this later) is the same for all of these problem solvers, then the diverse group finds better solutions. Though less surprising than the diversity-trumps-ability result, it helps us intuit for why diversity is beneficial.

To get started, we need a model of how a collection of people, diverse or not, solves a problem. We'll use the same process we described in the cup of coffee model: we order the members of the group and have them apply their problem-solving skills sequentially. One person searches until she gets stuck at a local optimum, then the next person searches beginning from that point. In this way, each person builds off the best solution found by the previous problem solvers. We have people literally standing on the shoulders (the solutions) of those who came before them. Only when no problem solver can find an improvement does the process stop.

Don't fret, the sequential search assumption is a convenience; it is not necessary for any of our results. We could also model all of the problem solvers working on the problem simultaneously and having any problem solver who locates a better solution post it to a common message board. The other problem solvers could then immediately begin searching for new solutions from this new, better solution.

Diversity Trumps Homogeneity

To see how diversity trumps homogeneity, we'll construct a model with two collections of problem solvers. Everyone in the first collection is unique. Each has a distinct perspective and set of heuristics. In light of the example that we just constructed with Sam and Maddie, we will assume that this internal diversity results in different approaches to solving the problem. Everyone in the second collection is identical. Every person uses the same perspective and the same heuristics. We further assume that all of the problem solvers in both collections have approximately the same individual ability, by which we mean that working alone on the problem, each does equally well.

If these assumptions hold, then the diverse collection generally outperforms the homogenous collection. The intuition behind this result should be clear: *the homogeneous collection may just as well contain only a single person.*[11] Every person in the homogenous collection possesses the same perspective and heuristics, so they all have the same set of local optima. Therefore, after the first person in the collection locates an optimum, no one else can improve on it. They would all look at the solution and say something like "looks good to me" and be done with it. Two heads are not only not better than one in this case—they *are* one.

Next consider the diverse collection of problem solvers. The first problem solver applies his perspective and heuristic until finding a local optimum. The next problem solver then attempts to find an even better solution. As the second problem solver relies on different perspectives and heuristics, she might find a better solution. If, by chance, the first problem solver locates the best solution, the global optimum, then of course it must be a local optimum for the second problem solver as well. But if that occurs, the diverse collection has solved the problem perfectly. If the first problem solver fails to locate the global optimum, then the other one might improve on that solution. That possibility of improvement explains why diversity trumps homogeneity.

An example clarifies this logic. This example relies on only two problem solvers in each group. The problem is to figure out a way to get as many objects as possible into a box. If it helps, think of a shoe, a soda can, a book, a toy car, a desk telephone, and so on...that must be put in a box. Imagine two homogenous problem solvers, each of whom relies on the Steven Covey "deal with the big items first" heuristic. This heuristic might result in three local optima to this problem. One of these must be the global optimum in which ten objects fit into the box. Let's suppose that in the other two local optima, eight and nine objects fit into the box, respectively.

Each of these three local optima is equally likely, and which of these local optima is found depends on which objects are put in first. Assuming equal sized basins of attraction, the expected value of a local optimum (in this case, the expected number of objects) for each problem solver equals one-third times ten plus one-third times nine plus one-third times eight, for an average of nine. The expected value for the two of them working together sequentially is also nine. Once the first person proposes a solution, the second person will not see a way to improve on it—because she sees the problem in the same way.

In the diverse collection, the first problem solver, Blair, uses a perspective and heuristics that almost always lead her to fit nine objects in the box. The ten-object solution is a local optimum for her as well—it has to be—but she almost never finds it. Her expected value is approximately nine, the same as that of the problem solvers in the first collection. The second problem solver, Karl, uses a different perspective and heuristics. He gets stuck at two local optima. The first is the best solution. In the second, he can place only eight objects in the box. Let's assume that these two local optima are equally likely, so that his expected value is also nine. Here's the key insight: *if Blair and Karl work together on the problem, they always find the optimal solution.* Their expected value equals ten.

To see this, suppose that Blair goes first. She either finds the global optimum (which is unlikely) or finds her local optimum that puts nine objects in the box. Let's assume the latter; otherwise, they've found the global optimum and the proof is complete. By construction, her nine-object solution is not a local optimum for Karl. He gets stuck only at solutions with eight objects or ten objects. If he is not at a local optimum, he can find an improvement starting from that solution. Thus, if he starts at a solution with nine objects, he must be able to find the global optimum, since his only other local optimum has fewer than nine objects.

Suppose instead that Karl goes first. Here the logic is the same but it requires one more step. If Karl finds the solution with ten objects, then they've done it. They have found the optimal solution. So let's suppose that he finds the solution with only eight objects (see figure 6.8). Blair can then improve on this solution. Why? No solution with eight objects is a local optimum for her, so she must find either her solution with nine objects or find the global optimum. If she finds the former, then following the logic above, Karl can then find the ten-object solution. Thus, Karl and Blair always find the solution with ten objects.

The characterization of problem solvers by their local optima clarifies the intuition behind the finding that diversity trumps homogeneity. That clarification rests on the *Intersection Property*, which says that the only way for two people to be stuck on a local optimum is if both are stuck. Yes, that sounds circular, but it's deeper than it seems. It means that the only local optima for

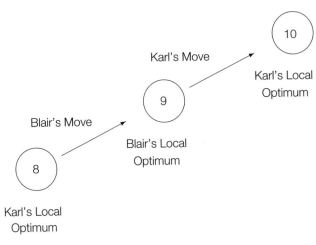

Figure 6.8 Blair and Karl Finding the Global Optimum

a collection of people are points that are local optima for *every* person in the collection. We previously saw this in the example of finding the car with the highest gas mileage.

The Intersection Property: *The local optimum for a collection of problem solvers equals the intersection of the individuals' local optima.*

We can use this property to recast our example. The analysis becomes a little more technical, but let's keep in mind that our goal is to move beyond metaphor to a logical understanding. Each of the two homogenous problem solvers has three local optima called *X, Y,* and *B* (for best). These have values eight, nine, and ten, respectively. The intersection of those sets of local optima remains the set *X, Y,* and *B*. Two heads are no better than one. In contrast, Blair has only two local optima, *Z* and *B*. Karl also has two local optima, *W* and *B*. The intersection of these two sets of local optima {*W, B*} and {*Z, B*} equals the single solution *B*. Regardless of how they interact, Karl and Blair must locate *B*. It is the only solution that is a local optimum for both problem solvers. Using the logic of the intersection property, we can see why diversity trumps homogeneity.

The Diversity Trumps Homogeneity Theorem: *If two collections of problem solvers contain problem solvers of equal individual ability, and if those problem solvers in the first collection are homogeneous and those in the second collection are diverse, that is, they have some differences in their local optima, then the collection of diverse problem solvers, on average, outperforms the collection of homogenous problem solvers.*

The proof of this claim is straightforward. The homogenous problem solvers all have the same local optima. Thus, the expected value of a solution located by the collection of agents cannot be better than that of any individual. This result does not hold for the diverse collection of problem solvers. Their local optima differ. In this way, just as in the example earlier, one problem solver gets stuck at a local optimum, and then another problem solver finds an improvement. The intersection property gives us a logic underpinning for the notion of standing on the shoulders of giants. What is a local optimum for one person's perspective and heuristics need not be for another's. As Emerson puts it,

> Every ultimate fact is only the first of a new series. Every general law only a particular fact of some more general law presently to disclose itself. There is no outside, no inclosing wall, no circumference to us. The man finishes his story, —how good! How final! How it puts a new face on all things! He fills the sky. Lo! On the other side rises also a man and draws a circle around the circle we had just pronounced the outline of the sphere.[12]

Emerson didn't believe that we ever got to the global optimum, whereas we allow for that possibility, but we can put such small quibbles aside. Emerson's prose and our logic agree: diversity creates iterative improvements. And these improvements continue until the collection finds a solution that lies in the intersection of the local optima for all of the problem solvers.

To some, the claim that diversity trumps homogeneity may not be surprising.[13] Fair enough, but we learn from dotting our *i*'s and crossing our *t*'s. Many intuitive insights turn out not to be true— Newtonian physics being just one example. So although this claim is not difficult to understand, it is important. It's better for two people to be diverse than for them to be the same when solving problems.

Diversity Trumps Ability

We now turn to the more surprising claim, namely that diversity trumps ability. This claim differs from the previous one in an important respect. This claim rests on different assumptions. The diversity-trumps-homogeneity claim assumes that all of the problem solvers have equal ability as measured by their expected value on the problem. The diversity-trumps-ability claim assumes lower average ability for the collection of diverse problem solvers. It also allows for variation among the collection of the best problem solvers. We're not assuming that every person in the group of the best is identical. We're only assuming that they're good.

We begin with an initial pool of potential problems solvers from which we draw the collections of problem solvers. We assume there are N of these people. N could equal everyone who works for a firm or every faculty member at a university. We then compare the collective performance of the M best problem solvers against the collective performance of M randomly selected problem solvers. The theorem provides sufficient conditions under which the random collection outperforms the collection of the best.

To demonstrate the logic of this result, we'll characterize the problem solvers by the local optima they find and the probabilities that they attain them. This approach has advantages over looking at their perspectives and heuristics directly. The best problem solvers get stuck at fewer local optima, and these local optima tend have higher values. Less effective individual problem solvers have more local optima, and many of these may have low values.

Before we go too far, let's keep in mind that the diversity-trumps-ability result doesn't always hold. It holds given certain conditions. We take up these conditions one at a time. Then we look at the formal claim, and then go back over the conditions in a slightly different way to hammer home the intuition. What follows can't be skimmed and fully understood.

The first condition takes into account that if the problem is so easy that a problem solver (or several problem solvers) can always finds the best solution, then the collection of the best problem solvers (which necessarily contains this best problem solver) always locates the best solution. In contrast, the collection of randomly selected problem solvers need not contain anyone who always finds the optimal solution. So for diversity to trump ability, the problem must be difficult. For example, if we need to find the answer to a calculus problem, we can often just ask an expert. The expert can give us the correct answer. A random group might not. However, if we have a difficult, previously unsolved math problem, we would want to ask a diverse collection of mathamaticians. Diversity benefits to kick in when the problems we face are hard—designing products, curing diseases, improving our educational system. We need not think of this as a limiting assumption.

Condition 1: The Problem Is Difficult. *No individual problem solver always locates the global optimum.*[14]

This condition requires some thought. We have assumed problems have an associated difficulty. This assumption seems to contradict our earlier discussion of perspectives in which we discussed how difficulty lies in the eye of the beholder. One person's rugged landscape is another's Mt Fuji. So, we need to be a bit more precise. What we're assuming is that the problem is difficult given any of the problem solvers' perspectives.

This second condition concerns the ability of the problem solvers. All of the possible problem solvers must have some ability to solve the problem. Their perspectives cannot create overly rugged landscapes. We cannot set loose a bunch of people from the humanities in the chemistry lab. We'll call this the *Calculus Condition* because people who know calculus can take derivatives. Derivatives tell the slope of a function. The slope of a mountain is either positive (uphill), negative (downhill), or zero (on a peak or a plateau). On a peak the derivative equals zero; the slope goes neither up nor down. So, people who know calculus can find peaks. People who do not know calculus could get stuck anywhere. They would not add much to a group trying to solve a problem. People who know calculus relative to the problem have perspectives that capture some of the structure of a problem. They have a reasonable number of peaks.[15] This condition trivially holds when the number of solutions is finite, such as in the traveling salesperson problem.

Condition 2: The Calculus Condition. *The local optima of every problem solver can be written down in a list. In other words, all problem solvers are smart.*

To see the importance of the Calculus Condition, suppose that it fails to hold. If a great many of the problem solvers had an infinite number of local optima, then the random collection could be just many monkeys on typewriters trying to peck out a little Shakespeare. They could not possibly do as well as a collection of the best problem solvers. To bring this more down to earth, a collection of random people would not outperform a collection of top statisticians on a statistical problem. Relative to the problem, most people would not satisfy the calculus assumption. They would get stuck on almost any solution.

The third condition requires that for any solution other than the global optimum, some problem solver can find an improvement on that solution. In other words, the intersection of all of the problem solvers' local optima contains only the global optimum. We'll call this the *Diversity Condition*, as it assumes diversity among the problem solvers.

Condition 3: The Diversity Condition. *Any solution other than the global optimum is not a local optimum for some nonzero percentage of problem solvers.*

This condition does *not* say that given any solution, some problem solver exists who immediately can jump to the global optimum. That assumption would be much stronger and would rarely be the case. Our assumption says, instead, that some problem solver exists who can find an improvement. That improvement may be small. In the example of the group of people playing Kasparov, this assumption may not have held. The collection of people may not have included someone to prevent a bad move. More than likely, though, Kasparov's advantage resulted from the collection's inability to evaluate moves properly, as they lacked experience in such high-level games—an observation we make more explicit in the next two chapters.

To see this in a more formal context, think back to the traveling salesperson problem. Imagine a collection of problem solvers each of whom has some collection of heuristics. Some of these heuristics might involve switching the order of four or five cities in the route. The Diversity Condition implies that given any nonoptimal route, there exists a problem solver who has a heuristic who can find an improvement in that route. This person doesn't have to be capable of finding the best route, just an improvement. That improvement could reduce the route by only a few miles or even just a few feet.

The final condition requires that the initial set of problem solvers must be reasonably large and that the set of problem solvers that form the collection must also not be too small. The logic behind this condition becomes clear when we consider extreme cases. If the initial set consists of only fifteen problem solvers, then the best ten should outperform a random ten. With so few problem solvers, the best ten cannot help but be diverse, that is, have different local optima. And as they individually perform best, they should do better collectively than the random ten problem solvers. At the same time, the collections that work together must be large enough that the random collection can be diverse. To see this, suppose that the collections contain only one problem solver. By definition, the collection with the best problem solver outperforms the collection with a random problem solver. Even with two problem solvers in the collections of problem solver, the collection of the best problem solvers would almost certainly do better. So we need to be picking from a big pool—firms, organizations, and universities do this, by the way—and we need to be picking collections of more than two or three people.

Condition 4: Good-Sized Collections Drawn from Lots of Potential Problem Solvers. *The initial population of problem solvers must be large and the collections of problem solvers working together must contain more than a handful of problem solvers.*

There is no explicit size that these collections have to be for the result to hold. The exact number depends on the difficulty of the problem and on the amount of diversity in the initial set of problem solvers. More difficult problems have more local optima and require more problem solvers to overcome the problem of overlapping local optima. The more diversity in the problem solvers, the smaller the collections can be. Diverse problem solvers get stuck at different local optima, so when working together on a problem they rarely get stuck at the same local optima.

These four conditions—the problem has to be hard, the people have to be smart, the people have to be diverse, and the group size has to be bigger than a handful and chosen from a large population—prove sufficient for diversity to trump ability. They're not the only conditions under which the result holds, but if they're satisfied, diversity trumps ability.

The Diversity Trumps Ability Theorem: *Given Conditions 1–4, a randomly selected collection of problem solvers outperforms a collection of the best individual problem solvers.*

This theorem is no mere metaphor or cute empirical anecdote that may or may not be true ten years from now. It's a logical truth.[16]

To see why it's true, let's go back to our beginning, a good place to start. Problem solvers have perspectives and heuristics. To make the logic as transparent as possible, we will assume that each person has a single perspective/heuristic pair. We can represent the space of perspectives and heuristics as being a box (figure 6.9). And as we have done with the problems themselves, we can create a landscape by setting the height of a perspective/heuristic pair equal to its average value when applied to our difficult problem. This landscape, the landscape of problem solvers, must have

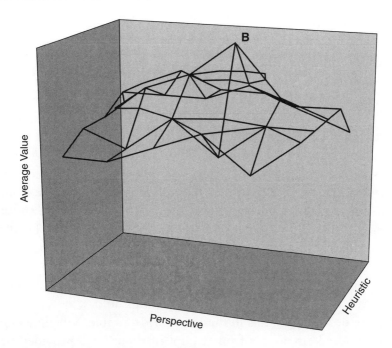

Figure 6.9 The Perspective/Heuristic Box

a global optimum.[17] That global optimum represents the best individual problem solver. We denote her by B. Note, though, that by Condition 1 (The Problem Is Difficult), no single perspective/ heuristic pair locates the global optimum every time.

Now let's generate lots and lots of problem solvers. We can represent these by dots in the figure. If we create enough problem solvers, most of the best ten or twenty will all lie near α, the global optimum on the problem solver landscape. Why? If we randomly tossed out billions of people in the Himalayas, most of the people at highest elevations would be on Everest (Everest in the space of problem solvers). However, even the best problem solver—the one atop Everest—cannot solve our problem alone. Why? On hard problems, even the globally optimal problem solve can't find the global optimum to the problem. Conversely, if we create only a few dozen problem solvers, the best ten or twenty are scattered throughout the perspective/heuristic box. Herein lies the key insight. When the initial set of problem solvers grows large, clustering of the best problem solvers near α becomes unavoidable, which is why we need Condition 4 (lots of initial problem solvers to choose from).

Because they are clustered near B, or at one or two other places, these best problem solvers all have similar perspectives and heuristics. And it follows that they do not perform much better as a collection than they do individually. In contrast, the random collection's members will most often lie all over the perspective/heuristic box. This diversity allows them to collectively perform much better than they do individually. That alone is not sufficient for them to outperform the best. They must be smart. Hence, the need for Condition 2 (the Calculus Condition). Finally, these diverse problem solvers cannot all get stuck at the same bunch of solutions with low values. Thus, we need Condition 3 (the Diversity Condition). And so we have it: Diversity trumps ability. Not always, but when the conditions hold.

How do we apply this in the real world? Simple. When picking two hundred employees from a pool of thousands, provided the people are all smart, we should keep the theorem in mind and not necessarily rank people by some crude ability score and pick the best. We should seek out difference. When picking four students from a class of sixty to work as a team to compete in a science competition, keep the theorem in mind as well, but pick the best four—unless they're demonstrably similar in skills.

Does the claim imply that a group of only chemists might benefit from having a poet join them? No. But perhaps they'd benefit from adding a physicist. Does it imply that a team of people with high test scores all trained at the same school in the same techniques might not do as well as a group that contains diversely trained people with diverse experiences and slightly lower average SAT, GRE, or IQ scores? Probably. If you work at a big firm filled with Harvard, Wharton, and Michigan Business School MBAs, you might question whether your firm shouldn't seek a little more diversity in educational background.

We should recall that Conditions 1 through 4 are sufficient but far from necessary for diversity to trump ability—just as ice cream is sufficient but not necessary to quiet my two boys. There are other conditions under which the results hold. The strongest of the conditions, the Diversity Condition, can often be relaxed. In fact, in the agent-based models that stimulated the formal analysis, it was almost never satisfied. So long as the solutions that lie in the intersection of the diverse agents' local optima do not have low values, the diverse groups perform better for the simple reason that they have fewer local optima.

DARWIN'S BRASS TACKS

As I mentioned earlier, the veracity of the diversity trumps ability claim is not a matter of dispute. It's true, just as $1 + 1 = 2$ is true. However, the claim applies to mathematical objects and not to people directly. It is a claim about how diverse perspectives and heuristics aggregate. Returning once again to the traveling salesperson problem helps us understand the implications of this distinction. We consider two thought experiments. In the first, we gather a group of one thousand undergraduates, explain the traveling salesperson problem to them and ask each to create a problem-solving algorithm. An algorithm consists of an encoding of the problem (a perspective) and ways to manipulate solutions (heuristics), so this fits our model perfectly. We rank those algorithms from best to worst based on how they performed on a sample eighty-city problem. We might well find substantial diversity among the thousand algorithms and also find that the best algorithms were similar. If so, a random collection of twenty algorithms would probably outperform the collection of the best twenty algorithms.

In the second thought experiment, we take the same one thousand students and we give them a general intelligence test. We then take the best twenty and put them in a group, and we take a random twenty and put them in a group. Suppose we then ask these two groups to come up with a solution to our eighty-city traveling salesperson problem. Would we still expect the random group to do better? The answer is less clear. Scores on general intelligence tests correlate with factors such as ambition, effort, and concentration, suggesting that the high-IQ group would do better. Even more relevant to our discussion, people with similar IQs might go about solving the traveling salesperson problem differently. So the high-IQ group could well be diverse.[18]

These two thought experiments reveal subtleties in how we think about the perspectives and heuristics. In the first, we need not care whether people came with those perspectives and heuristics already in their heads or if they developed them on the spot. In the second, this distinction matters. If people create their heuristics on the fly, then group dynamics matter even more. For example, the high-IQ group might recognize that they need to have diverse ways of solving the problem. If so, they probably would do better than the random group.[19]

Returning to the toolbox model helps us to make sense of how these two scenarios differ. People who score high on general intelligence tests probably possess more tools. Either that or the people who don't score well just know lots of stuff that test makers think is unimportant, such as how to speak backward in Pig Latin. (You say, "ooh;" they say, "yahoo.") If we compare a collection of people with high general intelligence to a collection of people with random general intelligence on some problem, we should find that each member of the first group has more tools. We might also think that the number of unique tools in their combined collections of tools exceeds the number for the other group and that therefore the high-IQ group would do better.

We have to be careful not to jump to conclusions. Let's dump out the toolboxes and see what we get. Suppose that each high-IQ person has on average thirty tools and the members of the random collection have on average twenty-five tools. With twenty members per collection, the high-IQ group has six hundred tools (twenty people times thirty tools each), whereas the other group has on average about five hundred tools. The point is that not all of these tools are unique. The relevant comparison is between the numbers of *unique* tools in each set. Now, we might think that the set with more tools should have more unique tools as well. *But that thinking is flawed.* By construction, the tools of the people in the high-IQ group are not random. They are tools that allow a person to do well on an IQ test. And IQ tests choose questions that people with high IQs do well on; so do SAT tests and ACT tests. This rule for choosing questions makes the tools of high scorers more similar than they would be if questions were chosen randomly. Nothing in the construction of the random group makes their tools similar.

This effect becomes even more pronounced the more accurate our test. If we were to select the "best" group according to how they do on the traveling salesperson problem, its members would be even more likely to have similar perspectives and heuristics. Why? Because the heuristics that enable someone to do well on a traveling salesperson problem are things like flip pairs of cities or flip pairs of cities separated by a city. They're specific heuristics. A group of the best might well all be thinking about the problem in one or two ways. Their overlap in tools would work to their disadvantage.[20]

This phenomenon of diversity reduction created by picking the best on either the IQ test or the traveling salesperson problem should sound familiar. We can find it in Darwin: *selection reduces diversity*. Even though we might think that we are selecting on something called ability, ability depends on tools. So, ultimately, selection takes place over the tools. By selecting those who perform better, we get people with more tools. That helps collective performance. But we also get people who are less diverse, and that hurts collective performance. That's why groups of the best need not be the best groups.

THE CONTEXTUAL PROBLEM OF VALUING DIVERSITY

The diversity-trumps-ability result also reveals the contextual nature of an individual's contribution. How much someone improves the current solution depends on her individual talents, to be sure, but her contribution also depends on her diversity relative to the other people working on the problem. She may be standing on the shoulders of the others and peering in a slightly different direction and therefore be able to make a small local improvement that no one else saw. Or she may be standing in a different place altogether and make a huge improvement. We don't care which. What we do care about is that the necessary condition for making a contribution is trying something different. And being different, as should be obvious, is not the property of an individual in isolation but a property of an individual relative to others. Try as he might, a person standing alone in a forest cannot be diverse.

This contextual nature of a person's contribution makes assigning credit difficult. Let's play with an example. Suppose that Belinda and Gordon work as civil engineers. Both are trying to solve the same difficult problem—namely how to pump sewage from five hundred houses up a steep hill at minimal cost. This problem has many possible solutions. To inject some diversity, let's assume that Belinda and Gordon have different perspectives and heuristics that they use to search for solutions. One day, Gordon happens on a one hundred thousand–dollar improvement in the current best solution, which involves using a pump with an enormous motor. Gordon realizes that if they reduce the circumference of the pipe, they could reduce the size of the motor. He announces his improvement in an email. Everyone, including Belinda, rejoices in this breakthrough. It's a good solution but not a great one because the smaller pipes require custom fittings. Two weeks later, Belinda finds an even better solution that builds on Gordon's breakthrough. Her idea is to put the small pipes inside regular-sized pipes, thereby obviating the need for the costly fittings. The added value of her solution is five hundred thousand dollars Belinda receives accolades near and far. After all, only a brilliant engineer could have solved this problem. Right? Maybe not. Let's consider three scenarios.

> **Scenario 1: Lucky Belinda.** Given the status quo solution, Gordon's perspective and heuristic pair might have led him to many improvements. He happened to have first found the small-pipe solution that had an added value of $100,000. Belinda's perspective/heuristic pair was stuck at the current solution, and the *only* solution that her perspective/ heuristic pair mapped to her better solution was Gordon's

breakthrough. Perhaps, as a child she enjoyed putting straws inside of straws when drinking milkshakes. So Belinda was lucky that Gordon announced his small-pipe solution.

Scenario 2: Deserving Belinda. Belinda's perspective and heuristic were such that she too would have thought of the small-pipe solution and then from there thought of the pipe-inside-a-pipe trick.

Scenario 3: The Coin Flip. Belinda might have first suggested the current pipe inside an even larger circumference pipe. This suggestion might have been thought silly. From there, Gordon would have realized that the internal pipe could be made smaller. If so, he would be the one who found the big breakthrough.

Belinda finds the big improvement and gets the related acclaim, while Gordon is considered a minor player. Yet only in the second scenario is Belinda's fame deserved. In the first scenario, Belinda's success was to a large extent a random event. Had Gordon found a different solution, Belinda would not have been able to use her experience with straws and milkshakes. In the third scenario, Belinda is deserving, but so was Gordon. Ironically, Belinda benefits because Gordon reveals his improvement first. Had she moved faster, her contribution would have been perceived as less significant.

Though these scenarios leave out perspectives and heuristics—they neglect to show how or why Belinda and Gordon got stuck—these details are relatively unimportant. What the scenarios reveal is the difficulty of determining the value of someone's contribution. The modern economy consists of many people who solve problems for a living. A great many of these people—doctors, engineers, scientists, architects, consultants, computer programmers, and so on—work collectively to solve problems. Figuring out who should receive credit for an improvement can be difficult. As the first and third scenarios show, the person who made the biggest contribution to the eventual solution may not deserve the credit.

This finding holds with some generality. Problem solvers of equal individual ability (i.e., equally good perspectives and heuristics for a specific problem) can generate arbitrary individual contributions to the final solution when working collectively.

Arbitrary Contributions Theorem: *Given problem solvers of identical ability, their contributions can be arbitrary, that is, any problem solver can make any contribution.*[21]

We should be careful not to make strong inferences about ability from how much someone contributes on a particular problem. One great discovery can be a stroke of luck. But, if we see someone consistently make contributions, we can probably infer that that person has an impressive toolbox, or at least a unique one.

Humans versus Computers: The Power of Perspectives

Before summarizing, we take a brief detour from our path. Much of what we have covered in this chapter could apply equally to people—who have perspectives and heuristics—or to computer search algorithms, which also encode the set of solutions and then search for improvements. We like to think that people differ from computers. And we do. In fact, we can use our frameworks to see an important way in which they do which gives us some hope for the continued value of human problem solvers. We can also use the frameworks to see the value of creating artifacts.

Recall that a few pages back in the example with Sam and Maddie, we saw an equivalence between pairs of perspectives and heuristics on a cube. Though different, their perspective/heuristic pairs resulted in identical problem-solving approaches. Another way to understand that result is to think of some perspectives as equivalent to heuristics. The same heuristic applied to a new perspective can be equivalent to new heuristics applied to an existing perspective.

This mathematical equivalence between perspectives and heuristics notwithstanding, in the real world the distinction has important consequences. If people use the same perspective, they can communicate new solutions easily. One person can say, "let's make the chocolate chips rockier looking," and the other person knows exactly what she means even though the words lack precision. Computers that perform parallel search or parallel computations exploit this ease of translation. When one computer finds an improvement, the new solution can be passed on to other computers, as the solution is represented in the same way—in binary code. Computers need not even send a complete description of the new solution. They need only send the changes from the old best solution.

When people have different perspectives, communication can be difficult. When one person finds a better solution, she may not be able to explain to others what that solution is. Recall Emerson's famous quotation, "To be different is to be misunderstood." If Barry's wife were to suggest that they choose an "earthier" color of yellow for the room they're painting, he might have only a crude idea of what she means. (He would, of course, still agree with her.) If a person who sees a problem differently lacks the ability to communicate his perspective, he may be ineffective. Others may ignore his ramblings about making the rear fender of the car "less male" and more "evocative of a beach lifestyle." Miscommunications across perspectives can have dire consequences. In 1999, NASA's 125 million–dollar Mars Climate Orbiter was lost forever owing to miscommunication across perspectives. The orbiter had traveled some 416 million miles to get to Mars, only to have its navigators misinterpret English measurements for metric measurements. Imagine someone telling you that you have two inches of space between your car bumper and the curb, but you think she means two meters and step on the gas with too much gusto. The story of the orbiter's demise is that simple. Lockheed Martin programmed the computer using pounds, an English unit of force. Jet propulsion Laboratory navigators thought that their instructions were being sent in Newtons, a metric unit of force. One pound equals about four and a half Newtons. The thruster rockets had been fired many times during the voyage but the discrepancy between the designated force and the actual force had gone unnoticed. But on

September 23, the difference in units of measure resulted in too much force (imagine asking for two pounds and getting nine), and the orbiter crashed into the atmosphere. Oops.

Diverse perspectives also reduce incentives to construct elaborate heuristics. A heuristic that works in one perspective may not be useful in another. Heuristics that scale peaks in one landscape may head toward the shallows in another. These two problems, difficulty communicating and reducing incentives to create sophisticated heuristics, might lead to the conclusion that efforts to increase diversity should emphasize heuristic diversity, but this intuition is flawed. Diverse heuristics tend to be more modest changes, more iterative. A new heuristic is not likely to make a problem simple. So if the common perspective creates a rugged landscape, a collection of people may be far better off considering alternative perspectives than wasting their time climbing the abundant local peaks. And though it is possible to mimic a perspective with a heuristic, that heuristic might be complicated. It might not be a heuristic that anyone would arrive at without backward engineering it from a perspective.

Perspectives, therefore, matter, though they create problems. We need diverse perspectives. Think back to our earlier discussion about breakthroughs in science. They rely on perspective diversity, not heuristic diversity. Moreover, the ability to work across diverse perspectives may be the one big advantage that humans have over computers. We possess remarkable abilities to communicate across diverse perspectives through artifacts, physical representations of solutions. These artifacts reduce communication errors. Imagine a team confronting a design problem—how to design a chair, a car, or a laser printer. Each person in the team probably thinks about the problem differently. Each has a different perspective. Suppose that the team uses artifacts, that they build prototypes. They may make cars out of Styrofoam and clay or sketch chairs on paper. These artifacts create a common perspective for communication and allow people to maintain their individual diverse perspectives, ignoring the deep philosophical question of whether we all see the same reality. In this way, we can exploit artifacts. They give us the same solution in our heads. They allow us to leverage our differences.

THE BENEFITS OF DIFFERENCE

If this chapter has a central message, a deliverable, it is that when solving problems, diversity may matter as much, or even more than, individual ability. From this we can infer that organizations, firms, and universities that solve problems should seek out people with diverse experiences, training, and identities that translate into diverse perspectives and heuristics. Specifically, hiring students who had high grade point averages from the top-ranked school may be a less effective strategy than hiring good students from a diverse set of schools with a diverse set of backgrounds, majors, and electives.

A second message is that the benefits of diversity also apply within individuals. People should acquire diverse sets of perspectives and heuristics so that they can make larger contributions. These tools should be diverse—but not too diverse; otherwise they can't be combined. We may be collectively better off if we're collectively diverse. We probably do best with a diversity of diversities—with some people being diverse and others specializing but with everyone having lots of tools. With more tools, a person is more capable of being diverse, of amassing more interesting perspectives, heuristics, and combinations of perspectives and heuristics. Paradoxically, the best way to be diverse is to be able— to have lots of tools.

A third message relates to the application of these ideas. One can easily come up with examples where ability trumps diversity. After all, Kasparov won. And had he played a group of random people, he'd have crushed them. Point taken. The blurry line that identifies people who satisfy the calculus condition is one that must be learned over time. Where that line lies may vary in different contexts. I take this up in greater length in the last part of the book.

A final, and less pragmatic, application of this logic relates to fun. Diverse perspectives and heuristics can be engines of joy. One reason that children bring such happiness into the world is that they employ diverse perspectives and heuristics. They attempt to solve problems in ways that are unimaginable to an adult. They rewrap bananas after opening them because they've changed their minds. They eat spaghetti with a straw. They put their socks on over their shoes. They tell you that the flour smells bad (because it doesn't smell like a flower).

Childlike perspectives and heuristics may help in the development of new fun things. And new fun things, just like scientific breakthroughs, often combine superadditively. First came the Frisbee. Now we have Frisbee golf, Frisbee football (Ultimate Frisbee), and, best of all, Frisbee fetch. Leveraging our diversity to make advancements in science and businesses is well and good, but we should also put it to use toward having some fun.

CHAPTER 7

Models of Information Aggregation

MINDLESS SIGNALS

I was brought up to believe the only thing worth doing was to add up the sum of the accurate information in the world.
—MARGARET MEAD, quoted in *New York Times*,
August 9, 1964

WE turn now to the role of diversity in helping collections of people make accurate predictions, the so-called wisdom of crowds. People often think of predictions in the contexts of weather (it's going to rain) or sports (Tiger will win the masters), but predictions are widespread. Firms predict sales. Colleges predict how many students will enroll. Governments predict the effects of policy changes. Society would not function if we could not predict with at least reasonable accuracy.

We might think that a collection of moderately informed and knowledgeable individuals would not make very accurate predictions, but that's not necessarily true. Substantial evidence suggests that diverse collections of people often predict rather well. If not, then how could we ever expect markets and democracies to function? After all, what is a stock price but a prediction? What is a choice in an election or a referendum but a prediction of what a politician will do or what forces the referendum will put into play? Sure, prices and outcomes don't have to be perfectly accurate for markets and democracies to work, but they can't be consistently far off the mark. Otherwise, we'd have far more stock market crashes and wrestler governors. Not that those don't exist. They do. But they're not so widespread that we've abandoned either markets or democracies. To the contrary, some think that market-based democracies represent the end of history.

Stock market prices and election outcomes are predictions by huge numbers of people. In addition to these society-level predictions, we also make lots of predictions in small and moderately sized groups—in juries, management teams, boards of directors, bargaining teams, and department faculties. Many, but not all, of the real-world examples that we'll consider in this chapter and the next describe a reasonably large number of people, a crowd, making a prediction. Somehow, a thousand people making an accurate collective prediction seems more amazing than three people doing so. But the logic, in the case of three or three thousand, remains the same; it relies on equal parts individual accuracy and collective diversity. For that reason, our not-so-real-world examples will include only a few people.

In this chapter, we consider several types of information aggregation models. These will not be based on our frameworks. Instead, these are representative of the models typically constructed by social scientists. We get to why we're doing this in a few pages. First, we need to understand what information aggregation is and how it differs from predictive model aggregation. In information aggregation, people get "signals" about the outcome. We can think of these signals as information. We can also think of them as predictions, but we see why that involves sloppy thinking and hand waving—two things we're trying to avoid. We take up predictive model aggregation in the next chapter.

In both this chapter and the next, we emphasize individual diversity and the central role it plays in collective accuracy. The only way a collective prediction can be accurate if the individual predictors are not diverse is if most of the individual predictors are accurate. But then we have a result that says good individual predictors make accurate collective predictions. That result is not at all surprising. Yet, we have many examples in which people are not individually accurate but the collection of them is. That mystery is what we seek to explain.

Surowiecki proposes three necessary conditions for a collection of people to make accurate predictions. These are that people have diverse predictive models; that people are independent (they are not allowed to influence one another); and that the prediction process be decentralized (people do not communicate with one another). All three of these conditions imply a diversity of predictive models. If people are not independent, they are not likely to have diverse predictive models. And if the process that aggregates predictions is not decentralized, then participants likely share predictive models, thereby lessening the diversity of the models used. Thus, in a way, the third condition can be seen as implied by the second.

To provide some grist for our cognitive mills, we start with some examples in which collections of people make accurate predictions. Some of these are anecdotes, but most present systematic evidence that collections of people can make accurate predictions. This distinction matters. We might put forth a theory that men are from Venus and women are from Mars. If this theory accurately predicted correctly the behavior of only 10 percent of men and women, it would be consistent with millions of anecdotes. Hence, we need systematic evidence. After looking at the evidence, we ask whether the models from the information aggregation models from social science prove up to the task of explaining these examples. The answer is no!

EXAMPLES OF WISE CROWDS

Many of the specific examples in which collections of people predict correctly seem almost unbelievable. We relate some from Surowiecki's *Wisdom of Crowds* here; see his book for even more. These examples are not laboratory experiments with ten subjects; they come from Las Vegas, county fairs, and game shows. Evidence also comes from the stock market. Stock market prices encapsulate the predictions of a crowd of people about future dividend streams. These predictions can be freakishly accurate: In 1986, the stock price of Morton Thiokol fell soon after the 1986 Space Shuttle Challenger disaster. Only later was it discovered that the O-rings that Morton Thiokol manufactured were primarily to blame. We can dismiss this accurate pricing as pure luck, but in repeated settings markets have proven to be quite capable predictors.[1] Futures markets for the price of orange juice determined by market traders have often proven more accurate than weather forecasts of the likelihood of freezes.[2] Obviously, market prices are not perfect predictors. Market bubbles and crashes occur with some regularity. But, as Surowiecki notes, markets create bubbles partly because they have no known end date, which creates an incentive for people who trade on trends to ride an increasing wave of prices.

Predictive markets other than the stock market include the Hollywood Stock Exchange (HSX), the Iowa Electronic Markets (IEM), and Tradesports.com.[3] On HSX, people buy stocks that pay dividends depending on ticket sales for movies. People also buy bonds on future ticket sales of movies for certain stars. Angelina Jolie, for instance, might sell for more than Burt Reynolds. A test showed that HSX performed as well as a leading expert in predicting the revenues for fifty movies released between March and September of 2000. HSX's predictions were off by an average of 31 percent, while the predictions of the expert, Brandon Gray of Box Office Mojo, erred by 27 percent on those same fifty movies.[4]

Later, we will see evidence showing the accuracy of the IEM and the sports betting lines. This evidence is important. We could always find two or three cases where a crowd of people miraculously predicted an outcome correctly, but that does not prove that crowds do so on average any more than my father's hole-in-one at Mullenhurst Golf Course in Yankee Springs, Michigan, in the mid-1990s would be proof that he's on a par, or under par as the case may be, with Tiger Woods. He's not.

Systematic evidence convinces social scientists, but that doesn't mean that anecdotes don't have their place. Anecdotes are more captivating—both times I've asked crowds of students to guess my weight, their average guess has been within a pound. Within a pound! When I weighed 194, they guessed 193 on average. The next year, they predicted me a leaner 186. I weighed 185. Anecdotes such as this provide us with a point of analytic entry and intellectual motivation. The anecdote that leads off Surowiecki's book plays both roles. Here's the short version: In 1906, Francis Galton analyzed predictions of the weight of a young steer by attendees of the West of England Fat Stock and Poultry Exhibition. The average (mean) of 787 contestants' estimates of the weight was 1,197 pounds. The actual weight of the steer was 1,198 pounds. There was no consensus about how tasty the steer was. Incidentally, Galton wouldn't be happy with Surowiecki's analysis because he advocated the median as the predictor, not the mean. One crazy guess can manipulate the mean.

Despite Galton's objection, we keep Surowiecki's mean-based analysis in mind as we walk through the information aggregation models of how collections of people make accurate predictions. Social scientists have devoted substantial effort to modeling how collections of people predict in economic and political settings. These models highlight the information that people possess and the incentives they have to truthfully reveal it. None of these models, though, explain the steer, but the model that we cover in the next chapter—based on the predictive model framework—does. I might add that lest we get too carried away with this last example, guessing the weight of a steer is not that difficult. As a former amateur cattleman (my wife and I owned nine steers for a short time), I can say from experience that a person can estimate the weight of a steer within a hundred pounds without mastery of Galois Theory or differential equations. It's like guessing the weight of really, really big people. Galton's was not an experiment in which random people on the street were asked to guess the viscosity of a mixture of Jell-O and motor oil in some obscure unit of measure. People know what a pound is. People know that steers weigh more than men but less than elephants. Nevertheless, as Thomas Schelling once wrote, if you are in the mood to be amazed....

INFORMATION AGGREGATION MODELS

We now look at standard social science models of information aggregation. The distinction between information aggregation and predictive model aggregation is subtle and often blurred. If we ask people to name the capital of Oregon, then we are asking them for information, for facts (not a prediction). If we ask those same people to predict the outcome of the next U.S. Senate race in Oregon, we are asking them to apply models to their information to predict the future.

In information aggregation models, people get signals about the answer. The various types of information aggregation models make one of three assumptions about what people know. These end up being assumptions about the signals, but we describe them here in terms of the information they provide. The models assume that people either know the answer with some probability, know pieces of the answer, or get blurry signals of the answer. The first assumption states that some people know the answer and others do not. The process of aggregation allows the people who know the answer to reveal it. The second assumption states that people know parts of the answer and that those parts can be aggregated to reveal the answer. As Aristotle puts it in what some call the "summation argument," what Jeremy Waldron more sublimely refers to as "the doctrine of the wisdom of the multitude,"[5]

> For each individual among the many has a share of excellence and practical wisdom, and when they meet together, just as they become in a manner one man, who has many feet, and hands, and senses, so too with regard to their character and thought. Hence the many are better judges than a single man of music and poetry, for some understand one part, and some another, and among them they understand the whole. (Aristotle, *Politics*, book 3, chapter 11)

Aristotle's interests run to poetry and music, not the price of Microsoft stock or the capabilities of politicians, but his insight applies in those cases as well. He proposes that because each person knows a part of the solution, the collection of people can know the whole. This whole-as-sum-of-the-parts logic may explain some wise crowds but it fails to describe people making predictions based on models.

The third common assumption, that people see a blurry picture of reality, captures situations in which something blocks or distorts our view. With some bending and stretching this can be framed as an assumption about predictions. We can think of the distortions as errors in predictive models, but this assumes that the noise is an addition to the true state, to the right answer. That's not likely to be true of actual predictions, that they're perfectly accurate but they just have extra stuff added in (or left out). Thus, this last assumption captures only situations in which people do not see the outcome or the event clearly.[6]

In all of the real-world examples listed earlier, people predict a future or unknown event: a future price or a current weight. People do not just recall bits of information, though sometimes that does happen—we consider a case involving a game show in a few pages—but it is the exception and not the rule in market and political settings. Some defend the social science models of information aggregation by claiming that their abstraction—the assumption that people get signals—allows them to be recast as models of people who make predictions. That can be done. But, as we shall see, doing so implicitly builds in diverse predictive models. Otherwise, how could these people receive different signals?

In what follows, we consider the standard assumptions about signals using toy models of information aggregation. Yes, these models reveal the limits of the information aggregation approach, but that's not why we study them. We're not constructing straw men to knock them down. To the contrary, we want to pull them off their sticks and walk them along a yellow brick road toward relevance. By looking at these simple models, we can begin to understand how to add information. Adding one plus one is easy. Adding information in the form of signals is a bit harder. Adding predictive models is harder still and almost impossible without first learning to add signals. Thus, we first look at models that, in the end, we find lacking. But by doing so, we gain the expertise—the tools—necessary to understand how information aggregates.

A Million Tiny Pieces

In our first toy information aggregation model, each person in a crowd has partial information about the correct answer to a question. They aggregate their partial information by voting. I frame this model using yet another example from *The Wisdom of Crowds*, one that involves the game show *Who Wants to Be a Millionaire*. On the show, a contestant must choose from among four possible answers. If the contestant is correct several times in a row, she can win one million dollars. If the contestant is stumped on a particular question, she can use "lifelines." One lifeline is to call a friend. This friend is presumably an expert, not a buddy from junior high. Another lifeline allows the contestant to poll the audience. By the way, the audience at a game show consists of few editors of the *Encyclopedia Britannica* or University of California at Berkeley faculty.

Data from the show reveals that the friends (who we again assume were called because they were ostensibly experts) proved correct only two-thirds of the time. We can assume that the experts get the call only on hard questions. No one phones a friend to learn the number of people in the Jackson Five. To paraphrase the 1980s rock icon Meatloaf: on difficult questions, two out of three ain't bad. And yet this level of accuracy pales in comparison to the accuracy of the audience's prediction. When polled, the audience predicted correctly nine times out of ten. Nine times out of ten is far better than ain't bad. It is amazing, astounding, and some might even say magical.

Though some think that the crowd's accuracy emerges from some deep and mysterious process, we should know better. There's no mystery here. Mistakes cancel one another out, and correct answers, like cream, rise to the surface. To explain how that occurs, I construct a model (big surprise).

Let's suppose that the question concerns the four members of the Monkees, a made-for-television band from the 1970s.

Question: *Which person from the following list was not a member of the Monkees?*

IDENTIFY THE NON-MONKEE

(A) Peter Tork
(B) Davy Jones
(C) Roger Noll
(D) Michael Nesmith

We can assume that the Monkees are not familiar to everyone (and thank goodness for that!). Those people who can identify the three Monkees on the list correctly identify Roger Noll as not being a Monkee. They vote for him. (Few of these people, probably, could further identify Roger as a Stanford economist and all-around good guy.) We next assume that those people who do not know any of the Monkees choose randomly from among the four names (more on that later). Now things get a little trickier. For those people who can identify two of the Monkees, we assume they randomize between the two names that they do not know. And for those people who know only one of the Monkees, we assume they randomize among the other three names.

We next imagine a hypothetical crowd of one hundred people, seven of whom know all three Monkees listed, ten of whom know two of the Monkees, fifteen of whom know only one of the Monkees, and sixty-eight of whom know none of the Monkees. On average, the individuals in this crowd are not well informed. Fewer than 10 percent know the answer and more than two-thirds have no clue.

Let's now have these people vote. Roger Noll gets seven votes from the seven people who know the answer. And, on average, he also gets five votes from ten people who know two Monkees on the list because these ten people randomize between just two names, Roger and one other person, who we can assume is random. Roger also gets five votes from the fifteen people who know only one

Monkee on the list and randomize among three names. Finally, he receives (again, on average) seventeen, or one-fourth, of the sixty-eight votes from people who have no clue as to the correct answer. If we sum these votes, we get that, on average, Roger Noll gets thirty-four votes.[7]

If, as assumed, people are randomizing, each of the other three names should split the remaining sixty-six votes and each get about twenty-two votes. Thus, Roger Noll should win. Thirty-four is larger than twenty-two. The crowd of not so wise people is wise. Even more amazingly, Roger Noll might win *even if no one in the crowd knows the correct answer.* To see this, suppose that each person knew that the correct answer was either Roger Noll or one of the other names. If every person votes for either Roger or one of the other names (chosen randomly), then Roger gets on average one-half of the votes. Each of the others gets one-sixth of the votes. Here, the crowd knows something—the identity of the person who is not the Monkee—that no one in the crowd knows.

In practice, Roger Noll wouldn't always be the prediction. Remember, the audience predicted correctly only nine times out of ten, not ten times out of ten. As so many votes are random, another person might randomly get more votes. Just as it is possible to flip a coin ten times and get eight heads, it is possible for the random choices to disproportionately favor one of the wrong choices. The probability of this type of error can be predicted using statistics. With the numbers from this example, the probability that the crowd would be wrong would be in the ballpark of 10 percent.[8] A second reason why Roger Noll might not be selected is that the people who do not know the answer may not pick randomly. They may suffer from a common bias that leads them to predict one of the other names frequently. Correlated errors might arise if a previous question had been about seamen, in which case Davy Jones might be thought of as a comical reference to Davy Jones's locker (a grave injustice), and this might lead to a correlated error.

This model is simple and elegant, but it goes only partway toward explaining the wisdom of crowds. It explains how, if some members of the crowd have the correct information and others do not, then the incorrect information can cancel out through randomness. It characterizes some, but not all, of Aristotle's logic using mathematics. Unfortunately, it explains none of the examples that began the chapter. In none of those cases did some members of the crowd know the correct answer. There were not, so far as we know, some subset of people who knew the exact weight of the steer at the fair Galton visited, the outcome of the horse races, or the outcomes of elections. I'm also pretty sure no one in my classes had ever seen me step on a scale.

Regional Sales

A second type of information aggregation model applies to situations in which each member of the crowd knows a part of the answer. It formalizes the logic of Aristotle. As an example, imagine a business that has sales staffs that serve five subunits representing Europe, Asia (including Australia), Africa, North America, and South America. Each has a manager who knows his or her own region's sales, but has little or no idea about sales from the other regions. The task of the managers is to predict aggregate sales. On the surface, this appears easy. If each manager reveals the sales from his or her region and those sales are totaled, this gives the correct answer. But the logic is a bit more complicated than that because the sales managers are predicting total sales, not just revealing regional sales.

Let's do an example. Suppose that the actual sales for each region are as shown in table 7.1.

How then should the managers make predictions? We'll consider two scenarios. Under the first scenario, the managers have some knowledge of past sales. Let's suppose that in the past, the average sales for each region have been 50K and that total sales have averaged 300K. These assumptions mean that each manager would predict total sales to be 300K plus or minus the difference between actual sales in his or her region and 50K. The Asian manager would predict $300K + (60K - 50K) = 310K$. We will call this the Past Sales Scenario. The predictions for each of the five managers would be as shown in table 7.2.

TABLE 7.1:
Actual sales

Region	Sales in Region
Asia	60K
Europe	50K
Africa	95K
North America	75K
South America	40K
Total Sales	320K

TABLE 7.2:
Managers' predictions under past sales
scenario

Region	Predicted Total Sales
Asia	310K
Europe	300K
Africa	345K
North America	325K
South America	290K
Average Prediction	314K

The aggregate prediction shown in the bottom line of table 7.2 equals 314K. The prediction is not perfectly accurate because sales were higher than expected. Their reliance on average past sales lowers their prediction. Nevertheless, the direction of their prediction is correct. Sales were above average; they predicted above-average sales. Under the Past Sales Scenario, this will always be true. The predicted direction of sales will always be correct. It just won't go far enough.

In the second scenario, let's assume that the managers lack past sales data to rely on. They therefore assume that the other regions will have sales identical to their own. Let's call this the Correlated Sales Scenario. The Asian manager predicts sales of 360K and the European manager predicts sales of 300K. The predictions for all six regions are shown in table 7.3.

TABLE 7.3:
Managers' predictions under correlated sales
scenario

Region	Predicted Total Sales
Asia	360K
Europe	300K
Africa	570K
North America	450K
South America	240K
Average Prediction	320K

This prediction is exactly correct. And if the managers use this rule, it always will be. The logic behind this result is easy to follow; it's just based on averaging the predictions.[9] Although this rule will always produce the correct answer, the managers may not choose to use it if they have knowledge of the past. The manager of the African market, who had sales of 95K, would know that these were high sales figures. He would probably not expect every other region to do as well. At the same time, he might expect some correlation between the other regions' sales and his own. So his prediction might be somewhere in between his prediction in the Past Sales Scenario and in the Correlated Sales Scenario, as might everyone else's predictions. The resulting collective prediction might then lie somewhere in between 314K and 320K—a prediction that, we might add, is also remarkably accurate.[10]

Though we've framed this as prediction, this example primarily involves aggregating diverse information. Each person knows a piece of the answer and these pieces can be pulled together. This logic might explain some situations, but it remains inadequate to address others. In this example, each manager knows a part of the relevant information, while in Galton's steer example it doesn't hold true—if it did, one person would have to know the weight of the hooves, another the weight of the tail, another the weight of the head, and so on until all of the parts were covered.

That's not to say that this way of aggregating information doesn't work. It does. The logic is powerful and useful. Suppose that you are a manager. There may be an instance when you need to recall some piece of information buried deep in the company files, such as which of two product designs had been less costly to produce. You could search for the information in your company's files, or you could quickly poll your subordinates. You could send out a quick group email and ask people which product had been cheaper to produce. Those people who recall the correct answer will provide you with the correct information. Those who do not recall will (you hope) randomize, and in the aggregate you'll find the correct information.

Staying in this hypothetical managerial role, suppose that you need to know the total number of employees who have called in "sick" the day before a three-day weekend. You could ask each of the directors of the divisions under you to report how many people called in sick from their divisions. They may be unwilling to tell you this information because it reflects badly on them. You might instead ask them to predict how many people they thought called in sick company-wide. In this case as well, people may have an incentive to lie, but less of one. The average of their predictions might well be a good estimate.

The Gravity of Truth

Our last two models differ only slightly. In the first, we will assume discrete signals—heads or tails, yes or no; the second assumes that they are continuous, that they can take any real value, such as the weight of a person or a steer. Both of these models are taught in probability classes and used by economists and political scientists to explain why markets and democracies work as well as they do. Most people find these probability models confusing and not much fun. They requires making lots of calculations using p's and $(1 - p)$'s and the like. Sometimes to make sense of things, we have to trudge through ugly calculations.

The first model we consider relies on two possible discrete signals. One is accurate. The other is inaccurate. The probability that a person gets the accurate signal equals three-fourths. To frame the model, we will assume the predictive task is to determine whether sweaters just shipped in from Guatemala are made of wool (W) or of artificial fibers (A). For the purposes of this example, we assume that all of the sweaters in question are, in fact, knitted from artificial fibers, despite the "100% wool" tags sewn inside the back of their collars. (Perhaps the tags are made of wool, so the tags—technically speaking—are accurate.)

In this model, each of three product testers picks up a different sweater and gets a signal as to its composition. What is this signal? No bells ring or sirens go off, so we have to assume that the product testers have skin allergies to wool. Each rubs a sweater on her arm. If she breaks out in hives, she believes the sweater is wool; otherwise, she believes the sweater to be made of artificial fibers. This skin test is not always accurate. Let's assume that about one-fourth of the time product testers do not break out when testing a wool sweater, and that about one-fourth of the time they do break out when testing an acrylic sweater. (The latter occurs because of the wool tags.) Given these assumptions, 75 percent of the time a person gets the signal A for artificial fiber, and 25 percent of the time a person gets the signal W for wool. In the language of probability theory, these signals can be said to be correct with probability three-fourths.

Let's further assume that these signals are *independent*: the signal that one product tester receives depends in no way on the signals that the other receives. Formally, this property is called *independence conditional on the state of the world*. In our example, the state of the world is the stuff of which the sweaters are made. Assuming independence (conditional on the state) implies diversity, and lots of it. If people reacted to the sweaters the same way, then they would get the same signal. Therefore, to get diverse signals, they must either react differently or test different sweaters.

Using a little math, we can compute the probabilities for all possible combinations of signals. Here come the detailed mathematical calculations that engineers love but that cause poets to skip entire paragraphs. Call our three product testers Howard, Mita, and Rick. One possibility is that all three sweater testers get the signal A. By assumption, each gets the correct

TABLE 7.4:
Individual signals and collective predictions

Signals			Collective Prediction	Probability of Outcome
Howard	Mita	Rick		
A	A	A	A	$\frac{3}{4} * \frac{3}{4} * \frac{3}{4} = \frac{27}{64}$
A	A	W	A	$\frac{3}{4} * \frac{3}{4} * \frac{1}{4} = \frac{9}{64}$
A	W	A	A	$\frac{3}{4} * \frac{1}{4} * \frac{3}{4} = \frac{9}{64}$
W	A	A	A	$\frac{1}{4} * \frac{3}{4} * \frac{3}{4} = \frac{9}{64}$
A	W	W	W	$\frac{3}{4} * \frac{1}{4} * \frac{1}{4} = \frac{3}{64}$
W	W	A	W	$\frac{1}{4} * \frac{1}{4} * \frac{3}{4} = \frac{3}{64}$
W	A	W	W	$\frac{1}{4} * \frac{3}{4} * \frac{1}{4} = \frac{3}{64}$
W	W	W	W	$\frac{1}{4} * \frac{1}{4} * \frac{1}{4} = \frac{1}{64}$

signal with probability $\frac{3}{4}$. As these signals are independent, the probability that both the first and second product testers get the signal A equals $(\frac{3}{4}) \cdot (\frac{3}{4})$, and the probability that all three get the signal A equals $(\frac{3}{4}) \cdot (\frac{3}{4}) \cdot (\frac{3}{4})$. Similar calculations for all possible combinations of signals are provided in table 7.4.

To show the wisdom of crowds, we let Howard, Mita, and Rick vote on the purchase lot of sweaters. When voting they reveal the signals they received.[11] Table 7.4 shows that these collective predictions are correct in the first four cases and incorrect in the last four cases. The table also shows that the first four cases are far more likely than the latter four. A little addition reveals that the crowd (three is, after all, a crowd) makes the correct prediction with probability $\frac{54}{64}$, or about 84 percent. This exceeds the probability that each person was correct individually, which was only 75 percent.

The collection of people predicts more accurately because a force pulls the group toward the correct answer. The underpinnings of this force can be seen best with a metaphor. Imagine two rooms. One has a door marked *A*, for artificial fibers, and the other has a door marked *W*, for wool. Imagine a long line of people standing outside the two doors. One of the two rooms represents the correct answer. Suppose that each person is handed a card that tells them the correct door with probability *p* and the incorrect door the rest of the time. Assume *p* is greater than one half. These signals are passes to get into the rooms. To enter the room with the door marked *A* requires an *A* pass. To enter the room with the door marked *W* requires a *W* pass. After ten people have entered the rooms, the expected number of people who have entered the correct room will be $10p$. The expected number of people who enter the incorrect room will be $10(1 - p)$. On average, more people will have entered the correct room than the incorrect room.

If *p* is close to one-half, then it is possible that more people will enter the wrong room, provided there were not many people in the original line. Suppose, though, that a million people have entered the rooms. Even if *p* is close to one-half, $1,000,000p$ will be much larger than $1,000,000 (1 - p)$, so more people will have entered the correct room. Statisticians explain this phenomenon using the Law of Large Numbers. As more independent signals get produced, the true value of *p* reveals itself. And if we assume that *p* is greater than one-half, then a large crowd eventually gets the right answer.

A not-so-obvious implication of this reasoning is that we should be willing to trade off some accuracy for group size. Specifically, a group of three people each of whom gets the correct signal (independently) with probability $\frac{3}{4}$ will not be as accurate as a group of eleven people, each of whom gets the correct signal (again independently) with probability $\frac{3}{5}$. Bernie Grofman refers to this as the trade-off between accuracy and group size. We'd be willing to sacrifice some accuracy if we could have more people in the crowd.[12]

This model might seem to explain the wisdom of crowds. The gravity of the truth wins out in the long run. If this seems all too convenient, it is. On what basis can we assume that people get independent signals? Though social scientists often assume this form of independence, why should we believe it to exist? Can each person in a crowd get an independent signal? We will consider those questions at the end of this chapter and in the next one. For the moment, we need only recognize that this model implicitly assumes a tremendous amount of diversity across the signals. And by doing so, it makes the crowd wise. It's what some call a heroic assumption.

In this stark form, this model fails to apply to any of our earlier examples. None of those predictive tasks involved making a binary choice. Each required predicting a numerical value. No one received a correct signal of the weight of the steer with probability p (or an incorrect signal with probability $(1 - p)$). Nevertheless, the model remains helpful by showing how *independent random errors cancel*. If we can find a way to guarantee that members of the crowd make random errors, then we have a wise crowd.

The Averaging of Noise

Our final model also assumes that people get blurry signals but these take on real values. As usual, we analyze this model in the context of an example. Suppose that a collection of people is assigned the task of determining whether or not McDonald's policy is to keep its coffee at 170 degrees. If these people go to McDonald's and get coffee, provided that they do not go to the same restaurant at the same time, we can assume that each receives something close to an independent signal conditional on the true state of the world, which in this case is McDonald's policy.

If in fact the thermostats in McDonald's coffeemakers keep the coffee at 170 degrees, the distribution of temperatures should have a mean 170 degrees plus or minus small errors. For the cup of coffee purchased by the ith person, call this error E_i. This person's signal equals the true temperature as set by policy, call this T, plus the error term. Letting S_i denote the signal that the ith person receives, we then have that $S_i = T + E_i$. (Sorry about all of these subscripts, but in a moment we'll see why they are needed.) If these assumptions hold, a collection of McDonald's coffee drinkers could, with high accuracy, uncover McDonald's policy. Each person's belief of the true temperature equals the temperature set by policy plus a small error. The prediction from the crowd, which we assume here to be the average and denote by T^{Pred} equals the sum of the six predictions divided by six.

$$T^{Pred} = \frac{T + E_1 + T + E_2 + T + E_3 + T + E_4 + T + E_5 + T + E_6}{6}$$

Summing up all of the T's gives

$$T^{Pred} = T + \frac{E_1 + E_2 + E_3 + E_4 + E_5 + E_6}{6}$$

This prediction will be close to T, provided the sum of the error terms is close to zero. If some of the individual error terms are negative and some are positive, the average of the error terms should be smaller in absolute value than any of the individual error terms. If we assume that the errors have an average value of zero and that they are independent, then the average will be close to zero. With an even larger crowd of predictors, the average will be even closer. This size of this reduction in error can be made formal using the Law of Large Numbers, but we won't bother. We want to focus on the underlying logic. Rousseau describes it quite accurately in his discussion of the difference between the general will and the will of all.

> There is often a great difference between the will of all (what all individuals want) and the general will; the general will studies only the common interest while the will of all studies private interest, and is indeed no more than the sum of individual desires. But if we take away from these same wills the plusses and minuses which cancel each other out, the balance which remains is the general will. (Jean-Jacques Rousseau, *The Social Contract, Or Principles of Political Right*, 1762)

This quotation from Rousseau describes in words what social scientists explain with all of those mathematical symbols—*the errors cancel out*. Crowds can be wise if each person sees the true answer plus an error (possibly a large one) so long as these errors have mean zero and are independent. The independence assumption guarantees that with enough people, the errors cancel out one another. Could this happen? Sometimes. The case of the coffee at McDonald's may be just such a case.[13]

As elegant and general as this last model seems, does it describe the wisdom of crowds? Does it explain how people predict election outcomes, stock prices, or the winner of sporting events, much less the weight of a steer? If we apply this model to the steer example, why should we assume that people's guesses were draws from some distribution that had the correct mean and independent errors? No Ray Kroc–trained employee was handing out pieces of paper with the true value of the steer (plus or minus some error term) at Galton's fair. The model lacks any explanation of the source of the signals. They're black boxed. The model fails to explain what goes on in the heads of the people making the predictions. The model contains no interpretations and no predictive models. Instead, the model describes signals. And as if by magic, each signal has the correct mean and is independent of the others. How does either of these things happen? *Does either happen?* Probably not, except in rare cases. The averaging-of-noise model, therefore, fails as a model of prediction, though it is a good model of blurry vision and easy to apply.

THE SPACE BETWEEN

The four information aggregation models all produce valuable insights. Let's quickly review. Crowds can predict the correct answer even if only a small set of people in the crowd know it (Model 1). As we may not know which people in the crowd know the answer, we may therefore choose to rely on crowds to reveal information. We also saw that if individuals who each know a piece of information make predictions based on history or on an assumption that the other pieces are like their own, then they collectively make accurate predictions (Model 2). Both of these models can explain cases where crowds predicted accurately, but neither fully explains our examples. We also saw that if people receive independent, generated signals, be they discrete (Model 3) or continuous (Model 4), their errors cancel. Their collective prediction is highly accurate. The last two models apply to situations in which people see the quality or the value plus or minus a small error. They apply less neatly to situations in which people make predictions based on models.

Implicitly, all of these models assume some diversity. That's what we want to keep in mind: even though we didn't know it, all of those assumptions about independence were also assumptions about diversity. However, the connections between the two concepts—diverse predictive models and independent predictions—are not formalized. We are left to rely on our intuitions as to whether predictions are independent, and whether on average they are correct. In some cases, these statistical assumptions may be valid. In others, they may be hiding the great and powerful Oz behind a flimsy curtain. So, to understand the role of diversity in contributing to the wisdom of crowds, we must unpack where those predictions come from and how they differ. We need to look at differences directly. Once we have done that, we can then come back to these models with a deeper understanding of when they make sense and when they don't.

In sum, if we hope to understand the wisdom of crowds, we need a model in which people make predictions. For a preview of how that model might work, let's return to the steer example. The estimates by fair goers were not true signals plus an error. It wasn't as though they each saw the steer standing on a scale from different angles, and as a result, each saw the true weight with some error. More likely, each had some primitive model of what a steer weighs. These models led to predictions of the steer's weight. The predictions were not naïve shots in the dark. In 1906, people knew a lot about steers. The farmers at this exhibition probably categorized the steer based on its attributes (big head, thin haunches, tall at the shoulders, large barrel chest, and so on), and then made educated guesses. Based on Galton's data, they all had slightly different models. Otherwise, their predictions would have been the same.

But certainly, the diversity of their predictions cannot explain why they were collectively so accurate, can it? Amazingly, combined with their moderate abilities, their diversity drove them to accuracy. So it would seem that we need both some level of individual accuracy and some amount of collective diversity for a crowd to be wise. But that's just crude intuition. We need to build a logic.

CHAPTER 8

Diversity and Prediction

THE CROWD OF MODELS

Prediction is very hard, especially about the future.
—YOGI BERRA

IN this chapter, we will apply the predictive model framework to explain the wisdom of crowds. The analysis culminates in two theorems: *The Diversity Prediction Theorem* and *The Crowds Beat Averages Law*. The first states that a crowd's collective accuracy equals the average individual accuracy minus their collective predictive diversity.[1] So for predictive tasks, the answer to the question, "how much does diversity matter?" is "just as much as ability." No less. No more. The second states that the accuracy of the crowd's prediction cannot be worse than the average accuracy of its members. Thus, the crowd necessarily predicts more accurately than its average member. So, groups are, on average, above average. Furthermore, the amount by which the crowd outpredicts its average member increases as the crowd becomes more diverse.

In this chapter, we also see how crowds of people using diverse interpretations can predict more accurately than models based on independent signals would suggest. Though convenient, an assumption of independence may understate the predictive ability of small crowds. We also see that it overstates the ability of large crowds. In addition to looking at crowds alone, we'll compare the performance of crowds to that of experts. We will learn conditions under which we would expect the crowd to predict more accurately and conditions under which we would not. We even consider crowds of experts—what we call the *crowd of models*. These crowds may predict best of all. Finally, we show how incentives can improve the accuracy of collective predictions, thus making the case for information markets.

We will restrict our discussion in this chapter to crowds of people, though we could also include examples of other species— ants, crows, and bison—as well as examples of machines and algorithms. The bison example provides a hint of how other species exploit diversity. Bison take different routes across a mountain range. Each bison leaves a trail. Two trails, in fact. A continuous foot trail and a discrete trail that we ignore. More heavily traveled routes become more beaten down and encode the collective wisdom of the bison. The collective trails over time become efficient.[2] Norman Johnson has constructed models that demonstrate this phenomenon.

Covering this substantial terrain requires moving back and forth between several types of models. This may prove challenging for many readers. The analysis includes quite a few mathematical calculations. Though no one calculation takes much effort (the hardest require squaring the difference of two numbers), we make a lot of them. The payoff at the end proves worth this effort. We get the theorems. These theorems are not political statements, but mathematical truths. To understand those theorems we must roll up our sleeves and work through a few simple formulas.

Before we begin, keep in mind that we will implicitly limit attention to challenging predictive tasks and intelligent predictors. Any easy predictive task (which will be warmer on January 8, 2006, at noon: International Falls, Minnesota, or San Diego, California?) requires neither a crowd nor an expert. Similarly, if the individual predictors do not know much of anything, the crowd may not predict well. If we ask ten thousand first graders to guess the weight of a fully loaded Boeing 747 (about forty tons), we should expect their average guess to be well off the mark. Some might guess as low as one hundred pounds. Some might guess as

TABLE 8.1:
The screenplay attribute to movie
quality mapping

	Violence			
Sex	*None*	*Low*	*Mod.*	*High*
None	B	B	G	B
Low	B	B	B	G
Mod.	G	B	G	G
High	B	G	G	G

high as a billion billion tons. You cannot make a silk purse out of a crowd of sows' ears.

THE WISE CROWD FROM SCREENING SUCCESS

To lay a foundation for the remainder of the chapter, let's return to Screening Success (discussed in chapter 4) and consider Ray, Marilyn, and Deborah as a crowd. We find this crowd to be wise indeed. In a few pages, we will show why crowds must be wiser than the people in them and why this particular crowd does so well. For the moment though, let's revel in the mystery of their wisdom.

Recall that the task in Screening Success was to predict whether a given screenplay would produce a profitable movie. Ray, one of our predictors, considered the amount of sexual content. Another predictor, Marilyn, considered the level of violence. These were their interpretations of the screenplays. Our third predictor, Deborah, used a much more complicated interpretation that relied on balancing the amount of sexual content and violence. We'll revisit her predictive model as well as Ray and Marilyn's in the next paragraph. Table 8.1 presents the mapping from screenplay attributes to whether the movie would be profitable (i.e., good, denoted by *G*) or unprofitable (i.e., bad, denoted by *B*).

Remember that Ray predicts that those screenplays with moderate or high levels of sexual content will be good and that others

TABLE 8.2:
Ray's predictive model

| | Violence | | | |
Sex	None	Low	Mod.	High
None	B	B	B	B
Low	B	B	B	B
Mod.	G	G	G	G
High	G	G	G	G

TABLE 8.3:
Marilyn's predictive model

| | Violence | | | |
Sex	None	Low	Mod.	High
None	B	B	G	G
Low	B	B	G	G
Mod.	B	B	G	G
High	B	B	G	G

TABLE 8.4:
Deborah's predictive model

| | Violence | | | |
Sex	None	Low	Mod.	High
None	B	G	G	B
Low	G	B	B	G
Mod.	G	B	B	G
High	B	G	G	B

will be bad; Marilyn predicts that those screenplays with moderate or high levels of violence will be good; and Deborah predicts that those screenplays that are balanced will be good. Their predictive models can be written in tabular form as shown in tables 8.2, 8.3, and 8.4.

TABLE 8.5:
Ray and Marilyn's agreement set

Sex	Violence			
	None	Low	Mod.	High
None	B	B		
Low	B	B		
Mod.			G	G
High			G	G

To capture how these three predict as a crowd making a prediction, we assume that they vote based on their predictions. As each person predicts either a good or a bad outcome, we cannot have any ties. If Ray and Marilyn agree that a screenplay is either good or bad, they leave Deborah with no say in the matter. Given our assumptions, Ray and Marilyn make the same predictions on screenplays that have relatively low sexual content and violence (these fall in the four upper left boxes) and on screenplays that have relatively high sexual content and violence (these fall in the four lower right boxes). Call this their *agreement set* (see table 8.5). Extra terminology helps us keep track of what's what.

Inside their agreement set, Ray and Marilyn have total say. Deborah is irrelevant. Outside of this agreement set, Deborah becomes all-powerful. Political scientists call her pivotal—her prediction determines the crowd's prediction. Looking at table 8.5, we see that Ray and Marilyn make different predictions for eight of the boxes—the boxes not in their agreement set. Filling in Deborah's predictions in those eight cases gives the predictions from the crowd shown in table 8.6.

This table should look familiar. It is the original table that maps from attributes to outcomes. The crowd predicts accurately every time. Amazing? Yes. But given that my parents are named Ray and Marilyn and my older sister is named Deb, shouldn't we have expected something like this? Clearly this example was carefully crafted, but for a purpose. The example shows how diverse predictive models can aggregate in ways far more subtle

TABLE 8.6:
The crowd's predictions

Sex	Violence			
	None	Low	Mod.	High
None	B	B	G	B
Low	B	B	B	G
Mod.	G	B	G	G
High	B	G	G	G

and sublime than the putting together of distinct pieces described by Aristotle. The Law of Large Numbers cannot get you to 100 percent, and neither can canceling errors.

To make sense of how the crowd can be 100 percent accurate, we need to compare this example to the sweater example in the Gravity of Truth Model (from chapter 7). In both examples, each individual predicts correctly three-fourths of the time. However, in the sweater example, the crowd predicted correctly only 84 percent of the time. What accounts for this difference? In the sweater example, we assumed independent individual signals: One person's reaction to the wool was independent of another's. We made no such assumption in Screening Success. The predictions in Screening Success must not be independent. They must be better than independent somehow. And they are. In those cases that Ray predicts incorrectly, Marilyn predicts correctly more than three-fourths of the time. Thus, she purposefully, as opposed to randomly, cancels out his errors. (That's true of my parents as well.) This reduces the probability that the crowd makes an error. Statisticians call this *negative correlation*. As will become clear, the wisdom of crows resides partly in the presence of negative correlation or the lack of positive correlation.

To show negative correlation mathematically, we need that when Ray predicts correctly, Marilyn is *less* likely to predict correctly, as this implies that when Ray predicts incorrectly, Marilyn is more likely to predict correctly. So she cancels out his mistakes. To do this, let's first write down the screenplays that

TABLE 8.7:
Correct predictions by Ray

	Violence			
Sex	None	Low	Mod.	High
None	B	B		B
Low	B	B	B	
Mod.	G		G	G
High		G	G	G

Ray predicts correctly, and then highlight those screenplays among them that Marilyn also predicts correctly (see table 8.7).

The table shows that Ray predicts correctly in twelve of sixteen cases. Marilyn predicts correctly in just eight of those twelve cases, or $\frac{2}{3}$ of the time. If her probability of predicting correctly had been independent of Ray's probability, then she would predict correctly $\frac{3}{4}$ of the time, or in nine of the cases. Eight is less than nine; therefore Marilyn predicts correctly less often than would be the case if her predictions were independent of Ray's. Thus, put in the formal language of statistics: the correctness of their predictions is negatively correlated.[3]

As I have already admitted, this example is contrived. However, it reveals a deeper truth. Ray and Marilyn's negatively correlated predictions provide the key insight. Notice that they look at different attributes of the same perspective. Earlier, we called these *projection interpretations*. Ray and Marilyn's projection interpretations do not contain any of the same attributes, so let's get precise and call them *nonoverlapping projection interpretations*.[4] In yes-or-no, good-or-bad predictive tasks such as the one considered here, nonoverlapping projection interpretations *always* create negatively correlated predictions.[5]

The Projection Property: *If two people base their predictive models on different variables from the same perspective (formally, if they use nonoverlapping projection interpretations) then the correctness of their predictions is negatively correlated for binary predictions.*

Understanding the Projection Property requires careful thought. It says that if two people look at different attributes of the same perspective (that is, different dimensions), and if the task is to predict success or failure, or any other binary outcome such as good or bad, or yes or no, then when one person is correct, the other person is less likely to be correct. Thus, they're better at collectively predicting than they'd be if they got independent signals.

At first, this result might seem hard to believe, or at least unintuitive. Yet it has a simple explanation that goes as follows: We know that it must be possible for two people to make predictions so that when one is right, the other is more likely to be wrong. The obvious way to do this would be to make diverse predictions. How better to make diverse predictions than to look at different attributes?

The projection property implies that crowds containing people who look at diverse attributes will be wise. Unfortunately, this insight cannot be leveraged as much as we might hope. The dimensionality of the perspective defines the number of nonoverlapping projection interpretations. A perspective that creates a five-dimensional representation of an event or situation can support at most five nonoverlapping projection interpretations. A perspective that creates ten dimensions can support at most ten nonoverlapping projection interpretations.

To avoid positive correlation as the number of people in the crowd becomes larger, people must either use cluster interpretations or they must base their interpretations on different perspectives. Deborah's interpretation is an example of the former. Though based on the same perspective, it is not a projection interpretation. Many papers, in fact, even seminal papers in political science and economics, assume infinite numbers of people getting independent signals (believe it or not, using infinity makes the math easier). If these signals come from predictive models, that assumption just doesn't have logical foundations. Constructing cluster interpretations that lead to independent signals is possible, but such examples are contrived. It's convenient, but so would be self-toasting bread. In writing good models, we shouldn't confuse

Table 8.8:
Predictions of the Rudy G. Bee

	Micheala	Juliana	Average	Outcome
Maggie	6	10	8	6
Cole	3	7	5	5
Brody	5	1	3	1

convenient assumptions with good ones. By assuming independent signals, these scholars assume more diversity than may exist.[6]

THE DIVERSITY PREDICTION THEOREM

Now that we've worked through an example, we're ready to turn to the more general theorems that reveal the importance of diverse predictive models among the members of a crowd. Versions of these theorems can be found in computer science, statistics, and econometrics.[7] To describe these theorems, we'll need two measures. The first captures how much a collection of predictive models differs. The other captures how accurate the models are. Both are based on the same accuracy measure: *squared errors*. In statistics, errors are squared so that negative errors and positive errors do not cancel one another out. If errors were added, a person who was equally likely to overestimate or underestimate an amount on average would make no errors $(-5 + 5 = 0)$. If we first square the errors, then the negative and positive errors do not cancel $((-5)^2 + 5^2 = 25 + 25 = 50)$. To build the logic of the theorem, we first construct an example. Suppose that Micheala and Juliana have developed models to predict where three students—Maggie, Cole, and Brody—will place in an upcoming spelling bee at Rudy Giuliani Elementary. Table 8.8 shows their individual predictions, their average prediction, and the actual outcome from the bee.

We first compute the squared errors of Micheala and Juliana's predictions. Michaela picks Maggie to take sixth place and she takes sixth, an error of zero. She picks Cole to take third and he takes fifth, an error of two. And she picks Brody to take fifth, but he takes first place, an error of four. Squaring these three errors gives zero, four, and sixteen. The sum of the her errors equals twenty.

Micheala's Individual Error: $(6 - 6)^2 + (3 - 5)^2 + (5 - 1)^2 =$
$0 + 4 + 16 = 20$

We next make the same calculation for Juliana. She misses Maggie's placement by four, she misses Cole's by two, and gets Brody's place exactly right. Squaring these errors gives sixteen, four, and zero, for a total squared error of twenty.

Juliana's Individual Error: $(10 - 6)^2 + (7 - 5)^2 + (1 - 1)^2 =$
$16 + 4 + 0 = 20$

The sum of each of their squared errors equals twenty, so their average sum of squared errors also equals twenty. We call this the *average individual error*. Here that's easy because their errors are the same.

Average Individual Error: *Average of the individual squared errors*

$$\frac{20 + 20}{2} = 20$$

We next compute the error of their *collective prediction:* the average of their individual predictions. They collectively predict that Maggie will take eighth place. She takes sixth, for an error of two. Their collective prediction for Cole, fifth place, is correct, and their prediction for Brody is off by two. Squaring these errors gives four, zero, and four, for a total of eight. We call this their *collective error.*

Collective Error: *Squared error of the collective prediction*

$$(8 - 6)^2 + (5 - 5)^2 + (3 - 1)^2 = 4 + 0 + 4 = 8$$

Notice that their collective prediction is more accurate than either of their individual predictions. The explanation for this can be found in the diversity of their predictions. When one of them predicts too high, the other predicts too low and their mistakes, while not canceling entirely, become less severe. To make this relationship between the diversity of their predictions and the accuracy of their collective prediction more formal, we calculate how much their predictions differ. We do this by calculating Juliana's squared distance from their collective prediction and Micheala's squared distance from their collective prediction. We then average these two numbers. Statisticians call this the *variance* of their predictions. We will call it the *prediction diversity*.

We first compute Micheala's squared distance from the collective prediction. The collective prediction for Maggie is eighth place. Micheala predicts sixth place for a difference of two. The collective prediction for Cole is fifth place, and she predicts third place for a difference of two. Finally, the collective prediction for Brody is third place, and she predicts fifth, a difference also equal to two. The squares of these differences are four, four, and four, which sum to twelve.

Micheala's Squared Distance from the Average:
$$(6 - 8)^2 + (3 - 5)^2 + (5 - 3)^2 = 4 + 4 + 4 = 12$$

As there are only two predictors in this example, Juliana's distance from the average in each case must be the same as Michaela's. That calculation can be made as follows:

Juliana's Squared Distance from the Average:
$$(10 - 8)^2 + (7 - 5)^2 + (1 - 3)^2 = 4 + 4 + 4 = 12$$

The *prediction diversity* equals the average of these two distances; in this case, it equals twelve.

Prediction Diversity: *Average squared distance from the individual predictions to the collective prediction.*

$$\frac{12 + 12}{2} = 12$$

Notice the relationship between the collective error (8), the average individual error (20), and the prediction diversity (12): *Collective error equals average error minus diversity.* This equality is not an artifact of our example. It is always true. And, even better, it holds for any number of predictors, not just two predictors as in our example. Thus, we call this the *Diversity Prediction Theorem*.

The Diversity Prediction Theorem: *Given a crowd of predictive models*

$$Collective\ Error = Average\ Individual\ Error$$
$$-Prediction\ Diversity$$

We have to be careful not to over- or understate what this theorem means. It doesn't say that you don't want all accurate people. If individual people predict perfectly, they cannot be diverse. (If average individual error equals zero, then diversity must also equal zero.) Notice also that prediction diversity equals the *average* squared distance from the collective prediction, so adding someone who predicts differently need not increase overall prediction diversity. Prediction diversity increases only if the additional person's predictions differ by more, on average, than those of other people. This implies a limit to the amount of predictive diversity we can have. If a collection of people has an average individual error of one thousand, then their prediction diversity cannot exceed one thousand. Any more diversity and the collective error would become negative, an impossibility.

Fine, we've got some caveats. But they just reveal some of the theorem's subtleties. What's important is that we keep in mind the core insight: individual ability (the first term on the right-hand side) and collective diversity (the second term) contribute *equally* to collective predictive ability. *Being different is as important as being good.* Increasing prediction diversity by a unit results in the same reduction in collective error as does increasing average ability by a unit.

Contrasting the Diversity Trumps Ability Theorem with the Diversity Prediction Theorem reveals important differences. In making a prediction, a group of randomly selected predictors might or might not predict more accurately than a group of the best predictors. Randomly selected predictors will be more diverse, to be sure, but they will also be less accurate. The two effects work in opposite directions. So, we cannot expect that a random intelligent group will predict more accurately than the group of the best. Yet, that stronger claim holds in the problem-solving context. The reason why is that poor performers fail to drag down problem-solving teams. If we bring Larry, a social scientist, into our cheese-making business, his lack of relevant tools won't hurt our cheese making. We just ignore him. He may cause delay or frustration, but if he has only bad ideas—peppermint cheese—those ideas won't be adopted. However, if we're predicting how much cheese to make, we won't know that he doesn't know and his prediction gets averaged along with everyone else's. And he could make the crowd less wise.

An implication of the theorem is that a diverse crowd always predicts more accurately than the average of the individuals. This runs counter to our intuition. We can call this the Crowd Beats the Average Law.

The Crowd Beats the Average Law: *Given any collection of diverse predictive models, the collective prediction is more accurate than the average individual predictions*

Collective Prediction Error < Average Individual Error

The Crowd Beats the Average Law follows from the Diversity Prediction Theorem. The Diversity Prediction Theorem says that collective error = average individual error − prediction diversity. Prediction diversity has to be positive if the predictions differ. Therefore, the collective error must be larger than the average individual error. There's no deep math going on. But the insight is powerful nonetheless.

We now have a logic for the wisdom of crowds. In an ideal world, these formal claims would replace pithy statements such as "two heads are better than one," but they may not be catchy enough. We can try though. We might replace the Diversity Prediction Theorem with "the wisdom of a crowd is equal parts ability and diversity" and the Crowd Beats the Average Law with "the crowd predicts better than the people in it." Not memorable, but accurate.

A Crowd of Draft Experts

To cement our understanding of the logic, let's consider some real data. Die-hard theorists prefer constructed examples because they are neater and cleaner. But sometimes even a theorist cannot help but peek out the window. So if we're going to look at data, we might as well look at something important: football draft selections. Table 8.9 shows predictions for the top dozen picks in the 2005 NFL draft from seven prognosticators. The players are listed in the order that they were selected. Each predictor provides a ranking of the draftees. We use the NFL draft because it has clean, integer-valued data, because it can be seen as a ramped-up version of our earlier example that involved Juliana and Michaela, and because these experts' predictions came from detailed analyses. They don't call them draft experts for nothing. These people, er men, devote long days and nights evaluating team needs, player skills, and a host of other factors.

If we look at their predictions, we see that they differ in their accuracy. The table reveals that some do far better than others. The last column, by the way, shows the crowd's prediction.[8] Here the crowd is just the collection of all seven predictors.

These data show the Crowd Beats the Average Law in full force. The average of the individual errors equals 137.3. The collective error, shown in the last column, equals about one-fourth of that, 34.4. In this example, the crowd predicts more accurately even than its most accurate member even though the Crowd Beats the Average Law makes no such claim.[9] The example also shows the power of diversity. These predictors are so diverse that they collectively predict well.

Even more amazing, note that this comparison between the crowd and its most accurate member is unfair. In selecting the best person after the fact, we stack the deck against the crowd. No one, other than perhaps Clark Judge himself, would have predicted Judge (despite his name) to be more accurate than the others. In the future, Judge may not be the best predictor. To take

TABLE 8.9:
Experts' predictions of 2005 NFL draft

Player	Predictor							
	Wright	Alder	Fanball	SNews	Zimm	Prisco	Judge	Crowd
Alex Smith	1	1	1	1	1	1	1	1.0
Ronnie Brown	2	2	4	2	2	5	2	2.7
Braylon Edwards	3	3	2	7	3	2	3	3.3
Cedric Benson	4	4	13	4	8	4	8	5.9
Carnell Williams	8	5	5	5	4	13	4	6.4
Adam Jones	16	9	6	8	6	6	9	8.1
Troy Williamson	13	14	12	12	13	7	7	9.7
Antrell Rolle	6	6	8	10	9	8	6	7.9
Carlos Rodgers	9	8	9	9	16	9	9	9.9
Mike Williams	7	7	7	6	7	12	12	8.0
Demarcus Ware	11	15	14	24	11	11	13	13.9
Shawn Merriman	12	11	3	11	12	10	11	10.1
Error^2	158	89	210	235	112	82	75	34.4

another example with higher stakes, successful investment funds differ from year to year. If at the beginning of the year, we could pick the fund that would do best at the year's end, investing would be fun and easy. But we cannot, so we diversify. By going with the crowd, we take on less risk. We should go with the expert only if we know that person to be far more accurate than the others and the others to make similar predictions.

Points and Ranges

Up until now, we have focused on the difference between the predictions and the outcomes. In many instances, we may want to know best- and worst-case scenarios. We want to know the range of possibilities. In building a stock portfolio, an investor may care about the range of possible prices. How high might the stock price go? How low might it go? In predicting a potential political uprising, a policy analyst may care less about having an accurate point prediction than about knowing worst- and

TABLE 8.10:
Range of predictions of 2005 NFL draft

Player	Actual	Low	High
Alex Smith	1	1	2
Ronnie Brown	2	2	5
Braylon Edwards	3	2	7
Cedric Benson	4	4	13
Carnell Williams	5	4	13
Adam Jones	6	9	16
Troy Williamson	7	7	14
Antrell Rolle	8	6	9
Carlos Rodgers	9	8	21
Mike Williams	10	6	12
Demarcus Ware	11	11	15
Shawn Merriman	12	3	13

best-case scenarios. We can look at the best and worst predictions and the actual outcomes (see table 8.10). In every case, the outcome falls within the range of predictions.

Amazing? No, not given the diversity of the predictions.

THE MADNESS OF CROWDS

Up to now, we have not discussed communication among crowd members. If people can share predictions, then they might become less diverse. To paraphrase Socrates, it's much easier to go with the flow, and people often change their predictions to match those of others. And, rather than seeing wisdom emerge, we might see madness—we might see speculators buying tulips at crazy prices. We can use the Diversity Prediction Theorem to explain the madness of crowds. When we think of a crowd being mad, we think of a collection of people all taking an action that in retrospect doesn't make sense. The madness of crowds led people to drink the green Kool Aid. The madness of crowds leads people to burn cars and sometimes even houses after sporting events. The madness of crowds explains stock market bubbles and stock market crashes.[10]

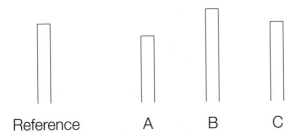

Figure 8.1 Asch's Lines

For a crowd to be mad, its members must systematically make the same bad decision. If people make these decisions in the heat of the moment—such as when burning a couch—we can chalk it up to the human tendency to join in, a topic we will return to in the epilogue. If though, people have time to construct what they believe to be reasonable predictive models, then we can often blame a lack of diversity. The Diversity Prediction Theorem implies that a crowd can make egregious errors only if the crowd members lack both accuracy and diversity.

Thus, the theorem shows the double-edged sword of deliberation. If people communicate with one another, if they share information and criticize one another's models, they can increase the accuracy of their models. However, they can also reduce their diversity. And it has been shown time and again that people often choose to abandon accurate predictive models in favor of inaccurate models. In a classic experiment, Solomon Asch asked people to compare the lengths of several lines. Each was given pictures with a reference line and three other lines marked A, B, and C.[11] Figure 8.1 provides an approximation of Asch's pictures.

Subjects were assembled together in a room and sequentially asked which lines were longer than the reference line, which lines were the same length as the reference line, and so on. The first subjects to answer were planted by Asch. They purposefully gave wrong answers. Asch found that others follow the majority—giving wrong answers—about one-third of the time. Given that people abandon their stated beliefs on the lengths of lines, we can hardly be surprised that they would abandon their beliefs in their predictions about the stock market, housing prices, or winning number combinations in the lottery.

More than just conformity leads to the madness of crowds. Often, in a group setting, people move too far in the direction of the majority opinion. So, if on average people think that prices are going to rise, then the group may work itself into a frenzy and begin to believe that because most people think prices are going up, prices are going to rise substantially.

DIVERSITY'S FREE LUNCH

To make the next step in our analysis of why and how crowds can be wise, we can build from an earlier insight that diverse interpretations lead to diverse predictive models. In Screening Success we saw how diverse interpretations lead to negatively correlated predictions using the Projection Property. This told us how crowds can sometimes be far wiser than we might expect.

To make this connection more explicit, we next analyze a class of examples in which people use diverse projection interpretations. In these examples, all of the interpretations rely on a common perspective. We then analyze an example in which the crowd members base their interpretations on different perspectives. We see that, in some cases, interpretations based on diverse perspectives can make a predictive task easier than it would be using predictive models that rely on interpretations based on either perspective alone. We have some magic after all. That magic results from diverse perspectives.

Different Parts of the Same Vision

If asked to make an important prediction such as who will win an election, whether an economy will grow, or the likelihood of armed conflict, we have to include many variables or attributes to make an accurate prediction. We've got to keep lots of variables in our heads. We might try a single-variable model, but they rarely work. A while back Thomas Friedman noticed that no two countries with McDonald's restaurants had ever gone to war. The Golden Arches Theory held up until 1999, when NATO began dropping bombs on Serbia.[12] Basing foreign policy on the location of fast-food restaurants wouldn't be a bright idea.

However, people just aren't that willing to spend hours developing sophisticated models with lots of variables. We're more likely to use simple, one- or two-variable models. We might think, for instance, that the economy improved and so the incumbent president is likely to be reelected. Or we might think that the incumbent president failed to pass a major policy initiative and so he's likely to lose. Each of these models makes sense. Each looks at only a single variable.

To see how these simple models aggregate to be collectively accurate, or at least reasonably so, imagine that we want to predict the annual sales for a hot dog stand on the Jersey shore. Assume for the moment that sales can be written as a linear function of a set of ten attributes (in statistics these would be called variables). These attributes include things such as the average summer temperature, the amount of rainfall, the price of gas, the level of construction on the roads, and possibly even the price of beef. (We're assuming the hot dogs contain beef—a leap of faith in some cases.)

Next, let's gather a crowd of people and ask each person in it to predict the change in sales from the previous summer. Each member of our crowd would probably consider some subset of these attributes in making her prediction. Let's suppose that these crowd members randomly choose attributes. In this way, the crowd may or may not include all N attributes.[13] For convenience, let's assume each person in the crowd uses a linear regression model. A linear regression model predicts an outcome as a constant added to each relevant variable multiplied by a coefficient. A regression model that predicts sales based on temperature might look as follows:

$$Sales = 0.3 + 1.2 \; temperature$$

In this example, sales will be a linear function of these ten attributes. To keep the model as simple as possible, we will assume that the coefficient of each of these variables equals one. We further assume that each attribute takes a value between minus one and one making expected change in sales equal to zero. If we denote the attributes by a_1 to a_{10}, then we get the following formula for the change in total sales:

$$S = a_1 + a_2 + \cdots a_{10}$$

We next assume that each person in the crowd makes a prediction based on the three attributes that she chooses randomly. When running a regression with sparse data, coefficient estimates are approximations. Therefore, a crowd member who looks at attributes one, four, and eight may have the following model:

Individual i's Predictive Model: $S^i = 1.1a_1 + 1.08a_4 + .991a_8$

By summing up the predictions of a crowd of models and averaging their predictions, we get that the crowd's predictive model looks something like the following:

The Crowd's Predictive Model: $S^C = .32a_1 + .42a_2 + .28a_3 +$ $.37a_4 + .36a_5 + .35a_6 + .33a_7 + .38a_8 + .29a_9 + .34a_{10}$

The crowd's predictive model includes all of the attributes, but its coefficients are far from accurate. This lack of accuracy is not just due to the individuals' errors in approximation, though these exist. The larger cause is that, on average, only 30 percent of the crowd members consider each variable. Therefore, when the predictions are averaged, even if the estimates of the coefficients by each crowd member were correct, the collective prediction understates the effects of each attribute. The averaging dampens each person's predictive model.

This example reveals two features of predictions by diverse crowds: the *Coverage Property* and the *Crude Approximation Property*.

The Coverage Property: *A crowd's predictive model includes the effects of any attribute or combination of attributes included by any member of the crowd's predictive model.*

The Crude Approximation Property: *A crowd's predictive model crudely approximates the effect of any attribute or combination of attributes on outcomes.*

These two properties combine to ensure that the crowd will make good predictions on average, but indicate that expecting perfect accuracy may be asking too much. Because the crowd includes lots of variables, it won't be caught by surprise if some subset of the variables takes on unexpected values. So, even though the crowd's coefficients only approximate the actual values, most of the time the crowd won't make enormous mistakes. In our hot dog model, it might be that only a couple of people take road construction into account. If major construction takes place, those people will make low estimates and they'll dampen the crowd's estimate, making it more accurate.

This formal investigation lacks the sexiness of real-world examples of crowds that predict the weight of a steer within a pound or the number of jellybeans in a jar within one or two. But we should not expect such outcomes every time. Our analysis suggests that diverse crowds predict pretty well, not that they will be freakishly accurate in all cases. Sometimes though, the crowd will get lucky. They'll be incredibly accurate. Let's see how that can happen. Let's put some magic back in the bottle before this all becomes too clinical and statistical.

Magic in the Bottle

Our example of the hot dog stand limited the amount of diversity by assuming that everyone chose from the same set of variables. In our formal language, they all used interpretations derived from the same perspective. Yet we have no reason to think that people would do this in all cases. And if people don't, then we can have some magic. In our next example, both the Coverage Property and the Crude Approximation Property hold, but in more interesting ways.

TABLE 8.11:
Energy as a function of
compounds present

Compounds Present {A,B,C}	Energy Produced
{0,0,0}	0
{0,0,1}	1
{0,1,0}	1
{0,1,1}	0
{1,0,0}	2
{1,0,1}	1
{1,1,0}	1
{1,1,1}	2

We'll rely on a rather complicated function that gives the energy produced by a chemical reaction based on the presence or absence of three compounds. Each of these three chemical compounds, A, B, and C, can be assigned a value of one if it is present and zero if it is not present. The function mapping compounds to outcomes looks as follows:

Energy Produced: $E = 2A + B + C - 2AB - 2AC - BC - 6ABC$

It's functions like this that give math a bad reputation. But just as beauty is in the eye of the beholder, so is ugliness. So we must hang in there; we'll turn this into a swan in just a page. To apply this ugly-looking function, we just plug in the values of A, B, and C. Fortunately, these variables take only two values, 0 and 1. So, if $A = 0$, $B = 1$, and $C = 1$, the value of the function equals $B + C - BC$, which equals 1 $(1 + 1 - 1)$.

We consider here a crowd of two children, Orrie and Cooper, with deep interests in scientific phenomena. We assume that they have no idea how complicated this function is. They're just trying to predict outcomes. Orrie's predictive model considers only the presence of the first compound A. To determine his prediction of total energy, we need first to determine total energy for each combination of compounds (see table 8.11).

TABLE 8.12:
Energy versus predicted energy

Compounds Present {A,B,C}	Process Outcome	Crowd's Prediction
{0,0,0}	0	0.5
{0,0,1}	1	1
{0,1,0}	1	1
{0,1,1}	0	0.5
{1,0,0}	2	1.5
{1,0,1}	1	1
{1,1,0}	1	1
{1,1,1}	2	1.5

In the cases, where A is present, the average energy produced equals 1.5. In the cases in which A is not present, the average energy produced equals 0.5. Orrie's predictive model, therefore, would be as follows:

Orrie's Predictive Model: $E^O = 0.5 + A$

This looks nothing like the original function. But then again, Orrie's just a kid.

The second member of the crowd, Cooper, relies on a different perspective. He's known for his unique way of looking at things. Rather than consider the chemical compounds alone, he looks at the combinations of compounds present. He then uses an interpretation that considers only whether the number of compounds included is even or odd. Based on this construction, his predictive model looks as follows:

Cooper's Predictive Model: $E^C = 0.5$ *if* $A + B + C$ *is even and* $E^C = 1.5$ *otherwise*

Again, this appears to have no resemblance to the ugly formula they're trying to predict. Orrie and Cooper's joint prediction equals the average of their two predictions. Our expectations here should be pretty low. Table 8.12 shows their average prediction and the actual energy level for each combination of compounds.

Incredibly, Orrie and Cooper predict four of the eight cases perfectly and miss by only one-half on the other four. This occurs despite the simplicity of their models and the complicated underlying function that they are trying to predict. How does this happen? Here the crowd seems far wiser than either member.

Their amazing accuracy can be explained by the diversity of their perspectives. Orrie's considers the compounds present. Cooper's considers combinations of compounds.[14] We see the magic of diverse perspectives when we translate Cooper's predictive model into Orrie's A, B, C perspective. It looks like a swan.

Cooper's Predictive Model: $E^C = 1.5A + 1.5B + 1.5C - 2.5AB - 2.5BC - 2.5AC + 4.5ABC$

Checking this takes a little effort, but any odd number of compounds gives a value of 1.5 and any even number gives a value of 0.5. Despite how complicated this formula looks, Cooper is not doing anything sophisticated. He's just counting the number of compounds and determining whether it is even or odd. Yet when written in the other perspective, his model appears complicated and it eerily approximates the true function. If we average this with Orrie's predictive model, we get the Crowd's Predictive Model:

Crowd's Predictive Model: $E = 0.25 + 1.25A + .75B + .75C - 1.25AB - 1.25BC - 1.25AC + 2.25ABC$

As in our example of hot dog sales on the Jersey shore, here again, the coefficients are crude approximations of the real values. But these crude approximations allow the crowd to predict with amazing accuracy.[15]

What we have just seen is that the crowd's predictive model can be complicated if it combines two simple predictive models based on diverse perspectives. This reinforces a point that we made in the chapter on perspectives. What is easy to represent (i.e., linear) in one perspective may be complicated to write in another perspective. So, crowds of unsophisticated people might be able to predict a complicated function if they use interpretations based on diverse perspectives.

We will next see that predictive models based on clumping interpretations can play a similar role. These also can capture interactions between variables. Recall Deborah's predictive model from Screening Success. To turn the example from Screening Success into a mathematical function, we need only represent the sex and violence attributes that range from none to high with the numbers 0 to 3. We then let S and V denote these values for a particular screenplay. If we assign an outcome value of 1 to a profitable screenplay and a value of 0 to an unprofitable one, then (with quite a bit of effort) we can write Deborah's predictive model as follows:[16]

Deborah's Predictive Model: $V = \frac{1}{2}(3S^2V + 3SV^2 - S^2V^2 - 9SV - S^2 - V^2 + 3S + 3V)$

This equation is hideous. And that's the point. Predictive models based on clumping interpretations include interaction terms. By definition, clumping combines variables. For this reason, good clumping interpretations may be difficult to explain. Emerson was right: to be different often is to be misunderstood.

This potential for diverse perspectives (such as Cooper's) and clumping interpretations (such as Deborah's) to include interactive effects suggests a nearly magical property of diverse predictors: simple, diverse models can be sophisticated. To contrast this with the No Free Lunch Theorem, which states that no heuristic is better than any other across all problems, let's call this the *Crowd's Possibly Free Lunch Theorem*.

The Crowd's Possibly Free Lunch Theorem: *Clumping interpretations and interpretations based on diverse perspectives result in predictive models that include interactive effects. A crowd of these predictive models can sometimes predict a complicated function.*

We will call this the possibly free lunch because we have no guarantee that these interaction terms will be the appropriate ones, and, by the crude approximation property, we know that the crowd's model's coefficients of these interaction terms err as well. Even so, there remains the possibility, as was true in the last example and in Screening Success, that the sublime is possible.

Groups versus Experts

We have seen how crowds can make accurate predictions, but often the relevant comparison is between a crowd and an expert. We talk about this more later in the book. Who should decide—a diverse group or a lone expert? Should Warner Brothers hire someone to predict DVD sales of a movie or should they just have forty people in the firm make off-the-cuff predictions? Should the government hire an office of people to predict the budget surplus or deficit or should they just create a prediction market on the Web?

Our analysis up to now has given us some insight into the trade-off between the crowd and the expert. The crowd's predictive model will include lots of attributes and possibly even interactions among these attributes, but the coefficients that it places on them will be crude. Relatively speaking, the expert's model will be more elaborate than any member of the crowd's individual model but starker than the crowd's collective model. Though the expert will include fewer variables and fewer interaction terms, we can assume that the expert's estimates of the coefficients will be more accurate.

To deepen our understanding, we begin by investigating when the expert's predictive model is more accurate than the crowd's. This will always be true if the expert's interpretation refines each crowd member's interpretation. When this happens, we say the expert *dominates the crowd*.

An expert **dominates the crowd** *if any set in any member of the crowd's interpretation contains a set in the expert's interpretation.*

This condition implies that the expert's model contains any attribute or interaction among attributes that a member of the crowd includes in his predictive model. Or, in less technical

TABLE 8.13:
Suebee's interpretation and predictions

Set	Suebee One	Suebee Two	Suebee Three	Suebee Four	Suebee Five
Bowlers	A,B,C	D,E,F	G,H,I	J,K,L	M,N,O
Scores	110 120 130	140 150 160	170 180 190	200 210 220	230 240 250
Prediction	120	150	180	210	240

language, the expert parses reality more finely on every attribute than does any member of the crowd.

The next claim states that an expert who dominates the crowd predicts more accurately, on average, than the crowd.

The Dominance of Experts: *The predictive model of an expert who dominates the crowd is more accurate (has a smaller squared error) than the crowd's predictive model.*

The logic of this claim is easy to comprehend. Within any set in her interpretation, the expert minimizes the squared error. The crowd's sets lump together sets of the expert, so the crowd can, on average, do no better than make the same prediction as the expert. Often, the crowd will fail to do that. Thus, the expert must predict more accurately on average.[17]

Now we hit on a subtle point. Even though the dominant expert does better on average, the expert won't be more accurate in every case. Moreover, we can find patterns in those cases when the crowd predicts more accurately.

Let's imagine a bowling tournament with fifteen participants whose last names conveniently begin with the letters *A* through *O*. Each person has an average bowling score somewhere between one hundred ten and two hundred fifty. In this example, the higher the letter that begins the person's name, the higher that person's average. We compare the ability of an expert, Susan, who goes by the funkier name of Suebee, against that of a crowd consisting of a certain Larry, Moe, and Curly. We will set this up so that Suebee dominates this crowd of stooges. Suebee partitions the participants into five sets of size three (see table 8.13).

TABLE 8.14:
Larry's interpretation and predictions

Set	Larry One	Larry Two	Larry Three
Bowlers	A,B,C	D,E,F,G,H,I, J,K,L	M,N,O
Scores	110 120 130	140 150 160 170 180 190 200 210 220	230 240 250
Prediction	120	180	240

TABLE 8.15:
Moe's interpretation and predictions

Set	Moe One	Moe Two	Moe Three
Bowlers	A,B,C,D,E,F	G,H,I	J,K,L,M,N,O
Scores	110 120 130 140 150 160	170 180 190	200 210 220 230 240 250
Prediction	135	180	225

Larry's interpretation creates three sets (see table 8.14). He lumps together Suebee's sets number two, three, and four.

Similarly, Moe lumps together Suebee's sets number one and two, and number four and five. He considers Suebee's set three separately (see table 8.15).

Finally, Curly lumps all five of Suebee's sets into one set. Thus, Curly predicts that everyone will bowl a one hundred and eighty game. One could do worse. At least he's got the average correct.

Notice that each set in Larry's, Moe's, and Curly's interpretations contains a set in Suebee's. Thus, Suebee dominates the stooges, as we had desired. This does not mean that Suebee is always more accurate. Table 8.16 shows the predictions of Suebee and the crowd for each of the fifteen possible bowlers, as well as the more accurate predictor. The horizontal lines delineate the sets in Suebee's interpretation.

Even though Suebee dominates the crowd, she predicts more accurately than the crowd in only ten of the fifteen cases. The crowd predicts better in two of the fifteen cases, and in three of the cases, the stooges and Suebee make equally accurate predictions. Thus, even a dominant expert can be less accurate than a crowd

TABLE 8.16:
Suebee versus Larry, Moe, and Curly

Bowler's Initial	Bowler's Score	Suebee's Prediction	Crowd's Prediction	More Accurate
A	110	120	$\frac{120+135+180}{3} = 145$	Suebee
B	120	120	$\frac{120+135+180}{3} = 145$	Suebee
C	130	120	$\frac{120+135+180}{3} = 145$	Suebee
D	140	150	$\frac{180+135+180}{3} = 165$	Suebee
E	150	150	$\frac{180+135+180}{3} = 165$	Suebee
F	160	150	$\frac{180+135+180}{3} = 165$	Crowd
G	170	180	$\frac{180+180+180}{3} = 180$	Tie
H	180	180	$\frac{180+180+180}{3} = 180$	Tie
I	190	180	$\frac{180+180+180}{3} = 180$	Tie
J	200	210	$\frac{180+225+180}{3} = 195$	Crowd
K	210	210	$\frac{180+225+180}{3} = 195$	Suebee
L	220	210	$\frac{180+225+180}{3} = 195$	Suebee
M	230	240	$\frac{240+225+180}{3} = 215$	Suebee
N	240	240	$\frac{240+225+180}{3} = 215$	Suebee
O	250	240	$\frac{240+225+180}{3} = 215$	Suebee

of stooges. The possibility that a not-so-wise crowd can predict more accurately than a dominant expert should lead us to be suspicious of collections of anecdotes of wise crowds. We can always find cases where crowds did better than experts. The ease with which one can accumulate anecdotes (especially with the Internet) explains why social scientists place such emphasis on systematic evidence.

Let's return to the example. A careful look at the table reveals a pattern to when the stooges predict more accurately than Suebee. The stooges predict more accurately only when the outcome lies between Suebee's prediction and the average outcome. For example, the stooges predict bowler *F*'s score to be 165 when his actual score is 160, whereas Suebee predicts a score of 150. The stooges' prediction lies halfway between the mean score of 180 and Suebee's prediction of 150. This bias toward the mean occurs because of the stooges' crude interpretations.

A Crowd of Projection Interpretations against an Expert

Our analysis of Suebee and the stooges shows how even crowds of moderately accurate models can hold their own against much more sophisticated experts. Clearly though, allowing the expert to dominate the crowd stacks the deck in favor of the expert. So, we now put the crowd on more equal footing with the expert. We do this by extending our previous example of predicting hot dog sales on the Jersey shore, by systematically varying the ability of the expert and crowd members and making some comparisons.

We start by assuming that our expert constructs a predictive model based on E of the ten attributes. The bigger is E, the more sophisticated the expert. If $E = 6$ and if the expert considers the first six attributes, then the expert's predictive model could be as follows:

Expert's Predictive Model: $S = 0.994a_1 + 1.02a_2 + 1.003a_3$
$$+.98a_4 + .992a_5 + 1.04a_6$$

In contrast, we assume that each person in the crowd constructs a predictive model based on C randomly chosen attributes. We make sure that $C < E$; otherwise, the members of our crowd are more expert than the expert. We can then run experiments varying C and E. The bigger C, the wiser the crowd. The bigger C relative to E, the more likely the crowd is more accurate.

Tables 8.17 and 8.18 compare the crowd against an expert. In table 8.17, C varies while E remains fixed at eight. In table 8.18, E varies while C is held constant at four.[18]

These two tables show what we expect. The more sophisticated the people in the crowd, the better the crowd predicts. And the more sophisticated the expert, the better the expert predicts.

TABLE 8.17:
The informed expert versus
crowds of varying ability
($E = 8$)

Sophistication of Crowd	Probability Crowd Wins (percent)
$C = 2$	33
$C = 3$	40
$C = 4$	44
$C = 5$	54
$C = 6$	66

TABLE 8.18:
Crowds versus experts of
varying ability ($C = 4$)

Sophistication of Expert	Probability Crowd Wins (percent)
$E = 5$	71
$E = 6$	65
$E = 7$	46
$E = 8$	44

The Overfitting Paradox

These examples beg an intriguing question: why doesn't the expert just include more attributes in her model? The expert could then have coverage over the attributes. If the expert also made precise calculations of the effects of each attribute and combination of attributes, then she would predict more accurately than any crowd because of the crudeness of the crowd's predictive model.

Would that this were possible. Unfortunately, this logic suffers from three flaws, and as a result, we always need crowds. First, it assumes that the expert writes down her model and performs a careful regression. Otherwise, all of the usual arguments about cognitive constraints and biases might cause her to predict even less accurately if she took in too much information. Second, it fails to take into account the possibly free lunch. It could be that the crowd members' models rely on multiple perspectives and clumping interpretations. If so, the expert may not be able to construct a model as sophisticated as the crowd's. This possibility exists, but it is probably not one on which someone advocating the use of crowds would want to hang his hat. The free lunch is possible, but we have no reason to think it always exists.

Third, and most important, the logic assumes that sufficient data exist and that the expert has access to them. In practice, the expert may not be able to construct a sophisticated model with lots of attributes. Without sufficient data, if the expert considered all of the attributes, she would overfit her predictive model.

Overfitting means that the predictive model uses too many variables relative to the amount of data *and* tries to estimate the coefficients for those attributes precisely. Doing so runs the risk of getting inaccurate estimates. An example helps us see what we mean by overfitting.

Suppose that a consulting company hires an expert, Magda, fresh from a top MBA program. The company assigns her the crucial task of predicting the number of waffles to make for the company breakfast. This company consists of a group of slothful partners who demand that their young associates work long hours and stay in great shape. The true model of how many waffles W that need to be made is as follows:

$$\textit{Waffle Reality:}\quad W = 4P + 2A + F$$

where P denotes the number of partners, A is the number of associates, and F equals the number of waffles dropped on the floor.

Our interest here is in overfitting, so we don't want to give Magda much information on which to base her model. So we assume that Magda has only two data points from which to construct her predictive model: the April breakfast and the

March breakfast. At the April breakfast, ten partners and twenty associates attended and no waffles fell on the floor. If we do the math, we learn that eighty waffles were made.[19] At the March breakfast, fifteen partners and fifteen associates attended and fifteen pancakes fell on the floor. This requires 105 waffles. Let's assume that Magda's predictive model includes the number of partners and the number of associates, but not the possibility of waffles falling to the floor. It therefore takes the following form.

Magda's Predictive Model: $W = \beta P + \alpha A$

With a little effort, we can show that Magda's predictive model can be written $W = 6P + A$.[20] If we plug in the numbers, we see that her model perfectly fits the existing data. However, it fails as a predictive model because she has overfit the data. The true coefficients are not anywhere close to six and one.

Next, we construct a model for a crowd. Our crowd contains only two people: Josh and Anna. Josh's model takes into account the number of partners, and Anna's takes into account the number of associates. Using the same data, we get the following predictive models:[21]

Josh's Predictive Model: $W = 7.4P$

Anna's Predictive Model: $W = 5.3A$

If we average these two models, we get the crowd's predictive model

The Crowd's Predictive Model: $W = 3.7P + 2.65A$

The crowd's predictive model more closely approximates the true function: $4P + 2A + F$. Most of the time it will be far more accurate than Magda's.[22]

What went wrong with Magda's estimate? In including both partners and associates together, Magda underestimates how much the associates eat. This occurs because at the first breakfast, more associates than partners attend, but fewer waffles fall on the floor. Therefore, she cannot but infer that associates do not eat many waffles.

This example speaks to a larger issue. Some econometricians believe that models with more than a few variables are dubious, precisely because of this problem.[23] Models with only a handful of variables suffer no such problems. Yet we can add up those simple models and in doing so create a larger model. That aggregate model will not suffer from overfitting. And it may be a better predictor. However, it will be only a crude approximation.

Why don't experts average over multiple models? One answer is that often the expert's goals go beyond just prediction. They also want to explain the effects of attributes. An expert might want to know the effect of education on income as well as predict income levels as accurately as possible. A second answer is that they do, and they have done so for a long time. The idea of combining forecasts became popular among economists in the 1970s.[24] As computer power has increased, the combining of multiple models has become a well-established approach to making predictions. These *ensemble methods*, as they are called, often prove more accurate than any of the models within them.[25] We know that the average of models must be better than the average model by the Crowd Beats the Average Law, but we cannot be certain it beats the best, though often it does.

Ensemble methods need not assume equal weighting of the models, though equal weighting is a good benchmark. One approach used to improve on equal weighting relies on Bayesian statistics. This approach, Bayesian Model Averaging, averages across possible models but chooses weights based on the likelihood that each model is correct given the data.[26] Unlike with crowds of people, crowds of statistical models can get only so big (at least at the moment). Computation takes too much time if more than twenty or so models are combined. Bayesian model averaging is not the only way to weight the models. Another popular approach, bootstrap aggregation, or bagging, adds weight to models that catch the errors of the other models.[27] As we see next, weighting models by accuracy has advantages, and, as we also see, markets create incentives for this to happen.

INCENTIVES: POLLS VERSUS INFORMATION MARKETS

Polls weight everyone's predictions equally, even the bad ones. A better method would be to weight models according to their accuracy. Information markets can place more weight on some models than on others.[28] In an information market, people bet money. Those people who believe their predictive models to be accurate can place larger bets and those who are unsure can bet less. Incentives drive out the less accurate predictors. Markets also reduce incentives for people to make different predictions. If some other intelligent person thinks that the stock price is below what you think, then you should probably lower your prediction. In fact, if there exists common knowledge of both rationality and optimizing behavior, then all predictions should be the same.[29]

Let's assume that our information market includes many participants and that participants can place bets of different sizes. Let's also assume that the more accurate a person's model, the larger her bet. In other words, people know when their models are accurate. In some contexts, this can be a strong assumption.[30] If the size of the bet and predictive accuracy are positively correlated, information markets would seem to have an advantage over equally weighted voting, but that's not necessarily true. We can see why using the Diversity Prediction Theorem. Under the assumption that more accurate predictions get more weight, the average accuracy of the predictions increases. However, the diversity of the predictions may decrease. The answer as to whether the information market produces a more accurate prediction than a poll (an averaging of all of the model) hinges on whether the increase in average ability outweighs the decrease in diversity.

Think back to our comparison of crowds versus experts. We can consider the expert to be a crowd that places all of its weight on its best predictor. In many instances, the expert fails to predict as accurately as the crowd because loss of diversity more than offsets the gain in accuracy. Placing all weight on a single predictor is an extreme case, as is giving all equal weight. Information markets lie between these two extremes. Does this mean that they predict

TABLE 8.19:
Poll, expert, and information
markets, 2005 NFL draft

	Squared Errors
Best Expert	75
Poll of All Seven	34.4
Poll of Best Five	40.7
Weighted Bets	31.4

better? The answer depends on the weighting. One condition that often ensures the gain in accuracy exceeds the loss in diversity is that highly inaccurate predictors drop out of the information market. We call this the *Fools Rush Out* condition.

Fools Rush Out: *People with highly inaccurate predictive models answer poll questions but do not wager money in information markets.*

If the most inaccurate models leave, the gain in accuracy can be substantial. Though some diversity is lost, that loss will be offset by the accuracy gain.[31] To see this in an example, let's return to our NFL draft data. Let's assume that the two least accurate predictors lack the confidence to enter the information market. They rush out of our information market. We consider two weighting schemes after we have dropped these least accurate predictors. In the *equal weighting* scenario, the remaining predictors all place equal sized bets. In the *weighted bets* scenario, the predictors place bets proportional to their rank. The best predictor gets a weight of five, the second best a weight of four, and so on, with the worst predictor assigned a weight of one. Table 8.19 shows the squared errors from poll (the crowd's prediction), the best individual predictor, Clark Judge (whom we call the expert for the purposes of this analysis), and the information markets' predictions under the two scenarios.

The best expert, Clark Judge, fares worst overall and the weighted bets scenario performs best. Interestingly, the poll of all seven predictors does better than the poll of the best five. This example shows that even though dropping the worst predictors put more weight on more accurate models, it can reduce diversity and collective performance. We have to be careful not to read too much into this one example, but it vividly reinforces that ability and diversity merit equal weight.

The Double Power of Incentives

Information markets create incentives for less confident people to stay out, and for confident people to bet more. Both incentives can improve aggregate predictions as long as they are not too powerful. Otherwise, only the single most accurate predictor bets. Thus, we should include incentives but only in moderation. Tempering incentives may be difficult for some economists. Economists love incentives the way that botanists love plants. (And rightly so.) Incentives are powerful forces. They give information markets huge advantages over polls. They're why free markets work. But we must keep them in check to maintain some diversity. We want to toss out some of the bad models but not all of them.

Incentives also operate in a deeper, more subtle way that we have yet to discuss. In many information markets, payoffs depend not only on being correct but also on the probability that other people are correct. If you are the only person who bets on a particular horse to win a race, your payoff is much larger than if a majority of people bet on that horse. This negative correlation between winnings and the number of people making the winning prediction occurs because the markets have to be balanced: the amount paid out must equal the amount bet. (At the horse races, only a percentage of the money bid is paid back, but the logic still applies.) So if one person predicts correctly, she gets all the money. If a thousand people predict correctly, they must split the money one thousand ways.

This the-larger-the-upset-the-bigger-the payoff feature of many markets creates an incentive to construct diverse predictive models. Suppose that you could construct a model that predicts correctly when most other people are wrong. That model would generate large payoffs on average because when it predicted correctly, the winnings would be split only a few ways. Thus, markets create two incentive effects that polls lack: *an incentive to be correct and an incentive to be diverse*. Both effects improve collective predictive ability. By predicting correctly, a person makes money. By predicting diversely, a person makes even more money.

All this talk of money is a bit crass. Money is only one coin of the realm. Prediction markets can also pay out in reputations. Consider our NFL draft experts. One reason that their predictions differed as much as they did may well have been because of the incentives for diversity. These predictors compete in a market for our attention. So each prognosticator has incentives to make predictions that run counter to the consensus.

THE CROWD OF MODELS

A summary of this chapter might read like this: for a crowd to be wise its members must be individually smart or collectively diverse. Ideally, they would be both. And sometimes, when their members' models rely on diverse interpretations, crowds can even enjoy a free lunch. Simple, diverse predictive models can form sophisticated crowd-level predictions. These crowds can perform better than experts, provided their increased coverage more than makes up for the crudeness of their estimates. This surely happens when one of the attributes or variables considered by the crowd and ignored by the expert takes on an unexpected value. And if instead of polling the crowd, we create an information market so that people can place bets of various sizes, we can make the crowd even more accurate. Market incentives can drive out the least accurate predictors and place more weight on the more accurate ones, so long as the accurate predictors know that they are accurate. Both of those effects would seem to lead to greater crowd accuracy, but we can take that logic too far. If only the best predictors remain or get most of the weight, we end up with a single expert who may not be better than the crowd. Finally, if people know that an information market will be used, they have incentives to be diverse as well as accurate. This further improves the performance of the crowd.

All of this leads to the conclusion that ideally we would have a *crowd of models* competing in a market. The best predictions should come from collections of diverse models. These models should parse reality differently. They should rely on interpretations based on diverse perspectives that look at different attributes in the same perspective, or interpretations that slice up the same perspective into different clumps. If so, each model will be accurate, and the collection of models will be diverse. This combination of accuracy and diversity makes for a wise crowd.

The recipe for creating a crowd of models might look as follows: create incentives for a collection of people with diverse (and relevant) identities, experience, and training, and add in a few wild cards. Training in chemistry may be less relevant than training in sociology or psychology if predicting which of five marketing plans to pursue, but adding a chemist guarantees some diversity. Then create incentives for those people to construct models— not necessarily mathematical or empirical models, but coherent predictive models. Do not train them in how to think about the problem; that would destroy their diversity. Finally, create an entry barrier, so that only those who think that they can make a reasonable prediction join the crowd. The crowd need not be large. It could contain only seven or eight people. With smaller crowds, such as management teams, juries, hiring committees, boards of directors, and the like, making efforts to ensure that people use diverse models may be even more important. With a larger crowd some diversity is almost sure to be present. Eighty-seven people are not likely all to think alike, but eight might.

Individuals can also amass their own crowds of models. Some of the best investors on Wall Street do exactly this. In fact, the legendary Charlie Munger, who, along with Warren Buffett, made Berkshire Hathaway investors billions of dollars, bases his investment decisions on what he calls a lattice of mental models: a collection of logically coherent diverse models that combine to help him make accurate forecasts. His crowd of models, we can only surmise, is an intelligent, diverse bunch.

Part Three

DIVERSE VALUES: A CONFLICT OF INTERESTS (OR IS IT)?

CHAPTER 9

Diverse Preferences

WHY TAPAS

Do not do unto others as you would they should do unto you. Their tastes may not be the same.
—GEORGE BERNARD SHAW, "Maxims for Revolutionists: The Golden Rule"

WE all differ in what we prefer. Some of us like old Craftsman houses. Some of us like modern houses with open floor plans. Some of us enjoy Latin jazz. Some of us prefer heavy metal. Some of us like spicy cooked food. Some of us are vegetarian. That's fine. That's the reason for tapas restaurants. Little plates, lots of different stuff. As has often been said, there's no accounting for taste.[1] (Less often said is the equally true claim that there's no taste for accounting.) Though we cannot account for taste, we can model it. And in this chapter, that's what we do.

We need to model tastes, or what we call diverse preferences, because they create problems—huge problems. If we value different ends, we may not agree on what good solutions are or what outcomes to predict. This potential for disagreement may create incentives to misrepresent how we feel. We may try to manipulate processes and agenda, creating distrust and dislike. Thus, much of the good created by a diverse toolbox might be undone by diverse values. Of course, we needn't care about diverse preference so much if the same people who have diverse toolboxes don't also have diverse preferences, but often they do.

To understand the severity of problems caused by diverse values, we need to see the root causes of the problems. We need frameworks and models. So, we build them. In this chapter, we learn the basics. In the next, we apply them. This treatment of preference theory is by no means complete nor is it traditional. Entire books from multiple disciplines are devoted to preferences and preference theory.[2] Most books present preference theory with an abundance of notation complicating the connection to the real world. We err in the other direction, forgoing variables whenever possible. This treatment is not traditional because it emphasizes the distinction between *fundamental preferences* (preferences about outcomes) and *instrumental preferences* (preferences about how we get what we want). Preferences about outcomes—fish tacos, healthy knees, or economic growth—are fundamental. Preferences about actions or policies—diets, stretching exercises, or tax policies— are instrumental. Actions are not ends in themselves; they are not outcomes, but they are the means to those outcomes.

Diverse fundamental preferences need not imply diverse instrumental preferences and vice versa. This finding has implications for how we think about preference diversity. People who have different fundamental preferences might be said to have different *values*. People who have different instrumental preferences but the same fundamental preferences have the same values but different *beliefs about how the world works*. In either case, people disagree over what policy or action to choose, but only in the first case does preference diversity create a problem. In the latter case, it can prove useful.

We highlight this distinction because diverse instrumental preferences derive from diverse predictive models. And it's easy to confuse the two types of diversity. So even if we don't like accounting, we have to do some. This linking of diverse predictive models to diverse perspectives offers a hint of the complexity to come. The frameworks—perspectives, heuristics, interpretations, predictive models, and preferences—can all be connected, and in many cases, diversity in one domain begets diversity in another.

Preference Orderings and Utility Functions

To describe preferences, we first note that they are distinct from choices. Preferences describe how much we value or desire things. Choices are what we select. Our preferences guide our choices, and our choices reveal (partially) our preferences. When we meet someone new, we try to infer something about that person's preferences by his choices. What clothes does he wear? What car does he drive? What does he order for lunch? You can even use your own choices as information about your preferences. In looking at a closet filled with black shirts, you might suddenly realize that you like black, or that you like Johnny Cash.

As is standard, we assume a set of alternatives about which people have preferences. These may be locations, product designs, public policies, or political candidates. They could be *outcomes* or they could be *actions* or *policies*.[3] That difference proves important. It is the basis for the distinction between fundamental and instrumental preferences.

The most basic way to think about preferences is to conceive of them as imposing an ordering over a set of actions, policies, or outcomes. For ease of presentation, I refer to these as the *set of alternatives*. A *preference relation* describes an ordering of alternatives, $>$. The statement $A > B$ means that alternative A is preferred to alternative B. If, for example, Joe is asked his preferences among a burrito, a taco, and an enchilada, and if he most prefers the burrito and least prefers the taco, then his preferences can be written as follows:

$$burrito > enchilada > taco$$

He might also be indifferent between two outcomes. He could like burritos and tacos equally well. If so, he is indifferent between burritos and tacos, and his preferences would be written

$$burrito \equiv taco$$

Preferences are typically assumed to be *rational*. The term *rational* has a formal definition. It means *complete* and *transitive*.

Preferences are complete if they compare any two alternatives.

> Preferences are **complete** *if given any two alternatives, A and B, either $A > B$, $B > A$, or $A \equiv B$.*

We might think that everyone's preferences satisfy completeness, that everyone can compare any two alternatives. Yet it is not a vacuous assumption because people often have conflicting or deep feelings about some pairs of outcomes. They either cannot or would be reluctant to make decisions among them. If someone asks you which of your parents or children you prefer, you might find the question impossible to answer.

Preferences are *transitive* if they do not admit cycles. A person with transitive preferences cannot prefer papers to rocks, rocks to scissors, and scissors to papers.

> Preferences are **transitive** *if they do not admit cycles; for example, if apples are preferred to bananas and bananas are preferred to pears, then apples are preferred to pears.*

The condition that preferences are transitive may also seem as though it states an obvious condition in technical language. At the individual level, it does. If Ravi prefers ice cream to yogurt and prefers yogurt to tofu, then he must prefer ice cream to tofu. For individuals, transitivity usually holds. When an individual must choose from among outcomes, she is not likely to have a preference cycle unless she is not thinking clearly. In comparing alternative plans for which gift to buy her mother (an action) in order to make her happy (an outcome), Laura might think that her mother would prefer a necklace to flowers (it lasts longer), flowers to garden tools (flowers are prettier), and garden tools to a necklace (they're more practical). This would be a preference cycle over actions, but one that should go away if Laura thought more carefully.

Though preference cycles may be rare within an individual, they are common within collections of people. In chapter 10, we analyze the aggregation of diverse preferences, we see that it is possible for a group of people to violate transitivity, to have cycles, even though none of the individuals themselves do. A collection of rational people may prefer tofu to ice cream, even though they prefer ice cream to yogurt and yogurt to tofu.

Preferences are **rational** *if they are complete and transitive.*

An assumption of rational preferences seems reasonable. Completeness and transitivity are mild assumptions, but they severely restrict the amount of preference diversity that can exist. To see this, we work within a restricted framework that rules out indifference, that is, we do not allow people to be indifferent between two alternatives.

In what follows, we consider preferences about five possible actions with respect to a man's facial hair: *a goatee, muttonchops, a mustache, a full beard*, and *a Van Dyke beard*. These could also be thought of as outcomes, but we want to think of these as actions that create an outcome called attractiveness. Preferences about attractiveness would surely satisfy *monotonicity*. People prefer to be more attractive. A rational preference relation without the possibility of indifference creates a complete ordering, a ranking, over the alternatives from best to worst. One such ranking would be the following:

full beard > goatee > Van Dyke > mustache > muttonchops

We can calculate the total number of such orderings as follows. Any of the five facial hair styles can be ranked first, leaving four that can be ranked second, three that can be ranked third, two that can be ranked fourth, and one that can be ranked last, or be least preferred. The total number of such orderings equals 5 * 4 * 3 * 2 * 1, or 120. If we up this to twenty alternatives, we get more then two million, billion orderings; that's why we're considering only five alternatives.

We can compare our 120 rational orderings to the number of possible irrational preference relations. Notice that we say relations and not orderings. The word *ordering* makes no sense when preferences are irrational. Irrational preferences do not necessarily order all of the alternatives. We first relax the transitivity assumption. This implies that for each pair of alternatives, a person still must have a preference, but it places no restriction on cycles.

PAIRWISE FACIAL HAIR RANKINGS

Van Dyke	>	full beard
Van Dyke	>	goatee
Van Dyke	>	mustache
muttonchops	>	Van Dyke
muttonchops	>	full beard
mustache	>	muttonchops
goatee	>	muttonchops
mustache	>	full beard
goatee	>	mustache
goatee	>	full beard

To compute the number of preference relations that are not transitive, we begin with these ten pairs of facial hairstyles. For each pair, one of the two must be chosen. That creates two times two times two... (ten times), or two to the tenth power, possible preference relations. Two to the tenth power equals 1,024. Almost ten nontransitive preference relations exist for each of the 120 rational preference orderings. Most of these preference relations contain cycles (904 of them, to be precise.) Here is one: mustache is preferred to muttonchops which are preferred to the Van Dyke, but the Van Dyke is preferred to the mustache.

Were we also to allow preferences to violate completeness, we would get an even larger number of possible preference relations. Now for each pair of alternatives, in addition to either being preferred, it could also be that the alternatives are noncomparable. This creates three possibilities for each pair of alternatives. With five alternatives (and, therefore, ten pairs of alternatives) the number of preference relations that violate both transitivity and completeness equals three (not two) raised to the tenth power, 59,049, or nearly five hundred times as many as the number of rational preference orderings.[4]

These calculations demonstrate the many ways to be rational. They also show the many, many more ways to be irrational. They have implications when we study preference aggregation. Collections of people need not have transitive or complete preferences. The billions of preference orderings that an individual might have over a set of twenty alternatives are a mere drop in the bucket compared to the number of irrational preference relations that a collection of people might have.

Spatial Preferences

Up to now, the alternatives were arbitrary, so we had no reason to attach any significance to preferring A to B or B to A. But suppose that we construct a *perspective* of these alternatives. Sometimes creating a perspective is easy. If we were to analyze how much people enjoy work, play, and sleep, we might describe an outcome as a vector (*work, play, sleep*) where the three variables denote the time spent working, playing, and sleeping, respectively. Decompositions like this into separate dimensions are a common approach in economics and political science.

Other times, representing alternatives in a perspective becomes complicated. Consider someone's preferences for food. Listing the particular food items, such as nachos, sushi, and pretzels, would be cumbersome. We could create *dimensions* that characterize food items based on ingredients. In the Ben and Jerry's example, this worked great. The number and size of chunks characterized the pints of ice cream. These two dimensions allowed Ben and Jerry to make a *spatial* representation of the various pints. However, this won't always work. Many of the items at Taco Bell contain the same ingredients in the same proportions. A taco salad is just a taco in a new arrangement.

But let's suppose that we can map the alternatives to a single-dimensional perspective. We can then distinguish between three types of preferences along that dimension. In defining each type, we take the other dimensions as fixed and ask what happens to preferences as we vary the level on one dimension. The first type of preference applies to those dimensions for which more is better.

Preferences are **increasing** *if more is always preferred to less.*

Preferences about money are usually assumed to be increasing. More money is better. Preferences are also increasing about health, gas mileage, and computer speed.

The second type of preferences apply to things that people do not like, such as pollution or noise, for which less is better.

Preferences are **decreasing** *if less is always preferred to more.*

Preferences about pollution are decreasing, as are preferences about the amount of time spent doing our taxes.

For most things, including sleep, salmon, and software, more is not always better and neither is less. We like more up to a point, and then we like less. Consider the size of an ice cream cone. One scoop is nice. Two are better. Three may be a bit much. And four borders on outrageous (unless you happen to be fourteen years old). We call such preferences *single-peaked* because graphical representations of our happiness, or what economists call utility, have a single peak. We call the amount that provides the highest utility the *ideal point*.[5]

Preferences are **single-peaked** *if there exists an* **ideal point.** *If the current amount is less than the ideal point, more is preferred. If the current amount is more than the ideal point, less is preferred.*

The powerful implicit assumption in the spatial formulation is that the dimensions used to define the alternatives, as defined by the *perspective*, capture those attributes of the alternatives that drive preferences. Otherwise, the assumptions of increasing, decreasing, or single-peaked preferences do not make sense. Think back to the masticity-based perspective on ice cream. Masticity was a measure of how long it took to chew a spoonful of ice cream. Most people would not have increasing, decreasing, or single-peaked preferences about masticity. This discussion reiterates a point made at length earlier: making sense of the world, in this case making sense of preferences, requires a good perspective.

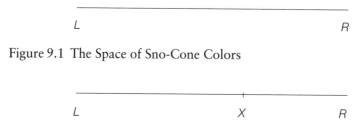

Figure 9.1 The Space of Sno-Cone Colors

Figure 9.2 An Ideal Sno-Cone

Raspberry and Bubble Gum Sno-Cones

Spatial representations of the set of alternatives, combined with assumptions that structure preferences, limit the number of possible preference orderings. To see this, consider preferences about the color for raspberry sno-cones. First some background for those unfortunately not in the know about raspberries and sno-cones. In the wild, raspberries can be black, red, and even yellowish orange. Raspberry-flavored sno-cones vary in color as well. In some regions of the United States, you will find dark red raspberry sno-cones. In others, you will find that they are light blue. Had we the time and energy, we might even make a map of the country coloring some states red and other states blue depending on the more common color of their raspberry sno-cones. (Maps of red and blue states are important to political scientists.)

Here we consider preferences within Ohio, a blue state, at least for raspberry sno-cones. We represent the range of possible blue colors on a line with light blue (denoted by L) on the left, and royal blue, denoted by R, on the right (see figure 9.1).

Each Ohioan has an *ideal point*, a color that she most prefers. A person with an ideal point L (resp R) has a decreasing (increasing) preference, and a person with an ideal point in the interior has a single-peaked preference. In what follows, distance to the ideal point determines preference: the closer a color lies to a person's ideal color, the more the person prefers that color. Though not necessary, this assumption simplifies the presentation. Figure 9.2 shows a person's ideal point at X.

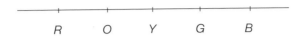

Figure 9.3 Five Alternative Sno-Cones

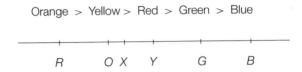

Figure 9.4 Brenda's Preferences

We now explore the implications of our three assumptions: (i) that the alternatives can be placed on a single line, (ii) that people have ideal points, and (iii) that preferences about alternatives are determined by the distance of the alternatives from the ideal point.

To see the restrictiveness of these assumptions, let's consider the task of assigning a color to bubblegum sno-cones. Bubblegum sno-cones could be any color. We won't use all of the colors—just the familiar ROYGB (red, orange, yellow, green, and blue) arranged along the spectrum. To make the comparison exact, we place these five colors on a line (see figure 9.3).

Suppose that Brenda most prefers the color orange. Her ideal point could be right at O; it could lie between R (red) and O or it could lie between O and Y (yellow). Let's suppose that her most preferred color lies between O and Y. For the purposes of this example, we assume that the colors are evenly spaced on the line and that Brenda's preferences about colors depend on the distance from the color to her ideal point. If we look at figure 9.4, we see that she must then prefer yellow (Y) to red (R), and she must also prefer red to green (G) and green to blue (B).

Thus, once we place her ideal point on the line, we uniquely define her preferences and limit preference diversity. We can calculate how many possible preference orderings can exist if we represent preferences on a single line. As before, we rule out ties. If a person most prefers red, she must like orange second best, then yellow, then green, and then blue. A person who most prefers blue must have preferences that go in the opposite order. Someone who most prefers orange could like yellow next best (as in our example above) or could like red next best. Either way, once we know her second favorite color, we know her full preferences. Therefore, two preference orderings have orange as the favorite color. The exact same logic applies to preferences that rank green or yellow first.[6]

Adding up all of these possibilities: only one preference ordering each for red and blue being ranked first, and two each for the other three colors, makes a total of only eight possible spatial preference orderings. If we relax the equal spacing assumption, then with a little effort we can see that only fifteen possible orderings exist. Either number is small when compared to the 120 possible rational orderings, the 1,024 intransitive relations, and the 59,049 relations that are neither complete nor transitive.

Thus, we see that assuming single-dimensional preferences reduces the number of possible preference relations—just as does imposing completeness and transitivity. If we increase the dimensionality of the perspective—say, moving from a line to a square—we allow for more preference orderings. The higher dimensional the perspective needed to make sense of preferences, the more diverse rational preferences can be. We might ask if we can always represent preferences spatially. We can, but we might have to make the number of dimensions large. It may even have to equal the number of alternatives.

Getting More Serious

We may disagree about what we believe to be pressing problems. Some of us believe it to be poverty, others believe it to be environmental sustainability, and still others believe it to be international stability. No one believes it to be selecting a type of beard or the color for a sno-cone. What we learn from fun examples, though, also applies to more serious contexts.[7] And we can think of the one dimension as representing an ideological spectrum from left to right. In fact, the sno-cone model provides a logical foundation for much of how we think about political ideologies. When we describe senators or congressional representatives as liberal, conservative, or moderate, we are placing them on a line.

These one-dimensional ideologies can be thought of as an interpretation. We can use this interpretation to construct a model to predict how representatives will vote on a bill. That crude predictive model works well. If we add a second ideological dimension, then we can do even better.[8]

Instrumental Preferences

Now that we have seen two basic preference frameworks—one based on orderings and one based on spatial representations—we turn to the distinction between fundamental and instrumental preferences, which is a big reason we're studying this in the first place. This distinction can be alternatively described as the distinction between preferences about ends and preferences about means. A person's preference about ends might be to live a long life and to minimize his chances of getting cancer and heart disease. His preferences about means may be to eat a low-fat diet that includes lots of fruits and vegetables.

We focus here on how interpretations and predictive models influence our instrumental preferences but not our fundamental preferences. Two people can have the same values, the same fundamental preferences, but have different instrumental preferences. To show this, we'll construct an example that includes government policies and the outcomes that those policies produce. Disconnecting ends and means is meaningful only so long as the mapping from policy choices to outcomes is difficult to infer, that is, if the mapping from policies to outcomes creates a rugged landscape. For nonrugged landscapes, even crude interpretations lead to correct predictions.[9]

We'll assume that everyone has the same preferences about outcomes. This assumption is not as strong as it seems. Sure, people disagree about abortion and the right to own guns. But our preferences agree more than we think. Try to think of any politician who doesn't claim to want a better educational system, less crime, more growth, less inequality, greater international security, cheaper health care, and enhancing sustainability. Now try to think of any two politicians who agree on how to achieve those outcomes.[10] One politician may claim that markets generate greater efficiency than bureaucracies and that we should have vouchers for education. Another may claim that markets benefit the wealthy at the expense of the poor and that we should not create vouchers. This political posturing on policies continues year after year, decade after decade because the policy problems remain difficult. If confronted with simple problems, voters would learn the correct policy and demand that politicians adopt it. But policy problems are rarely simple. To predict the likely outcomes of proposed policies, we rely on predictive models.

We Reduce Crime by...

To see the linkage between interpretations, predictive models, and instrumental preferences as well as the disconnect between instrumental and fundamental preferences, consider policies for crime reduction. Assume that crime-fighting policies have a fiscal and a social dimension. On the fiscal dimension, each policy can be left (L), moderate (M), or right (R). The same is true for the social dimension. We distinguish the social dimension by using lowercase letters, l, m, and r.

Policies either increase crime, reduce crime, or have no effect. The policy space and the mapping from policies to outcomes look as shown in table 9.1.

So, for example, the policy Lm reduces crime, and the policy Rm increases crime. Now, let's imagine two politicians, Arun and Rebecca, running for office. Each interprets the policy space differently. Arun sees only the social dimension of a policy. He looks at the columns. This interpretation resembles Marilyn's interpretation in Screening Success. Given this interpretation, Arun's predictive model looks as shown in table 9.2.

TABLE 9.1:
A policy mapping

	Social		
Fiscal	l	m	r
L	increase	reduce	reduce
M	no effect	increase	reduce
R	reduce	increase	increase

TABLE 9.2:
Arun's predictive model

	Social		
Fiscal	l	m	r
L	increase	reduce	reduce
M	no effect	increase	reduce
R	reduce	increase	increase
Prediction	no effect	increase	reduce

TABLE 9.3:
Rebecca's predictive model

	Social			
Fiscal	l	m	r	Prediction
L	increase	reduce	reduce	reduce
M	no effect	increase	reduce	no effect
R	reduce	increase	increase	increase

Arun predicts that socially liberal policies have on balance no effect, that socially moderate policies increase crime, and that socially conservative policies reduce crime. Rebecca looks only at the fiscal dimension of a policy. She predicts that fiscally liberal policies (*L* to her) reduce crime, that fiscally moderate policies have no effect, and that fiscally conservative policies increase crime (see table 9.3).

Suppose that Arun and Rebecca compare two policies: one that is moderate on both dimensions (*Mm*) and one that is conservative on both (*Rr*). Rebecca predicts that the latter policy, which she interprets as conservative, will increase crime and that the first policy, which she interprets as moderate, will have no effect. Arun predicts that the conservative policy will reduce crime and that the moderate one will increase it.

In this example, Arun and Rebecca have identical preferences about outcomes—they both want reductions in crime—but their diverse predictive models lead them to have opposing policy preferences. Arun prefers the conservative policy, and Rebecca prefers the more moderate one. This example, more than any other in this chapter, reveals the interplay between preferences and tool boxes. Think back to the landscape metaphor where high elevations represent better solutions. Arun and Rebecca don't agree on which end is up in policy space even though they want the same outcome.

LINKING PREFERENCES AND TOOLBOXES

We have just seen how diverse interpretations can result in diverse instrumental preferences. The causality can also go in the other direction. Diverse preferences, in this case fundamental ones, can result in differences in interpretations. How a politician interprets a welfare policy depends on his preferences. How a businessperson interprets a strategic plan or a potential product launch depends on her preferences. College applicants who want to study drama look at schools differently than do physics applicants: In considering a school such as Carnegie Mellon University, which is strong in both disciplines, students interested in drama ignore the computer facilities and laboratory spaces, attributes that budding physicists find of utmost importance.

Our brains are not large enough to keep track of everything we need to know. We look at what is important to us. When what we look at is large, metaphorically, when it has many parts and dimensions, we abandon perspectives for interpretations. We can have a perspective on a route between ten cities. But we cannot have a perspective on the design for the car we drive between those cities. As a result, for most problems, the dimensions we include depend on what we value. The link between what we prefer and what we notice is so obvious that it requires little elaboration.

How we experience events or draw aesthetic pleasure from them is a function of our knowledge of what we see and experience. The dimensions that we see and experience are partly choice-driven, though not entirely so. Politicians, and some might say the media, exploit our susceptibility to manipulate how we think. But they are not alone in doing so. Writers, performers, film makers, in fact all artists, manipulate and focus our attentions to create certain understandings. Advertisers do the same thing. How else to explain our worries about gingivitis?

A related connection can be made between preferences and cognitive tools generally. The tools that people choose to acquire are those that help them achieve their preferences. People who have different preferences likely acquire different tools. People who love good food often learn tools that enable them to become excellent cooks. People who love to hike may cognitively represent regions of the country based on the number and types of trails they have. This powerful, widespread influence cast by preferences on perspectives, interpretations, and tools suggests the centrality of preferences in any discussion of diversity and its influences.

CHAPTER 10

Preference Aggregation

FOUR (NOT SO) DEPRESSING RESULTS

*We all do no end of feeling, and we mistake it for thinking.
And out of it we get an aggregation which we consider a
Boon. Its name is Public Opinion. It is held in reverence.
It settles everything. Some think it the Voice of God.*
—MARK TWAIN, "Corn-Pone Opinions"

NOW that we have a grounding in preference theory,
we can analyze how diverse preferences aggregate—how diverse
teams, communities, and societies make collective choices. We
find problems. The results may at first seem depressing, but I
suggest that the problems may not be as severe as we might
think; I show that when preference diversity is instrumental but
not fundamental, these problems may not be problems at all.
Moreover, as we see in the next chapter, without preference
diversity, we might not have as much of the other types of diversity.
Because we differ in what we want, we differ in how we represent
things, how we look for solutions, and how we interpret things.
Thus, preference diversity, though it has negative direct effects, has
positive indirect effects. Taking all the plusses and minuses into
account, some optimistic readers might even say that preference
diversity is (to quote Martha Stewart) a good thing.

Before we can reach a balanced view on the effects of preference diversity, we must first open up our dog-eared copies of Dante and descend into the depths of the inferno. The reference to Dante may seem overblown, but I have to be honest: the literature on preference aggregation paints a depressing picture. Diverse preferences create a litany of problems. I highlight four: *collective preferences may fail to exist, an unconstrained voting process may result in arbitrary choices, people may have incentives to manipulate the choice process,* and *common resources (public goods) may be underprovided.* These problems produce individual-level frustration that sometimes escalates into conflict.

In what follows, we survey a substantial literature written to analyze entire societies and legislative bodies. We interpret this literature broadly. We consider collections of all sizes. Size matters little here. The same problems that beset an entire country or even a federation of countries such as the European Union can frustrate small groups of people making a decision within an organization, a firm, or even a family. To reverse a phrase, what's bad for America—preference diversity—is also bad for General Motors.

While we do see some differences between the political and business contexts, the similarities are stronger than we might think. In the political context, people want different outcomes. Some people care about a clean environment. Others care more about economic growth. Within an organization or a firm, most everyone might be thought to have a common goal, such as maximizing the value of the firm or the number of members in an environmental awareness group. However, that is not always true. The organizational incentive structure may create variation in fundamental preferences. A plant manager may not prefer a new overtime pay policy that helps the corporate bottom line if, given the current incentive structure, that policy hurts *his* bottom line. These types of preference diversity can be thought of as *fundamental,* as can some diverse political preferences. In both cases, people want different outcomes.

However, even though ample preference diversity exists, much of the preference diversity that we see may in fact be *instrumental* diversity. People often want the same outcome: less crime, better schools, and the like, but they advocate different policies to attain those ends. (Again, try to think of a major party candidate in any democracy who ran on a platform that promised poorly educated children or more sickness.) Everyone wants well-educated children and healthy citizens. The differences arise in how to achieve those outcomes. Much of political preference diversity is instrumental and not fundamental. Instrumental diversity exists as well in firms and organizations. People may want approximately the same outcome—a higher stock price, more members, or a better reputation—but may differ in how they propose to achieve it. If so, they have different instrumental preferences.

In the models, we will take preference diversity as a primitive. We assume it. Therefore, whether it is fundamental or instrumental matters little. But when we interpret the models, the distinction becomes crucial. Under fundamental preference diversity, realized outcomes affect people in different ways. Some people are pleased and some are not. When an electorate votes to dam a pristine stream to produce hydroelectric power, the people who wanted lower energy prices reap benefits while the people who fished and canoed in the stream suffer a drop in happiness. No decision can make everyone happy, but some decisions are better compromises than others.

Under instrumental preference diversity, everyone experiences outcomes in the same way. The managers of a company that makes designer reading glasses may all want to maximize the company's long-term value but advocate diverse company policies. But when a choice is made to produce a retro cat eye line of glasses, the implications of that choice affect them all in the same way. If the company's value goes up, everyone is pleased. If the value goes down, they are not.

Instrumental preference diversity arises because people have diverse predictive models. If diverse predictive models cause instrumental preference diversity, is it a good thing? Didn't we learn that in chapter 8? Yes, but we can learn more. Let's think back to our analysis of collective prediction. We can reinterpret much of that analysis as the aggregation of diverse instrumental preferences by assuming that everyone has the same fundamental preference: to make an accurate prediction. (People have diverse instrumental preferences created by the diverse models that they use to predict.) What we previously called averaging their diverse predictions we might now call aggregating their diverse instrumental preferences. Thus, prediction can be seen as analogous to preference aggregation. And, provided that the choice we're making is not an easy one, instrumental preference diversity—that is, diverse predictive models—should be a good thing.

In our analysis of predictive models, however, we averaged or took a weighted average of the predictions to obtain the crowd's prediction. That's because all of our predictions were one-dimensional. People were predicting values, so averaging made sense. We avoided situations where averaging was not possible. If a firm must choose whether to locate a new office in London or Miami, the average preference may lie somewhere in the middle of the Atlantic. We also ignored the possibility of new alternatives being introduced. We considered predictions over a fixed set of possibilities. In choice contexts, new alternatives can be introduced. These new alternatives can be used to manipulate outcomes. That's one of the many problems that we have to come to grips with in this chapter. New alternatives aren't all bad, though. They can soothe tensions if they forge the right compromise.

COLLECTIVE PREFERENCES

We begin with a seminal result, proven by Kenneth Arrow fifty years ago. Though familiar to most scholars of politics, this result may shock others, so it's best to read this section sitting down. It shows how diverse individual preferences can fail to aggregate into collective preferences. This means that no reasonable collective preferences may exist. We may not be able to define the preferences of a society or even a family. We may have no coherent way of characterizing the preferences of the American people. More to the point, we may not be able to say whether our family prefers pizza to tacos or tacos to burgers.

The lack of collective preferences has profound implications. It means that we cannot say, "This is what the American people want." We can sit in cafés wearing predominantly black clothing, smoking cigarettes, and discussing the deep philosophical concepts of the "general will" and "will of all" until we're blue in the face and black of lung. It won't matter; this problem won't go away. The cause of this problem: diversity.

To show Arrow's result, we first define what reasonable collective preferences would be and then what it would mean for them not to exist. To do this, we return to the model of preferences from the previous part of the book. Suppose that we wanted to write down the preferences for the people of the great state of Ohio, for the board of directors of Cisco, or for the faculty of the arts and sciences at the University of Memphis. We would want these preferences to satisfy some normative properties, what academics call *desiderata*.[1]

Before getting to these desiderata, we need to be aware of some key assumptions in Arrow's formulation. He considers a finite set of alternatives over which individuals have rankings. He also precludes information other than these preference rankings to be used in constructing collective preferences. People can't pay other people money or IOUs (as they do in Congress) to demonstrate strength of preference. Arrow considers only functions that map individual preference orderings into collective preference orderings: each person submits a ranking of alternatives and Arrow asks whether the collective has such a ranking.

The first desideratum for collective preferences is that they be *rational*: they are complete (any two alternatives can be compared) and transitive (no rock-paper-scissors cycles are allowed). Without rationality, a collective could be handcuffed, unable to move. Forget big policy questions for a second. This problem also exists for family decisions. Where does our family go to dinner if we prefer Chinese food to Mexican food, Mexican to Italian, and Italian to Chinese? (The answer "Denny's" will not be countenanced.)

The second desideratum is that collective preferences reflect individual-level unanimity. If everyone prefers A to B, then so must the collective. If every person in Ohio prefers buckeyes to oranges, then so should the people of the great state of Ohio. If the predictive models of every officer at Google show that Ann Arbor, owing to its friendly, intelligent, diverse people makes a far better place to open a new office than Boston, then Google, as a collective, should prefer Ann Arbor to Boston as well.

Preferences **reflect unanimity** *if all individuals prefer X to Y, so then the collective prefers X to Y.*

Individuals, by the way, always reflect unanimity. If a person prefers X to Y, then she prefers X to Y.

The third desideratum requires that preferences over alternatives do not depend on the existence of other, less attractive alternatives. Writing this down makes this sound more complicated than it is.

Preferences satisfy **independence of irrelevant alternatives** *if X is preferred to Y when Z is not a possible outcome, and if both X and Y are preferred to Z, then making Z a possible outcome should not cause Y to be preferred to X.*[2]

Without independence of irrelevant alternatives, people could introduce new alternatives and manipulate outcomes. This again is not a concern for an individual, only for a group.

The final desideratum is that no dictator exists. A dictator is someone whose preferences determine the collective preferences.

Preferences are **nondictatorial** *if no individual's preferences determine collective preferences.*

If we allowed a dictator, then constructing collective preferences would not be a problem. They could be the dictator's preferences. Having a dictator undermines the original goal—to aggregate the preferences of the individuals.[3]

These desiderata underpin the first part of our analysis of preference aggregation. When not directly in play, they lurk in the background. When people's preferences are sufficiently similar, these desiderata prove harmless, but when individuals have diverse preferences, the desiderata conflict.

Arrow's Possibility Theorem

As mentioned, Kenneth Arrow proved the inherent conflict of these desiderata. Assuming that individual people have rational preferences, the following result can be shown:[4]

Arrow's Theorem: *No complete, transitive collective preference ordering based on individual preference orderings exists that satisfies unanimity, independence of irrelevant alternatives, and nondictatorship if all possible preferences are allowed.*[5]

Arrow's Theorem remains one of the great paradoxes of social science. It says that *any rule for aggregating preferences, including majority rule voting*, cannot satisfy the desiderata. Let's be honest. That sucks. It's not a happy result. Note also that when we say that voting among rational people can result in irrational collective preferences, that is, preferences with cycles, we imply that this can occur with either fundamental or instrumental preference diversity. Later give an example of each.

To construct a fundamental preference cycle we need only include three people and three alternatives. Suppose that Liz, Skip, and William must decide where to hold the summer Olympics. The three candidate cities are London; Washington, DC; and Hamburg. The preferences for Liz, Skip, and William are as follows:

> **Liz:** Hamburg > London > Washington
> **Skip:** Washington > Hamburg > London
> **William:** London > Washington > Hamburg

When these three vote, Washington defeats Hamburg two votes to one, Hamburg defeats London two votes to one, and London defeats Washington two votes to one. The collective preferences determined by voting create a cycle. Though the individuals have rational preferences, the collective does not. This type of cycle is called a Condorcet cycle after the Marquis de Condorcet, who first discovered it. He might have gone even further with this logic had he not lost his head—literally—in the French revolution.

TABLE 10.1:
A policy mapping

	Social		
Fiscal	l	m	r
L	increase	reduce	reduce
M	no effect	increase	reduce
R	reduce	increase	increase

TABLE 10.2:
Arun's predictive model

	Social		
Fiscal	l	m	r
L	increase	reduce	reduce
M	no effect	increase	reduce
R	reduce	increase	increase
Prediction	no effect	increase	reduce

To construct an instrumental preference cycle, we build from the earlier example involving policies and their effects on crime rates (see table 10.1). A policy had a social dimension (the column) and a fiscal dimension (the row).

Recall that we read the table as follows: The policy *Lm* reduces crime, and the policy *Rm* increases crime. Recall also our two politicians, Arun and Rebecca, who use who different interpretations. Arun sees only the social dimension of a policy and Rebecca sees only the fiscal dimension. They therefore have distinct predictive models (see tables 10.2 and 10.3).

We now place Arun and Rebecca on a committee with a third person, Mary. Mary partitions the policies into three sets: *left-wing*, *right-wing* and *political*. Mary interprets a policy as left-wing if it has a liberal position on at least one dimension and is not conservative on the other (see table 10.4). A policy is right-wing if it is conservative on at least one dimension and not liberal on

TABLE 10.3:
Rebecca's predictive model

	Social			
Fiscal	l	m	r	Prediction
L	increase	reduce	reduce	reduce
M	no effect	increase	reduce	no effect
R	reduce	increase	increase	increase

TABLE 10.4:
Mary's interpretation

	Social		
Fiscal	l	m	r
L	left wing	left wing	political
M	left wing	political	right wing
R	political	right wing	right wing

the other. A policy is political if it is a compromise: liberal on one dimension and conservative on the other or moderate on both.

Of the three policies she sees as political, two lead to reductions in crime, so she predicts crime reductions for political policies. Of the three policies she sees as right-wing, two of them increase crime, so she predicts crime increases from right-wing policies. Of the three policies she sees as left-wing, one reduces crime, one increases crime, and one has no effect, so she predicts no effect (see table 10.5).

Now consider three policies: Lm, Mr, and Rl. With a little effort, we can figure out the predictions of Arun, Rebecca, and Mary (see table 10.6). We consider Arun's here. Arun looks at the social dimension (the capital letters) and believes moderate policies are better than policies from the right, which in turn he believes to be better than policies from the left.

TABLE 10.5:
Mary's predictions

		Social	
Fiscal	l	m	r
L	no effect	no effect	reduce
M	no effect	reduce	increase
R	reduce	increase	increase

TABLE 10.6:
Predictions about policies

		Policy	
Person	Lm	Mr	Rl
Arun	increase	reduce	no effect
Rebecca	reduce	no effect	increase
Mary	no effect	increase	reduce

Assuming that everyone most prefers decreasing crime and least prefers increasing crime, we get the following preference orderings:

Arun: $Mr > Rl > Lm$
Rebecca: $Lm > Mr > Rl$
Mary: $Rl > Lm > Mr$

These preferences create a voting cycle. The policy Lm defeats the policy Mr in a vote, which in turn defeats Rl, which then paradoxically defeats Lm.[6] Even though everyone has the same fundamental preferences, when they vote they create a cycle. The cycle emerges from their diverse predictive models. We no longer have the wisdom of crowds in which diverse predictive models aggregate into an accurate prediction. We have the circularity of crowds. The crowd plays Rock, Paper, Scissors.

The Faustian Bargain over Desiderata

Arrow's desiderata, like all wish lists, characterize the best that we can hope to attain. The conflicting desiderata oblige a choice. We must abandon one or more or them. One way to avoid cycles is to use a scoring rule, such as the one developed by Jean-Charles de Borda in the eighteenth century. Under the Borda rule, each person's ranking determines points for each of the alternatives. With three alternatives, a person's top choice gets three points, her second gets two points, and her third gets only one point. The alternative that gets the most points wins. Each alternative gets a score, so cycles become impossible. If eight is bigger than seven and seven is bigger than six, then six cannot be bigger than eight. That's good.

But wait. Arrow's Theorem tells us that something else must go wrong. And it does. The Borda rule fails to satisfy independence of irrelevant alternatives. New, irrelevant alternatives can change the rankings of the other alternatives. Think back to our example of Liz, Skip, and William picking a host city for the Olympics. Suppose that they use the Borda rule; the result would be a three-way tie. But if Skip were to introduce Bethesda as an alternative, and if everyone thought Bethesda to be little more than a less attractive version of Washington, their preferences might look as follows.

Liz: Hamburg > London > Washington > Bethesda
Skip: Washington > Bethesda > Hamburg > London
William: London > Washington > Bethesda > Hamburg

Now, if we apply the Borda rule, Hamburg gets four points from Liz, two points from Skip, and one point from William, for a total of seven points. London gets three points from Liz, one point from Skip, and four points from William, for a total of eight points. Washington gets two points from Liz, four points from Skip, and three points from William, for a total of nine points. And Bethesda gets one point from Liz, three points from Skip, and two points from William, for a total of six points. Bethesda was seemingly

| L | M | R |

Figure 10.1 The Median Ideal Sno-Cone

irrelevant. It took last place. Yet it changed the outcomes so that Washington wins.

We might ask, what does Arrow's theorem have to do with diversity? Recall that Arrow's theorem allows all possible preference orderings. This was a condition of the theorem. If preferences are restricted, that is, not allowed to be diverse, then the desiderata do not necessarily conflict.[7] In the extreme case, where everyone has identical preferences, all of the desiderata are satisfied. The desiderata are also satisfied if preference diversity is limited to a single dimension—an admittedly strong assumption. To see this, we return to the sno-cone model from chapter 9, and we consider majority rule voting among pairs of alternatives as our rule for aggregating preferences.

A Return to the Sno-Cone Model

Recall that in the sno-cone model, people have preferences about sno-cone colors that were determined by their ideal sno-cones. For the moment, we do not care whether these preference differences are fundamental or instrumental. In either case, we say that one sno-cone color is *collectively preferred* to another if a majority of people prefers it.

We next consider a set of potential sno-cone colors and have people vote for their favorite color. We pay special attention to the person whose preferred color is the *median* among preferred colors. Let's call this person Chad (yes, he has dimples). We denote Chad's ideal point by M (see figure 10.1). We will assume an eleven-person sno-cone committee. To make Chad the median, we must place five people's ideal points to the left of M, and five to the right of M.

We now show that the color M defeats any other color in an election. To see this, suppose that some other color to the right of

M is paired in an election against M. Chad prefers M to this other color as do all people with ideal points to the left of M. Similarly, if the other color lies to the left of M, then Chad prefers M as does everyone with an ideal point to the right of M. Thus, M would be the winner. The preferred color of the sno-cone committee would be M. We can also use the majority voting rule to determine collective preferences. These collective preferences satisfy all of the desiderata.[8]

This example shows that a little diversity—whether it is fundamental or instrumental—doesn't cause any problems. However, not everyone may be happy with the collective choice (or ranking). If these preference differences are fundamental, then Chad's preferred outcome balances the concerns of those on the left with those of people on the right. Even so, some people may be thrilled with the alternative chosen. And, as we discuss later, people who participate in groups with diverse members are, on average, less happy with the outcomes. Some dissatisfaction is unavoidable. To quote Mick Jagger, "you can't always get what you want." Whether you get what you need is open to debate.

If preference differences are instrumental, whether people are happy or not depends on how good the choice is as a prediction. If the committee cares only about sales of sno-cones, then Chad's preferred color can be thought of as a policy. Whether the outcome of that policy, the total sales, will be good or bad depends on the accuracy and the diversity of the individual predictions. (We know this from the Diversity Prediction Theorem.) Everyone will be happy if this prediction is good and unhappy if it is not.

PLOTT'S THEOREM: GREATER DIVERSITY AND AGGREGATION FAILURE

Given that we're okay if preferences differ along a single dimension, we cannot help but ask whether it's also okay if they differ along two dimensions. Unfortunately, it's not okay. To see why, we assume that, in addition to choosing a color for the sno-cone, our committee must also choose a size. Everything else is as

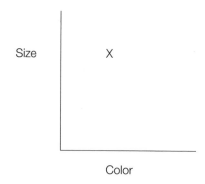

Figure 10.2 Two-Dimensional Sno-Cones

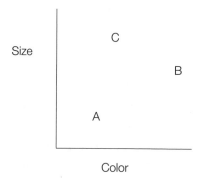

Figure 10.3 Two-Dimensional Sno-Cones, with Three People's Ideal Points

before. We'll refer to the color and size of a sno-cone as its design. We can plot each possible sno-cone design in two-dimensional space, where color is on the horizontal axis and size is on the vertical axis (see figure 10.2).

By adding this second dimension, we create a bunch of problems. The first is that Chad, our median person, disappears. In one dimension, Chad was situated so that half of the people had ideal points to the left and half had ideal points to the right. In two dimensions, it's not likely that we can find a person whose ideal point satisfies this property on both dimensions. To see why Chad is left dangling, consider figure 10.3, which shows three people's ideal designs denoted by *A*, *B*, and *C*.

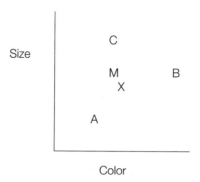

Figure 10.4 Defeating the Median

To be the median on a dimension, a person's ideal point must lie in between the ideal points of the other two people. In this figure, person *B* has the median ideal point on the size dimension, but person *C* has the median ideal point on the color dimension. This lack of a median need not create a problem. We could define the *median sno-cone* as the median on each dimension. We could, in effect, create a *virtual Chad*. Let's denote his ideal point by *M*.

We might think that we're okay, that this trick gets us a policy that wins. However, when we check to see if *M* wins a vote against any another alternative design, if it's the winner of any majority rule vote, we see that it is not. Defeating *M* requires little effort. Consider the sno-cone design *X* that lies just to the right and below *M* (see figure 10.4).

By inspection, we can see that the people with ideal points at *A* and *B* both prefer *X* to *M*. The policy *M* then cannot be a winner against every other proposal as we had hoped.

Even though the virtual Chad's ideal point, *M*, can be defeated, perhaps some other design is most preferred. Charlie Plott showed this not to be true. He showed that if preferences exist in more than one dimension, then *any alternative can be defeated*.

Plott's No-Winner Result: *In more than one dimension, generically, there will be no alternative that defeats every other alternative in a pairwise vote.*[9]

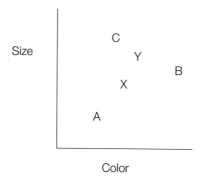

Figure 10.5 Defeating X

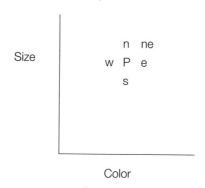

Figure 10.6 The Plott No-Winner Result

We will define what *generically* means in a moment. First, we describe the intuition behind the result and why it's so important. Rather than look at M, let's consider the design X that defeats M. It, in turn, can be defeated by Y, as both B and C prefer Y to X (see figure 10.5).

Extending this logic to a general proof is not hard and is worth doing. Consider an arbitrary sno-cone design denoted by P. We can surround P by sno-cone designs in every direction (see figure 10.6).

We're hoping that P can win a vote against any other sno-cone design, including the one below it, s. This implies that fewer than half of the people must prefer designs smaller than P. P must also win a vote against the design denoted by n, so fewer than half of the people must prefer designs larger than P. Similarly, fewer than half of the people must prefer darker colored sno-cones and lighter colored sno-cones—the designs denoted by e and w, respectively. Applying this same logic to designs that differ from P in both size and color, we see that fewer than half of the people must have ideal points that lie to the upper right of P. If they don't, P would lose a vote to ne.

Putting all of this together, for P to win a vote against all other designs, it has to be the median in every direction. The ideal points of the committee members must be equally distributed in every direction from P. Mathematicians call this *radial symmetry*. Preferences could be symmetrically arrayed, but it's not likely. In fact, it's almost impossible; hence the use of the word *generically* in Plott's claim.

This looking in every direction should remind us of something— the looking in every direction for a good cup of coffee that began chapter 6. These two models show diversity's double-edged sword. Differences in how we see things allow us to search in lots of directions and find better solutions. Differences in what we desire lead people to make policy proposals in lots of directions. This makes almost any policy or outcome unstable.

We have to be a bit careful here. The implications of Plott's result differ depending on the source of preference diversity. If the diversity is fundamental, as is usually assumed to be the case, people may have incentives to keep proposing alternatives nearer to their own ideal points. Ideal points represent outcomes in this case, and people want to get outcomes closer to what they prefer.

If preferences differ instrumentally, this same logic need not hold. In this case, the designs may be company policies and outcomes may equal sales. People have incentives to propose designs that they think are likely to increase sales (designs near their ideal point), but they would also be cognizant that a median design (our virtual Chad's ideal point) might be a pretty good prediction. Thus Plott's result creates fewer problems in this case, unless people are enamored of their own predictions (imagine!) and fail to recognize the wisdom of crowds.

McKelvey and Rock, Paper, Scissors

The Plott result alone need not be serious cause for alarm. We should worry only if diverse preferences could lead to bad choices or predictions. Yet as we now see, these worries may be justified. We will see that absent institutional constraints, a sequence of votes could lead anywhere—literally, wrestler governors.

We can see this using our two-dimensional sno-cone model. We again suppose that our committee begins at design P, and then moves to some other design that defeats it in a vote. Call this design P_1. We next consider a sno-cone design that defeats P_1; call it P_2. If we do this forever, and Plott's result tells us that we can, eventually one of two things must happen: either we find a small rock-paper-scissors-like cycle, where P_7 loses to P_8 and P_8 loses to P_9 and P_9 loses to P_7, or the sno-cone designs wander through some large region of the space of sno-cone designs.

The first outcome—policies alternating among some small good set of choices—doesn't sound so bad, and it isn't. The second outcome—the wandering aimlessly around the space of possibilities—doesn't sound appealing. It might make us rethink whether democracy is such a good thing after all. Unfortunately, we get wandering. To see why, recall how we constructed a sno-cone design that defeats M (virtual Chad's ideal point). We created a sno-cone that A and B preferred to M. We did not care at all about how C felt about that design. That's the key insight: build a coalition that makes some people unhappy. Then create a sno-cone that makes those people a little less unhappy that attracts just enough other voters to win a majority. We did that earlier when we choose Y, which B and C preferred to X. At design Y, person A is unhappy. So a sno-cone design that lies far from A but close to B can defeat Y. Call this Z (see figure 10.7).

At Z, person C would be furious. And, even though person A voted for Z, person A doesn't like his design much either. Person A's ideal point lies a long way from Z. Person B doesn't much like the Z either. So, now we have done it. We have a terrible

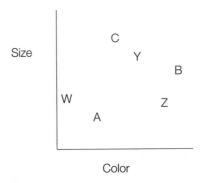

Figure 10.7 Leaving the Space of Reasonable Designs

winning alternative Z (it's a long way from anyone's ideal point), and we got there through a series of votes. We could continue on in this way, and show how through a sequence of votes we can get anywhere—we can have little tiny light blue sno-cones lose to huge dark blue sno-cones.

What we now have is a troubling finding: a sequence of votes could traverse the space of alternatives. We have no guarantee that we don't get a completely arbitrary outcome.

McKelvey's Cycling Theorem: *If preferences are multi-dimensional, then (generically) given any alternative, through a series of votes it is possible to reach any other alternative.*[10]

To give full credit where credit is due, this result was subsequently generalized by Norman Schofield, who showed that continuous paths of majority preferred choices lead from anywhere to anywhere else.[11] This sounds technical, but what it means is that we could walk a smooth path from any one policy to any other. It wouldn't take some sophisticated trick for democracy to be led astray.

These first few theorems led scholars to talk about the "chaos of democracy." To infer chaos would be to misread the theorems. These theorems describe characteristics of collective preferences, not what would happen in a real election. If the people proposing designs have an incentive to get as many votes as possible, then the winning design tends to be near virtual Chad's ideal point.[12]

Electoral institutions can also include procedural rules that prevent choices from spiraling out into the nether regions of design space. Think back to the example in which the sno-cone design W defeats Z. Everyone should know that W is a bad design. Any one of the people could propose his or her ideal point and it would defeat W unanimously. Thus, another effective way to prevent cycles is to demand supermajorities. If two-thirds of the people must approve any change to the status quo, cycles become impossible with large numbers of voters.[13]

So let's go back to McKelvey's result that a collection of voters could get from any sno-cone design to any other if they wanted to do so. Such paths exist. The tendency for choices to escape the central region of design space hinges on the incentives of people to make proposals away from the median and their ability to get these passed. These incentives differ depending on whether the preference diversity is fundamental or instrumental. If it is fundamental, then people with nonrepresentative preferences have incentives to propose outcomes that they like. They might get lucky and win.

If preference differences are instrumental, then although a series of votes could lead anywhere, people have little incentive to propose policies that head away from the collective prediction. This incentive would exist only if people think that their predictive models were much better than everyone else's. If everyone thinks that way, then problems could arise. If only one person thinks that way (and if that person is correct—if her model is more accurate), then, as we saw in chapter 8, this might not be all bad. So, once again, the problems that arise when aggregating diverse preferences have less severe implications for instrumental preferences.

All else being equal, then, greater preference diversity should imply less representative choices by the electorate. This holds in large elections: the representativeness of choices made by voters appears to be negatively correlated with preference heterogeneity. Using ballot data from Los Angeles County voters, Elizabeth Gerber and Jeffrey Lewis estimated the heterogeneity of preferences within a congressional district by looking at votes cast in fifty-five races. They found that representatives from districts with greater preference heterogeneity were less closely related to the district's median voter than were representatives from more homogeneous districts.[14] The evidence agrees with the logic, or at least what we have does.

GIBBARD-SATTERTHWAITE AND MANIPULATION

The results we have covered so far have been so negative that we might want to just fold up our tents and go home. Fortunately, concluding our analysis of collective decision making and diverse preferences at this point would be premature. We can put these results in a more favorable light. Before things get better, however, they get worse, a lot worse.

Up until now, we have assumed that people voice their true preferences. This assumption rests on a naïve view of human nature. People can—and do—misrepresent their preferences in order to achieve good outcomes. People do this by voting for candidates that they think can win rather than the candidates that they would like to win.[15] Evidence even exists that cardinals do this when selecting a pope.[16]

To see how these incentives to lie might arise, let's consider an example involving the "members of the academy" who vote for the Oscars. In what some regard as one of the great upsets in the history of the Oscars, Adrien Brody won the 2003 best actor award over Michael Caine, Nicholas Cage, Daniel Day-Lewis, and Jack Nicholson. What follows is pure speculation. All that we know is that Brody received more votes than anyone else, a plurality of the votes. But for fun, let's suppose that the vote percentages were as shown in table 10.7.

We might suppose that those people who voted for Nicholson preferred Caine to Brody, Nicholson and Caine both being part of Hollywood's old guard. Had these voters known, or even thought, that Brody would win, they could have misrepresented their preferences and voted for Caine. If so, Caine would have won his first Oscar, and the people who switched their votes—who

TABLE 10.7:
2003 best actor vote totals

Actor	Percentage of Total Votes
Adrien Brody	25
Michael Caine	20
Nicholas Cage	20
Daniel Day-Lewis	20
Jack Nicholson	15

manipulated the outcome—would have been happier. They preferred Caine to Brody.

This may seem contrived, but it's not. Allan Gibbard and Mark Satterthwaite have shown that this incentive for misrepresentation always exists. So long as at least three alternatives exist and people have diverse preferences, then any decision rule can be manipulated (unless we appoint a dictator—but dictators can be manipulated in other ways).

The Gibbard-Satterthwaite Theorem: *Any nondictatorial rule for aggregating diverse preference orderings over more than two outcomes is manipulable.*[17]

We already saw that even if people tell the truth, voting—or any other decision rule—has problems. We now see that people don't have an incentive to tell the truth. To make sense of this result, we first assume fundamental preferences. We discuss instrumental preference diversity in a few paragraphs.

Our interest is in understanding the two roles that diversity plays in the Gibbard-Satterthwaite Theorem. One condition requires at least three alternatives. The second condition requires that all preference profiles must be allowed, that preferences can be diverse. We first explore why we need at least three alternatives. Clearly, no one can have an incentive to misrepresent her preferences with only a single alternative. Some U.S. congressional primary elections have only a single candidate, and we can rest assured that no voters misrepresent their preferences in these races.

TABLE 10.8:
Scenarios not including Valerie's vote

Scenario 1	jasmine leads by more than one vote
Scenario 2	jasmine leads by exactly one vote
Scenario 3	jasmine and basmati are tied
Scenario 4	basmati leads by exactly one vote
Scenario 5	basmati leads by more than one vote

Let's next consider a vote over two alternatives and show that even in this case no problems arise. We consider a vote over type of rice: jasmine or basmati. Specifically, let's assume that a committee of people writing a cookbook is voting over which type of rice to include in a recipe for slow-cooked tarragon chicken with carrots. Our protagonist in this morality play, Valerie, prefers jasmine to basmati. To determine if Valerie would ever have an incentive to misrepresent her preferences, we need to consider five possible scenarios (see table 10.8).

In scenarios 1 and 5, Valerie's vote cannot influence the outcome, so we can ignore them. She doesn't even have an incentive to vote. But she would anyway, just to be a good team player. In the other three scenarios, her vote could matter. In scenario 2, if she votes for jasmine, then jasmine wins. If she votes for basmati, the vote ends in a tie and would have to be decided by a coin flip or some other procedure. In this scenario, Valerie should vote for jasmine, because she prefers jasmine. In scenario 3, Valerie's vote determines the outcome. Valerie prefers jasmine, so again she should vote for jasmine. Finally, in scenario 4, basmati wins unless Valerie votes for jasmine, in which case basmati and jasmine tie. So she should again vote for jasmine.

In each of the three scenarios where Valerie's vote matters, she should vote for jasmine, her preferred choice. She has no incentive to misrepresent her preferences. Next, we increase the number of alternatives by adding wild rice. Now, there exist scenarios in which Valerie should misrepresent her preferences. We again assume that Valerie prefers jasmine to basmati. We also assume that she prefers basmati to wild. If Valerie expects jasmine to

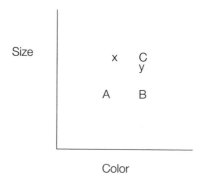

Figure 10.8 Three Sno-Cone Colors in One Dimension

Figure 10.9 Sno-Cone Designs in Two Dimensions

receive around 10 percent of the votes and basmati and wild to split the other 90 percent equally, her best strategy would be to switch her support to basmati. (She would be doing the same thing that the Nicholson voters did in switching to Caine in our previous example.) If she does, she might swing the vote in basmati's favor.

We've just seen that it takes three alternatives in order for manipulation to rear its ugly head, but that alone is not enough. Even with three or more alternatives, manipulation may not be possible. Manipulability requires that preferences must also be diverse. Consider an example with three potential sno-cone colors along a single dimension (figure 10.8).

Suppose that an informal poll is taken and color *B* gets the most votes, followed by color *C*. People who prefer *A* have no incentive to misrepresent their preferences. They prefer *B* to *C*; it's closer. If we add a second dimension, size, then the incentives to misrepresent become greater. This possibility can be seen in figure 10.9.

A person with an ideal point at *x* most prefers design *C*, but *A* is her next favorite design. A person with an ideal point at *y* also most prefers design *C*, but *B* is his next favorite design. In

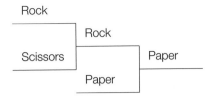

Figure 10.10 A Rock, Paper, Scissors Tournament

two dimensions, knowing a person's preferred alternative places fewer restrictions on her preferences about the other alternatives than is the case in one dimension. Therefore, the incentives for misrepresentation increase.

To briefly summarize, if we have more than two alternatives and diverse preferences—that is, preferences that we cannot put on a line—then we are likely to have the possibility of manipulation through misrepresentation. Manipulation is not good, but it is a larger problem for diverse fundamental preferences than for diverse instrumental preferences.

Agenda Manipulation

We now go one step deeper in the morass of problems created by diverse preferences by showing that diverse preferences create an incentive for agenda manipulation. Consider the task of constructing a tournament to determine the champion among the strategies rock, paper, and scissors. If rock plays scissors in the first round, and the winner plays paper, then paper wins the tournament (covering rock after rock's first-round smash of scissors) (see figure 10.10).

Consider a second tournament in which paper plays rock in the first round with the winner playing scissors. Now, scissors wins (see figure 10.11).

Comparing the outcomes of these two tournament structures helps us see the importance of setting the agenda.[18] In one tournament, paper wins. In the other tournament, scissors wins. This same phenomenon occurred in our analysis of the Colonel

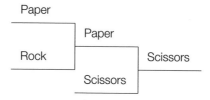

Figure 10.11 A Second Rock, Paper, Scissors Tournament

Blotto game, where the "national champion" turned out to be the team that played Oklahoma first.

This potential for gains from manipulating the agenda has two consequences—both bad. Not only can outcomes be less than representative—often, people can manipulate the agenda in ways far more severe than we've considered—but also these manipulations breed mistrust. When someone proposes an agenda, how can others not wonder whether that agenda was designed so as to manipulate outcomes?

Implications

The effects of misrepresentation and agenda manipulation can be seen in two ways. If we look at outcomes, the effects need not be harmful. Had members of the academy misrepresented their preferences and Michael Caine won, wouldn't the outcome be just as good, if not better? Thus, misrepresentation of preferences can improve outcomes. For this reason, many political scientists refer to incentive-based misrepresentation as strategic voting, not as lying. By voting strategically, a person avoids wasting a vote on a favorite alternative and chooses one that has a chance to win.

Further, if preferences differ instrumentally, the incentives to misrepresent preferences (or to manipulate the agenda) are weak. If people have a common goal, they have little reason not to reveal their predictions. People even have incentives to share information, models, and experiences so that people can refine their predictive models to improve the collective choice.

The second way to look at the effects of strategic voting and agenda manipulation focuses on group relations. Misrepresentation can reduce trust among group members. Let's return to our example of the Academy Awards. Suppose that the winner is chosen by a committee whose members sit in a room and discuss each nominee. A committee member who states a strong preference for Nicholson but then votes for Caine might infuriate other members of the committee. If so, in diverse preference groups we might expect people to be less open, less willing to share their preferences. We need say little about the effects of attempts to manipulate agendas on group relations.

These problems might be more severe with fundamental preference diversity. If the differences are instrumental, no person prefers a particular policy. People care only about the outcome. Unfortunately, people can be as attached to their ideas as they are to their preferences. If a member of a committee believes himself to have a far more accurate predictive model than everyone else, he might try to manipulate the outcome. In fact, everyone might feel that way, and they might all act strategically. They might be so attached to their own models that even after the outcome has been realized, they might still believe that their choice would have resulted in an even better one.

DIVERSITY CAUSING UNDERCONTRIBUTION

Our analysis so far has concentrated on choosing a single alternative. In many cases, a collection of people must allocate a budget across several projects. In these instances, fundamental preference diversity creates other problems. Most notably, it results in underprovision of resources relative to what would be chosen by a homogenous society. Imagine two families of four, each with the same fixed budget that they can allocate to building a house. Each family has a mother, a father, and two teenage boys.

The members of the first family all enjoy the same activities: singing, playing cards, and making elaborate buildings from popsicle sticks. They build a house with a moderate-sized kitchen, a large family room, a music room, and two modest bedrooms.

The members of the second family have diverse fundamental preferences. The mother, Ellen, likes to weld. The father, Daniel, builds model airplanes. Their elder son, Zachary, plays drums, and their younger son, Evan, enjoys calligraphy. They build a house with a tiny kitchen and living room combination, a large garage for welding, three bedrooms, and a workshop in which Daniel can build his airplanes. To satisfy their diverse preferences, they are left with little common space.

This tendency for diverse fundamental preferences to result in underprovision of common resources holds generally. If people want the same things, they can spend more money on those same things and jointly benefit. If they want different things, then they have to spread their money thinly. As the logic is so straightforward, we won't bother with a formal model, but instead comment on the implications of diverse societies, organizations, and families. More diverse fundamental preferences should result in fewer resources allocated to collective goods and projects—things that everyone can use. The collective pie has to be sliced into many thin slices consumed by individuals. If preferences were more similar, the pie could be cut into a few large wedges that could be shared by everyone.

Sobering Differences

Our analysis of diverse preferences leads to some sobering observations. Individuals with diverse preference can form collections that, formally speaking, are not rational. The results of votes can be somewhat arbitrary when preferences are diverse unless proper procedures are put in place. And no procedures work perfectly; individuals have incentives to misrepresent their preferences and to manipulate the agenda. The best check on this strategic behavior may well be strategic behavior by others. However, even if this strategic behavior results in good outcomes, when all is said and done, people may not like each other or the process. The implications are not as dire as we might think, however. The incentives to act strategically when preferences differ instrumentally may not be that strong. In fact, the lessons of chapter 8 on prediction suggest rather strongly that instrumental preference diversity may be a good thing. Diverse instrumental preferences are, after all, nothing more than diverse predictive models.

Throughout this chapter, we have assumed either purely fundamental or purely instrumental preference diversity. Quite often, both types of diverse preferences may be in play. For example, many localities have passed referenda establishing greenbelts. We might first assume that everyone cares only about maximizing the value of his or her home. If so, votes on the referenda could be considered as predictions about the effect of greenbelts on housing prices. Those people whose models predict that the greenbelt will increase demand for existing houses—by reducing the supply of new housing—vote for these referenda. And those people who believe that the greenbelt will reduce growth in the region and decrease overall housing demand vote against them. But we might also assume that people care about preserving green space and native species. If so, their votes for the referenda might be based on those fundamental preferences. Most likely, people care both about housing values and about preserving green space. And most likely, people do not know the outcome of these policies. Therefore, preferences differ both fundamentally and instrumentally.

The differences between fundamental and instrumental preference diversity influence how we think about the composition of decision-making bodies. If we believe that most preference diversity is fundamental, then when putting together a committee to make a decision that has society-wide impact, we want representatives with diverse preferences. In fact, we want the preferences of our committee to *reflect* those of society so that any choice, and here choices mean outcomes, will be acceptable to most of society. For this simple reason, creating diverse committees that include men and women, people of different ethnic and racial groups, people from different age groups, and people from different professions and parts of the country often makes sense.

Carrying this logic even further, we may want, in addition, to put in place some safeguards against those people with the majority preference tyrannizing those people in the minority, or so thought James Madison. And so think many others.

We take up reflectiveness again later in the book, but for the moment recognize that we do not want to reflect people with highly inaccurate predictive models. Instead, what we would like, again provided the predictive task is not easy, are diverse and accurate predictive models. Therefore, we would like a committee composed of people who think intelligently and differently. Otherwise, their collective prediction won't be accurate.

The implications of diverse preferences also apply within individuals. A person may be a husband, a father, a son, a brother, a friend, and a marketing representative. What a person prefers in any particular context depends on the role he is performing. Some refer to these various roles as identities. Different identities get evoked in different contexts. When voting or investing, we may think only of our families. When deciding which books to read, we may think only of our careers or friends. When multiple roles or identities get evoked contextually, then we may fail to be rational: We may have diverse fundamental preferences that contain cycles. Similarly, we have in our heads many predictive models. These models may give conflicting events and even create cycles. We find this recognition in Walt Whitman, who wrote, "Do I contradict myself?/Very well then I contradict myself,/(I am large, I contain multitudes)," and in Maxine Hong Kingston, who wrote, "I learned to make my mind large, as the universe is large, so that there is room for paradoxes." In both cases, the fullness of their lives produces these inconsistencies. Most of us would accept this trade-off. We would willingly accept contradictions in exchange for a fullness or richness of roles and ideas. Teams, groups, and entire societies might well accept this same compromise, for to be large enough to contain contradictions also makes them large enough to solve problems and make accurate predictions, as we are about to see.

CHAPTER 11

Interacting Toolboxes and Preferences

GO ASK ALICE

Alice: It would be so nice if something made sense for a change.
—Lewis Carroll, *Alice in Wonderland*

So far we have considered the effects of diverse toolboxes and diverse preferences in isolation. The brief summary goes as follows: diverse toolboxes good, diverse preferences not so good (but not so bad either). Our unpacking and careful recombining of parts allowed us to see the effects of each type of diversity. However, piece-by-piece unpackings lose the interplay between the various parts—in our case, the types of diversity. For this reason, we now explore the interactions between diverse toolboxes and diverse preferences on the various tasks.

Our analysis of interactions will be far from exhaustive. I just want to provide a glimpse of how the frameworks connect and interact. We will see that sometimes one type of diversity creates another and that the contexts to which they apply overlap, and their effects intertwine. We therefore do well to accept all of the various types of diversity, just as we accept the people who possess them, warts and all.

The logic presented in this chapter turns some, but thankfully not all, of the logic of the previous chapters on its head. It produces a bit of an Alice in Wonderland sensation. Everything will appear upside down. Fundamental preference diversity, which created nothing but problems in chapter 10, may be a driver of perspective, toolbox, and predictive model diversity, and therefore improve problem solving and prediction. Perspective and heuristic diversity, which previously were these wonderful things that result in more potential solutions, may produce more outcomes over which fundamental preference diversity can arise, and, by our previous logic, in which there exist more opportunities for manipulation.

These interactive effects, powerful as they may be, mitigate but do not overwhelm the isolated effects of each type of diversity. To say that everything we've learned so far is wrong would miss the point. Everything we have covered so far considered isolated tasks. When we fold tasks together the analysis becomes more interesting, more nuanced, and more fun.

We will begin by seeing how diverse fundamental preferences affect the other types of diversity. This resurrects preference diversity, turning it from something that causes problems to something that helps solve them—and helps make better predictions. When we say that people have diverse preferences, we will mean that we have different goals, desires, wants, and needs. And we acquire diverse cognitive tools to satisfy these preferences. If a person wants to be a great artist, she acquires the tools to become one. If a person wants to open a coffee shop, he learns how to select beans and foam milk. In this simple, direct way, diverse preferences translate into diverse tools: perspectives, heuristics, interpretations, and predictive models. Preference diversity begets toolbox diversity. And therefore, preference diversity has a strong and positive indirect effect on problem solving.

The Problem of Problems

Up to now, we've discussed topics such as ice cream, the NFL draft, and the Academy Awards. To some, this may have seemed flippant. We make up for that now. We get serious. When people differ in their preferences, they differ not only in what kinds of food they like to eat and music they enjoy. They also differ in what they think important. When people choose how to spend their days, to what purpose to devote their lives, their preferences guide them. What we see as problems or opportunities depends on what we value.

People who value greater social equality may believe poverty to be a problem. If so, they may choose to work to eradicate poverty. By deciding on poverty as a problem, they then may choose to develop relevant cognitive tools. They may develop perspectives, interpretations, heuristics, and predictive models to allow them to make sense of whether the consumer price index accurately categorizes people as poor. Other people may think that male pattern baldness is an important problem and may devote their lives to finding a cure. Some people—those with lots of hair—may not think baldness a pressing social concern. Though it is far better that we care about humanity's fate than its pate, value judgments lie outside our analysis. My point is only that the cognitive tools required to cure male pattern baldness probably differ from those required to eradicate poverty.

Our decisions about what problems to apply ourselves to solving need not be conscious. We can leave it to historians to decide why people choose what they do. Consider the case of Louis Pasteur, who developed the germ theory of disease. Early in his career, he helped the French wineries develop fermentation processes that killed germs. The Pasteurization process later was applied to beer, milk, and other foods. Later on, Pasteur advocated that doctors clean their surgical instruments and wash their hands. Initially, few doctors believed him, and so the germ theory of disease took a while to catch on.[1]

Pasteur had training in physics, chemistry, mathematics, Latin, and art. He could have studied anything. Why study wine? Why study germs? The choice of wine may well have been cultural. Pasteur was French. Had he been German, he might have studied beer. His decision to study germs and disease may have been based on personal reasons: three of his children died of typhoid at young ages.

If, like Pasteur, we choose the tasks to which we devote our lives through some combination of opportunity, culture, and preferences, then we cannot separate preference diversity from toolbox diversity. We acquire tools that enable us to contribute to what we think important. The tools chosen by someone who wants to cure breast cancer differ from the tools chosen by someone who wants to cure diabetes. Thus, our preferences about what we want to achieve play an enormous role in why the insides of our heads differ as much as they do.

Now let's jump up a level. The question of what problems a society should tackle, or attempt to tackle, might well be called *the problem of problems*. We can think of deciding on which problems to address as being determined by preferences—some people think equality is more important than environmental sustainability or economic growth. But we might also think of this choice as being a problem—a problem of which problem to address first. It may be that some problems are more pressing than others, that we would collectively be much happier if we addressed them first. And, as we saw in our discussion of problem solving, if we want a good solution to a problem—including the problem of problems—we want to include people with diverse perspectives and heuristics.

The Force of Diverse Preferences

To see formally how diverse preferences can lead to diverse perspectives, we return to and expand on the rugged landscape model. Recall that the height of a point on the landscape denotes its value. In the Ben and Jerry's example, we assumed that the altitude of an ice cream summit represented how good the ice cream tasted. In our toy model, Ben and Jerry had the same fundamental preference: to make the best ice cream.

Now let's suppose that Ben's preferences change, that he becomes concerned with profits. He wants to make as much money as possible so that he can donate it to charity. Some pints of ice cream cost more to produce than others. Cream from small Vermont farms comes at a cost. So do real chocolate chips. Although taste and profits may be positively correlated (the better it tastes, the more it sells, the higher the profits), they would not produce the exact same ranking of the pints. So Ben's profit landscape might now differ from Jerry's taste landscape. If so, Ben and Jerry would assign different values to each pint: *each searches on a different landscape.*

This multiple landscapes metaphor highlights the distinction between diverse perspectives and diverse fundamental preferences. Diverse perspectives create different encodings of the set of possible solutions. Diverse fundamental preferences produce different values (the elevations on the landscape) for the set of solutions.

Why then would diverse preferences create diverse perspectives? The answer should be obvious. Recall that ineffective perspectives create extremely rugged landscapes (badlands) and that good perspectives create smooth landscapes (Mount Fujis). A problem solver searches for a perspective that results in a smooth landscape. If people have diverse preferences, the values that they assign to solutions differ. A perspective that makes the landscape smooth for one person would not necessarily make the landscape smooth for another.

We can see this by returning to the Ben and Jerry's example. Suppose that increasing the calorie count in ice cream has a large effect on costs. For Ben, newly concerned with profits, lining up the pints of ice cream according to caloric rank may create a single-peaked landscape: profits rise with calories as the improved taste more than offsets the increase in costs and then fall as the cost increases swamp the taste improvements. For Jerry, the calorie perspective may have lots of peaks—far more than the size of chunks/number of chunks perspective.

In keeping with our attempt to be a bit more serious, we next apply this same logic in the context of a scholarship decision. Suppose that a committee of two people has to search among five hundred applicants to find three finalists for a single science scholarship winner. Much of the information about the applicants may exist in a spreadsheet, but some information, such as letters of recommendation, may exist only in paper form in application files. Suppose that Mike cares only about academic skills. His valuation of a student might be strongly correlated with the student's grade point average in science courses. The spreadsheet, though, might contain only total grade point average. Mike's perspective might be to arrange the students according to their overall grade point average (using the "sort" command on the spreadsheet), as that likely would be highly correlated with their science grade point averages. His heuristic might then be to start at the top of the list, pull the corresponding files, and compute the applicants' grade point averages in science courses. He might then work his way down the list until he becomes convinced that he is not likely to find someone with a higher grade point average in science courses.

A second committee member, Mahmoud, may care about creativity, energy level, and a hard to define attribute that he calls "spark." Very little about desire, creativity, effort, and spark can be gleaned from the information on the spreadsheet, but Mahmoud knows those qualities when he sees them. How then to arrange the files? What perspective does he employ? Arranging the files by grade point average would not be useful to Mahmoud. Grade point average may have almost no correlation with desire, creativity, and spark and at most a mild correlation with effort level. Mahmoud might hit on the idea of opening the file cabinets, pulling out all of the files, and arranging them by their thickness. Thickness of file might be correlated with desire and effort. It might also be positively correlated with creativity, and it is almost surely correlated with the length of the letters of recommendation. As for what heuristic to use, Mahmoud might begin with the thickest file first and then move to the next thickest. He might only stop searching when he believes that the remaining files lack sufficient thickness to reveal spark.

In this example, the two members of the committee use similar heuristics. They search along their single dimensional perspectives until they do not believe that any of the remaining files is likely to be better than their current best file. This similarity of heuristics does not hold generally. Had one of them used a two-dimensional perspective, he would have needed a different heuristic—one that tested files in both directions. People with diverse preferences therefore also can be led to construct and acquire diverse heuristics. But our main point is that Mike and Mahmoud have different preferences. And as a result, they search for solutions differently.

We can also connect diverse preferences to diverse interpretations. We bias our interpretations toward dimensions we believe most important. If we differ in what we think important, we likely differ in the dimensions we include in our interpretations. If Tom cares about energy conservation, he may ask to see the heating bills before buying a house. If Bonnie cares about interior light, she may count the number of windows and their size. These attributes become part of how they interpret a house. Because their preferences differ, so do their interpretations. Since interpretations provide the basis for predictive models, diverse preferences also cause people to construct diverse predictive models.

Diversity Goes Bump

We've just seen how preference diversity can create other, more beneficial types of diversity. We now see how some of the other types of diversity can bump into one another—how the presence of one type gets in the way of, or symbiotically improves, another. This bumping into one another creates complexities that we might like to ignore, but cannot.

We'll start with the good news. We see a positive interaction between diverse preferences and problem solving. Following this analysis requires a little effort because we combine ideas and frameworks.

We return yet again to the rugged landscape model, this time without Ben and Jerry. We consider two doctors, Cathy and Yeong, confronting the problem of how to build an artificial elbow. Let's assume that these two doctors were both trained at the same medical school, took internships together, and even work in the same elbow, knee, and hip clinic, and that because of this they use exactly the same perspective and heuristics to search for solutions.

We will not assume that they have the same preferences about outcomes, however. The first doctor, Yeong, has a deeps aesthetic sense. He cares about how the elbow looks. Does it appear

TABLE 11.1:
Cathy's results

Starting Design	Ending Design
A	A
B	D
C	G
D	H
E	I
F	D

natural? Does it posses the beauty and grace of a human elbow? His colleague, Cathy, cares primarily about functionality. Yeong chalks this up to Cathy's experience as a former tennis prodigy.

Let's assume that prior to Yeong and Cathy working on this elbow project, a team of medical engineers developed six prototypes, which have been assigned the letters A to F. Cathy and Yeong use these six prototypes as starting points in their search for even better elbows. By convention, new prototypes that Cathy or Yeong develop will be assigned letters beginning with G.

Table 11.1 shows the results of Cathy's efforts to find improvements. The first column in the table gives the starting design. The second column gives the design she developed. When she started from design A, she could find no better design. When she started from B, she wound up at D, which she prefers to B. When she started at C, she wound up at a new solution, which we denote by G.

Using the same notational convention, we can write Yeong's progress as in table 11.2.

These tables reveal that the local optima for Cathy differ from the local optima for Yeong. Cathy moves from *B* to *D*, and Yeong does the opposite. We can infer from these local optima that elbow *D* is highly functional but not so attractive. We can also infer that elbow *B* (a local optima for Yeong, but not for Cathy) must be attractive but not functional. These differences in local optima arise not from differences in how they search but from differences in what they value.

TABLE 11.2:
Yeong's results

Starting Design	Ending Design
A	B
B	B
C	I
D	B
E	E
F	J

Recall from our discussion of collective problem solving the importance of the intersection of the sets of local optima. Diverse groups found good solutions because their local optima did not intersect at many points. Previously, we talked about how this arose if people had diverse perspectives and heuristics. Now we see that it also holds if they have diverse preferences. People with diverse preferences are not likely to get stuck on the same solutions. Thus, if two people have diverse preferences, they may do well on problem solving.

This logic has limits. The preferences cannot be too diverse. If so, any improvement for one person would make matters worse for the other. If we think back to our discussion of error-allowing heuristics and simulated annealing, we come to a conclusion that a little preference diversity would probably be a good thing, and that ideally, preference diversity would reduce over time. That could happen. Yeong could learn to appreciate the importance of functionality, and Cathy could recognize the value of aesthetics. If so, the design they develop would probably be quite good.

TOO MUCH OF A GOOD THING

We just saw how diverse preferences can have positive effects. Previously, we saw how diverse perspective and heuristics enable a group of problem solvers to generate more solutions

TABLE 11.3:
Values of solutions found
without diverse perspectives and
heuristics

Elbow Design	Values for (Cathy, Yeong, Monica)
H	(2,1,3)
I	(7,5,6)
J	(5,7,5)
Best	???

and to have fewer common local optima. We might therefore think that having *both* diverse perspectives and heuristics *and* diverse preferences would be even better, but alas, we can have too much of a good thing. Too many solutions combined with diverse preferences can be a lethal combination. When people have diverse preferences, each solution has multiple values, one for each problem solver. This can result in preference cycles, manipulation, and misrepresentation.

Let's suppose that Cathy and Yeong add a third doctor, Monica, to their team and that Monica cares only about costs. The cheaper the artificial elbow, the more people who can afford it. Let's first suppose that Monica has the same perspectives and heuristics as Cathy and Yeong. If so, they're relying totally on their preference diversity to lead them to lots of potential solutions. Let's suppose that the three of them identify three possible solutions. Table 11.3 identifies the solutions by letters and their values for the three problem solvers by a vector of three values—one for each person. These values lie between one and ten, with the better the elbow design the higher the value.

If Cathy, Yeong, and Monica vote among these solutions, they decide on *I*. It defeats both other designs in pairwise votes. It is a good solution. It's Cathy and Monica's top choice and Yeong's second favorite.

Now, let's extend the example and assume that Cathy, Yeong, and Monica also have diverse perspectives and heuristics

TABLE 11.4:
Value of solutions found with
diverse perspectives and
heuristics

Solution	Values
H	(2,1,3)
I	(7,5,6)
J	(5,7,5)
K	(1,2,2)
L	(3,4,3)
M	(5,5,5)
N	(4,6,7)
O	(3,5,3)
P	(5,5,5)
Best	???

(table 11.4). This would enable them to locate even more solutions.

Elbow design *I* now loses in a pairwise vote to design *N*. Unfortunately, *N* loses to *J*, and, as we know, *J* loses to *I*. So, we once again have a preference cycle.

We do not know what outcome will result from this cycle, but it could be *J*. And previously, we argued that *I* was better than *J*. But this was based on having only three alternatives. Even if the three doctors do choose *J*, the discussions and procedures that result in *J* could include misrepresentations and attempts to manipulate the agenda. The same outcome, then, could be worse because people are unhappy with the process that produced it.

THE WORLD TURNED UPSIDE DOWN

In interacting the types of diversity, we have highlighted two effects. First, we saw how diversity begets diversity. Diverse preferences can create diverse perspectives, heuristics, interpretations, and predictive models. And, as we know, diverse predictive models create diverse instrumental preferences. By implication, we cannot consider these types of diversity in isolation. Second, we saw that the implications of diversity in one context seep into other contexts. Diverse perspectives and heuristics result in more potential solutions. This can only improve the problem-solving capabilities of a collection of people with identical preferences, however, this intuition need not hold if they have diverse preferences. This good news/bad news result holds in other places as well. Diverse preferences create distinct local optima, which can improve problem solving but can also lead to disagreements about what is an improvement.

These aren't the only interaction effects between types of diversity. The set of experiences from which we construct our predictive models often consists of the solutions that we have generated. Thus, diverse perspectives and heuristics influence our predictive models. This discussion of interactions paints a complicated picture of how individual diversity influences our collective performance on tasks. We should not lose sight of the larger picture by overemphasizing these more subtle details. Sure, people might disagree sometimes, and they might even try to manipulate outcomes, but on the whole, diversity proves beneficial. With it, we can solve hard problems and make accurate predictions.

Part Four _____

THE PUDDING: DOES DIVERSITY
GENERATE BENEFITS?

CHAPTER **12**

The Causes of Cognitive Diversity

FAMILY VACATIONS, COLLEGE, OR IDENTITY?

*I don't know if I think the way I do because I am a physicist or
if I am a physicist because of the way I think.*
—KEN HAAS

THE time has come to look at the evidence, to see whether
toolbox diversity improves problem solving and prediction, and
to see whether fundamental preference diversity leads to conflict
and frustration. Time and space permit only so much, but we
don't need much of either. The evidence speaks clearly: *diversity
produces benefits* (cognitively diverse societies, cities, and teams
perform better than more homogenous ones), *fundamental preference diversity creates problems* (public goods are underprovided
and people don't get along), and, finally, *collections of people with
diverse cognitive toolboxes and diverse fundamental preferences
have higher-variance performance* (they locate better outcomes
and produce more conflict). As identity diverse collections of
people often contain both types of diversity, they perform both
better and worse than homogenous groups as well. Put differently,
identity diverse teams, cities, and societies *can* perform better, but
they often fail to do so. These findings all agree with the models.
To think different is good. To want differently isn't, at least not
necessarily.

As we move forward, it is important to note that we are not testing the logical truth of the models. The models hold up mathematically, just as the equation $5+4 = 9$ does, regardless of whether empirical evidence supports them. We're interested in whether the hypotheses and insights developed in these stark models shed any light on the complex multifaceted real worlds in which we live. Before we begin, two caveats are in order. First, the models that we covered do not provide the only candidate explanations for the empirical phenomena we discuss. Other models might better explain some or all of these empirical regularities. Second, even if the evidence does align with the models, it need not always do so: social scientific facts are temporal regularities. Boys may score better than girls on tests of verbal skills in one decade and worse in another. A tax rebate may have a large effect on spending at one point in time and no effect in another. We can contrast these with facts about the physical world, which remain fixed. The water molecules streaming from your faucet contain two hydrogen atoms and one oxygen atom. They will tomorrow. And they will next year as well.

Before we can make sense of the empirical evidence, we need a better understanding of the causes of cognitive diversity. That's our mission in this brief chapter—to explain what causes cognitive diversity. Without this understanding, we have no way of distinguishing between cognitively homogeneous and cognitively diverse groups. In this chapter, we discuss two direct causes, training and experiences, and one indirect one, identities. The direct causes require no justification and the indirect one requires only a little. We'll ignore genetics, not because genes don't matter. They do.[1] Genes even correlate, however slightly, with identity classifications such as ethnicity and gender.[2]

We will leave out genes because compared to training, experience, and identity, genes play a minor role. Let's allow them briefly to strut and fret and then be heard no more. The case against genes begins with the advice given to young Benjamin Braddock (Dustin Hoffman) in *The Graduate*: "plastics." Our brains possess amazing plasticity—both in structure and function. Neuroscientists have only just begun to understand the former, but they do know that as we learn, we physically alter the structure of our brain. Thinking is weight lifting for the mind. Just as curling weights builds our biceps, so does thinking spatially build our hippocampi.[3] Juggling develops both biceps *and* hippocampi.[4]

This plasticity decreases with time, which increases ethnic and cultural effects. Try as we might, we cannot escape our parents—not just their genes, but all of those other effects they had. This functional plasticity provides one reason for ignoring genetics: *our genes differ little from those of our ancestors of a few hundred years ago, but our cognitive tools differ markedly.* Our ancestors did not know about DNA, bacteria, or viruses. They did not know about the elements, molecules, or atoms, let alone quarks or muons. They did not know the conservation laws from physics. They did not know about electricity, evolution, plate tectonics, or carbon cycles. They did not know calculus. They did not know either Pascal—the man or the computer language. They had similar genes but different toolboxes.

A second reason for ignoring genes relies on economics, preferences, and combinatorics. Think back to the example of Bobbi and Carl and their cognitive toolboxes. Let's make the strongest case we can for genes playing a role in the number and type of tools that they acquire. Bobbi might be genetically predisposed to acquire some tools more easily than Carl does and some tools less easily. These differences could be thought of as determining their costs of acquiring different tools. Their genes might also influence their total budget—how many tools they can acquire. Thus Carl and Bobbi face different prices and have different budgets. We could apply the logic of Economics 101 and think that we'd get fairly accurate predictions about their purchases. For example, suppose Bobbi has twenty dollars and can buy science tools for one dollar apiece and artistic tools for two dollars. And suppose Carl has eighteen dollars and can buy science tools for two dollars apiece and artistic tools for one dollar. Can we then expect Bobbi to acquire more science tools than Carl? No. We cannot. If Carl likes science and Bobbi likes art, he'll buy more science tools. They have billions and billions of possible choices.

The supermarket of tools is so large that other factors swamp the price effects (the impact of latent abilities). Therefore, we can hardly avoid taking an anti-essentialism approach and assume that human potential varies little across people or across identity groups.[5]

TRAINING AND EXPERIENCE

Let's first consider how training and experience cause cognitive diversity. Strong relationships exist in both cases. People trained differently acquire different cognitive tools. Someone trained as an actuary learns different cognitive tools—different perspectives, interpretations, and heuristics than someone trained as a doctor or as a lawyer. Two people who have different experiences also develop different toolboxes. A city-dwelling banker acquires tools such as navigating a transportation system and balancing a stock portfolio. A farmer learns quite different tools, perhaps even balancing on a transportation system (a horse) and navigating stock, tools that the banker has no incentive to acquire.

We begin with the obvious link between training and cognitive tools. Much of schooling consists of the accumulation of perspectives: polar and Cartesian coordinates, and even rational trigonometry. Children also learn heuristics—lots of them. They learn to diagram sentences. They learn to deconstruct arguments and plots. They learn how to hold a paintbrush and how to draw lines to capture movement. As they get older, children learn more general heuristics that they can apply across contexts. They learn that they can tie themselves to the mast like Odysseus (often a good idea). They learn that, like Cortez, they can burn their ships behind them to create a strong commitment to move forward. (My lingering sadness about having sold my 1985 Toyota Land Cruiser compels me to recommend following Cortez only in extreme circumstances.)

Training influences our interpretations—the boxes we use to categorize what we see and learn. When we learn about magnetism, we gain an interpretation that separates objects into two boxes: one labeled magnetic and the other labeled not magnetic. Training also contributes to the set of predictive models that we carry around in our heads. These can be simple predictive models or more elaborate ones based on the theory of evolution or the law of conservation of energy. The examples we've given have been limited to educational training, but training does not end in school. Our training continues through life. Those best-selling books to the contrary, we do not learn everything we need to know (the perspective, heuristics, categorizations, and predictive models) in kindergarten. We don't even learn them all in college.

The causal relationship between training and preference diversity pulls in both directions. Diverse preferences can lead to diverse training, and diverse training can lead to diverse preferences. The first causal relationship also applies to fundamental preferences. What we fundamentally desire influences how we choose to be trained. The second causal relationship applies to instrumental preferences. Training changes our instrumental preferences by providing us with more tools—more ways of seeing the world and deeper understandings of causality. This increased cognitive depth and breadth enables us to see situations, events, and problems differently and, we hope, more productively. We choose different means to ends than we would have without training.

I do not mean to suggest that all training is equal. Memorizing long lists of unrelated facts is far less valuable than accumulating tools and understandings. Training in core skills and understandings is necessary. A person cannot accumulate a sophisticated and diverse toolbox without some foundations: knowledge of basic mathematics, an understanding of the fundamental laws of physics and chemistry, knowledge of various interpretations of great works in literature, and an understanding of important events in history. People should learn deeply *and* differently. Otherwise, collectively we won't be able to solve problems and more predictions.

We next turn to experience. We learn cognitive tools that help us make sense of our experiences. If confronted with different sets of experiences, we likely acquire and develop different tool sets to succeed in our endeavors: many people who live near water learn the tools required to fish. Desert dwellers have little need for such tools. Experience also shapes the attributes we use in our interpretations and our predictive models. A person who has dropped and broken a laptop computer considers the durability of his next purchase.

The process of developing a model requires structuring our experiences in categories. And the problem of choosing the best set of attributes for a given predictive task (of creating the Soccer Mom category) has been shown to be difficult in a formal sense.[6] Thus, we should not expect people to find the best possible predictive model. And even if people could find the best model, it might not be unique. More than one predictive model may be consistent with experiences, as we saw in Screening Success.[7]

History offers many examples of predictive model refinement. Fifty years ago, a fair percentage of doctors performed tonsillectomies on children with mildly recurrent sore throats. Now, few do. We should not take an entirely optimistic view of how we learn from experience. As teachers go, experience counts among the harshest. We learn some of life's most valuable lessons—to bring lots of water on hikes, to leave plenty of time to get to the airport, and to wear protection (in the rain)—the hard way. To give just one example, in the 1980s, the Coca-Cola Corporation attempted to replace Coke with what they called New Coke. New Coke outperformed the original Coke in blind taste tests, yet the public response to New Coke was harsh and swift. People hated it. Not the taste—they liked the taste. They hated the idea of tampering with an American icon. The Coca-Cola Corporation had the wrong predictive model. They had categorized Coke as a consumer product that people drank because of its taste. They quickly learned—consumers held rallies demanding the return of the original Coke—that Coke occupies a special place in American culture, and not to mess with the secret formula.

Experience can also affect both types of preference diversity. Experience influences the creation of predictive models, so it has a direct effect on instrumental preferences. Experience can also change our fundamental preferences. Often, the more we experience something, the more we like it. Children learn to enjoy food that they eat frequently. With repeated interactions, people even learn to like others who made bad initial impressions.[8] On the flip side, familiarity can breed contempt. Either way, experiences affect preferences.

Finally, much of our creative thinking relies on analogies.[9] This implies a central role for experiential diversity in creating cognitive diversity. In his introductory physics lectures, Richard Feynman claims that people have difficulty understanding the principles of modern physics because our everyday experiences provide us with no good analogies. We experience Newtonian physics. We can see how force equals mass times acceleration. Seeing is both believing and understanding. That's why Newton's laws make so much sense to us and that's why quantum mechanics seems so obscure. We don't experience many quantum effects, or at least, we're not aware of them. If some group of people had quantumlike experiences, if they saw things that existed in probabilistic waves that only became particles when observed, these people would probably make good physicists—provided that they also acquired all of the necessary mathematical heuristics.

IDENTITY

The importance of analogies in creative thinking provides an entry into a brief discussion of the role of identity differences in creating cognitive differences. Our cultures are part of our identity. Cultures contain stories. These stories can provide the basis for understanding and analogies. Cultures also contain languages and perspectives. We hold onto our cultural traits so long as we connect to people who share them. Sometimes this comes at an economic cost.[10]

Evidence that cultures influence the perspectives and heuristics that people develop takes many forms.[11] When looking at a fish tank, people from Eastern countries tend to notice patterns in the swimming fish, and people from Western countries more often notice individual fish. When asked to identify a person as happy or sad, people from Western countries less often take into account the happiness of surrounding people.[12]

Everyday routines and rituals create differences in how our brains are structured. Abundant evidence shows that societies develop tools and representations necessary for their survival and success. Not that they always succeed. Some societies collapse.[13] Consider an example from Ed Hutchins's book *Cognition in the Wild*. Micronesians rely on a navigational perspective that confounds most outsiders. Their perspective assumes their boats to be fixed in the water. Rather than seeing the boat move toward an island, they see the islands move past the boat. As islands pass, the navigator knows his location. Micronesians have even invented imaginary islands to help them know their location. Imagine getting in your car and driving from Ohio to Georgia and having a Micronesian in the backseat. Whereas you might say, "We're now driving over the Ohio River and entering Kentucky," the Micronesian would say, "The Ohio River just passed underneath the car and Kentucky is heading right at us." One can only imagine what fun it would be to teach geometry to Micronesians.

Cultural differences exist, to be sure, but they may be swamped by the variation that exists within cultures. Our identities also include our races, genders, physical abilities, sexual orientations, religions, and even our training. Some of these characteristics are socially constructed (race and gender); others (sex) are biological. The socially constructed attributes can be hard to pin down. Race can be defined externally (how others see us), internally (how we see ourselves), and expressively (how we present ourselves to others).[14] Sometimes all three of these line up. Sometimes they don't. For decades, the movie star Raquel Welch presented herself as Anglo and was perceived as Anglo, but internally she felt Latina. Only recently have all three of her constructed identities aligned.

Attributes such as race shape our experiences. They limit, steer, and even guide our choices. Thus, identity attributes cause us to construct different sets of cognitive tools. Sometimes these are not chosen so much as forced on us. So to think that people possess the traits that they do because they are somehow essential, somehow determined by their identities, is to commit what psychologists call a fundamental attribution error. Just because someone slips and falls does not mean that she is clumsy. It could mean that her front porch is icy. Similarly, just because someone thinks a certain way does not imply a genetic link. His way of thought could have been influenced more by his environment than by his genes. Thus, we cannot attribute difference to essential differences unless environments are the same.

Though identity matters, we cannot equate individual tools or collections of tools with specific identities. We can expect, however, that identity differences lead to experiential differences that in turn create tool differences. We can see this in the context of gender differences. Most people treat and react to men and women differently. Almost anyone would be frightened more by a six-foot-four-inch, two-hundred-sixty-pound man than by a five-foot-one-inch, one-hundred-two-pound woman. This makes logical sense. The man can probably inflict more physical punishment. If you meet the man in a dark alley, you might run in fear. If you meet the woman, you might feel protective of her. Of course, not all men are larger than all women. Many women are taller than lots of men. The basketball star Lisa Leslie is taller than all but a small percentage of men. Nevertheless, the average man is more physically imposing than the average woman, and he's more violent. Here's the point: because we treat men and women differently, we provide them with different experiences. As a result, they learn to think about situations differently.[15]

Men and women may differ in the tools they choose to acquire, yet this does not in any way imply that they differ in the perspectives, heuristics, interpretations, and predictive models that they *could* acquire. More men than woman study physics. And more women than men learn to crochet. But, even at Harvard, women earn A's in physics. And some men learn to be surgical nurses (though not many). Even though women dominate some professions, such as elementary school teacher and veterinarian, men are capable of doing these jobs as well.

The effects of identity on experience and opportunities are hard to measure. But almost no one disputes that they are large. The relevant question for us is whether those differences translate into meaningful cognitive differences—different perspectives, interpretations, heuristics, and predictive models. The answer to that question depends on context. If we're trying to solve problems of poverty, we cannot but think that the answer is yes. Someone who has been poor or whose extended family and friends include poor people probably brings useful understandings to the table, and so does a good statistician. If we're trying to solve a problem in chemistry or physics, the answer becomes less clear. On the one hand, we shouldn't expect race or gender or anything else to matter too much. On the other hand, people reason by analogy or from experience. People belonging to different identity groups pull from different wells of experience.

Ideally, society would not discriminate based on identity characteristics. But even if a society did not, policies that encourage or mandate identity blindness could not immediately overcome the residue of past biases. Science has long been predominantly male. As a result, science has become infused with masculine features—think of all of the dropping, crashing, and exploding that takes place in a physics or chemistry classroom. Some have claimed that if we taught physics and chemistry in a more feminine way—through cooking (note the stereotyping)—we'd attract more women scientists.[16] John Dewey, by the way, taught science through cooking at his Lab School at the University of Chicago.[17]

Further, even if we did achieve gender, color, and cultural blindness and treated everyone equally, that would not mean that people from different identity groups would not differentiate themselves in ways that affect their cognitive tools. Even in a colorblind society, we would still expect identity differences to correlate with some cognitive differences. Not that color blindness is itself well defined. Many of us can look past skin color but cannot look past scarves and cornrows.

Let's get precise about what these differences might be. To capture differences in interpretations, a tool in our toolbox, anthropologists and sociologists use something called *pile sorting*. This technique captures differences in how people represent things.[18] Here's how it works. People are asked to sort a list of familiar items—types of food, plants, or animals—into piles. Pile sorting can also reveal cognitive differences created by experience or training. Suppose that you are given the following list of people and asked to sort them into piles.

- Gerald Ford
- George H. W. Bush
- Madonna
- Jodie Foster

Most people would create two piles. They'd put the two former presidents in one pile and the two entertainers in the other. But in two small subcultures, one located in Ann Arbor, Michigan, and the other in New Haven, Connecticut, the piles would differ. These people would put the two University of Michigan undergraduates, Madonna and Gerald Ford, in one pile and the two Yalies, George H. W. Bush and Jodie Foster, in the other.[19]

People who grow up in different cultures create different piles, though not everyone in the same culture creates the same piles. We won't find a "French pile sort" of a list of food items, but we will find strong similarities in the piles that French people produce. The French probably find snails more similar to shrimp than Americans do. In many cases, this distribution of piles has small variance—the collection of piles are relatively similar.

Empirical evidence shows that people who construct different ways of life also construct different interpretations and perspectives. This can result in different predictive models and should create incentives for learning different heuristics. Scott Atran and Douglas Medin have identified cultural differences in the cognitive maps for the Itza', Ladino, and Q'eche living in the Guatemalan lowlands. What Atran and Medin call *cognitive maps* we could call *predictive models*. These predictive models influence how they manage resources.[20] Psychologists can plot features of these cognitive maps, but that doesn't mean that people can easily learn to think like someone from a different culture. That takes time and effort, just as learning how to think like a chemist would take some time.

SERENDIPITY

Surely, then, our diverse training, experiences, and identities cause us to think differently. They cause us to have distinct cognitive tools. Even so, we have to be aware that we cannot know beforehand which person's tools will prove up to a given task. Many breakthroughs seem to be serendipitous.[21] Serendipity implies more than mere luck. A person's ability to contribute improves if she can see a problem in multiple ways and if she can apply diverse heuristics.[22] As Louis Pasteur wrote, "Chance favors the prepared mind." Newton, Curie, Edison, and Aristotle were, by any measure, prepared.

Serendipity would seem to be too elusive to model. Yet, the frameworks in this book deepen our understanding and appreciation of Pasteur's comment in particular and of serendipity in general. An event may create opportunity only for those minds representing the event in particular ways. Insights are often the recognition of a previously ignored dimension or causal relationship. They are new interpretations and new predictive models.

The invention of the phonograph is an example of a prepared mind seeing an event differently. Edison had been designing a device that could play back Morse code automatically. He noticed that the needle running across the spinning disk on his machine made a humming sound. The leap from the obscure humming to the reproduction of voice was then but a small step for Edison. Lots of things hummed. Only Edison thought deeply about what was causing the humming of his spinning disk and stumbled on the phonograph. His mind was prepared and he noticed a dimension (the humming) and a causal relationship that others had missed.

We need not go all the way back to Edison. Steven Jobs, the founder of Apple, took calligraphy courses in college. That experience taught him to care about fonts—something other designers ignored. Sometimes serindipity allows someone to directly apply an idea from the past to a current problem. Tom Plaskett, once the head of marketing for American Airlines, applied an idea he learned as a child in Raytown, Missouri: people like *getting something for nothing*. His mother was an avid collector of S&H Green Stamps. She traded her stamps for gifts. Plaskett took the Green Stamp idea and applied it to airlines. The result: frequent flier programs.[23]

Insights can come even from dreams. Nearly one hundred years ago, W. A. Kaempferrt described Elias Howe's invention of the sewing machine as follows.

> Howe had been making the needles of his early failures with a hole in the middle of the shank. His brain was busy with the invention day and night and even when he slept. One night, he dreamed that savages captured him and took him before their monarch.
>
> "Elias Howe," roared the monarch, "I command you on pain of death to finish this machine at once."
>
> Cold sweat poured down his brow, his hands shook with fear, his knees quaked. Try as he would, the inventor could not get the missing figure in the problem over which he had worked so long. All this was so real to him that he cried aloud. In the vision he saw himself surrounded by dark-skinned and painted warriors, who formed a hollow square about him and led him to the place of execution. Suddenly he noticed that near the heads of the spears which his guards carried, there were eye-shaped holes! He had solved the secret! What he needed was a needle with an eye near the point! He awoke from his dream, sprang out of bed, and at once made a whittled model of the eye-pointed needle, with which he brought his experiments to a successful close.[24]

Breathe deeply and put aside Howe's horrible reference to the dark-skinned warriors and all that they might represent in the recesses of Howe's psyche. Instead, look at this as another instance of the Costanza "do the opposite" heuristic leading to a breakthrough. Sewing needles have holes at their blunt ends. Sewing machines needed holes at their pointy ends. In his horrible dream, this insight became clear to Howe. This anecdote would seem to imply that our diverse experiences can work in the recesses of our minds, that we can derive new insights and connections even during sleep. This is true. Elias Howe was not the only person ever to solve a problem while sleeping. Scientific evidence shows that sleep helps us think.[25] These studies provide yet another reason to expose yourself to diverse ideas. Your brain may connect them to the difficult problems you're contemplating.

Almost by definition, breakthroughs require serendipity. That serendipity arises from diverse preparedness. It derives from someone noticing and knowing how to interpret strange phenomena. Albert Einstein wrote that "the most beautiful thing we can experience is the mysterious. It is the source of all true art and science."[26] In trying to come to grips with those mysteries, we apply our tools. The more tools we amass through training, refine by experience, and filter through our identities, the better.

CHAPTER **13**

The Empirical Evidence

THE PUDDING

The proof of the pudding is in the eating.
—MIGUEL DE CERVANTES, *Don Quixote*

W E'VE walked—and worked—through the logic of diversity, and seen when and how it applies. And we just discussed some causes of diversity, so we are now ready to look at some of the empirical and experimental research related to our logical claims that diversity produces benefits. If diversity is as powerful as the models suggest, then its effects should be borne out in the same way that gravity's effects are. The logic should be supported in data about economies and democracies, not just in cute examples about things like the NFL draft selections. So let's see if this works in the "real" real world.

We start with a brief glance at all of human history, then bear down and consider groups and teams, and then move to cities and countries. We look across levels because the logic should apply regardless of the scale (within the conditions that we set earlier) and to all human endeavor. We didn't care whether the groups included ten, ten hundred, or ten million people, nor did we care whether the problem solving took place on one afternoon or over a millennium.

In much of what follows, we distinguish between studies that focus on training and vocational diversity and those that look at identity diversity. Overall, the evidence agrees with our logic: cognitive diversity improves performance at problem solving and predictive tasks. The evidence for identity diverse groups, though, is far from unequivocal. Some identity diverse groups perform well. Others do not. The same is true of identity diverse cities and countries. This makes sense, given the conditional nature of the logic. First, the linkages between identity diversity and cognitive diversity may not be strong in all cases. Second, many identity diverse groups have differences in their fundamental preferences, which, as we've seen, cause problems. Third, people who differ often have trouble communicating and getting along. Nevertheless, if we look closely at the evidence across the scales— groups, cities, and countries—we find that well-managed identity diversity does produce benefits.

How to Read the Data

When we look at the data, we see some complications. One problem is that people who have undertaken studies on the benefits of diversity didn't have the benefit of good models. We cannot just take two groups—one homogenous and one diverse— and expect the diverse group to be better. The group has to be involved in a task, such as problem solving or prediction, for which diversity is beneficial. Some tasks, such as selling merchandise or completing phone surveys, consist primarily of individual work. These would not be considered tasks at which collections of people work together to find good solutions or make accurate predictions. Therefore, we should not expect diversity—be it functional or identity-based—to correlate with better performance. If anything, we should expect the opposite. We should expect differences to hurt collective performance.

Further, even in those cases where diversity should produce benefits, it will do so only if managed well. Lots of strange things can happen in a diverse group that would not be likely to happen among homogeneous people—including physical and verbal violence. We should thus expect diverse groups to be the best. And we should also expect them to be the worst. We should not expect to see study after study showing unequivocal benefits from diversity. So, for the moment, it's okay to look for evidence that diverse groups *can* perform better than more homogenous groups. What would concern us would be evidence that diverse groups never, or only rarely, do better than more homogenous groups.

To see why we can take what might appear to be a biased position, let's consider *the bicycle test*. The test goes like this. A group of empirical social scientists wants to determine whether bicycling or running is a faster form of transportation. Our intrepid social scientists venture into the depths of various Glendales, Glenbrookes, and Glenviews, and gather up one hundred five-year-old children. They divide these children into two equal-sized groups. They ask each child in the first group to run as far as possible in ten seconds. Perhaps the fastest child runs sixty or even seventy yards, and the slowest covers only twenty. Being good social scientists, they plot the distances that these children travel and compute an average of around forty yards. They place the other fifty children on bikes and ask them to peddle these bikes as far as they can in ten seconds. Again, the social scientists plot the data and find the average distance to be about forty yards. However, the variance in distance is enormous. Those children who know how to ride bikes travel well over a hundred yards. Those children who don't know how to ride bicycles fall down and skin their elbows and knees. (We can assume that our social scientists have a ready supply of bandages.)

If we look at the data, biking appears no better than running, and we might conclude that bikes are no better than feet. But if we look at the situation more carefully, we see that riding a bike requires training and experience. And we might expect that as people acquire those skills, the bicyclists will dominate the runners. This parable of the bicycle test is important because we're just beginning to have widespread diverse interactions. Globalization is a relatively new phenomenon, so is serious interdisciplinary research, and so are multiethnic teams. It may take some time to learn how to exploit diversity's benefits. Forty years may seem a long time by social science standards, but it's not. We have much to learn. Thus, a primary concern at this point should be whether studies show that diversity can produce benefits, not that it does every time.

DIAMOND IN THE ROUGH

Let's begin with a bit of fun, a sneak peek into the back of the fridge at some old pudding. Ten thousand years ago, human society consisted primarily of hunter-gatherers. Humans had domesticated only a few small animals. Now we send rovers out to survey adjacent planets, we eat toasted, sliced bread, and we read by electric lights that we can turn on and off with the clap of our hands. How did this happen?

Allocating credit to the varied causes of this transformation requires speculation. For instance, the fact that we've had good weather the last ten thousand years (relatively speaking) has played a role, but how big is a matter of conjecture. Fortunately, we can exclude some explanations. We can rule out theories that modern civilization arose because our brains grew. Most estimates place modern humans' arrival at around fifty thousand years ago but the rise of civilization at a mere ten thousand years ago.[1] Most explanations for the rise of modern civilization rely on a logic of accumulation. New ideas and innovations built on old ones. Diverse skills and ideas combined to produce the gains on which modern civilization was built. To borrow from a recent popular book that makes exactly this point, the story of modern civilization is the story of nonzero interactions.[2]

To see how this logic works, we revisit the rugged landscape metaphor. Imagine the human societies of ten thousand years ago as being stuck on many local peaks. By modern standards, these peaks had low altitudes—they would not qualify as ice cream summits. People lacked the necessary heuristics and perspectives to solve basic problems related to farming and animal domestication. We've since solved some of these problems, but we haven't solved them all. As Jared Diamond describes in vivid detail in *Guns,*

Germs, and Steel, even with all of our modern techniques, we have yet to tame any zebras or turn acorns into a crop.

Our inability to tame zebras proves crucial to Diamond's account of how modern civilization arose. According to Diamond, and he musters substantial evidence to support this claim, the cradle of civilization, the Fertile Crescent, offered easier problems: the crops had larger seeds and the animals were easier to domesticate. Metaphorically speaking, inhabitants of the Fertile Crescent confronted a less rugged landscape than people elsewhere faced. And, as we know, less rugged landscapes can be climbed more easily. Once people developed heuristics that solved these problems, complex human societies began to form. People could more easily share these heuristics horizontally—along the same latitude—because of similar climate and soil conditions. Think of it this way: you can bring an orange tree to Finland but you can't make it drink. As a result, complex modern society first spread east–west and then eventually north–south.

Diamond takes us from hunting and gathering to ground wheat, domesticated cattle, and nuts, but how do we get from there to steam engines, penicillin, and iPods? Joel Mokyr theorizes that this second leap came about as cognitive toolboxes diffused.[3] Mokyr shows that the transferability of technique and knowledge created a transition from a society of artisans to a society of mass production. Hence, we get the amazing productivity growth that we have experienced over the past three hundred years. Once people could share technologies, perspectives, heuristics, and predictive models, rapid economic rapid growth followed. Knowledge diffusion allowed cognitive skills to be used anywhere and by anyone confronting a similar problem.

In both Diamond's and Mokyr's accounts, the application of new heuristics (in the form of skills and techniques) and perspectives (in terms of how to represent the problems confronted) drove growth. And most important in both of their accounts, tools and techniques could be combined. Recall the example (from chapter 1) of solving the hard fill-in-the-blank problem. We derived the answer, 42, using two perspectives. Feeding large numbers of people presents a difficult challenge. Learning to harvest seeds helps a little; so does domesticating beasts of burden. Possessing both tools allows a society to use domesticated animals to plow the fields planted with the harvested seeds, and to tote the abundant yield to market. One plus one equals twelve.

We can extend these ideas into models. One approach would be to use *meme* theory, and to consider ideas as similar to genetic material. Martin Weitzman constructed a model that does this. It conceptualizes technologies and ideas as building blocks that can be combined and recombined to produce economic growth.[4] We can examine his impressive mathematics directly, or we can just look around. We see no shortage of examples. Chocolate plus peanut butter gives Reese's Peanut Butter Cups. Cars are fine. So is a radio. But when we put the radio in the car, we create the possibility of cruising down the road listening to the live version of Dire Straits' "Sultans of Swing" at high volume. We create the sublime.

Mokyr makes clear that combining diverse tools and solutions requires transferable technologies and cognitive tools. Once one person learns how to make steel, so can everyone else. Economists describe cognitive tools as *nonrival*—one person using the tool does not preclude someone else from using it simultaneously. If I'm using calculus at this moment to solve a problem, you can too. But if I'm using the bathroom, everyone else has to wait until I'm done (as my older sister would all too eagerly attest). This touches on an insight we explore in more detail when we look at cities: population density matters for the spread of diverse ideas. If an idea falls in a forest, no one hears it. Physical proximity causes ideas to bump into one another. This powerful phenomenon helps to explain the rise of modern civilization and scientific understanding.[5] Economic growth correlates strongly with population growth: the more people, the more ideas, and the more ideas, the more growth. One creative attempt to compare historical data shows that this relationship between size and growth holds not only over the past ten, fifty, or hundred years but over a million years![6] More, it appears, is better, but not just more of the same—more of the different, and especially more of the different that bumps into each other.

DIVERSE COLLECTIONS AND GROUPS OF PEOPLE

We now look at some of the empirical research on diverse group performance. In doing so, we have to keep in mind some of the perils of empirical work in the social sciences. Data involving people is rarely clean and nice. And we often don't have as much data as we like. We will focus on two distinct but related questions. First, we explore whether the evidence agrees with our models. And second, we explore whether identity diversity improves performance. We look at this second question because it's one that lots of people have studied, and because it's so salient in light of globalization. Also, given that we can look only at data that exist, we're stuck with lots of studies that consider that question. That question has been posed so frequently that it even has a name: *the Value in Diversity Hypothesis.*[7]

The Value in Diversity Hypothesis: *Identity diverse groups perform better than homogeneous groups.*

As mentioned earlier, if we look at collections of people who perform routine tasks, such as flipping burgers, we would not expect cognitive diversity to correlate with performance. And we'd be right. Flipping burgers does not require much collective problem solving or prediction. But if we look at teams of people who develop marketing strategies, we should expect to see diversity's benefits. Diverse perspectives, heuristics, interpretations, and predictive models can produce value only if they're put to work. Claims that diversity improves outcomes may be inaccurate if the task involves no problem solving or prediction.

We have a second problem with measuring the effects of diversity: noisy data mean that many studies may not find significant effects. This has to do with what statisticians call the "noise-to-signal ratio." Random factors can be large relative to the effects we're looking for, making it hard to find the effect. The noise-to-signal ratio in measuring someone's height with a ruler is low. The noise-to-signal ratio of measuring a man's age by the amount of hair he's lost is high. (James Carville and Karl Rove aren't that old!)

One reason that the noise-to-signal ratio is high in these studies is that the benefits, in absolute terms, should be modest. We should not expect cognitive and identity diversity to translate into 20 percent increases in performance. That'd be nice, but it won't happen. Even the computer didn't do that. Nor did the car. Let's not leave reality here. In an organization or an economy, a 2 to 5 percent increase in productivity would be a cause for celebration. Any gains from diversity will be small. However, we shouldn't expect these to be just one-time benefits. If diversity improves problem solving this year, it should also do so next year. Thus, we're not talking about a one-time shift in the level of productivity, but a potential permanent increase in productivity growth. Corporations spend billions on diversity training. They don't do this in the hope of getting a one-time gain. These permanent modest increases can have a huge effect. Remember the miracle of compound interest and the Rule of 72. If diversity improves performance 4 percent every year, annual productivity *doubles* in less than twenty years—that's twice as many pairs of Prada boots, twice as many Junior Mints, and twice as many red wheelbarrows for the same number of hours worked.

We also have a third problem: diversity can create communication problems, fundamental preference diversity, and problems with group dynamics. In some contexts, such as prediction markets, none of these costs exist and we should expect to see only diversity's benefits. So let's look at the evidence from prediction markets in a little more detail.

Prediction

Almost no one disputes the evidence that diversity improves collective performance in predictive tasks. In the Iowa Electronic Markets (IEM), people buy stocks related to political events. For example, one stock might pay a dividend if a particular candidate wins an election—say, George Bush in the 2004 U.S. presidential election. If this stock was selling for fifty cents, then the market thought that Bush had a 50 percent chance of winning. But, barring a change in the Constitution, the George Bush in 2008 stock would sell for nothing (or close to it), but Jeb Bush might have a significant share price. Over the past five presidential elections, the predicted vote total in the IEM missed by a mere 1.37 percent. For elections outside the United States, the average error has been only 2 percent.[8] Moreover, the only time the market has missed by significantly more than ten percent in more than fifty elections occurred on March 17, 1992, when Paul Tsongas unexpectedly tanked in Michigan and Illinois and Bill Clinton wrapped up the nomination. Overall, the IEM has proved far more accurate than final polls at predicting election outcomes.[9]

The IEM data can be challenged because the people buying and selling the stocks have access to the polling data and they might just be averaging lots of polls. So we might expect the IEM to do pretty well. That's fine. It fits the models. We have high-ability predictors who are also diverse, a crowd of models. As a result, they predict well. Even if the polls do give a baseline, the IEM does better than that baseline.

The baseline problem does not exist for sports betting lines. If we average over all games that the Las Vegas betting line has predicted that one professional football team will defeat another by, say, seven and a half points, the average margin of victory is almost exactly seven and a half points. In other words, the betting line exhibits no bias.[10] Similarly, studies of the final odds at racetracks show them to be more accurate than prerace predictions by experts.[11]

Let's look at one recent study of sports betting just to show how accurate these crowds can be. The point of this study was to examine whether betting real money made much of a difference in the accuracy of the crowd's predictions. To test this, the accuracy of Tradesports (a site based in Ireland that uses real money) was tested against the accuracy of NewsFutures (a site at which no money changes hands).[12] Both markets predicted with uncanny accuracy. This comparison involved predictions of the outcomes of 208 NFL games in the fall of 2003.

A good way to measure the accuracy of these markets is to ask: If the market predicted that a team would win with probability p, what was the actual probability that team won? Put another way, if for twenty of the games, the market price was at 80 percent, this would mean that we would expect sixteen of those games to be won by the favorite. We can compare this prediction with the actual outcomes. The correlation between the actual outcomes and the market data is 96 percent for the market that uses real money and 94 percent for the market that doesn't. These data, like the IEM data, seem almost impossibly accurate, but do they agree with our claims? Well, we know these markets contain people with diverse predictive models. And we know that the people betting in these markets are not on average that accurate. We know this because many bought and sold at other prices. They think they're getting a good deal. So, yes, we can see these results as direct support for the Diversity Prediction Theorem and for the benefits of diversity.

Problem Solving

We just saw that cognitively diverse groups are good at prediction, but how do they do on solving problems? Here, too, we can run into problems created by group dynamics and communication problems and we may or may not have some problems associated with fundamental preference diversity. If trying to solve social problems, we might differ about the outcomes we favor, but if curing male pattern baldness, we probably agree that more (hair, that is) is better. The benefits of cognitive diversity in problem solving can be found both in the real world of practice and in careful academic studies. The simple facts of the matter are that when society confronts difficult problems—putting people on the moon, curing diseases, designing new products, crafting changes in the tax code—we create teams of diverse people. We create small-scale versions of Bletchley Park. We wouldn't do this if it didn't work.

Careful empirical studies show this benefit to cognitive diversity as well: teams of people with diverse training and experience typically perform better than more homogenous teams.[13] Studies that isolate diversity in skills, such as between the types of engineers, show evidence that diversity improves performance.[14] Studies of creativity and innovation conclude that cognitive variation is a key explanatory variable.[15] Studies also show that management teams with greater training and experiential diversity typically introduce more innovations.[16] Based on this evidence, organizational scholars generally agree that cognitive diversity improves rates of innovation, though they might not accept that diversity improves performance in all tasks.[17]

This evidence from the world of business and organizations suggests that we should also expect cognitive diversity to produce benefits in scientific research. Advocates of interdisciplinary science certainly believe this to be true. And we're awash in anecdotal evidence of how someone from another field suggested an idea that led to a breakthrough. Less and less often do we read of the solitary scientist making a breakthrough. It's not that we lack smart people. To the contrary, James Gleick claims that we lack a current Einstein-like genius because we have too many smart people.[18]

Other reasons that we seem to have fewer individual geniuses and more teams of them include the facts that problems have become harder, that research projects have become larger (running a linear accelerator requires far more people than does running a light bulb), and that collaboration has become easier.[19] Just as teams now dominate modern corporations, they also dominate big science. The evidence is quite compelling. From 1901 to 1910, fourteen people shared the Nobel Prize in Physics. That's a lot of solitary geniuses in lab coats. From 1995 to 2004, exactly twice as many people were awarded the prize. This average of 2.8 scientists per prize becomes all the more remarkable in light of the fact that at most three people can win a Nobel. The same phenomenon has occurred in chemistry. The first ten prizes were awarded to ten people; the last ten have been awarded to twenty-seven.[20] When the going gets tough, even the best and the brightest rely on others.

Another place where we find support for the models is in experiments that compare teams to individuals. Recently, economists and central bankers have begun to question when an individual should make decisions on monetary policy and when a team should. In experiments with undergraduates, Alan Blinder, a former vice-chairman of the board of governors of the Federal Reserve System, and John Morgan, an economist at Berkeley, test this question. It's a big, important question. Who should decide: the chairman or the board? A single person or a committee? It's a question that extends far beyond monetary policy. Our models suggest that the board should. The board has more perspectives and more heuristics.

What Blinder and Morgan find agrees with the models.[21] We won't get into the details of the two quite different experiments that they ran, but in each case the group outperformed the individuals by about 3.6 percent. Recall from our discussion of the rule of 72 that, in the real world, such an improvement would be cause for celebration. Blinder and Morgan's results were so intriguing that a group of scholars at the Bank of England ran similar experiments and found similar improvements.[22] Even more compelling, on both sides of the ocean, the experimenters tested individuals after they had been part of groups. Even after the group experience—the sharing of perspectives and heuristics—the individuals still did not do as well as the groups.

Identity Diverse Groups

We now turn to what many readers, especially those interested in globalization and affirmative action, may consider a critical empirical question: How well do identity diverse groups perform? As I stated in the introduction, for identity diversity to be beneficial it must be linked with cognitive diversity. And the extent to which identity diversity translates into cognitive diversity depends on the context, so we should expect the empirical record to be mixed. It is. Moreover, we should expect it to be beneficial only for problem solving and for prediction, not for more routine tasks, for reasons already mentioned.

What we see when we examine the many studies that consider identity diverse groups is pretty much what we'd expect. Some studies show the benefits of identity diversity (because, in those contexts, there's a connection between identity diversity and diverse tools and it's a task in which cognitive diversity is useful), and some studies find no relationship between demographic diversity and success.[23]

We also see that identity diverse groups and teams often exhibit problems with group dynamics that hurt their performance. These problems result partly from behavioral differences: some people raise their hands to speak; others interrupt. Toss in unhealthy portions of communication problems and fundamental preference diversity and the potential it creates for manipulation and misrepresentation, and the result is unproductive (and unhappy) groups.[24] To help us work through what we know about demographically diverse group performance, we can write an equation relating the performance of homogenous and diverse groups.

$$\textit{Net Benefits of Diversity} = \textit{Gross Benefits of Diverse} \\ \textit{Tools} - \textit{Costs of Diversity}$$

Tests of the Value in Diversity Hypothesis measure the net benefits. But the models consider only the gross benefits. Aside from the problems of preference diversity, we've ignored the costs. These costs can be overcome if people learn to get along. Thus, we should expect to see that in some cases diverse groups do better and in some they do worse. That's oh-so-true. In a survey of around eighty studies, Katherine Williams and Charles O'Reilly find that crude tests of net benefits show weak empirical support for the hypothesis, but higher variance in the performance of the diverse groups.[25] One recent attempt to look for direct benefits from identity diversity in large corporations found net benefits to be nonexistent or small in most cases.[26] A second study, this one by Sarah Fisher Ellison, Jeffrey Greenbaum, and Wallace Mullin, analyzed a firm with many small offices in the United States and around the world and found that gender diversity correlated with higher revenues.[27] Their study also found that gender diversity correlated with reduced cooperation and lower employee satisfaction, which indirectly lower revenues. (We can reasonably expect that cooperation and satisfaction correlated positively with revenues.) Their study reveals in stark econometric detail the pluses and minuses of diversity. They found that, on average, the benefits of diversity outweighed the costs, but that won't always be true. Mixed evidence is not a reason to get rid of diversity; it's reason to learn to reduce its cost, an insight that we discussed earlier in the parable of the bicycle test.

And yet, nothing in these studies contradicts the claims. Most of the studies show two things: a modest net effect and evidence of costs. If we plug these stylized facts back into the accounting equation, we get that the gross benefits must be positive: zero equals one minus one. This does not mean that by looking only at part of one side of the equation, we've engaged in chicanery. We haven't. Our goal was to explore when and how diversity produces benefits. We accept that it has some costs.

To see if the logic of the claims holds up, we have to ask more precise questions of these studies. If it's true that identity diverse groups have more perspectives, they should generate more solutions. Many studies find this to be true.[28] If we separate out those studies where identity diverse groups do better from those where they do not, we see support for the models. First, we see that when identity diverse groups perform well, identity diversity correlates with cognitive diversity. In a *Harvard Business Review* survey article, David Thomas and Robin Ely, summarizing several studies of diverse group performance, suggest that we should not think of diversity as external physical differences: "Diversity should be understood as *the varied perspectives and approaches to work* that members of different identity groups bring."[29] To rephrase what they say, which is also what our logic suggests, on tasks where only weak connections exist between identity diversity and cognitive diversity, we have no logical reason to think that identity diverse groups would perform better than more homogeneous groups—unless we believe that some mysterious collective cognitive capability emerges from the interactions of people with diverse identities. But the whole point of this book has been to move beyond metaphor and mysticism and place claims of diversity's benefits on solid foundations. And those foundations are conditional. Identity diversity should produce benefits only when it somehow correlates with or causes cognitive diversity.

Let's keep pushing. The models showed benefits in problem solving and prediction. Substantial evidence suggests that functional and identity diverse groups are more innovative, which we would expect.[30] Studies also suggest that groups whose members have diverse preferences are more creative.[31] This fits the idea that diverse preferences may well cause diverse perspectives, which in turn lead to more solutions.

A recent study of prediction showed that racially diverse groups predicted better than all-white groups. The task was predicting the guilt or innocence of a black defendant, a task in which race might well matter. The evidence shows that whites constructed more subtle predictive models based on finer interpretations when in diverse groups.[32]

This deeper unpacking allows us to look at overall firm performance studies in a new light. Some of these studies consider firms whose employees perform repetitive tasks (ahem, that would be all firms) such as filling out loan forms and turning screws. These tasks do not involve lots of problem solving or prediction. So, we shouldn't expect any benefit. Yeah, someone at Burger King might develop a new technique for slicing onions or spreading ketchup, but for repetitive tasks like these, we're near the optimum. There's not much room for diversity to find improvements. If we restrict attention to firms that innovate—that is, try to solve new problems—we see that identity diverse firms perform better, not much, but better nonetheless.[33]

The models do not completely ignore the cost side of the accounting equation. Our models of preference diversity suggest that identity diverse groups should perform relatively better when they have a common goal. The evidence shows this to be true.[34] We would also expect diverse groups to perform better over time, as they learn to work through their preference differences. Evidence supports this as well. Diverse groups sometime start out performing worse but end up performing better than more homogenous groups.[35]

This still leaves the problem of getting along with others. People feel more comfortable and open when around people from their own identity groups. For diverse groups to perform well, people must feel as though their identities have been validated and their contributions verified. If a person's involvement in a group does not require abandoning her self view, the result is that the person contributes more and the group performs better.[36] Finally, and we come back to this later, Thomas and Ely also find that expectations play an important role in how identity diverse groups perform. If people belonging to an identity diverse group expect diversity to generate benefits, they're more likely to realize those benefits.[37]

Though this brief survey merely skims the surface of an enormous literature on identity diversity and performance, we can still draw some general conclusions. In many cases, identity diverse groups do perform better than homogeneous groups. And those situations in which they do perform better are far from random. Identity diverse groups perform better when the task is primarily problem solving, when their identities translate into relevant tools, when they have little or no preference diversity, and when their members get along with one another. These features translate into high benefits of diversity and low costs. And so overall, while the evidence is far from overwhelming, it supports our models. When those conditions don't hold, we shouldn't expect identity diverse groups to do much better. We have to be realistic. Hiring diverse people to clean hotel rooms may make for a better society, but it may not lead to many big performance increases.

In the end, we're left with the fact that across many studies the average performance for identity diverse groups and homogeneous groups is roughly the same, but the identity diverse groups have higher variance. This suggests that we just haven't quite figured out how to get along, and that when we do, diversity improves performance. We just have to get on those bikes and learn to ride.

City-Level Productivity and Diversity

We now jump up in scale and consider the role of identity diversity in the success of cities and countries. If diversity produces benefits, if collections of diverse cognitive tools produce benefits, this should be evident in the data. Cities provide a good place to start. All else being equal, larger cities should have more diversity. Cities also bring ideas and technologies in close proximity—people in cities bump into one another more often. As hinted at earlier, this should make workers in cities, on average, more productive. They are. And workers in more technologically diverse cities should be more productive than those in relatively homogeneous cities. And they are, as well. The evidence on these size effects borders on overwhelming. Economists estimate that a doubling in city size increases productivity per worker by somewhere between 6 and 20 percent.[38] The Nobel laureate Robert Lucas, among others, argues that this, and not good late-night Chinese food or opera, explains why cities exist.[39] Of course, this increase in productivity in cities can be explained by other factors. City workers could be more productive because of scale economies or because of lower transaction costs. They could be more productive because city firms can share inputs more easily. They could be more productive because of the economics of averaging: larger markets provide insurance and resale opportunities that smaller markets cannot (by the law of large numbers, the larger the market, the more predictable the average).[40]

Demonstrating that *diversity* explains these data requires a tighter link between diversity and productivity. We need evidence that what economists call *knowledge spillovers* and *technological externalities* correlate with higher productivity. A knowledge spillover is what we would call tool sharing. It's when one person shares a perspective, heuristic, interpretation, or predictive model with someone else. A technological externality exists when one technology can be applied in a new context—when we put the laser in the printer and in the pointer. Abundant descriptive evidence, building on the work of Jane Jacobs, supports the claim that knowledge spillovers—the sharing of cognitive tools—have a geographic bias.[41]

Accepting that these spillovers exist, we might debate the form they take. A model attributed to the economists Kenneth Arrow, Paul Romer, and others emphasizes spillovers within industries. In their model, one Silicon Valley programmer develops a new perspective or heuristic and it quickly spreads within the city. This contrasts with Jacobs's idea that spillovers leap across industries, that heuristics and models move across contexts and domains. At first, Jacobs's idea seems less plausible. Can firms that build cars learn from firms that sell milk? In fact, they have. A few decades ago, much was made of automobile manufacturers adopting innovative just-in-time inventory systems, but supermarkets had used a related inventory system for decades. If you're selling bananas and fresh fish, your inventory system must be just in time—no one wants old fish (except maybe a cat).

Both the Arrow-Romer model and the Jacobs model fit with this book's logic. Spillovers, whether within an industry or across industries, exploit diversity. Someone discovers a new way to see a problem (a perspective) or a new way to look for solutions (a heuristic) and others either use it in an identical situation or apply it in another, seemingly unrelated context. The Jacobs model, though, fits the logic better: in her model, ideas move across industry borders. The existing evidence to distinguish the two models is preliminary at best but points in favor of the Jacobs model. Maryanne Feldman and David Audretsch find more support for the Jacobs model in a direct comparison with Arrow-Romer, and John Wagner and Steven Deller find a significant positive relationship between industrial diversity and economic growth across America's fifty states.[42] These findings suggest that cognitive tools often spread outside of their initial domains.[43]

In the realm of economic productivity, we have good reasons to expect a strong positive relationship. Diverse perspectives, interpretations, heuristics, and predictive models should improve problem solving and prediction, which play crucial roles in an economy: The better the people in an economy can solve problems, the faster they can innovate. The more precisely they can engineer, the quicker they can respond to unexpected events. The better the people in an economy can predict future outcomes, the better they can choose among technologies, the more accurately they can anticipate swings in demands, and the better they can allocate resources. Toolbox diversity is the stuff on which economies grow.

We can ask the same question of identity diverse cities. Are they more productive? Once again, though, we have the problem that identity diversity can be positively correlated with other features that hurt growth. We discuss these problems in more detail in a moment. First, we look at the good news. Many historical cases and some recent evidence demonstrate that cities with greater identity diversity can be more productive. As Jane Jacobs writes, "city areas with flourishing diversity sprout strange and unpredictable uses and peculiar scenes. But this is not a drawback of diversity. This is the point... of it."[44] Amsterdam's golden age provides a compelling historical example of the power of cultural diversity. In the late sixteenth century, a thriving trade industry driven by the Dutch East India Company contributed to Amsterdam's explosive economic growth. With trade came immigrants from all over the world. Jewish refugees poured in from Spain and Portugal, and Protestants came from nearby Belgium after Spanish troops took over Antwerp, a leading business center at the time. The combination of Belgian businessmen and Calvinist craftspeople proved economically powerful. French Huguenots, Germans, and others followed these groups in search of religious freedom and economic opportunity. These diverse peoples combined to form an economically productive, culturally advanced, and religiously free city unrivaled in Europe for one hundred years.

The story of Amsterdam plays out today in places such as Hong Kong, Paris, New York, London, Miami, and Singapore. Recently, economists have attempted to connect identity diversity to growth in cities. In U.S. cities, greater ethnic diversity correlates with higher growth in wages and rents.[45] Rents might go up because the city becomes more interesting culturally, but that would not explain the wage increases.

Any analysis of the relationship between identity diversity and productivity cannot avoid the effects of preference diversity. Recall our brief discussion of how preference diversity leads to underprovision of public goods. Empirically, whether we look at cities or countries, we find that the more ethnically diverse groups, the fewer resources devoted to public goods. The pie has to be split too many ways, leading to underprovision of public goods. This proves true in many African countries whose relatively poor economic performance can be largely attributed to the low investment in public goods resulting from ethnic diversity.[46] The problem of underprovision is not unique to democratic forms of government. With a dictatorial government, we might expect this problem to go away, but it doesn't. If anything, the underprovision is more pronounced in ethnically diverse dictatorships. Even though dictators do not face elections, in order to remain in power, they must placate the ethnic groups within their country.[47]

This correlation between ethnic diversity and public good provision also holds in advanced countries. After accounting for economic and sociological variables, levels of productive public goods and services within cities—schools, trash collection, sewer, infrastructure, and so on—decrease with a rise in the level of ethnic diversity. The more different we are, the less we agree on what we would like to do.[48]

Richard Florida, a researcher at George Mason University, attempted to discern what creates growth in cities by focusing on the attributes of the city and the people in it. He constructed a measure of creativity based on four indices—a high-tech index, an innovation index, a gay index, and a percentage of people who belong to what he calls the creative class. His analysis, which he restricts to American cities, reveals a link between growth and his creativity index.[49] His creativity index is at best a crude proxy for diverse toolboxes, but it's a start. I might add that tests of productivity of cities against racial diversity show no positive relationship. Given racial tension and the problem of undercontribution to public goods, this should not surprise us, nor does it imply racial diversity doesn't produce benefits, just that those benefits are cancelled out by costs.[50]

In sum, the evidence we do have suggests that in cities, cultural diversity correlates with growth but racial diversity does not. This agrees with the country-level evidence. A more ethnically diverse country should possess abundant toolbox diversity which should result in more innovation and better collective predictions. Ethnic diversity also correlates with fundamental preference diversity, however, resulting in underinvestment in public goods and less political stability.

Whether ethnically diverse countries perform better or worse would then seem to depend on whether the single positive effect outweighs the two negative ones. In a survey article covering ethnic diversity and its effects on economic performance, two economists, Alberto Alesina of Harvard University and Eliana La Ferrera of Italy's Bocconi University, describe the relationship between diversity and country-level growth as follows: "As for the productive effects of diversity, the picture is complex. It is somehow easy to point to economic failures of fractionalized societies, but this is not a general phenomenon. Rich, democratic societies work well with diversity, in the case of the United States, very well in terms of growth and productivity."[51]

One way to make sense of these findings is to apply the toolbox analogy. If people have small toolboxes, owing to poor health and educational systems, the potential benefits from diversity may not be as large. If no one possesses many tools, no matter how many people you group together it's unlikely that you will generate benefits. A second problem stems from communication problems. In linguistically diverse countries, people have difficulty sharing tools because they cannot communicate across ethnic groups. Jonathan Pool, a political scientist, puts it this way: "A country whose entire population, more or less, speaks the same language can be anywhere from very rich to very poor. But a country that is linguistically highly heterogeneous is always underdeveloped or semideveloped." The Pool hypothesis, which is descriptive not causal, has strong empirical support when we look at per capita income, but less support if we consider growth rates.[52]

The other half of the Pool hypothesis—that the diverse can be rich—also passes a sniff test. The United States, Switzerland,

and Canada, all of which are ethnically diverse, have among the highest per capita gross domestic products (GDPs).[53] But, some of the poorest countries in the world are also diverse. To paraphrase Alesina and La Ferrara, we cannot look at this evidence and jump to any strong conclusion either way. But given this evidence, we cannot help but think that diversity *can* produce benefits if harnessed.

Not surprisingly then, a large study by Alberto Alesina and Errico Spolaore suggests that ethnic diversity creates diverse demands for resources and leads to underinvestment in infrastructure, education, and other public goods. This points toward a strong incentive for ethnic groups to pull apart and form nation-states. By the way, this has been happening—in 1946, there were 74 countries. In 2004, the United Nations recognized 191 countries.[54] Many of these new countries are small—around half have fewer than ten million people—and most are ethnically homogeneous. But countries cannot become too small or they lose the benefits of diversity and returns to scale that correlate with size. And they may be vulnerable to military attack. These economic benefits from agglomeration must be balanced against the political desire for ethnic sovereignty. In principle, countries would have an ideal size given their ethnic diversity. Evidence shows that many countries come close to striking the right balance.[55]

This tension between the benefits of agglomeration and the desire for ethnic homogeneity can be seen most vividly in Europe, which wants to reap the benefits of its diversity in the economic and scientific realms but whose member countries want to maintain political self-determination.[56] Viewed through this book's models, this all makes sense. These new nations seek less ethnic diversity to limit fundamental preference diversity, but they seek to maintain size to ensure cognitive diversity.

A Clean Bowl

We have finished eating our pudding. And what do we know? We know that whether we look at economic growth over the course of human history, at the current rate of productivity of countries or cities, or the performance of small groups, we cannot but come to the conclusion that cognitive diversity improves collective performance. We see strong evidence that collections of people with diverse training perform well. We also see that the evidence on identity diverse collections—be they countries, cities, or groups—is less clear. However, the increase in the variance of outcomes suggests that we don't yet know how to manage identity diversity, not that potential benefits don't exist. Two important and unsurprising caveats also apply: If diverse collections of people fight over common resources, they will not be as productive. And if they refuse to or lack the ability to communicate with one another, they will also fail to reap benefits. These caveats apply regardless of whether the diversity comes from experience, training, or identity, but they may be most pronounced for identity differences.

To sum up, the benefits of diversity do exist. They're not huge. We shouldn't expect them to be huge. But they're real, and over time, if we can leverage them, we'll be far better off. We'll find better solutions to our problems. We'll make better predictions. We'll live in a better place.

Part Five

GOING ON THE OFFENSIVE

CHAPTER 14

A Fertile Logic

PUTTING IDEAS TO WORK

There is a great satisfaction in building good tools for other people to use.
—FREEMAN DYSON, *Disturbing the Universe*

N OW, we go on the offensive. The implications of this logic should be more than merely explanatory. Explanation has its place. Far better, though, that we leverage our understandings to make our lives and our world more interesting, more secure, more sustainable, and more productive. So in this final part of the book, I discuss how to apply what we've learned to building teams, hiring employees, admitting students, and designing political institutions. The scope is grand. We will contemplate estimating the amount of leather in a cow (as disgusting as that may be to animal rights activists), the functioning of democracies, and a whole lot in between.

MOVE BEYOND THE PORTFOLIO ANALOGY

Many people compare a diverse collection of people to a stock portfolio. The analogy goes as follows: a financial advisor building a stock portfolio chooses stocks so that regardless of what happens in the economy, some of the stocks perform well. The advisor advocates investing in rainy day bonds, sunny day stocks, and cloudy day cash. Regardless of the weather, the investor earns a positive return. As a result, good portfolios often leave out some stocks with among the best expected individual returns.

Stock diversification provides insurance through its broad coverage. And as analogy, it gives some intuition for why we might not always want the best individual performers when constructing a team: just as an investor might avoid buying the best-performing individual stocks, so might a firm or university also reject some of the best individual people. Stocks pay off in states of the world, and portfolio theory explains why a firm might hire someone with strong statistical skills even though that person has a low IQ. In the event that a vexing statistical problem arises, the firm can turn to their statistics person—even if he might not perform well under other conditions. This person provides insurance for a state of the world that might be called "firm encounters statistical problem."

As compelling as it may be, the portfolio analogy misses a key part of our logic: *the superadditivity of diverse tools.* People have perspectives, heuristics, interpretations, and predictive models. When a collection of people work together to solve a problem, and one person makes an improvement, the others can often improve on this new solution even further. Problem solving is not the realization of a state but a process of innovation in which improvements build on improvements.

Diverse perspectives and diverse heuristics apply sequentially; one gets applied after the other, and in combination. As we've seen throughout, one plus one often exceeds two.[1] The parts of the portfolio can be combined to create new solutions. Diversity is superadditive.

For example, one reason to offer diverse things to eat at a fair would be to cover all contingencies. Some visitors may want sweets. Others may want something more substantial. At the 1904 St. Louis World's Fair, attendees could choose from a diverse portfolio of alternatives. Unfortunately, one day the ice cream vendor ran out of cups. Ernest Hami, a Syrian waffle vendor in the booth next door, rolled up some waffles to make cones. The rest, as they say, is history.[2] The parts of the portfolio—the waffles and the ice cream—combine to create something new and better, the ice cream cone. Diverse people work the same way. Yes, they can handle any contingency owing to their differences, but they can also combine their differences to create even better solutions.

CONTAIN MULTITUDES: EXPERIMENT

The logic implies that rather than having a single perspective, interpretation, heuristic, or predictive model, we should have many. This requires accepting some dissonance. We might not be sure how to think about a situation. For that reason, we must become Whitmanesque and contain multitudes. And if we contradict ourselves sometimes, so what? We should be large. As different as Walt Whitman and Maxine Hong Kingston may be, they agree on this point, on the value of largeness and contradiction, as we saw at the end of chapter 10.

The advantages of containing multitudes should be all too clear from this book. Diverse perspectives and heuristics improve problem solving. Diverse interpretations and predictive models lead to more accurate predictions. Crowds are not wise, but crowds of models are. One way to maintain this diversity is to mimic evolution. From evolution, we know that diversity combined with crude selective pressures can solve hard problems. In evolution, genetic mutation maintains diversity. Those mutations that increase fitness survive; those that do not fall by the wayside. The same effects occur within groups of people. Good attempts survive. Bad ones don't. Experimentation can lead to a better "best" individual performer. More important, it can result in better collective performance. As we saw, increasing diversity improves our collective performance at prediction (the Diversity Prediction Theorem) and at problem solving (the Diversity Trumps Homogeneity Theorem).

Let's do a thought experiment. Suppose that we had to predict the amount of leather produced by a cow. This requires knowing the surface area of a cow. Even the complicated surfaces from calculus class pale in comparison to a cow. Fortunately, a book on modeling offers a solution to this problem. We can imagine a spherical cow.[3] (We ignore how we'd milk this spherical cow or how we'd walk it out to pasture.) We can calculate its surface area using tools we learned in high school math. We can then use that number as an estimate for the real cow. Our estimate won't be exactly right, but it won't be too bad either.

The logic suggests that we can do even better by considering diverse predictive models. We might also imagine cows shaped like boxes (we might even tape together a few Gateway Computer boxes until we've reached cowlike proportions) and elliptical cows. One of these other models may prove more accurate than the spherical cow model. If so, that's great. The greatest benefit from having diverse models may not be the models themselves, but the average of them. The crowd of cow models may well be better than the best. Experimentation not only allows the possibility of finding a better model. It creates a crowd of models. The crowd of models is itself a model, and a good one.

The amount of experimenting with diverse ideas that makes sense depends on the circumstances. Clearly, the lower the costs of experimenting and the more important the problem, the more we should experiment. We should also err on the side of more search when a problem is connected to other problems. If we can understand how proteins fold, we can make headway on lots of other problems. Cognitive tools flow freely between domains. And by combing tools, we can find even larger breakthroughs.[4]

LOOK OUTSIDE: CONSULTING DISSENTERS

When we solve problems, we climb landscapes. Individuals, teams, and organizations all climb. Unfortunately, some climb landscapes that are more rugged than they need be. We fall into particular ways of seeing problems. We encode our problem the wrong way—we use the wrong perspective. In an organization, common perspectives facilitate communication and the development of more advanced heuristics, but they also create common local optima. If one of us gets stuck and if we all think the same way, then we're all stuck. Now, it could be that our collective perspective makes the problem easy and the company is acting optimally. But experience suggests that the only companies that optimize lie nestled within the pages of introductory economics books. For this reason, every so often they need to bring in people from the outside. People from the outside can help us get unstuck by bringing in new perspectives. One quick caveat: outsiders do not stay outsiders for long. Recall the Asch experiments in which people went along with the crowd when comparing the length of lines. Outsiders must remain outsiders, otherwise they will cease to think differently.

To provide some grounding, let's start with an example from within the academy. Most universities organize themselves into departments. This hinders diversity for obvious reasons, but we look past that fact. These departments largely monitor themselves. Deans and provosts look for signs of external validation to see how these departments perform, including the placement of graduate students, the number of publications by faculty in top journals, and the frequency of attempts by other schools to hire away faculty. These signals indicate whether a department performs well, but they provide almost no clue to *how* a department could perform better. For this reason, universities periodically invite committees composed of scholars from other schools who work in the same discipline or in closely related ones. These visiting committees provide suggestions for how the department might improve. How do they do this? They gather information, make sense of the current state of the department, and advocate certain changes. Are these people who visit more able than the people in the department? If so, not by much. But they are different. And they leverage those differences to make improvements.

These visiting committees can be thought of as a type of consultant. In fact, they are consultants (they just do not get paid as much as real consultants). So, we can apply the same thinking to explain the benefits of consultants: they're able people who provide diversity to help companies improve. Sure, some companies trot out highly paid consultants in fancy suits to add credibility to decisions that directors have already made—"Look,

McKinsey agrees with me!" And yes, some consulting companies perform services that firms do not have the capacity or ability to do themselves, but many consultants actually consult. And they make improvements. Otherwise, there would not be so many consulting companies, and consultants wouldn't be paid so much money. But the fact that these consultants add value does not mean that they are giants of the Earth, smarter and more capable than others.

Let's be realistic: how could a consultant, who might be a freshly minted MBA, know more about dog food than Purina or more about manufacturing processes than General Motors or Toyota? She couldn't. Consultants may be talented and hard-working, but they're not smarter than everyone else, and they rarely know more about a company and its market than do the people who work at the company. That's okay. As the logic shows, the consultants need not be smarter according to some measuring stick. The consultants can add value just by being different, by possessing a different set of core tools than people at the company.

The careful reader will notice the subversive nature of this logic. We might have thought of visiting committees and consultants as experts, but we did not. Instead, we've thought of them as people who think differently. Visiting committees and consultants challenge the status quo. They are what Cass Sunstein might call "dissenters."[5] In politics, dissenters identify new policy dimensions, and they force us to abandon our existing predictive models. Dissent is useful. Without it societies would falter. Our consultants—whether academic or corporate—are dissenters, too, but they're not choosing to be dissenters. They're given incentives to be. (Lots of them.)

Leverage Relevant Diversity

The advice to contain multitudes and to look outside makes an implicit assumption that the diversity fits the task. Most universities do not pack visiting committees with unicyclists and manicurists. They choose academics and experts from the appropriate field. Consulting companies do not hire people from the hidden valleys of Papa New Guinea, dress them in suits, and ask them to help companies comply with the new Sarbanes-Oxley regulations. They hire graduates of MBA programs. Diversity must be relevant. In the context of problem solving, we discussed this at some length. Without the calculus condition, we have no assurance that diverse collections of people do well. That same logic applies to predictive contexts. For crowds to be wise, they must be able and diverse.

Encourage Diverse Citizens

According to the logic of the Diversity Prediction Theorem, a successful democracy requires either voters with accurate predictive models or voters with diverse predictive models. Because any one individual's vote matters little (although the vote of some guy named Chad in Florida mattered a lot in 2000) voters have weak incentives to be engaged, to construct accurate predictive models. As a rule, people do not have very accurate predictive models about policy outcomes. Most of us can't even predict what we're having for lunch. We're making a distinction here between having information—that's pretty easy nowadays—and having a way to interpret that information in order to construct a predictive model. For democracy to work, people need good predictive models. And often, the problems may be too difficult or too complex for that to be the case.

An alternative way to ensure good collective predictions—and a more realistic one—is to have each person make a moderately accurate but diverse prediction. Making a moderately accurate prediction requires making a relevant interpretation and constructing a predictive model. People can make decent predictions by drawing analogies or by concentrating on a few of the many dimensions involved in a policy debate. To borrow an insight from my colleague Arthur Lupia, making good predictions about welfare policy does not depend on the ability to name the fifty state capitals.[6]

Those who argue that everyone should read books like Garry Wills's captivating *Lincoln at Gettysburg* have it only half right.[7] Books like Wills's provide more than just facts. They help us to organize our thinking about historical events. They help us to develop predictive models. They also help create a stronger identity. These are all good things. But a deep understanding of Lincoln's speech will not guarantee good collective predictions about current policies. Someone whose only exposure to the Gettysburg address is Peter Norvig's hilarious PowerPoint version (www.norvig.com/Gettysburg/) may be perfectly capable of casting an intelligent vote on whether a city should offer free wireless hookup in its central business district.

For democracy to function, people must have reasonably accurate and diverse models. Often we do. Most of us can think through some of the implications of school location decisions or property tax increases. And thus the electorate becomes a crowd of models—sometimes these models are not as sophisticated as we would like, but they are models nonetheless. Often we don't have models and we look to experts, hoping that these experts have deep understandings based on elaborate models.[8] Such shortcuts often work, but if we all look to the same expert, we get just the expert's prediction, which may not be better than the crowd's prediction would have been.

If our predictive models are no better than random guesses, then collectively we make random choices. So if we're being asked to vote on which groundwater treatment system to implement, we won't perform like a crowd of models. We might be no better than a bunch of random rolls of a die. We've developed informal norms within our political institutions so as to limit direct votes on technical issues where people would not be informed. (That's true even in California.) Hence, we vote directly on issues of good government but not on arms treaties.[9]

For obvious reasons, when we make some decisions, such as whom to elect president, we allow everyone to vote (except felons and people who have recently moved). And in those elections, if we're all partially informed *and* use similar models, then we won't make good democratic decisions. Looking to the past to predict the future may make sense for individuals, but if everyone does it, we lack diversity, and we make poor choices. Politicians whose policies have resulted in a lower standard of living tend to get voted out of office. That's good. But, unfortunately, so do may politicians who happened to be in office during an unfortunate random event. Chris Achen and Larry Bartels have found evidence that voters punish presidents for acts of nature such as droughts and shark attacks.[10] People conflate human suffering with government policies, whether the government was to blame or not. Losing an election because of a shark attack is the result of voters having simple, similar models: "our situation is worse, let's vote him out." In those cases, the crowd is not wise. It's mad—not angry mad, but "let's spend our grocery money on tulips" mad.

The lack of incentive for voters to develop sophisticated predictive models for electoral decisions creates a fundamental challenge for democracy. Our hope for democracy cannot rest on informed, engaged citizens. It must include diversity as well. And so nations that have diverse market economies and diverse cultures may be at an advantage. In a market economy, people choose to specialize. We get up in the morning, pack our lunches, and go accumulate diverse experiences. We learn about trains, packaged goods, cat food, disease spread, real options, groundwater treatment, and graphic design. Each day, we construct diverse toolboxes. When asked a policy question, we filter it through these experiences and training as well through our identities.

Though we often hear that democracy creates a free rider problem, we less often hear how democracy catches a free ride from a diverse economy and society. The flip side of this happy symbiosis is that a society without a diverse economy may lack diverse predictive models. We can even speculate that lack of cognitive diversity might explain the lack of stability in developing countries. A society whose citizens possess fewer predictive models has fewer checks on bad ideas. An effective democracy, therefore, may depend as much on its citizens' having diverse predictive models as on their having accurate predictive models, or so says the Diversity Prediction Theorem.

CREATE PREDICTION MARKETS

In reading the analysis of how markets can aggregate mental models, an organization's leaders might ask, when they might use information markets to make predictions? Information markets have substantial appeal to businesses and organizations. They're accurate. And they often don't cost much. Currently, most large companies and organizations hire people to construct models to predict future demands, sales, or, in the case of political parties, votes. Without these predictions, long-range planning becomes difficult if not impossible. By creating an internal prediction market, an organization can leverage the wisdom of its own crowd. This prediction market could supplement or even replace an expert's prediction. Some companies such as Hewlett-Packard and Google have already done this. Hewlett-Packard used managers to predict printer sales. The managers' predictions proved to be as good as, and in some cases better than the experts'.[11]

To make this more tangible, let's consider an auto company that wants to predict what types of cars will sell best in the coming five years—a prediction that auto manufacturers make regularly, and one that they often get wrong. They could set up an internal market that includes all of the company's engineers. This probably would not work. Their engineers probably do not have much knowledge about consumer trends—they're engineers, for goodness sake! We may as well ask them to predict the Oscars. These information markets require that participants have reasonable models. But if these same engineers were asked to predict which of two vehicles would prove more durable, the information market should perform well. For this task, the engineers possess diverse and reasonable models (they understand different parts of the vehicle). Owing to that diversity, they can collectively predict well.

ENCOURAGE INTERDISCIPLINARY EFFORTS

Given that we face no shortage of difficult and complex problems, we have little choice but to leverage our differences.

Many of these problems intersect with many traditional disciplines and areas of thought. To put this in some context, consider four current large-scale issues: environmental sustainability, world poverty, international security, and disease. Significant break-throughs in any of these areas will require the perspectives of physicists, chemists, biologists, psychologists, sociologists, immu-nologists, economists, and political scientists—and more.[12] To make headway on these problems, we must apply the logic of physics to chemistry, and we must the logic of psychology to politics.

These interdisciplinary efforts can be as crude as having people work together and communicate across disciplines or they can re-sult in new terminologies and frameworks. What's most important is sharing perspectives, heuristics, interpretations, and predictive models across disciplines. This approach will enable us to get off local peaks.

DISTINGUISH THE FUNDAMENTAL FROM THE INSTRUMENTAL

Conventional wisdom suggests that teams and groups must overcome the problems created by preference diversity. They must get on the same page, so to speak. This intuition is only partly correct. If preference diversity is fundamental, then yes, some compromise must be reached before the group can move forward: if they're not aiming at the same goal, there's little chance that they'll work well together. Without a compromise, people will tug in opposite directions. They'll manipulate agendas and they'll even lie. But we also know that diverse instrumental preferences are a good thing (see the Diversity Prediction Theorem). If we agree on the end, then it may well be useful to disagree on the means to that end. In that case, there's no need for compromise, we need only aggregate the diverse predictive models.

We therefore need to distinguish which environment is which. If we agree on the ends but disagree on the means, we should not try to manipulate outcomes or misrepresent what we think. We should just accept the wisdom of the crowd. We should recognize that the choice being made is, on average, better than the average choice we would make (see the Crowds Beat Averages Law). Instrumental preference diversity shouldn't be seen as a problem.

Best-selling how-to-negotiate books such as *Getting to Yes* make a similar point. They advise people involved in a negotiation to emphasize interests, not positions. Two people who disagree about whether a window should be open or shut are arguing positions. It may be that one wants fresh air but the other hates bugs. If so, they can purchase a screen for the window and both will be happy.[13] These two people have compatible fundamental preferences but their initial instrumental preferences bump into one another. If we can learn to distinguish fundamental preference differences from instrumental preferences differences, then half of the time we find we don't have any problems at all. The other half of the time we must compromise.

DIVERSE FUNDAMENTAL PREFERENCES CAN HELP

Even with healthy group dynamics, compromise is tough (otherwise, there wouldn't be books like *Getting to Yes*). All else being equal, each person would prefer the other to make the compromise. This might lead us to see fundamental preference diversity as a bad thing, but it only creates problems for choice. It may actually produce benefits when groups are problem solving and predicting.

We don't choose perspectives and heuristics out of thin air. We choose them because we think they'll help us find better solutions. So if we want different outcomes, we may well choose different perspectives and heuristics. If Tess values outcomes differently than Gwen and Eric, then even if they share the same perspectives and heuristics, Tess may find a solution that she likes better. A peak for them need not be a peak for her. From Tess's improvement, Gwen may find a solution that everyone likes better. When solving problems, a little fundamental preference diversity may go a long way.

A similar logic applies to predictions. If we're making a prediction, we don't care about everyone's preferences. We only care that their predictions are accurate and different from our own. If someone has different preferences, or if a subunit in an organization has different goals, then this person or subunit may naturally look at different attributes; they may have a different interpretation.[14] As a result, the aggregate prediction may be more accurate. Part of the wisdom of crowds may lie in the diversity of the crowd's preferences.

USE THIS BOOK AS A REASON TO BELIEVE

When considering the evidence of identity diversity's benefits, we saw how difficult these benefits were to realize. Though practical, human resource–based particulars of how to manage diverse groups lie outside the scope of our analysis, one of the conditions that makes diverse groups effective merits deeper contemplation. Recall David Thomas and Robin Ely's finding that if people believe that interactions with people different from themselves produce benefits, they're more likely to realize those benefits. This link between expectations and outcomes should not surprise us. Expectations shape behavior, and behavior shapes outcomes. If we expect benefits, we get benefits. If we don't expect benefits—if we interpret efforts to be inclusive as promoting social justice—we're not likely to see benefits. Why would we? We're not likely to listen to what others have to say if we don't think it will help. As laudable as concerns of fairness and justice may be, they do not appear to create the proper expectations for the benefits of diversity to materialize.

An analogy helps make sense of all this. Suppose that you own a corner restaurant with copper-topped tables. One day, a customer notices a ketchup spill on his table and comments that even though some ketchup was lost, at least the copper will be shiny. You ask why, and he tells you that ketchup cleans copper. Let's assume that before this moment, you'd never considered the copper-cleaning capabilities of ketchup (and, before this moment, you probably hadn't either). So you test the claim. You take the ketchup bottle and squeeze out your name in ketchup on the table. You let it sit a moment, wipe, and voila! you can read your name. Now you can benefit from this new knowledge. You can have your wait staff squirt a little ketchup on tables before cleaning them and you'll have shinier tables as a result.

You can directly put to use the knowledge that ketchup cleans copper. It's not hard to identify ketchup or copper. And squirting ketchup and wiping it off don't require subtle combinations of skills (although the order does matter). That's not true of creating well-functioning diverse groups—which is why corporations spend billions on diversity training. They're teaching people the art of getting along. What Thomas and Robin Ely point out, which seems counterintuitive, is the importance of expectations and belief. If we want diverse groups to work better, it helps to believe that they do. We have to believe the ketchup can clean the table if it has any hope of doing so—if we don't, it won't. There's still hard work to do: belief in diversity's benefits alone is not enough—we can't reap the benefits of diversity by clicking the heels of our ruby slippers and heading off to Oz, baby. But we need to believe in the value of diversity. Belief may be a necessary condition. Hence, the importance of logic. It gives us (to quote Bruce Springsteen) a reason to believe.

ADMITTING, HIRING, AND APPOINTING DIVERSITY

Applying our logic to admissions, hiring, and appointment decisions requires some care. As sensible as the seeking people of individual ability may seem, the logic of this book shows it incomplete. In choosing a team, admitting a class, or hiring employees, our concern should not be the average ability of the people hired, chosen, or admitted. Our concern should be collective performance, which depends as much on collective diversity as it does on individual ability. The belief that the best group consists of the best individual people rests on faulty logic. Instead, the best collections contain people who are both diverse and capable.

In what follows, we first look at university and college admissions, move on to hiring decisions and government appointments, and then conclude with some more general implications.

Admissions

Let's begin by considering a university admission decision. We often think of these decisions as being competitions between two applicants. Let's name our applicants Francesca and Leslee. Francesca has a combined score of 1470 on her SAT, while Leslee's is 1340. Both have similar grade point averages. The logic steers us away from simply selecting Francesca based on her higher scores. To decide whom to admit, our university must first have an objective or mission. It could be to educate a cognitive elite to keep society running smoothly. It could be to educate the citizens of our state. It could be to maximize alumni donations forty years hence. Let's suppose that our hypothetical university wants to add to its students' toolboxes as much as possible to advance knowledge and understanding.

Given this mission, let's look again at Francesca and Leslee. We can think of them as collections of tools (and potentials to acquire tools). Higher SAT scores may correlate with the number of tools, but they don't tell us exactly what tools someone possesses. Suppose Francesca took mostly college prep course classes but avoided math despite scoring in the ninetieth percentile on the quantitative section of the SAT. She also played varsity soccer and was active in her church, even taking a trip to Florida to help clean up after a hurricane. She enjoys painting and music and dreams of one day running an animal rescue program in the third world. To pursue these goals, she hopes to major in ecology and then get a masters degree in public health.

Leslee likes chemistry and math and took lots of courses in those areas, but scored only at the eightieth percentile on the quantitative section of the SAT test. She was never involved in many extracurricular activities because she didn't have a reliable form of transportation. And in the future, she wants to become a doctor and live among the Navajo. Finally, we note that Francesca identifies as white and that Leslee identifies as mixed race. And whereas Francesca comes from a wealthy suburb, Leslee's family is poor.

Ideally, we'd know exactly what tools these two possess, but we don't (although we do have some clues). We know that Francesca knows lots about animals, biology, and religion. We know that she has the ability to acquire math tools quickly if they're needed. We know she's seen tragedy. She hasn't been shut up in her suburban home. We know that Leslee has acquired scientific tools but may struggle with some mathematics. We know she has an interest in Native Americans and that she's seen poverty up close. She's also experienced life as a racial minority. The books she's read, the stories she's heard, and the culture she's experienced differ from Francesca's. On her own, though, Leslee is not diverse. Diversity is not a property of an individual but a property of a collection of people.

We have no hope of ranking Francesca and Leslee absent some context. In a class on ecology and sustainability, Francesca would contribute more to her fellow students and probably would learn more as well. In a physical chemistry class, Leslee would bring more to the table, so she'd share more and she'd also learn more, not just because of her greater interest, but also because of her stronger science foundations. In a political science, philosophy, or sociology class, each would contribute and learn differently. How then to decide? We have to look at these two applicants in the context of all of the applicants. Some of these applicants will be truly outstanding—they'll have demonstrated tremendous ability and be diverse. We're still left with the task of filling in the rest. And we have to make choices. In some cases, those choices will be easy. If we do not have many students with interesting perspectives on the environment, Francesca would be a good person to admit. If we lack students with tools from science, we'd admit Leslee.

Leslee might also be a better choice if we have few poor students and mixed-race students because she would offer a relatively rare perspective in her social science and literature classes. More generally, her experiences would differ; inferences she'd draw would come from unique analogies. Leslee's mixed racial identity, her relative poverty, her interest in the sciences, and her concern for the Navajo make her an appealing candidate if we think these aspects of her application imply that she brings or will acquire diverse tools.

This may look like the equivalent of giving extra points to Leslee because of her racial identity. In a way it is, but she's not getting points because of her race. She's getting points because of her tools.[15] We're saying that we think because of her racial identity she's likely to bring different perspectives, interpretations, predictive models, and perhaps even heuristics. Could this diversity offset 300 points on the SAT? Probably not. Could it offset 100 points? Most math professors would say no, but you'd get lots of disagreement from professors of politics, sociology, history, or literature. They'd disagree not because they're liberal academics (although many are) but because they've taught classes filled with white suburban girls named Jennifer. These professors would want to accept Leslee. Others have taught classes filled with rural and poor students. They'd want Francesca. In schools in which most students cared about making money but not saving the planet, Francesca would add a unique perspective.

In graduate programs, the benefits of toolbox diversity are even more pronounced. Graduate seminars are like group learning projects. Students benefit by interacting with people who see a problem differently. A graduate program in biology benefits by having students with lots of mathematical training as well as students with experience in the lab. These students learn from one another while preparing for oral examinations. Without that diversity, the entire class performs less well. A social science program with all male students probably suffers from a similar lack of tool diversity. Does this mean a graduate economics department should accept a woman with a 3.4 grade point average over a man with a 3.8? Again, it depends on the context. Economics, as a field, may need more women. JSTOR, an online search engine for scholarly articles, spits out one-third more articles for "sports economics" than for "gender discrimination economics."[16] Not that sports don't matter, but . . . .

Hiring

We can apply this same reasoning to a company's hiring decisions. Again, keep in mind that we're ignoring problems of getting along and differences in fundamental preferences (most companies point you toward the goal that they want you to work on). For companies, what counts as relevant diversity and, again, how much to weigh diversity relative to individual performance depends on the context. Let's suppose that we're hiring people for a job for which we have a well-defined ability measure and that people work alone at this job. We might, for example, be hiring someone to paint houses or to deliver messages by bicycle. If ability correlates with identity—if women on average outperform men—then maintaining equal numbers of men and women would sacrifice performance. But let's not go crazy here. Most likely, some men could paint houses better than enough women to be worthy of hiring. To refuse to consider hiring men because women perform better on average would hurt performance—we'd miss out on a few good men. (It would also be discriminatory.)

In contrast, suppose that we're hiring people to design Web pages, and that these people must work together either directly or indirectly. In this case, we probably want to consider collective diversity as much as individual ability. We should look for people with diverse training, experiences, and identities. We should not forget that the crossword puzzle champion and the classicist both contributed at Bletchley Park. Nor should we forget the success of InnoCentive.

Unfortunately for human resources professionals, we can't just look at someone and see her perspectives or heuristics. That's why firms interview, administer tests, ask for recommendations, and sample previous work. They're trying to make inferences about the tools that applicants possess. We know, for example, that someone with a computer science degree probably knows more programming heuristics than someone with a degree in biology. We know that someone who has worked for five years selling cars probably brings finer and more interesting interpretations of consumer types than someone who has been confined to a cubicle writing manuals for DVD players. But what of the undergrad riding the skateboard with all of those tattoos and piercings? Many people in corporate America would think "he looks different from us." Should they hire him? The answer depends. If the kid on the skateboard knows the equivalent of calculus for the problem—if the job at hand is, say, designing bowling shirts or tennis shoes—they might want to think about doing so. But if the firm invests in derivatives and the skateboarder stopped taking math classes in fifth grade, then the firm would do better to look elsewhere.

Let's get specific. Consider a firm that hires people to design software, say, Google. Owing to its success, Google can hire almost anyone that it likes. If it wanted, Google could hire just the top students from top-ranked engineering schools such as MIT, Caltech, Stanford, Illinois, Michigan, Georgia Tech, and Cal–Berkeley. These people would all be smart, but they might be trained similarly. They also might have had similar college experiences. And they might be far from representative in their identities.

Like many modern corporations, Google organizes itself in work teams that solve problems. For these teams to be successful, people must be able to communicate, and they must also be diverse. That's why Google doesn't pursue a strategy of hiring only the people with the best grades from the best schools. In its own description of "Who we're looking for," Google's first criterion is diversity—"people with broad knowledge and expertise in many different areas of computer science and mathematics"— as is their last, "people with diverse interests and skills." People who think alike get stuck. So Google samples widely. It looks for diversity in training, experience, and identity. Computer science graduates from Santa Clara work alongside former math professors. But Google is also aware of the Calculus Condition. It seeks diverse people with knowledge in mathematics and computer science. It's not seeking poets. Though, if a good mathematical epidemiologist showed up at Google's door, it would hire her because she might possess novel understandings of how diseases spread across populations and these understandings might inform Google's efforts to organize information flows.

Firms should also consider identity. Identity attributes correlate with or influence how we think. Leveraging diversity requires more than greater racial and gender balance. Forgetting this results in lost opportunities. The U.S. Army has substantial identity diversity at every rank. But owing to the hierarchical nature of the military, it does not have much age diversity within a rank, so the people making the same kinds of decisions and giving advice to the same people are likely all about the same age. This makes their life and military experiences more similar than they would otherwise have to be and reduces perspective and predictive model diversity. Some of the strongest evidence in the empirical diversity literature relates to demographic diversity. Those who arrive at the same time think the same way.[17] A lack of age diversity hinders collective performance.

Appointing

When the government puts together a cabinet, panel, or commission, it strives to achieve identity diversity. It does this partly for political reasons. For a society to accept decisions as impartial and representative, some reflectiveness is needed. Further, to the extent that preference diversity correlates with identity diversity, appointing an identity diverse commission ensures some preference diversity. And as the government often makes decisions that affect everyone, it's important that everyone's preferences be considered.

This book's logic suggests another reason these commissions should be identity diverse. In policy domains we might expect the best-performing team to be identity diverse. To have a group of only wealthy people decide on busing policies probably would not be wise. Including people more affected by those policies, who probably have diverse perspectives and interpretations, would lead to better solutions and more accurate predictions. They'd help because busing is a hard problem. But we don't want to go too far in the other direction, either. We wouldn't want only poor people deciding on busing, either.

In some contexts—say, determining the cause of the space shuttle explosion—identity diversity probably matters less, though the potential for serendipity—for a unique experience in someone's life to lead to a breakthrough—implies that we shouldn't rule out identity as a possible factor. But, overall, we may be better served by seeking out people with diverse experiences and training.

More generally, in putting together these panels and commissions, we have to think about including multiple types of diversity. If every member of a government commission grew up in an upper middle-class household, went to the same prep school, and then went to Yale, where they studied the same texts under the same professors, they may not be that cognitively diverse, regardless of how diverse their identity classifications may be. Identity diversity need not imply cognitive diversity.

Seek Diversity and Create Diversity

As firms and universities seek more diversity, they encourage the creation of ever more diversity. Students believe, sometimes mistakenly and sometimes correctly, that employers and graduate programs place enormous emphasis on grades. As a result, students shy away from difficult classes. Surveying a random selection of undergraduate transcripts reveals that few students take extra physics, organic chemistry, or advanced mathematics courses. These classes demand lots of time and effort and earning a good grade in any one of them is difficult. Yet if someone wanted to be a good lawyer, wouldn't an upper-level mathematical logic class or some basic economic theory be beneficial? Of course. But that's hard work compared to taking a course that the student can ace. The History of Elvis course might be difficult (really, dude, it has, like, lots of reading), but it may not help the student develop relevant perspectives, interpretations, heuristics, or predictive models. It may just be a way for the student to apply existing tools to a new subject area and maintain that grade point average above

3.5. The cost to society of students pursuing high grades rather than accumulating knowledge is enormous. We would all prefer that our doctor knew a bit more chemistry or physics, or that our elementary school teachers knew a bit more math.

Test for Toolbox Diversity

So how do we find diverse people? Universities, companies, and other organizations can test for diverse toolboxes. As an analogy, at present many companies administer personality tests to employees. These personality tests help employees better understand their own behavior, and they provide information that firms find useful when trying to manage these employees. These tests show that some people strongly prefer explicit tasks—figure out a way to get this package to Fargo by Friday at the lowest price. Other people prefer more open-ended assignments—make our Web page more intuitive.

Firms can also test applicants for cognitive diversity relative to one another and to their current employees. Testing for diversity isn't as hard as it sounds. A few years ago, a consulting company asked job applicants to predict the annual sales for a standard household product, something like rubber bands, peanut butter, lug nuts, or size C batteries. This company wanted to identify applicants who understood that total demand equals the sum of individual demands (recall the Calculus Condition in the Diversity Trumps Ability Theorem). They also wanted to find people who thought differently. They could achieve both goals by learning if and how the applicants segmented the market of consumers, whether they created relevant or novel categories. Among those asked the question about the C batteries, the applicants who parsed households into those with male children probably had a good chance of getting hired. Those applicants who divided the country into regions probably didn't. And yet the company wouldn't want all people who identified young boys as big users of batteries. They'd want some people who identified other market segments, such as campers.

TABLE 14.1:
Application test results

Applicant	Q1	Q2	Q3	Q4	Q5	Q6	Q7	Q8	Q9	Q10
Spencer			X	X	X			X	X	
Jeff	X	X			X	X	X		X	X
Rose	X	X				X	X		X	X

Let's make this more tangible. Suppose we give a ten-question test to three people, Spencer, Rose, and Jeff, who are applying for two open positions on a research team. We might decide whom to hire by comparing how they performed on our test. Let's suppose that Jeff answered seven correctly, Rose got six right, and Spencer answered only five correctly. Does this mean that we should hire Jeff and Rose? Not necessarily, to do so is to ignore diversity. Far better that we look also at which questions they got right. Table 14.1 shows the questions, denoted by Q1 through Q10, that each applicant answered correctly.

Notice every question that Rose answers correctly, Jeff answers correctly as well. Notice also that Spencer, who gets the fewest questions correct, answers correctly every question that Jeff gets wrong. Thus, even though Rose does better than Spencer on the test, hiring Jeff and Rose doesn't make as much sense as hiring Jeff and Spencer. Spencer's more diverse relative to Jeff than Rose is.

Accept Toolbox-Created Difficulties

If we use a single measuring stick, decisions of whom to admit, hire, and appoint don't require much effort. We line people up, measure them, and choose from the top of the list. A college might do this by creating some weighted average of grade point average and SAT score, or an employer may look at grade point average plus some scores computed from letters of recommendation. If we apply toolbox logic, we think of people as collections of tools, and we want to put together a collection of people with as many tools as possible, making for a much more difficult hiring problem.

To see how much harder, let's consider a college choosing an entire freshman class. The college may have 5,000 applicants for 1,000 spots. Even if it can rule out 3,500 of these people based on their tool sets, the school leaves itself the onerous task of choosing a collection of 1,000 students out of 1,500. The number of possible combinations boggles the mind (think billions of billions of billions and then a lot more). We might think that this number of possible solutions makes choosing almost impossible, so the college should just construct a stick and use it.

Here's a heuristic that allows the college to do at least as well as if it used the measuring stick. It works as follows: First, use the measuring stick. Think of those thousand potential admittees as the status quo solution. Then, allow a set of diverse, talented people to look for ways to make changes that increase relevant diversity but have minor changes in average ability. If each change improves the class's constellation of tools, this heuristic cannot do worse than sticking with the original thousand. Such an approach may not give a school as much diversity as it would like. There just may not be many men who apply to a veterinary school or many people of Asian descent applying for PhDs in the romance languages. If so, then perhaps the firm or school won't be as diverse as it would ideally be or as diverse as the society it serves. But, at least, the university has used toolboxes, not quotas: nor has it exclusively used measuring sticks.

The Samuel Paul Bowie Caveat

We can go too far in pursuing skill difference. In our pursuit of diversity, we must keep in mind the need to balance diversity with ability. We need only recall the 1984 NBA draft in which Portland picked Samuel Paul Bowie, a seven-foot center from Kentucky, over a small forward from North Carolina named Michael Jordan. Reasons for this pick vary. Some claim that Jordan's talents had been obscured by North Carolina's team-oriented style of play. Regardless, in retrospect, the pick looks stupid.

Let's cut the Blazers some slack. Portland's error may have resulted from having the wrong predictive model. Portland executives had reason to believe in the value of a good center. They had won a title just a few years earlier with an injury-prone Bill Walton at the pivot. Further supporting their case, only one team from 1959 to 1984 had won an NBA title without an all-star center. Add to this the fact that Portland already had an excellent tandem at small forward and shooting guard—Clyde Drexler and Jim Paxson—and the Bowie decision looks reasonable.

The lesson: we should not forget that ability still matters. The theorems say that it matters as much as diversity. If you want a super duper basketball team, draft Michael Jordan even if you have to sacrifice some diversity.

Avoid Lumping by Identity

Employers often use identity as a crude proxy for cognitive diversity. It's true that the types of cognitive diversity that we've considered may sometimes correlate with identity, for reasons we've already discussed. Even so, we probably can do better than to rely on coarse identity classifications to categorize people. People are multifaceted and multitooled. We all have different experiences and training as well as different identities. Experiential and training differences also translate into diverse toolboxes.

By mapping people into identity groups, we're guilty of too much lumping. We lump a recent immigrant from Nairobi, Kenya, a grandson of a sharecropper from the Mississippi delta, and the daughter of a dentist from Barrington, Illinois, into the same category: African Americans. We place the granddaughter of a miner from Copper Harbor, Michigan, a son of Gloria Vanderbilt (that would be Anderson Cooper), and a recently married former au pair from Lithuania into the box labeled non-Hispanic white. And in the Asian American box we lump together people whose ancestors came from Singapore, Malaysia, China, Japan, and

Korea. Each of these lumps of people, if unpacked, would prove cognitively diverse.

This lumping also ignores combinations of identities. A group consisting of five French men, three Korean men, two Kenyan women, and a woman from Singapore contains men and Kenyans but it does not contain Kenyan men and therefore may not be able to look at the problem from the same perspective that a Kenyan man might. And keep in mind that there is no single way in which a Kenyan man would look at a problem.

This insight should temper our enthusiasm for pipelines used to recruit minorities. These programs nurture potential employees or students from underrepresented groups. They may improve numbers, but they can limit the amount of cognitive diversity that a firm gets. By hiring only African American engineers who graduated from Berkeley and attended the same summer internship program, a company such as Cisco sacrifices cognitive diversity on the altar of identity accounting. Its employees look different, but they may not think differently. Thus, the use of pipelines probably has a negative effect on the benefits of diversity. It probably reduces the performance of identity diverse firms. The greater identity diversity gained through the pipeline could be more than offset by the hires' lack of experiential, demographic, or training diversity.

Far better that Cisco forms a consortium of companies to create multiple pipelines to obtain what we might call within-lump diversity. Or even better, perhaps society might be structured in such a way that those pipelines are not needed.

Avoid Stereotypes

Lumping people by identity groups has other negative consequences as well. It results in stereotypes and stigmatization. Many people think men are smarter than women, that people who grew up on farms work harder, and that Italians can cook better than the English. We also describe people as typical Europeans or as fraternity boys. These stereotypes are predictive models. They place people in categories and make predictions based on those categorizations—if we invite those frat boys, they'll eat all our food (and drink all our beer). These inferences may be more accurate than not. On average, Italians probably are better cooks than English people, and frat boys do eat a lot of food (and drink a lot of beer). But they can be wrong too: men are not smarter than women.

However, stereotypes create problems. First, because stereotypes are predictive models about people, and not about physical phenomena, they influence behavior and can become self-reinforcing.[18] Suppose that a person has space in his head for only three categories of people. (A silly assumption, but we're using it to make a point.) If this person has experience working with white people, he might create two subcategories of white people: the first he might call "hard workers" and the second he might call "slackers." He might then have one category that lumps together all nonwhite people. Matt Jackson and Roland Fryer show that, given these mild assumptions, even if white people and nonwhite people are equally likely to be good workers, this person would hire only whites.

This biased hiring would occur because, based on his interpretation, our employer can distinguish between people like him (good workers) and slackers, but he cannot distinguish among nonwhites. As a result, he predicts that anyone who is not white is just average—some are good workers and others are not. Note that this person is not saying that all nonwhite people are bad workers. To the contrary, he's got an accurate model of the abilities of nonwhites. However, when making a hiring decision and faced with three applicants—a hard worker, a slacker, and a nonwhite person—the best choice would be the white person who is a hard worker.

In this example, the predictive model and hiring rule reduce the incentives for potential nonwhite applicants to acquire training so that they would do well on the job. Even if 90 percent of nonwhite applicants performed well, the average "person like me who works hard" would be a better employee. His predictive model is accurate, but it's accurate only because it's so crude. Even worse, given that the employer has this predictive model, nonwhite people have little incentive to become qualified. Why bother? They won't get hired regardless of their talents and skills.

Although we used a racial stereotype, we could equally well have used any common stereotype. People may evaluate women as less effective than men at task performance, even if by objective standards the women perform as well. This stereotyping can reduce incentives for women to work hard and become self-fulfilling. Any stereotype—that Asians do better in math, that Indians are better spellers, that British people are wittier, or that African Americans are more creative—can induce self-fulfilling behavior. If we make stereotypical inferences about people who belong to an identity group, we reduce their incentives to accumulate tools outside these stereotypes. We limit opportunity. To use Glenn Loury's phrasing, we stigmatize.[19]

The second negative implication of stereotypes is that they restrict people's ability to contribute by restricting how they think. People feel compelled to represent their identity groups when they are underrepresented in a group. Someone might try to act and think as a woman or an Asian, and not as herself. In doing so hurt group performance. We need not strip ourselves of our identities, but we shouldn't let our core identities confine us. To use the language of Kwame Appiah, our identities root us: they provide us with meaning and purpose, but they should not restrict us. We should be allowed to be diverse, to be cosmopolitan, to posses multiple identities and to pursue a range of experiences and training.[20] As Toni Morrison put it, "In *Tar Baby*, the classic concept of the individual with a solid, coherent identity is eschewed for a model of identity which sees the individual as a kaleidoscope of heterogeneous impulses and desires, constructed from multiple forms of interaction with the world as a play of difference that cannot be completely comprehended."[21]

If Joe goes through life wearing a Lance Armstrong bracelet with the acronym WWAWMD (What would a white man do?) to remind himself of his identity, he may lose himself and try to act like some amalgamation of white men everywhere. In doing so, Joe may fail to bring his full range of cognitive tools bear on a problem or situation. He might instead apply only those tools that align with his identity group. Even worse, he may tote along what he considers to be the fundamental preferences of his identity group and those preferences may be inappropriate for the situation at hand.[22] He may end up focusing on social justice and equality of opportunity—laudable goals, yes, but inappropriate ones if he's part of a team designing a calendar with pictures of Sharpei puppies.

Concerns with social justice and equality of opportunity have a place in our lives, a central one. We should not, like Mussolini, concern ourselves only with having the trains run on time. But at some point we must put our diverse shoulders to the wheel and find cures for diseases, policies that reduce poverty, and technologies that produce clean energy sources.

Finally, the use of stereotypes limits predictive diversity when evaluating people. By definition, stereotypes are widely shared predictive models. By applying stereotypes, we are not thinking differently at the individual level; therefore collectively, we won't make accurate predictions. We saw this in our analysis of the Diversity Prediction Theorem. Therefore, if we want to make good predictions, we should abandon stereotypes and construct diverse predictive models. In that way, collectively we can make accurate predictions about others.

Recognize That Reflection May Not Be Ideal

When selecting people for a group, be it for a committee, a panel, or even an entering class, we often seek identity reflectiveness—we want the demographics of our selections to reflect the population. Identity representation matters not just for symbolic reasons. Many people believe that fairness and justice require something approximating reflectiveness. Others feel less strongly about legislating reflectiveness but question collections of people that do not reflect the larger population. Why doesn't the panel include anyone who looks like me?

At times, groups become homogenous because of preferences. Few college students go to see Disney's theatrical performance of *The Lion King*. So, we needn't assume that some implicit or even explicit discrimination took place. Even so, we must be ever vigilant. Small amounts of discrimination can tip a system into segregation.[23]

Even if we care only about productivity, we must also be concerned with social justice. At the end of the day corporations want to turn a profit. To achieve this goal, their workers need to get along with and trust one another. Universities have an even stronger drive for promoting justice, but their missions also include producing top research. In either context, if our concern is balancing productivity and social justice, then our logic points to no special reason for reflectiveness—except that reflectiveness satisfies feasibility. It is at least possible to have every group reflect society in its composition, whereas it's not possible for every school to be more diverse than the society it serves.

However, a commitment to reflectiveness limits our ability to leverage diversity in two ways. First, it leads us to stop adding diversity at an arbitrary point—namely at the level that reflects society. Once a firm or organization reaches the reflective percentages of people from each identity group, once it has 10 percent African Americans and Latinos, 5 percent Asians (again in one giant lump), and 50 percent women, it stops. But, is this ideal? If people of diverse ethnic and racial backgrounds bring diverse perspectives to the problem, they should be included until they stop making the group more effective, not just until they reach numbers that reflect their percentage in the population.

Second, a commitment to reflectiveness makes the composition of every group similar. The logic of diversity's benefits also applies to group composition. Different groups, too, should be diverse. If a company creates ten teams that work independently to come up with a new marketing plan, why not have some teams be 80 percent women, others be 40 percent Asian, and still others be 75 percent African American? Why not have some teams that are all engineers and some that consist mostly of marketers? Companies, organizations, and governments could create some reflective teams, but also some majority-minority teams, and some teams with only a few minorities.

In the political context, Heather Gerken calls this creation of majority minority groups *second-order diversity*. Let's be clear on what second-order diversity would or could mean. It could mean having a majority Latina U.S. District Court of Appeals, a county planning board dominated by Arab Americans, and an all-white FCC. Thus, a second-order diversity policy allows people who've never been in the majority to call the shots sometimes. People who never have power gain some experience. This could create opportunities for them to acquire different tools.[24]

If people have fundamental preference diversity, they may feel uncomfortable with the idea of second-order diversity. If ethnic or racial identity correlates with fundamental preference diversity, then a majority-minority body could choose an outcome that lies far from the median voter's ideal point. Defenders of second-order diversity question why a minority group getting the outcome they most prefer 10 percent of the time is any less fair than that same group never getting the outcome they most prefer. And while second-order diversity could increase policy ping-ponging, a little jumping back and forth between policies can be good, as we discussed in our analysis of simulated annealing.

Organizations can encourage exploration by encouraging people to think differently, by giving them time off to pursue individual projects, or by creating skunk works.[25] Though the benefits of exploration are enormous, we have to balance this exploration with the exploitation of good solutions once we find them. Successful organizations achieve this balance. They can maintain balance if some people move slowly, if they do not leap to the next new idea along with everyone else.[26]

Maintain Humility in the Face of the Mystery

The final piece of advice returns us to the beginning. In the prologue, I mentioned that the logic could be used to support proactive diversity policies, and it can. If individual diversity contributes to collective benefits, we should pursue pro-diversity policies. Companies, organizations, and universities that hire and admit diverse people should not expect instant results. But, in the long run, diversity should produce benefits. I do not advocate sacrificing ability for diversity, but rather balancing the two. This balancing was made explicit in the Calculus Condition in the analysis of problem solving and in the Diversity Prediction Theorem.

Previously we discussed why Google wouldn't want only freshly minted graduates from MIT and Caltech. People with different training and experiences often add more than people who score better on measuring sticks. Most employers and universities understand this logic and hire and admit accordingly. The link between identity diversity and cognitive diversity is more subtle and mysterious. Nevertheless, for similar reasons, these companies and universities shouldn't want all white men or all Asian women. Identity diversity is likely to correlate with cognitive diversity, sometimes directly—this would certainly be true for most public policy problems—and sometimes serendipitously.

No one can claim to predict the sources of inspiration. Nevertheless, all else being equal, we should expect someone different— be their differences in training, experiences, or identity—to be more likely to have the unique experience that leads to the breakthrough, to recognize the organizing principle of atomic weight, or to not see space as seperate from time.

Epilogue

THE KETCHUP QUESTION

If we cannot now end our differences, at least we can help make the world safe for diversity.
—JOHN FITZGERALD KENNEDY

IN the summer of 2004, I gave a talk at the Ralph Bunche Summer Institute at Duke University for prospective graduate students in political science. The Bunchies, as they call themselves, comprise a diverse group of undergraduates from across the United States. I began my talk with a question that few expected, a question I have asked thousands of people, from CEOs to members of the military: Do you store your ketchup in the refrigerator or the cupboard?

Among the Bunchies, about half stored their ketchup in the refrigerator. This percentage contrasts with some Midwestern and Wall Street audiences where almost everyone does. My non-scientific sample reveals that around 80 to 90 percent of people store their ketchup in the fridge. Almost all white Midwesterners do, but many African Americans, Australians, New Zealanders, Indians, and Irish do not. They store their ketchup in the cupboard.

A person once responded to the question by saying that ketchup had to be refrigerated because it contains vinegar. (He later admitted that he stores his vinegar in the cupboard, so go figure.) As a point of fact, few brands of ketchup state on their labels that they must be refrigerated after opening. And oh, by the way, almost all diners keep ketchup on the table right next to the salt and pepper. Nevertheless, refrigerator people think the cupboard people are abnormal, when in fact, it's the ketchup in the fridge people who are wasting precious resources and adding to global warming.

When asking the ketchup question, I follow it with five others. Each question has two possible answers.

1. Do you cross the street when the don't walk sign is flashing but no cars are present?
2. Do you ask people to remove their shoes when they enter your home or apartment?
3. Do you keep the radio on in your home or apartment?
4. When you greet friends, do you hug them?
5. Do you read the newspaper at the breakfast table when others are present?

After posing the list of questions, I ask my audience to identify the common characteristic of the situations the questions describe. Most people first notice that all of the questions pertain to minor, unimportant behaviors. After a while, someone recognizes that each of these questions describes a situation where the incentives to coordinate overpower the desire to express individual preferences. Eric may slightly prefer his ketchup warm, and if he had his way he would store it next to the salad oil in the cupboard, and his wife, Sheryl, may prefer her ketchup cold. But, most likely, neither cares much about the ketchup's temperature. However, both care about finding the ketchup. They care about coordinating on a place to store it.

The other questions also capture situations with incentives for coordination. (If you ever get the chance, walk across a city with someone from Brazil and someone from Switzerland. The Brazilian will ignore the blinking don't walk signs and cross heavy traffic. The Swiss will wait for the walk light even with no cars near the intersection.) These questions reveal how our desire to fit in with others contributes to what we say, what we wear, where we go, and how we behave. We conform our behaviors to match those of the people with whom we interact.[1] This logic extends to decisions about criminal behavior, tattooing, and golfing, as well as to decisions about where to leave the car keys, whether to shake hands, hug, or kiss, and whether or not to send birthday cards. This coordination sometimes gets subsumed under the heading of *norms*. Norms differ slightly because they are reinforced socially. If someone deviates from the norm, that person is punished.[2]

When we see differences across peoples of different races, ethnicities, and regions, we cannot escape the idea that these differences are intrinsic, that they're innate, essential. Jumping to such a conclusion mistakenly identifies the benefits to coordination as genetic determinism. Geneticists will not find a ketchup in the refrigerator gene. It doesn't exist. Nor will they find a hugging gene or a kiss on the cheek gene. Thus, if someone differs from us, our initial reaction should be that those differences arise from coordination problems, not from intrinsic differences.

Coordination also occurs in more important domains of human interaction. Not only do we coordinate on the storage of ketchup, we also coordinate how we celebrate marriages and births and how we honor the dead. Cultural and ethnic identities are part ketchup and part rituals, a combination of coordinations big and small. These coordinations form what the poet Mark Strand calls our "continuous lives." As we carve out these lives, some of us choose to paint red dots on our foreheads. Some of us choose to eat with chopsticks. Some of us talk with clicking sounds.

These coordinated differences extend beyond behavior. We differ in the stories we tell and the values we hold dear. These differences create either of two reactions, or both. They can create discomfort—and a reason why people need critical mass. We feel uncomfortable around people who act differently. We even feel uncomfortable around people trained differently. Marketing people find engineers awkward, and almost everyone finds some frustration in dealing with lawyers, accountants, and economists (hence, the frequency with which we toss about the derogatory jokes). Alternatively, these differences can inspire wonder and curiosity. You eat fish for breakfast? You drink ninety-six-ounce colas? Impossible!

If the first reaction dominates the second, then we wind up hanging out with people who store their ketchup in the same place and tell the same stories about Hansel and Gretel dropping breadcrumbs. We pull apart. A preference for working with people who bring the same formal perspectives to bear on a problem leads to segregation by function in firms and by discipline in the academy. In each case, the tendency to interact only with people like us creates the same macro-level dynamic. Each culture in a society, each identity group in a city, each department in a university, and each functional area of a firm ends up building walls around itself. As these walls become higher, the members of each group—be they Evangelicals, African Americans, chemists, or accountants—find themselves inside silos of their own creation.

People often speak of tolerating differences. Toleration, be it of Tupac (pronounced *two-POCK*) or Wagner (pronounced *VAHG-ner*) requires effort: we have trouble finding the darn ketchup, or we don't know what those people from marketing mean. Who can blame us when, after engaging people different from us, we head right back to our silos rather than embracing a more cosmopolitan approach to life?

Imagine though that you had the opportunity to leave your silos to interact with people smarter than your collegues and coworkers. These smarter people would enable you to find better solutions to your problems (a new, more effective marketing campaign, a new cleaning compound) and make more accurate forecasts (of future stock prices or of political hot spots). You'd jump at the chance to meet these people. In this book, we've seen how people with diverse tools can help us find better solutions and make better predictions. So why not jump at the chance to hang out with them as well? We have no guarantees that these people will help us, but our logic and the weight at the evidence suggest that they can. What each of us has to offer, what we can contribute to the vibrancy of our worlds, depends on our being different in some way, in having combinations of perspectives, interpretations, heuristics, and predictive models that differ from those of others. These differences aggregate into a collective ability that exceeds what we possess individually. To quote Maxine Hong Kingston,

"To me success means effectiveness in the world, that I am able to carry my ideas and values into the world—that I am able to change it in positive ways."[3]

People often speak of the importance of tolerating difference. We must move beyond tolerance and toward making the world a better place. When we peer out of our silos and see people doing strange things with ketchup (in the cupboard? on eggs?), when we meet people who think differently than we do, who speak different languages, who have different experiences, training, and values, we should see opportunity and possibility. We should recognize that a talented "I" and a talented "they" can become an even more talented "we." That happy vision rests not on blind optimism, or catchy mantras.

It rests on logic. A logic of diversity.

Notes

Prologue: How Diversity Trumps Ability

1. H. Reingold (2002) *Smart Mobs* (Cambridge, MA: Perseus Press).

2. James Surowiecki (2004) *The Wisdom of Crowds* (New York: Doubleday Press).

3. E. Mannix and M. Neale (2006) "What Differences Make a Difference? The Promise and Reality of Diverse Teams in Organizations," *Psychology in the Public Interest* (forthcoming).

4. This is a loose paraphrase of a comment heard from a Ford Motor Company employee.

5. We are not equating identity diversity with cognitive diversity—the so-called congruence assumption. See B. Lawrence (1997) "The Black Box of Organizational Demography," *Organization Science* 8: 1–22. Nor are we denying that such identity along with other things can often be a cause of cognitive differences.

Introduction: Unpacking Our Differences

1. See Karim R. Lakhani, Lars Bo Jeppesen, Peter Lohse, and Jill A. Panetta (n.d.) "Solving Scientific Problems by Broadcasting Them to Diverse Solvers," working paper, Massachusetts Institute of Technology.

2. Ayn Rand (1957) *Atlas Shrugged* (New York: Signet), p. 178.

3. Cognitive differences should not be confused with personality differences as measured by a Myers-Briggs or OCEAN test. These tests capture differences in extroversion, openness, conscientious, and so on. For example, a person with a low conscientiousness score

(the "C" in the OCEAN model) is more likely to make tpyographical errors and introduce an acronym without explaining what each letter represents.

4. Evelyn Fox Keller (2002) *Making Sense of Life* (Cambridge, MA: Harvard University Press).

5. Thus, our usage of the word *heuristic* expands the common usage, which includes only rules of thumb. Gerd Gigerenzer, Peter M. Todd, and the ABC Research Group (1999) *Simple Heuristics That Make Us Smart* (New York: Oxford University Press).

6. Gerd Gigerenzer and Reinhard Selten, eds. (2001) *Bounded Rationality: The Adaptive Toolbox* (Cambridge, MA: MIT Press).

7. T. C. Chamberlain (1890) "The Method of Multiple Working Hypotheses," *Science* o.s. 15: 92–96; reprinted in *Science* 148 (1965): 754–75.

8. The models and examples summarize, condense, and synthesize existing models and ideas produced by some creative psychologists, organizational theorists, educators, computer scientists, economists, biologists, political scientists, and statisticians. These frameworks have various origins. The perspectives, interpretations, and heuristics frameworks extend work of mine with Lu Hong, but we did not construct these frameworks from whole cloth. All three exist in slightly different form in computer science and cognitive psychology. The predictive model framework is a stripped-down version of a causal network model. Judea Pearl (2000) *Causality: Models, Reasoning, and Inference* (Cambridge: Cambridge University Press). The diverse preferences model is borrowed from economics, political science, and social choice, though our treatment of it will be somewhat nontraditional.

9. To give a weightier example, Republicans and Democrats alike want to see a reduction in crime (a fundamental preference) but differ on how to achieve it. Republicans believe that harsher penalties for criminal behavior reduce crime more than increases in social services, while Democrats believe the opposite (instrumental preferences).

10. H. Triandis, E. Hall, and R. Ewen (1965). "Member Heterogeneity and Dyadic Creativity," *Human Relations* 18: 33–55.

11. For evidence that groups whose members possess diverse perspectives and skills perform better and that those with diverse values

do not, see D. A. Thomas and R. J. Ely (1996) "Making Differences Matter: A New Paradigm for Managing Diversity," *Harvard Business Review* 74 (5): 79–90. Surowiecki's *Wisdom of Crowds* demonstrates the second point. James Surowiecki (2004) *The Wisdom of Crowds* (New York: Doubleday Press). The excellent survey by Katherine Williams and Charles O'Reilly III shows evidence for the first and third points: that cognitive diversity improves solutions but value diversity creates problems. K. Y. Williams and C. A. O'Reilly III (1998) "Demography and Diversity in Organizations: A Review of 40 Years of Research," *Research in Organizational Behavior* 20: 77–140. A number of studies show that preference diversity, a lack of mutual respect, and stereotyping reduce the benefits of diversity. For a review of this literature, see E. Mannix and M. Neale (2006) "What Differences Make a Difference? The Promise and Reality of Diverse Teams in Organizations," *Psychology in the Public Interest* (forthcoming). See also G. Northcraft, J. Polzer, M. Neale, and R. Kramer (1995) "Diversity, Social Identity, and Performance: Emergent Social Dynamics in Cross-Functional Teams," in *Diversity in Work Teams: Research Paradigms for a Changing Workplace*, ed. Susan E. Jackson and Marian N. Ruderman (Washington, DC: American Psychological Association).

12. The claim is not that identity differences produce benefits directly, but rather that they do so through the diverse cognitive tools that the various identities foster. A person's age, race, ethnicity, gender, religion, sexuality, and physical appearance influence her life experiences. They contribute to how that person sees and interprets events, outcomes, and situations—that is, experiences change the composition of each person's toolbox. See Elizabeth Anderson's entry on "Feminist Epistemology and Philosophy of Science" in the online *Stanford Encyclopedia of Philosophy*.

13. T. Kochan, K. Bezrukova, R. Ely, S. Jackson, A. Joshi, K. Jehn, J. Leonard, D. Levine, and D. Thomas (2003) "The Effects of Diversity on Business Performance: Report of a Feasibility Study of the Diversity Research Network," *Human Resource Management Journal* 42 (1): 3–21.

14. Mannix and Neal (2006).

15. Though companies do make cultural mistakes, the legend of the failed release of the Chevy Nova in Mexico (no va means "no go"

in Spanish) is outlandish. As argued on www.snopes.com/business/misxlate/nova.asp, would Americans think that a dinette set called Notable means "no table"? Doubtful.

16. P. Frymer and J. D. Skrentny (2004) "The Rise of Instrumental Affirmative Action: Law and the New Significance of Race in America," *Connecticut Law Review* 36: 677–723.

17. R. T. Ford (2004) *Racial Culture: A Critique* (Princeton, NJ: Princeton University Press).

18. If you can still recite the quadratic formula—"negative *b* plus or minus the square root of b^2 minus $4ac$ divided by $2a$"—you'll sail through.

19. See especially Scott E. Page (1996) "Two Measures of Difficulty," *Economic Theory* 8 (2): 321–46; Lu Hong and Scott E. Page (2001) "Problem Solving by Heterogeneous Agents," *Journal of Economic Theory* 97 (1): 123–63; Lu Hong and Scott E. Page (2004) "Groups of Diverse Problem Solvers Can Outperform Groups of High-Ability Problem Solvers," *Proceedings of the National Academy of Sciences* 101 (46): 16385–89; Scott E. Page with Jenna Bednar (2006) "Game(s) Theory and the Emergence of Culture," *Rationality and Society* 18 (2); and Lu Hong and Scott E. Page (2005) "Interpreted and Generated Signals," working paper, University of Michigan–Ann Arbor. Posted online at www.cscs.michigan.edu/~spage/.

Chapter 1: Diverse Perspectives

1. Bill Bryson, in *A Short History of Everything* (New York: Oxford University Press, 1999), claims that the game of solitaire actually led to this discovery. The account given here is an abbreviated version of Richard Morris's 2003 book *The Last Sorcerers: The Path from Alchemy to the Periodic Table* (Washington, DC: Joseph Henry Press), which makes no mention of solitaire.

2. Steven Toulmin (1953) *The Philosophy of Science* (London: Hutchinson), p. 34.

3. See Michael Bradie (1999) "Science and Metaphor," *Biology and Philosophy* 14: 159–66.

4. I thank Richard Langlois for this anecdote.

5. Robert Wright (1999) "Time 100: Molecular Biologists," *Time*, March 29. Posted online at www.time.com/time/time100/scientist/profile/watsoncrick.html.

6. In a more complete treatment of a perspective, the set of possible objects in reality could be infinite, but here, to avoid unnecessary complications, we assume a finite set.

7. See Daniel Dennett (1996) *Kinds of Minds: Toward an Understanding of Consciousness* (New York: Basic Books), p. 39.

8. But wait a minute: each one of us does not have a single word for each of the situations that we experience, objects that we see, and possible solutions to a problem. This assumption is unrealistic in many contexts. Often, we place objects, experiences, events, and solutions in categories. We lump stuff together. We consider these categorizations in chapter 3, when we cover the interpretation framework. Here, I consider perspectives because they are much simpler to understand. Once we have a firm grip on the implications of diverse perspectives, we can move on to interpretations. Theories differ from perspectives. Theories are coherent sets of ideas that build from basic principles. They can include notions of cause and effect. Theories, though, must include perspectives.

9. Some problems prove difficult in both Cartesian and polar coordinates. To solve them, we need to represent solutions using other perspectives such as Norman Wildberger's rational trigonometry. Rational trigonometry's perspective relies on spread and quadrance (we won't go into what these are). By doing so, it gets rid of all of those messy cosines and sine calculations. All calculations become rational. Norman J. Wildberger (2005) *Divine Proportions: Rational Trigonometry to Universal Geometry* (Kingsford, Australia: Wild Egg Books). Rational trigonometry does not simplify every problem, but it does simplify many.

10. See Ariel Rubinstein (1996) "Why Are Certain Properties of Binary Relations More Common in Natural Language?" *Econometrica* 64 (2): 343–55.

11. Fred Lager (1994) *Ben & Jerry's: The Inside Scoop: How Two Real Guys Built a Business with a Social Conscience and a Sense of Humor* (New York: Crown Publishers).

12. Incidentally, the question for which 42 is the answer is "What is 9 times 6?" In base thirteen, $9 \times 6 = 42$.

13. One of a pair of new houses in a subdivision was dropped because it was identical to the other.

14. Each number can be included or not. Thus, any subset can be written as a binary list (a list of 0s and 1s) of length thirteen. The number of such strings equals 2^{13}.

15. With N objects, 2^{N-1} distinct perspectives create single-peaked landscapes.

16. For a more precise statement and proof, see Lu Hong and Scott E. Page (2001) "Problem Solving by Heterogeneous Agents," *Journal of Economic Theory* 97 (1): 123–63.

17. Roberto A. Weber and Colin Camerer (2003) "Cultural Conflict and Merger Failure: An Experimental Approach," *Management Science* 49 (4): 400–415.

18. Irving L. Janis (1972) *Victims of Groupthink: A Psychological Study of Policy Decisions and Fiascoes* (Boston: Houghton Mifflin); Paul T. Hart (1990) *Groupthink in Government: A Study of Small Groups and Policy Failures* (Baltimore: Johns Hopkins University Press); Paul A. Kowert (2002) *Groupthink or Deadlock: When Do Leaders Learn from Their Advisors?* (Albany: State University of New York Press).

19. S. Moscovici (1976) *Social Influence and Social Change* (New York: Academic Press).

Chapter 2: Heuristics

1. Barry Nalebuff and Ian Ayres (2003) *Why Not? How to Use Everyday Ingenuity to Solve Problems Big and Small* (Cambridge, MA: Harvard Business School Press).

2. Gerd Gigerenzer, Peter M. Todd, and the ABC Research Group (1999) *Simple Heuristics That Make Us Smart* (New York: Oxford University Press).

3. See Richard Cyret and James March (1963) *Behavioral Theory of the Firm* (Englewood Cliffs, NJ: Prentice-Hall).

4. Christopher Alexander, Sara Ishikawa, and Murray Silverstein with Max Jacobson, Ingrid Fiksdahl-King, and Shlomo Angel (1977) *A Pattern Language: Towns, Buildings, Construction* (New York: Oxford

University Press); Christopher Alexander (1979) *The Timeless Way of Building* (New York: Oxford University Press).

5. See Gigerenzer, Todd, and the ABC Research Group (1999) for a discussion of this trade-off.

6. Barry Schwartz (2004) *The Paradox of Choice: Why More Is Less* (New York: Hapercollins).

7. David H. Wolpert and William G. MacCready (1995) "No free Lunch Theorems for Search," Technical Report SFI-TR-95-02-010, Santa Fe Institute.

8. The one-dimensional gradient is called the derivative.

9. The formal version goes as follows: The probability of accepting a new solution equals

$$e^{\frac{-Decrease}{Temp}}$$

If the temperature is high, the value of this expression is approximately e^0, which is 1. When the temperature approaches zero, the value of this expression approaches $e^{-\infty}$, which is zero. The art of simulated annealing work rests in choosing the proper temperature schedule. If the temperature falls too quickly, the heuristic gets stuck. If it falls too slowly, the heuristic wanders the space of solutions without going uphill. See Scott E. Page (1996) "Two Measures of Difficulty," *Economic Theory* 8 (2): 321–46, for an introduction to simulated annealing.

10. Note that our linear formula has a logical flaw: If *Decrease exceeds Temp*, The probability becomes negative. We can get around this problem by setting negative probabilities equal to zero.

11. See Alex Osborn (1953) *Applied Imagination* (New York: Scribners).

12. Melanie Mitchell (1996) *An Introduction to Genetic Algorithms* (Cambridge, MA: MIT Press).

13. I thank Michael Ryall for this example.

14. Nalebuff and Ayres (2003)

CHAPTER 3: INTERPRETATIONS

1. Lu Hong and Scott E. Page (2005) "Interpreted and Generated Signals," working paper, University of Michigan–Ann Arbor. Posted

online at www.cscs.umich.edu/~spage/signals.pdf. See also the literature on PAC (probably approximately correct) learning.

2. Roland G. Fryer and Matthew O. Jackson (2003) "Categorical Cognition: A Psychological Model of Categories and Identification in Decision Making: An Extended Abstract," in *Proceedings of the 9th Conference on Theoretical Aspects of Rationality and Knowledge (TARK-2003), Bloomington, Indiana, June 20–22, 2003*, ed. Joseph Y. Halpern and Moshe Tennenholtz (New York: ACM Press), pp. 29–34.

3. See Brent Berlin and Paul Kay (1969) *Basic Color Terms* (Berkeley and Los Angeles: University of California Press).

4. These partial taxonomies exist across cultures. See Brent Berlin (1992) *Ethnobiological Classification* (Princeton, NJ: Princeton University Press).

Chapter 4: Predictive Models

1. Maris A. Vinovskis (2005) *The Birth of Head Start: Preschool Education Policies in the Kennedy and Johnson Administrations* (Chicago: University of Chicago Press).

2. See Malcolm Gladwell (2005) *Blink: The Power of Thinking without Thinking* (New York: Little, Brown).

3. Gerd Gigerenzer, Peter M. Todd, and the ABC Research Group (1999) *Simple Heuristics That Make Us Smart* (New York: Oxford University Press).

4. See www.jumptheshark.com.

5. Michael Lewis (2003) *Moneyball: The Art of Winning an Unfair Game* (New York: W. W. Norton).

6. See Robyn Dawes, David Faust, and Paul Meehl (1989) "Clinical vs Actuarial Judgment," *Science* 243: 1668–74; William Grove and Paul Meehl (1996) "Comparative Efficiency of Informal (Subjective, Impressionistic) and Formal (Mechanical, Algorithmic) Prediction Procedures: The Clinical-Statistical Controversy," *Psychology, Public Policy, and Law* 2 (2): 293–323.

7. Philip Tetlock (2005) *Expert Political Judgment: How Good Is It? How Can We Know?* (Princeton, NJ: Princeton University Press).

CHAPTER 5: MEASURING STICKS AND TOOLBOXES

1. P. F. Drucker (1993) *Post-Capitalist Society* (New York: Harper Business), p. 215.

2. L. Guinier and S. Sturm (2001) *Who's Qualified? A New Democracy Forum on Creating Equal Opportunity in School and Jobs* (Boston, MA: Beacon Press).

3. Gerd Gigerenzer and Reinhard Selten, eds. (2001) *Bounded Rationality: The Adaptive Toolbox* (Cambridge, MA: MIT Press).

4. Other countries vary in how much they believe in measured intelligence.

5. Howard Gardner (1983) *Frames of Mind: The Theory of Multiple Intelligences* (New York: Basic Books).

6. Robert J. Sternberg (1985). *Beyond IQ: A Triarchic Theory of Intelligence* (Cambridge: Cambridge University Press).

7. Of course, orderings by age are not set in stone. If Kathleen were to travel at a speed close to the speed of light, then she would age more slowly and could become younger than her brother Patrick.

8. I leave this exercise to the motivated reader.

9. Fan dissatisfaction has led to refinements of the ranking system over the years. One can show rather easily that had the formula not changed, different teams would have played in some recent championship games (calm yourself, Louisville fans, it's just a game).

10. Our use of three doors and one hundred pieces is arbitrary. In Blotto, the number of pieces must be relatively large when compared to the number of doors, and the number of doors must be odd.

11. If USC plays Oklahoma, USC wins. Michigan then defeats Florida. And USC defeats Michigan in the championship game. If Florida plays Oklahoma first, Florida wins. Meanwhile, USC again defeats Michigan, and Florida then defeats USC in the championship.

12. A criticism might be levied that this model assumes that each player has the same number of pieces. Better, more able players might have more pieces. Suppose that one player had 140 pieces to the other player's 100. This would be a substantial difference in what we might think of as "ability." But even with this arrangement, the first player can be defeated. The first player must have more than forty-one pieces

in front of one door. That means he must have fewer than ninety-eight pieces at the other two doors. The other players can arrange their pieces in front of only those other two doors.

13. What counts as a tool is obviously subjective. And the more finely we differentiate between tools, the larger these numbers become.

14. See Wayne A. Grove, Donald H. Dutkowsky, and Andrew Grodner (2005) "Survive Then Thrive: Determining Success in the Economics Ph.D. Program," manuscript, Le Moyne College.

CHAPTER 6: DIVERSITY AND PROBLEM SOLVING

1. See Thomas Homer-Dixon (2000) *The Ingenuity Gap* (New York: Knopf).

2. For an introduction, see John H. Miller and Scott E. Page (2006) *Complex Adaptive Social Systems: The Interest in Between* (Princeton, NJ: Princeton University Press.)

3. To model the agents, I built on the work of Allen Newell and Herb Simon, who characterized problem solvers as having problem representations (what we call perspectives) and heuristics. Allen Newell and Herbert Simon (1972) *Human Problem Solving* (Englewood Cliffs, NJ: Prentice-Hall).

4. To be mathematically precise, each agent had a pair of basis vectors that it could walk along on the landscape.

5. Lu Hong and Scott E. Page (2004) "Groups of Diverse Problem Solvers Can Outperform Groups of High-Ability Problem Solvers," *Proceedings of the National Academy of Sciences* 101 (46): 16385–89.

6. Recall that heuristics need not be elaborate methods such as simulated annealing or Fourier analysis. They can be rules of thumb or routines that we have acquired over time. As such, they may not lend themselves to description. In these cases, they could be thought of as *procedural knowledge*. See J. R. Anderson (1976) *Language, Memory and Thought* (Hillsdale, NJ: Erlbaum); J. R. Anderson (1993) *Rules of the Mind* (Hillsdale, NJ: Erlbaum).

7. The following 2005 model years cars were used: Acura RL, Nissan Ultima, Mazda 6, Toyota Camry, Honda Accord, Chrysler Sebring, Chevy Malibu, Hyundai Sonata, Dodge Stratus, Saturn L300,

Volkswagen Jetta, Kia Optima, Buick Century, Ford Taurus, Mitsubishi Galant, Mercedes C240, Suzuki Verona, Volvo S60, BMW 525, Pontiac G6, Lexus ES, Cadillac CTS, and Saab 9-5. The source for these data was Edmunds.com.

8. Brian Greene (2004) *The Fabric of the Cosmos* (New York: Alfred Knopf), p. 382. Emphasis in the original.

9. For a much more detailed treatment, see Lu Hong and Scott E. Page (2001) "Problem Solving by Heterogeneous Agents," *Journal of Economic Theory* 97 (1): 123–63.

10. Note, though, that people with diverse perspectives but common heuristics or people with a common perspective and diverse heuristics cannot.

11. For related logic in the predictive context, see B. Grofman, G. Owen, and S. Feld (1983) "Thirteen Theorems in Search of the Truth," *Theory and Decision* 15: 261–78.

12. From "Circles" in Ralph Waldo Emerson (1983) *Essays and Lectures* (New York: Library of America), p. 405.

13. Bernardo Huberman (1990). "The Performance of Cooperative Processes," *Physica* D42(38); S. H. Clearwater, B. A. Huberman and T. Hogg (1991) "Cooperative Solution of Constraint Satisfaction Problems, *Science* 254: 1181–83.

14. If the best problem solver finds the optimal solution 99.9 percent of the time, the collection of randomly selected problem solvers will not outperform the group of the best.

15. The formal condition requires that the set of all of the local optima for all of the problem solvers can be written down as a list. Mathematicians refer to this requirement as the set being denumerable. Any finite set is denumerable, some infinite sets, such as the integers $(1,2,3,\ldots)$ are also denumerable, but other infinite sets such as the real numbers are not.

16. See Hong and Page (2004).

17. We need the set of perspective and heuristics to be bounded for this to be true, which is why I've drawn it as a box.

18. If the two groups know how they were formed, then all bets are off. Owing to within- and between-group dynamics, we might not be able to say much at all. The members of the high-IQ group could put forth little effort, knowing that they are smarter, or they could

work especially hard to prove their greater intelligence. Members of the random group might well just decide to give up. Or they might work even harder.

19. I might add that since beginning this research I have been told dozens of stories by people who have conducted the equivalent of this experiment. They have let students form groups on their own to work on projects. This anecdotal evidence suggests that the groups formed by the students who were best as individuals do not do best.

20. One could argue that if only a small number of the students were able to find even reasonable solutions, the group of the best would do better. That intuition jives with the theorem because the Calculus Condition is violated.

21. Lu Hong and Scott E. Page (2001) "Problem Solving by Heterogeneous Agents," *Journal of Economic Theory* 97 (1): 123–63.

CHAPTER 7: MODELS OF INFORMATION AGGREGATION

1. Keep in mind that if the predictive task is too hard, no one will do much better than a dartboard. See Philip Tetlock (2005) *Expert Political Judgment: How Good Is It? How Can We Know?* (Princeton, NJ: Princeton University Press).

2. Justin Wolfers and Eric Zitzewitz (2004) "Prediction Markets," *Journal of Economic Perspectives* 18 (2): 107–26; R. Roll (1984) "Orange Juice and Weather," *American Economic Review* 74 (5): 861–80.

3. HSX and IEM use real money, as do Tradesports.com and Betfair.com. Other prediction markets, such as Ideosphere.com, use virtual money.

4. See David M. Pennock, Steve Lawrence, C. Lee Giles, and Finn Årup Nielson (2001) "The Real Power of Artificial Markets," *Science* 291: (February 9) 987–88.

5. Jeremy Waldron (1995) "The Wisdom of the Multitude: Some Reflections on Book 3, Chapter 11 of Aristotle's *Politics*," *Political Theory* 23 (4): 563–84.

6. For that reason, Lu Hong and I refer to these as *generated signals*. Lu Hong and Scott E. Page (n.d.) "Interpreted and Generated Signals," manuscript.

7. The formal calculation goes as follows:

$$7 * (100\%) + 10 * (50\%) + .5 * (33.3\%) + 68 * (25\%) = 34$$

8. An exact calculation of the probability that the audience predicts correctly is tedious but not difficult.

9. Each manager predicts five times his region's sales; then the average of these predictions is the sum of the five regions' sales.

10. If the managers weight past and current sales differently, the collective prediction could lie outside this range.

11. That assumption is not as innocuous as it may seem. In some models, rational people may choose not to vote informatively, but here they would. See Timothy Feddersen and Wolfgang Pesendorfer (1997) "Voting Behavior and Information Aggregation in Elections with Private Information," *Econometrica* 65 (5): 1029–58.

12. See B. Grofman, G. Owen, and S. Feld (1983) "Thirteen Theorems in Search of the Truth," *Theory and Decision* 15: 261–78.

13. This logic underpins the design of many modern multimirrored telescopes. Each of the mirrors can be thought of as a diverse, flawed telescope. When combined, the idiosyncratic blurriness from the various pictures cancels out, creating a clear vision of a portion of the night sky.

CHAPTER 8: DIVERSITY AND PREDICTION

1. By *accuracy* here we mean the distance between the model's predictions and the actual outcomes, and by *predictive diversity* we mean the average distance between each model's prediction and the average predictions of other models.

2. See Norman L. Johnson (1998) "Collective Problem Solving: Functionality beyond the Individual," Los Alamos Working Paper LA-UR-98-2227; Norman L. Johnson (1999) "Diversity in Decentralized Systems: Enabling Self-Organizing Solutions," presented at the Decentralization II Conference, UCLA.

3. The eager reader can calculate whether Deborah's predictions are also negatively correlated. (Hint: they are.)

4. If screenplays had a third attribute, say level of humor, and both included it in their interpretations, then they would overlap.

5. For a precise statement of the claim see Lu Hong and Scott Page "Generated and Interpreted Signals" on my web site.

6. The aggregation of predictive models through voting should not be confused with processes that generate *common knowledge*. Information becomes common knowledge when everyone knows that everyone knows that everyone knows something, and so on. So, for example, because Ray knows the rows and Marilyn knows the columns, they must collectively know the row and the column and between the two of them they can predict with 100 percent accuracy. To see this, suppose that they are considering an applicant with no sexual content and a moderate level of violence. Under an assumption of common knowledge, each would know the other person's interpretation as well as the outcome associated with each combination of attributes. They would therefore know that Marilyn's prediction is correct. See John Geanakoplos (1992) "Common Knowledge," *Journal of Economic Perspectives* 6 (4): 53–82.

7. The version of the theorem that we describe follows A. Krogh and J. Vedelsby (1995) "Neural Network Ensembles, Cross Validation, and Active Learning," in *Advances in Neural Information Processing Systems 7*, ed. G. Tesauro, D. S. Tourtetsky, and T. K. Leen, (Cambridge, MA: MIT Press), pp. 231–38. For more general background, see E. Leamer (1978) *Specification Searches—Ad Hoc Inference with Nonexperimental Data* (New York: John Wiley and Sons).

8. The analysts are Scott Wright from *NFL Countdown*, James Alder from About.com, the Fanball staff at Fanball.com, the *Sporting News*, Paul Zimmerman from *Sports Illustrated*, and Pete Prisco and Clark Judge from *CBS Sportsline*.

9. Dan Catlin performed a similar analysis on the 2005 NBA draft and found that Pete Prisco defeated the crowd, but he was the only one.

10. A complete theory of bubbles and crashes requires a bit more complication, for though we might blame a lack of diversity for collective predictions gone awry, we can sometimes blame diversity, at least a little bit of it, for bubbles. It's easy to see that diversity in predictive models can drive price increases. For a price to rise, someone must think that the

current price is too low. That person must have preferences that differ from those of other people, though they do not have to differ by much. See J. Sheinkman and W. Xiong (2003) "Overconfidence and Speculative Bubbles," *Journal of Political Economy* 111: 1183–1219.

11. S. E. Asch (1956) "Studies of Independence and Conformity: A Minority of One against a Unanimous Majority," *Psychological Monographs* 70: 416.

12. Someone in a Wikipedia entry wryly notes that NATO itself has no McDonald's.

13. This approach to having people use inaccurate but linear models to predict outcomes can also be found in Bob Axelrod and Michael Cohen (1984) "Coping with Complexity: The Adaptive Value of Changing Utility," *American Economic Review* 74 (1): 30–42.

14. Cooper's perspective is based on the Walsh Functions. See Scott Page and David Richardson (1992) "Walsh Functions and Schema Variance," *Complex Systems*: 125–35. I never would have believed that this paper would sneak into this book, but it's an example of how a perspective can move from one problem to another.

15. Just to put a bow on this, the crowd's accuracy also can be explained by the Diversity Prediction Theorem. Cooper's individual error equals two, as does Orrie's. The diversity of their predictions equals one. Subtracting this from their average individual error gives the collective error of one. Their collective accuracy stems from their diversity and their individual accuracy, just as we know it must.

16. To convince yourself that this formula works, plug in screenplay with no sex ($S = 0$) and no violence ($V = 0$). The formula spits out a value of 0, which is Deborah's prediction. Plug in a screenplay with low sexual content ($S = 1$) and no violence ($V = 0$). The formula gives a value of 1, which again aligns with Deborah's prediction.

17. To prove that experts who dominate the crowd predict more accurately on average, denote the sets in the expert's interpretations as $1, 2, \ldots N$. For convenience, assume that each of these sets contains the same number of situations that could arise and that all situations are equally likely.

Each person in the crowd is a nonexpert. Each also partitions the possible situations into sets. Their sets lump together the expert's sets. Or put another way, the expert's sets split the sets of each person in the crowd. Under this assumption, the expert sees the world more finely than do people in the crowd. Any distinction that someone in the crowd can make can also be made by the expert.

Let $S_{i1}, S_{i2}, \ldots S_{iM}$ denote the sets in person i's interpretation, where $iM < N$. The individual's sets are collections of the experts sets. The set S_{i1} might equal the union of expert's sets 1, 2, and 3. For convenience, assume that the sets 1 through N are arranged in such a way that the expert's predictions increase with the set number. In this way, the prediction from the set N is the highest and the prediction from the set 1 is the lowest.

Under this scenario, the expert sometimes predicts less accurately than the crowd, though he does predict more accurately on average. To see both of these results, choose a situation that belongs to some set i in the expert's interpretation. Let x be the value of this situation. The prediction made by the expert is the average value of situations within that set, call this V_i.

To compute the average prediction of the individuals in the crowd requires making some further assumptions. Suppose that the crowd contains five individuals and that each pairs the set i with exactly one other set from the expert's interpretation. Call these J_1 through J_5. The prediction of the person who lumps set i with set j_1 equals one-half the sum of V_i and V_{J_1}. It follows that the average prediction from the five individuals for a situation in the set i, $P(i)$ equals:

$$P(i) = \frac{\frac{V_i+V_{J_1}}{2} + \frac{V_i+V_{J_2}}{2} + \frac{V_i+V_{J_3}}{2} + \frac{V_i+V_{J_4}}{2} \frac{V_i+V_{J_5}}{2}}{5}$$

This reduces to

$$P(i) = \frac{V_i}{2} + \frac{(V_{J_1} + V_{J_2} + V_{J_3} + V_{J_4} + V_{J_5})}{10}$$

This equals the average of the prediction from the set i and the average predictions from the sets J_1 through J_5. This prediction might appear to be less accurate than the expert's prediction. And on average it is. It cannot be more accurate on average as V_i is the average value in the set i. However, if x is less than V_i, then the expert's prediction is too high. And if the average prediction made for situations in the sets J_1 through J_5 is less than the prediction from set i, then the crowd might predict more accurately than the expert.

To see this another way, assume that the average value in the sets J_1 through J_5 equals the average value across all situations. If a situation in set i arises, the prediction of the expert will be V_i. The average prediction by the crowd will be a weighted average of V_i and $\bar{V}$, the average value over all situations. The crowd's prediction is therefore biased toward the mean, and the crowd will predict more accurately than the expert in those situations whose value differs from the expert's prediction in the direction of the mean. So, even though the expert's interpretation is finer than the group's, the group may still outperform the expert in some cases.

This argument can be made more generally. Consider some set i containing several situations, each of which has a value. As above, let average value in that set equal V_i and consider a situation that has the value x. The expert's error equals the following:

Expert's Error: $(V_i - x)^2$

The crowd's prediction for situations in the set i is not V_i, but V_i plus some bias that results from some of the people in the crowd lumping set i in with other sets. The crowd's prediction equals $V_i + LB_i$, where LB_i denotes the sum of all of these lumping biases. The crowd's error can then be written as follows:

Crowd's Error: $(V_i + LB_i - x)^2$

V_i is the average value in the set i; therefore, on average V_i will be closer to the value for situations in the set i, but there may be cases in which $V_i + LB_i$ is closer to x than V_i is. These cases will be at the extremes of the values. If the lumping bias for set i is positive, then the crowd can predict better only for those situations in set i that have higher than average value. What this means is that even if the members of the group lump the categories of the expert, the group is still likely to predict more accurately than the expert in specific cases and those case have a pattern.

18. To generate their predictive models, the expert and the crowd estimated their models on a *training set* of three hundred points. Once they estimated their models, the crowd's and the expert's models were compared on a *testing set* consisting of one hundred points.

19. Using our formula, $W = 4 * 10 + 2 * 20 + 0 = 80$.

20. This calculation is not difficult. If her model is correct, then it should fit the data from the first breakfast:

$$80 = \beta 10 + \alpha 20$$

and from the second breakfast

$$105 = \beta 15 + \alpha 15$$

She has two equations and two unknowns. Solving these equations gives $\beta = 6$ and $\alpha = 1$. To get this, divide the first equation by 10 and multiply it by 15. This gives $120 = \beta 15 + \alpha 30$. Subtract this from the second equation to obtain $15 = \alpha 15$. This gives that $\alpha = 1$. Plug this value in to get $\beta = 6$.

21. We assume here that Josh takes the total number of waffles made in the two months, 185, and divides by the number of partners who attended those two breakfasts, 25. Anna makes the same calculation for the associates.

22. If, for example, twenty partners and ten associates show up for breakfast, Magda predicts that 130 waffles will be required ($130 = 6 * 20 + 1 * 10$). Josh and Anna collectively predict that only 100 are needed ($100 = 3.7 * 20 + 2.6 * 10$). The actual number needed equals 100 ($100 = 4 * 20 + 2 * 10$) plus however many waffles fall on the floor. Unless an enormous number of waffles falls on the floor, Josh and Anna's prediction will be more accurate than Magda's.

23. Chris Achen (1991) "Let's Put Garbage-Can Regressions and Garbage-Can Probits Where They Belong," *Conflict Management and Peace Science* 22 (4): 327–39.

24. See J. M. Bates and C. W. J. Granger (1969) "The Combination of Forecasts," *Operations Research Quarterly* 20: 451–68.

25. D. Opitz and R. Maclin (1999) "Popular Ensemble Methods: An Empirical Study," *Journal of Artificial Intelligence Research* 11: 169–98.

26. Chris Volinsky (1997) "Bayesian Model Averaging for Censored Survival Models," Ph.D. diss. University of Washington; David Madigan, Adrian E. Raftery, Chris Volinsky, and Jennifer Hoeting (1996) "Bayesian Model Averaging," *AAAI Workshop on Integrating Multiple Learned Models*, pp. 77–83.

27. L. Breiman (1996) "Bagging Predictors," *Machine Learning* 24 (2): 123–40.

28. See Robin Hanson (1999) "Decision Markets," *IEEE Intelligent Systems* 14 (3): 16–19.

29. See John Geanakoplos (1992) "Common Knowledge," *Journal of Economic Perspectives* 6 (4): 53–82.

30. See, for example, Bella M. DePaulo, Kelly Charlton, Harris Cooper, James J. Lindsay, and Laura Muhlenbruck (1997) "The Accuracy–Confidence Correlation in the Detection of Deception," *Personality and Social Psychology Review* 1 (4): 346–57.

31. Determining the optimal subset of models to include is a difficult problem, given that the number of subsets of predictors is exponential in the number of predictors. See Damien Challet and Neil F. Johnson (2002) "Optimal Combinations of Imperfect Objects," *Physical Review Letters* 89: 028701.

CHAPTER 9: DIVERSE PREFERENCES

1. Gary Becker (1977) "De Gustibus Non Est Disputandum," *American Economic Review* 67: 76–90.

2. David Austen-Smith and Jeffrey S. Banks (1999) *Positive Political Theory I: Collective Preference* (Ann Arbor, MI: University of Michigan Press).

3. Preferences can be defined over "states of the world." A state of the world describes all relevant information about outcomes.

4. The ratio of the number of irrational preferences to rational preferences grows even larger as the number of alternatives increase. Suppose that twenty alternatives exist. Using the same logic as earlier, the number of rational preference orderings equals twenty (the number of alternatives that could be ranked first) times nineteen (the remaining alternatives that could be ranked second) times eighteen times seventeen and so on all the way down to three times two times one (the number of alternatives that the person could least prefer once all of the others have been ranked). Plugging this into a calculator gives 2,432,902,008,176,640,000, or approximately two and a half billion million. That's a large number.

To compute the number of irrational preference orderings, we follow the same logic as earlier. Twenty alternatives create one hundred and ninety pairs of alternatives. For each pair, either alternative could be preferred. This creates 2^{190} possible preference orderings that violate transitivity, or approximately 1.6×10^{56}. To make sense of how large this number is, cubing the number of rational preference orderings would give a number only slightly larger. If preferences also violate completeness, then for each pair of alternatives three possibilities exist. This creates 3^{190} possible preference orderings, which equals 4.5 times 10^{90}. This number is enormous. It is approximately equal to the number of rational preference orderings raised to the fourth power. So, for each of those two and a half billion million rational preferences, billions and billions of irrational preference relations exist.

5. A person could have an ideal point but not have single-peaked preferences.

6. If a person's ideal point is closest to green, then that ideal point must lie closer to either blue or yellow. (We're ruling out ties.) If it lies closer to blue, then her preferences must go: green first, blue second, yellow third, orange fourth, and red fifth.

7. Harold Hotelling first described this model in the context of firms deciding on locations. Harold Hotelling (1938) "The General Welfare in Relation to Problems of Taxation and of Railway and Utility Rates," *Econometrica* 6(3): 242–69. Firm location decisions are not in one-dimensional space, but in two- or even three-dimensional space, with the third dimension being the floor on which the firm is located. Hotelling modeled a one-dimensional world because it was easier. Anthony Downs subsequently applied the Hotelling model to political competition. Anthony Downs (1957) *An Economic Theory of Democracy* (New York: Harper).

8. Keith T. Poole and Howard Rosenthal (1997) *Congress: A Political-Economic History of Roll Call Voting* (New York: Oxford University Press).

9. I ignore the possibility that the optimal policy depends on some unknown state of the world.

10. We do differ in how much weight we place on each of these universally good outcomes. Some of us care more about education, others about the environment, and still others about economic growth.

CHAPTER 10: PREFERENCE AGGREGATION

1. I sort through these desiderata with too much noise and haste; for a more complete treatment, see Ken Arrow's seminal 1951 work *Social Choice and Individual Values* (New York: Wiley).

2. Sometimes individuals violate this axiom. Suppose you are at a restaurant and your waiter offers you a choice between chocolate milk (*X*) and regular milk (*Y*). You might choose chocolate milk. Suppose he then asks, "Would you prefer a chocolate shake (*Z*)?" Being on a diet, you would never consider having a chocolate shake. But the existence of the chocolate shake option might cause you to reinterpret your choice of chocolate milk as decadent. You might reconsider your original choice and say, "You know what? Give me the regular milk."

3. Ruling out dictators might still permit someone with the same preferences as the collective, but this person would *reflect* collective preferences, not determine them. This person could not, irrespective of the preferences, of others, make the collective preference anything he wants. He would just happen to agree with the collective in all cases.

4. Arrow, Kenneth. 1951. *Social Choice and Individual Values*. New York: John Wiley & Sons, Inc.

5. The theorem also rules out interpersonal comparisons of preference differences. It assumes that people cannot attach single dimensional values to each alternative. If they could, their collective preferences could be determined by adding up those values.

6. I would like to thank James Joyce, a colleague from philosophy, for encouraging me to construct this example.

7. For a careful elaboration of this and other points related to the theorem, see Don Saari (2001) *Decisions and Elections: Explaining the Unexpected* (New York: Cambridge University Press).

8. They satisfy completeness: Given any two alternatives, one must be closer to *M* than the other. If not, they are an equal distance away and they tie. Thus, we can compare any two alternatives. These preferences satisfy transitivity. If alternative *A* is closer to *M* than alternative *B*, and if alternative *B* is closer to *M* than alternative *C*, then it follows that alternative *A* is closer to *M* than alternative *C*. Preferences therefore satisfy transitivity and completeness. They are

rational. Preferences trivially satisfy unanimity. If one alternative is closer to everyone's ideal point than another, that first alternative must be closer to M. Preferences also satisfy independence of irrelevant alternatives. If alternative A is preferred to alternative B, then A is closer to M than B. This relationship between A, B, and M is unaffected by the existence of some other alternative C. Our final desideratum is that the preferences be nondictatorial. Chad might appear to be a dictator, but he is not. He reflects collective preferences. He doesn't determine them. If Chad were to move his ideal point out of the middle, then he would no longer determine the winning alternative. If he were a dictator, he could change his preferences however he liked and the collective choice would remain his ideal point.

9. C. R. Plott (1967) "A Notion of Equilibrium and Its Possibility under the Majority Rule," *American Economic Review* 57: 787–806.

10. R. D. McKelvey (1976) "Intransitivities in Multidimensional Voting Models and Some Implications for Agenda Control," *Journal of Economic Theory* 18: 1–22.

11. N. Schofield (1978) "Instability of Simple Dynamic Games," *Review of Economic Studies* 45: 575–94.

12. See Ken Kollman, John H. Miller, and Scott E. Page (1992) "Adaptive Parties in Spatial Elections," *American Political Science Review* 86: 929–37.

13. See A. Caplin and B. Nalebuff (1988) "On 64% Majority Rule," *Econometrica* 56 (4): 787–814.

14. Elizabeth Gerber and Lewis, Jeffrey (forthcoming) "Beyond the Median, Voter Preferences, District Heterogeneity, and Representation" *Journal of Political Economy*.

15. See Avinash K. Dixit and Barry J. Nalebuff (1991) *Thinking Strategically: The Competitive Edge in Business, Politics, and Everyday Life* (New York: Norton).

16. See J. T. Toman (2004) "The Papal Conclave: How Do Cardinals Divine the Will of God?" working paper, University of Melbourne.

17. A. Gibbard (1973) "Manipulation of Schemes that Mix Voting with Chance," *Econometrica* 41: 587–600; M. A. Satterthwaite (1975) "Strategy-Proofness and Arrow's Conditions: Existence and Correspondence Theorems for Voting Procedures and Social Welfare Functions," *Journal of Economic Theory* 10: 187–217.

18. Note that we have assumed that people vote sincerely. If we allow people to vote strategically, manipulating the agenda becomes much harder. Those people who most favor paper and least prefer scissors would vote for rock over paper in the first round of a sequential vote in which the winner faced scissors because rock would then defeat scissors in the final vote.

CHAPTER 11: INTERACTING TOOLBOXES AND PREFERENCES

1. See Louise Robbins (2001) *Louis Pasteur: And the Hidden World of Microbes* (New York: Oxford University Press).

CHAPTER 12: THE CAUSES OF COGNITIVE DIVERSITY

1. Steven Pinker (2002) *The Blank Slate: The Modern Denial of Human Nature* (New York: Viking); H. Hamer, Peter Copeland, and Dean Hamers (1999) *Living Our Genes: Why They Matter More than You Think* (New York: Anchor Books).

2. On ethnicity, see Marcus W. Feldman and Luigi L. Cavalli-Sforza (1989) "On the Theory of Evolution under Genetic and Cultural Transmission with Application to the Lactose Absorption Problem," in *Mathematical Evolutionary Theory*, ed. Marcus W. Feldman (Princeton, NJ: Princeton University Press, pp. 145–73. On gender, see Anne Moir and David Jessel (1992) *Brain Sex: The Real Difference between Men and Women* (New York: Dell Publishing).

3. Eleanor A. Maguire, David G. Gadian, Ingrid S. Johnsrude, Catriona D. Good, John Ashburner, Richard S. J. Frackowiak, and Christopher D. Frith (2000) "Navigation-Related Structural Change in the Hippocampi of Taxi Drivers," *Proceedings of the National Academy of Sciences* 97 (8): 4398–4403.

4. B. Draganski, C. Gaser, V. Busch, G. Schuierer, U. Bogdahn, and A. May (2004) "Neuroplasticity: Changes in Grey Matter Induced by Training," *Nature* 427 (6972): 311–12.

5. Glenn Loury (2000) *Dubois Lectures*, Harvard University, April 27.

6. Enriqueta Aragones, Itzhak Gilboa, Andrew Postlewaite, and David Schmeidler (2005) "Fact-Free Learning," *American Economic Review* 95 (5): 1355–68. Some have questioned the relevance of computational measures of problem difficulty. See Roger Penrose (1989) *The Emperor's New Mind: Concerning Computers, Minds, and the Laws of Physics* (New York: Oxford University Press).

7. Judea Pearl (2000) *Causality: Models, Reasoning, and Inference* (Cambridge: Cambridge University Press).

8. J. Denrell (2005) "Why Most People Disapprove of Me: Experience Sampling in Impression Formation," *Psychological Review* 112 (4): 951–78.

9. K. J. Holyoak and P. Thagard (1995) *Mental Leaps: Analogy in Creative Thought* (Cambridge, MA: MIT Press).

10. Edward Lazear (1999) "Culture and Language," *Journal of Political Economy* 107 (6): S95–S126.

11. See S. J. Ceci and A. Roazzi (1994) "The Effect of Context on Cognition: Postcards from Brazil," in *Mind in Context: Interactionist Perspectives on Human Intelligence*, ed. R. J. Sternberg and R. K. Wagner (New York: Cambridge University Press), pp. 213–47.

12. Richard Nisbett (2003) *The Geography of Thought: How Asians and Westerners Think Differently—and Why* (New York: Free Press).

13. Jared Diamond (2005) *Collapse: How Societies Choose to Fail or Succeed* (New York: Viking).

14. I thank David Harris for bringing these distinctions to my attention.

15. Elizabeth Anderson (2005) "Feminist Epistemology and Philosophy of Science," *Stanford Encyclopedia of Philosophy* [CD-ROM] (Stanford, CA: Metaphysics Research Lab).

16. Evelyn Fox Keller (1983) *A Feeling for the Organism: The Life and Work of Barbara McClintock* (San Francisco: W. H. Freeman).

17. John Dewey (1907) "The School and the Life of the Child," chapter 2 of *The School and Society* (Chicago: University of Chicago Press).

18. A. Kimball Romney, Susan C. Weller, and William H. Batchelder (1986) "Culture as Consensus: A Theory of Culture and Informant Accuracy," *American Anthropologist* 88 (2): 313–38.

19. Ford went to Yale as well, for law school.

20. Scott Atran and Douglas Medin (forthcoming) *The Native Mind: Cognition and Culture in Human Knowledge of Nature* (New York: Oxford University Press).

21. Robert K. Merton and Elinor Barber (2004) *The Travels and Adventures of Serendipity: A Study in Sociological Semantics and the Sociology of Science* (Princeton, NJ: Princeton University Press); Royston M. Roberts (1989) *Serendipity: Accidental Discoveries in Science* (New York: Wiley).

22. Marcie J. Tyre and Eric von Hippel (1997) "The Situated Nature of Adaptive Learning in Organizations," *Organization Science* 8 (1): 71–83.

23. David Leonhardt, "What Price Loyalty? Something Free," *New York Times*, April 26, 2006.

24. W. Kaempffert (1924) *A Popular History of American Invention*, vol. 2 (New York: Charles Scribner's Sons), p. 385. Excerpted from Stephen LaBerge (1985) Lucid Dreaming (Los Angeles: Tarcher).

25. U. Wagner, S. Gais, H. Haider, R. Verlager, and J. Born (2004) "Sleep Inspires Insight," *Nature* 427 (6972): 352–55.

26. Quotation drawn from the web site http:/quotationspage.com/quote/1388.html.

Chapter 13: The Empirical Evidence

1. Jared Diamond (1997) *Guns, Germs, and Steel: The Fates of Human Societies* (New York: W. W. Norton).

2. Robert Wright (2000) *Nonzero: The Logic of Human Destiny*, New York: Vintage Books.

3. Joel Mokyr (2002) *The Gifts of Athena: Historical Origins of the Knowledge Economy* (Princeton, NJ: Princeton University Press).

4. Martin L. Weitzman (1998) "Recombinant Growth," *Quarterly Journal of Economics* 113 (2): 331–60.

5. Wright (2000).

6. See Michael Kremer (1993) "Population Growth and Technological Change: One Million B.C. to 1990," *Quarterly Journal of Economics* 108 (3): 681–716.

7. T. Cox, S. Lobel, and P. McLeod (1991) "Effects of Ethnic Group Culture Differences on Cooperative and Competitive Behavior on a Group Task," *Academy of Management Journal* 34: 827–47.

8. See the 2005 Nancy L. Schwartz Memorial Lecture, by John Ledyard.

9. Tom Reitz, Joyce Berg, Forrest Nelson, and Robert Forsythe (2003) "Results from a Dozen Years of Election Futures Markets Research," in *The Handbook of Experimental Economics Results*, ed. Charles Plott and Vernon Smith (Amsterdam: Elsevier Science).

10. This finding is a little less amazing that it first seems. The line could predict every game would end in a tie and would also exhibit no bias.

11. See Ray C. Fair and John Oster (Forthcoming) "College Football Rankings and Market Efficiency," *Journal of Sports Economics*; S. Figlewski (1979) "Subjective Information and Market Efficiency in a Betting Market," *Journal of Political Economy* 87 (1): 75–88.

12. See Emile Servan-Schreiber, Justin Wolfers, David M. Pennock, and Brian Galebach (2004) "Prediction Markets: Does Money Matter?" *Electronic Markets* 14 (3).

13. See K. Y. Williams and C. A. O'Reilly III (1998) "Demography and Diversity in Organizations: A Review of 40 Years of Research," *Research in Organizational Behavior* 20: 77–140.

14. Keld Laursen, Volker Mahnke, and Per Vejrup-Hansen (2005) "Do Differences Make a Difference? The Impact of Human Capital Diversity, Experience, and Compensation on Firm Performance in Engineering Consulting," DRUID working paper, posted at www.druid.dk.

15. L. R. Hoffman (1959) "Homogeneity of Member Personality and Its Effect on Group Problem-Solving," *Journal of Abnormal and Social Psychology* 58: 27–32; N. R. F. Maier (1930) "Reasoning in Humans: On Direction," *Journal of Comparative Psychology* 12: 144–55; and T. Amabile (1983) *The Social Psychology of Creativity* (New York: Springer-Verlag).

16. See Sydney Finkelstein and Donald C. Hambrick (1990) "Top Management Team Tenure and Organizational Outcomes: The Moderating Role of Managerial Discretion," *Administrative Science Quarterly* 35: 484–503; and K. A. Bantel, and S. E. Jackson (1989) "Top Management and Innovations in Banking: Does the Demography of the Top Team Make a Difference?" *Strategic Management Journal* 10: 107–24.

17. See also Howard Gardner (1993) *Creating Minds: An Anatomy of Creativity Seen through the Lives of Freud, Einstein, Picasso, Stravinsky, Eliot, Graham, and Gandhi* (New York: Basic Books); Rosabeth Moss Kanter (1983) *The Change Masters: Innovations for Productivity in the American Corporation* (New York: Simon and Schuster).

18. See James Gleick (1993) *Genius: The Life and Science of Richard Feynman* (New York: Vintage Press).

19. Thomas Homer-Dixon (2000) *The Ingenuity Gap* (New York: Knopf).

20. I thank Thomas Wilcher for this example.

21. A. Blinder and J. Morgan (2005) "Are Two Heads Better Than One? An Experimental Analysis of Group versus Individual Decision Making," *Journal of Money, Credit and Banking* 37 (5): 789–811.

22. Clare Lombardelli, James Proudman, and James Talbot (2002) "Committees versus Individuals: An experimental Analysis of Monetary Policy Decision-Making," *Bank of England Quarterly Bulletin* (Autumn).

23. Martin Kilduff, Reinhard Angelmar, and Ajay Mehra (2000) "Top Management-Team Diversity and Firm Performance: Examining the Role of Cognitions," *Organization Science* 11: 21–34.

24. Susan E. Jackson, A. Joshi, and N. L. Erhardt (2003) "Recent Research on Team and Organizational Diversity: SWOT Analysis and Implications," *Journal of Management* 29 (6): 801–30; Susan E. Jackson (1992) "Consequences of Group Composition for the Interpersonal Dynamics of Strategic Issue Processing," in ed. P. Shrivastava, A. Huff, and J. Dutton, *Advances in Strategic Management, vol. 8*, (Greenwich, CT: JAI Press); Susan E. Jackson and A. Joshi (2004) "Diversity in Social Context: A Multi-Attribute, Multi-Level Analysis of Team Diversity and Performance," *Journal of Organizational Behavior* 25: 675–702; Deborah H. Gruenfeld, Elizabeth Mannix, Katherine Y. Williams, and Margaret A. Neale (1996) "Group Composition and Decision Making: How Member Familiarity and Information Distribution Affect Process and Performance," *Organizational Behavior and Human Decision Processes* 67: 1–15; Katherine W. Phillips, Elizabeth Mannix, Margaret Neale, and Deborah Gruenfeld (2004) "Diverse Groups and Information Sharing: The Effects of Congruent Ties," *Journal of Experimental Social Psychology* 40: 497–510; T. Kochan, K. Bezrukova, R. Ely, S. Jackson,

A. Joshi, K. Jehn, J. Leonard, D. Levine, and D. Thomas (2003) "The Effects of Diversity on Business Performance: Report of a Feasibility Study of the Diversity Research Network," *Human Resource Management Journal* 42 (1): 3–21.

25. Williams and O'Reilly (1998). See also Marian N. Ruderman, Martha W. Hughes-James, and Susan E. Jackson, eds. (1996) *Selected Research on Work Team Diversity* (Greensboro, NC: American Psychological Association and Center for Creative Leadership); K. A. Jehn, G. B. Northcraft, and M. A. Neale (1999) "Why Differences Make a Difference: A Field Study of Diversity, Conflict, and Performance in Work Groups," *Administrative Science Quarterly* 44: 741–63; H. Tajfel and J. C. Turner (1986) "The Social Identity Theory of Intergroup Behavior," in *Psychology of Intergroup Relations,* ed. S. Worchel and W. G. Austin (Chicago: Nelson-Hall).

26. Kochan et al. (2003).

27. Sarah Fisher Ellison, Jeffrey Greenbaum, and Wallace Mullin (2005) "Diversity, Social Goods Provision, and Performance in the Firm," MIT Department of Economics working paper (September).

28. A. C. Filley, R. J. House, and S. Kerr (1976) *Managerial Process and Organizational Behavior* (Glenview, IL: Scott, Foresman, and Co.); E. Hoffnan (1979) "Applying Experiential Research on Group Problem Solving to Organizations," *Journal of Applied Behavioral Science* 15: 375–91; Joseph E. McGrath (1984) *Groups: Interaction and Performance* (Englewood Cliffs, NJ: Prentice-Hall); R. A. Guzzo and M. W. Dickson (1996) "Teams in Organizations: Recent Research on Performance and Effectiveness," *Annual Review of Psychology* 47: 307–38; F. J. Milliken and L. L. Martins (1996) "Searching for Common Threads: Understanding the Multiple Effects of Diversity in Organizational Groups," *Academy of Management Review* 21: 402–33.

29. D. A. Thomas and R. J. Ely (1996) "Making Differences Matter: A New Paradigm for Managing Diversity," *Harvard Business Review* 74 (5): 79–90. Emphasis added.

30. C. Nemeth (1986) "Differential Contributions of Majority and Minority Influence," *Psychological Review* 93: 23–32.

31. N. Triandis, E. Hall, and R. Ewen (1965) "Member Heterogeneity and Dyadic Creativity," *Human Relations* 18: 33–55.

32. Samuel R. Sommers (forthcoming) "On Racial Diversity and Group Decision-Making: Informational and Motivational Effects of Racial Composition on Jury Deliberations," *Journal of Personality and Social Psychology*. A jury determines the outcome. Therefore we cannot say precisely whether it was right or wrong, but juries can make more or fewer mistakes in reasoning or logic, and they can be more or less consistent with the law.

33. Orlando C. Richard, Amy McMillan, Kenneth Chadwick, and Sean Dwyer (2003) "Employing an Innovation Strategy in Racial Diverse Workforces: Effects on Firm Performance," *Group and Organization Management* 28 (1): 107–26.

34. Williams and O'Reilly (1998).

35. W. E. Watson, K. Kumar, and L. K. Michaelsen (1993) "Cultural Diversity's Impact on Interaction Process and Performance: Comparing Homogeneous and Diverse Task Groups," *Academy of Management Journal* 36: 590–602; Warren E. Watson and Kamalesh Kumar (1992) "Factors Associated with Differences in Decision-Making Regarding Risk Taking: A Comparison of Culturally Homogeneous and Culturally Heterogeneous Groups," *International Journal of Intercultural Relations* 16: 53–65.

36. William B. Swann, Jeffrey T. Polzer, Daniel Conor Seyle, and Sei Jin Ko (2004) "Finding Value in Diversity: Verification of Personal and Social Self Views in Diverse Groups," *Academy of Management Review* 29 (1): 9–27; Robin J. Ely and David A. Thomas (2001) "Cultural Diversity at Work: The Effects of Diversity Perspectives on Work Group Processes and Outcomes," *Administrative Science Quarterly* 46 (2): 229–73.

37. Ely and Thomas (2001).

38. See John M. Quigley (1998) "Urban Diversity and Economic Growth," *Journal of Economic Perspectives* 12 (2): 127–38.

39. I'm borrowing this line from James Boyd of Resources for the Future.

40. See Quigley (1998).

41. This bias is more pronounced among innovations produced by firms than those produced by universities. See Adam B. Jaffe, Manuel Trajtenberg, and Rebecca Henderson (1993) "Geographic Localization of Knowledge Spillovers as Evidenced by Patent Citations," *Quarterly Journal of Economics* 108 (3): 577–98.

42. Jane Jacobs (1984) *Cities and the Wealth of Nations* (New York: Random House); Maryanne Feldman and David Audretsch (1999) "Innovation in Cities: Science-Based Diversity, Specialization and Localized Competition," *European Economic Review* 43: 409–29; John E. Wagner and Steven C. Deller (1998) "Measuring the Effects of Economic Diversity on Growth and Stability," *Land Economics* 74 (4): 541–56.

43. Barry Nalebuff and Ian Ayres (2003) *Why Not? How to Use Everyday Ingenuity to Solve Problems Big and Small* (Cambridge, MA: Harvard Business School Press).

44. J. Jacobs (1961) *The Death and Life of Great American Cities* (New York: Random House).

45. G.I.P. Ottaviano and G. Peri (2006) "The Economic Value of Cultural Diversity: Evidence from US Cities," *Journal of Economic Geography* 6 (1): 9–44; G.I.P. Ottaviano and G. Peri (2004) "Cities and Culture," *Journal of Urban Economics* 58 (2): 304–37.

46. William Easterly and Ross Levine (1997) "Economic Africa's Growth Tragedy: Policies and Ethnic Divisions," *Quarterly Journal of Economics* 112 (4): 1203–50. The Easterly and Levine model relies on a measure of ethnic linguistic fractionalization, a rather crude proxy for politically relevant divisions. Daniel Posner has constructed a more politically relevant measure of the number of ethnic groups and found similar results. Daniel M. Posner (2004) "Measuring Ethnic Fractionalization in Africa," *American Journal of Political Science* 48 (4): 849–63.

47. Paul Collier (2005) "Ethnicity, Politics and Economic Performance," *Economics and Politics* 12 (3): 225–45.

48. Alberto Alesina, Reza Baqir, and William Easterly (1999) "Public Goods and Ethnic Divisions," *Quarterly Journal of Economics* 114 (4): 1243–84.

49. Richard Florida (2002) *The Rise of the Creative Class: And How It's Transforming Work, Leisure, Community and Everyday Life* (New York: Basic Books).

50. E. Glaeser, J. Scheinkman, and A. Shleifer (1995) "Economic Growth in a Cross-Section of Cities," *Journal of Monetary Economics* 36: 117–43.

51. Alberto Alesina and Eliana La Ferrara (2005) "Ethnic Diversity and Economic Performance," *Journal of Economic Literature* 43 (September): 762–800. Quotation from p. 794.

52. Jonathan Pool (1972) "National Development and Language Diversity," in *Advances in the Sociology of Language*, ed. Joshua A. Fishman (The Hague: Mouton), vol. 2, p. 222; Daniel Nettle (2000) "Linguistic Fragmentation and the Wealth of Nations: The Fishman-Pool Hypothesis Re-Examined," *Economic Development and Cultural Change* 48 (2): 335–48. A problem with using growth rates is that poorer countries can exhibit high average growth rates over short time horizons and yet remain poor. A 20 percent increase over nothing is still nothing. Of course, over long periods of time growth rates should correlate with performance. See Brad Lian and John R. Oneal (1997) "Cultural Diversity and Economic Development: A Cross-National Study of 98 Countries, 1960–1985," *Economic Development and Cultural Change* 46 (1): 61–77.

53. If we ignore small countries such as San Marion, Jersey, Guernsey, and Luxembourg, then these three countries all rank in the top seven of GDP per capita. Two of the others, Iceland and Norway, benefit from large energy reserves. The other two, Denmark and Ireland, would not count as diverse.

54. The UN's count omits Taiwan and the Vatican City, which fit most people's criteria for separate countries.

55. Alberto Alesina and Enrico Spolaore (2003) *The Size of Nations* (Cambridge, MA: MIT Press). See also Alberto Alesina, Enrico Spolaore, and Romain Wacziarg (2000) "Economic Integration and Political Disintegration," *American Economic Review* 90 (5): 1276–96.

56. Jenna Bednar (n.d.) "The Robust Federation," manuscript.

Chapter 14: A Fertile Logic

1. If, for example, each of three people makes a mistake with probability p, then the probability that all three make a mistake equals p^3.

2. Unbeknownst to Hami, Italo Marchiony, a recent Italian immigrant to New York, had patented the ice cream cone in 1903.

3. John Harte (1985) *Consider a Spherical Cow: A Course in Environmental Problem Solving* (Los Altos, CA: W. Kaufmann).

4. For a more detailed analysis of when to allow diversity in a complex system, see Robert Axelrod and Michael D. Cohen (1999) *Harnessing*

Complexity: Organizational Implications of a Scientific Frontier (New York: Free Press).

5. Cass R. Sunstein (2003) *Why Societies Need Dissent* (Cambridge, MA: Harvard University Press).

6. Arthur Lupia and Matthew D. McCubbins (1998) *The Democratic Dilemma: Can Citizens Learn What They Need to Know?* (New York: Cambridge University Press).

7. Garry Wills (1992) *Lincoln at Gettysburg: The Words That Remade America* (New York: Simon and Schuster).

8. Lupia and McCubbins (1998).

9. See John G. Matsusaka (1992) "Economics of Direct Legislation," *Quarterly Journal of Economics* 107: 541–71.

10. Christopher H. Achen and Larry M. Bartels (2002) "Blind Retrospection: Electoral Responses to Drought, Flu, and Shark Attacks," paper prepared for presentation at the Annual Meeting of the American Political Science Association, Boston.

11. Kay-Yut Chen and Charles R. Plott (2002) "Information Aggregation Mechanisms: Concept, Design, and Implementation for a Sales Forecasting Problem," working paper, California Institute of Technology.

12. See *Facilitating Interdisciplinary Research* Committee on Facilitating Interdisciplinary Research (2004) National Academy of Sciences, National Academy of Engineering, Institute of Medicine. 2004.

13. Roger Fisher and William Ury (1981) *Getting to Yes: Negotiating Agreement without Giving In* (Boston: Houghton Mifflin).

14. Michael D. Cohen (1984) "Conflict and Complexity: Goal Diversity and Organizational Search Effectiveness," *American Political Science Review* 78 (2): 435–51.

15. Some people object to the diversity promotes benefits logic because they see in it a form of exploitation—other students benefit from the unique experiences of the diverse student. That's true, but calling this exploitation misses the mark. These interactions produce mutual benefits.

16. Approximately 8,100 to 6,100.

17. For an overview of this research, see J. Pfeffer (1983) "Organizational Demography," in *Research in Organizational Behavior*, vol. 5, ed. L. L. Cummings and B. M. Staw (Greenwich, CT: VAI Press).

18. This is a simple version of a model by Jackson and Fryer. Matthew O. Jackson and Roland G. Fryer Jr. (2002) "Categorical

Cognition: A Psychological Model of Categories and Identification in Decision Making," Working Papers 1144, California Institute of Technology, Division of the Humanities and Social Sciences.

19. Glenn C. Loury (2000) "Lecture 1: Racial Stereotypes," lecture delivered at Harvard University as part of the DuBois Lectures; and Glenn Loury (2002) *The Anatomy of Racial Inequality* (Cambridge, MA: Harvard University Press).

20. See Kwame Anthony Appiah (2005) *The Ethics of Identity* (Princeton, NJ: Princeton University Press).

21. Quotation posted on http://womenshistory.about.com/od/quotes/a/toni-morrison.htm.

22. M. B. Brewer and R. J. Brown (1998) "Intergroup Relations," in *The Handbook of Social Psychology*, ed. D. T. Gilbert, S. T. Fiske, and G. Lindzey (Boston, MA: McGraw Hill); J. E. McGrath, H. Arrow, and J. L. Berdahl (2000) "The Study of Groups: Past, Present, and Future," *Personality and Social Psychology Review* 4 (1): 95–105; H. Tafjel and J. C. Turner (1986) "The Social Identity Theory of Intergroup Behavior," in *Psychology of Intergroup Relations*, ed. S. Austin and W. G. Austin (Chicago: Nelson Hall).

23. Thomas Schelling (1978) *Micromotives and Macrobehavior* (New York: W. W. Norton and Company).

24. Heather K. Gerken (2005) "Second-Order Diversity and Disaggregated Democracy," 118 *Harvard Law Review* 1099.

25. A skunk works is a group of people who work on a problem in an unusual way. Some claim the term from a moonshine operation in Al Capp's *L'il Abner* cartoon. For olfactory reasons, the modern business literature refers to skunk works as greenfields.

26. J. G. March (1991). "Exploration and Exploitation in Organizational Learning," *Organization Science* 2 (1): 71–87.

Epilogue: The Ketchup Question

1. In the academic literature, the desire to coordinate has many names—*homophily, peer pressure, conformity, herd behavior,* and *jumping on the bandwagon.* See M. Kandori, G. Mailath, and R. Rob (1993) "Learning, Mutation, and Long-Run Equilibria in Games,"

Econometrica 61: 29–56; Glenn Ellison (1993) "Learning, Local Interaction, and Coordination," *Econometrica* 61 (5): 1047–71; and H. Peyton Young (1998) *Individual Strategy and Social Structure: An Evolutionary Theory of Institutions* (Princeton, NJ: Princeton University Press).

2. J. Bendor and P. Swistak (1997) "The Evolutionary Stability of Cooperation," *American Political Science Review* 91: 290–306.

3. Quotation from
http://en.thinkexist.com/quotes/maxine_hong_kingston/.

Index